DALITS IN MODERN INDIA

DALITS IN MODERN INDIA
Vision and Values

SECOND EDITION

Edited by
S.M. MICHAEL

SAGE Publications
Los Angeles • London • New Delhi • Singapore

First published in 1999 by Vistaar Publications

This Second edition Published in 2007 by

Sage Publications India Pvt Ltd
B1/I1, Mohan Cooperative Industrial Area
Mathura Road, New Delhi 110 044
www.sagepub.in

Sage Publications Inc
2455 Teller Road
Thousand Oaks, California 91320

Sage Publications Ltd
1 Oliver's Yard, 55 City Road
London EC1Y 1SP

Sage Publications Asia-Pacific Pte Ltd
33 Pekin Street
#02-01 Far East Square
Singapore 048763

Published by Vivek Mehra for Sage Publications India Pvt Ltd, typeset in 10.5/12.5 Garamond at InoSoft Systems, Noida, and printed at Chaman Enterprises, New Delhi.

Library of Congress Cataloging-in-Publication Data

Dalits in modern India: vision and values/editor S.M. Michael.—2nd ed.
    p. cm.
  Originally published: Untouchable. Boulder, Colo.: Lynne Rienner, 1999.
  Includes bibliographical references and index.
  Untouchability and stratification in Indian civilisation/Shrirama—who is a Dalit?/John C.B. Webster—Colonialism within colonialism: Phule's critique of Brahmin power/Mahesh Gavaskar—Dalit vision of a just society in India/S.M. Michael—Ambedkar, Buddhism and the concept of religion/Timothy Fitzgerald—The Dalit movement in mainstream sociology/ Gopal Guru—Liberation movements in comparative perspective: Dalit Indians and black Americans/K.P. Singh—Sociology of India and Hinduism: towards a Method/S. Selvam— Hinduisation of Adivasis: a case study from South Gujarat/Arjun Patel—Ambedkar's daughters: a study of Mahar women in Ahmednagar District of Maharashtra/Traude Pillai-Vetschera—The BSP in Uttar Pradesh: whose party is it?/Christophe Jaffrelot—Ambedkar's interpretation of caste system, its economic consequence and suggested remedies/Sukhadeo Thorat—Dalits and economic policy: contributions of Dr B.R. Ambedkar/Gail Omvedt— Reservation policy and the empowerment of Dalits/P.G. Jogdand—Scheduled castes, employment and social mobility/Richards Pais.

  1. Dalits—India—Political activity. 2. India—Politics and government—20th century

DS422.C3U54   305.5'688—dc22   2007   2007001590

ISBN: 978-0-7619-3571-1 (PB)   978-81-7829-732-3 (India-PB)

The Sage Team: Ashok R. Chandran, Gayatri E. Koshy and Rajib Chatterjee

To

Dr Stephen Fuchs

Srirama p48

Thorat p288

Webster

Contents

Part IV

List of Tables

Acknowledgements

Dr Stephen Fuchs, the founder of the Institute of Indian Culture, a research centre specialising in anthropology and sociology in the mega city of Mumbai, has been a source of inspiration to a large number of scholars who have undertaken research on the marginalised people of India. After a long period of committed scholarly work, spanning more than 60 years in India, he passed away in January 2000. This volume is in his honour, in appreciation of his enormous contribution to Indian anthropology and sociology.

Dalit sociology is product of teamwork. I express my profound sense of gratitude first to Professor J.V. Ferreira for his valuable suggestions throughout this work. I am indebted to Teresa Menezes for typing the manuscript. I am also grateful to Elizabeth Reuben, Kaj Tougaard and Mark R. Hooper for their editorial assistance.

Last, but not least, to the contributors to this volume, I express my sincere thanks.

S.M. Michael

Introduction

S.M. MICHAEL

Sociology grows and changes continually in response to new phenomena within world societies, to discoveries and insights within the discipline itself and to the mandate for ever-increasing relevancy that comes from the very people whom sociologists study. Today, prominent aspects of world economic, political and social relations revolve around issues of inequality, those based on class, caste, race and gender. In the context of India, anthropological and sociological attention to the study of the Untouchables, now known as Dalits, represents a major trend in Indian sociology.

As has been rightly argued by scholars, those who occupied the bottom rungs of society were invisible owing to the cognitive blackout perpetuated by the upper caste, middle class, urban, male researcher. Today, however, they are in full view and demand their legitimate share of representation of knowledge. It is further argued that the attempts to create their own knowledge system are essentially aimed at destroying the caste system that is constructed through the complex hierarchies of labour, sexuality and knowledge.

Throughout history, sociocultural and political situations have been changed by the power of certain ideals and visions. Such a tremendous change is in progress in traditional India and the old values related to caste relationships are under great strain. It will not be an exaggeration to say that one of the profound changes in contemporary Indian society has been the Dalit transformation of our times. As will be shown in brief in this introduction and more fully in several chapters in this volume, the Dalit vision of Indian society is different from that of the upper castes. The Untouchables have come to a new sense of their new humanity and are forging ahead to shape a new modern India. It is appropriate, therefore, to explore the social, economic and cultural content of this transform-ation. We also need to focus upon its relevance for the nation and its possible implications for our future. Dalit sociology studies this aspiration and struggle of the marginalised masses for a new humanity based on the values of equality, social justice and human dignity.

It might be suggested that we dispense with visions entirely and deal only with reality. But that may, in fact, be the most utopian vision of all, for reality is far too complex to be comprehended by any single mind. Visions are like maps that guide us through a tangle of bewildering complexities, and like maps, visions have to leave out many concrete features in order to enable us to focus on a few key paths to our goals (see Sowell, 1987: 13–17). The term used here, 'vision', is not a dream, a hope, a prophecy, or a moral imperative, though any of these things may ultimately derive from some particular vision.

The aspirations of contemporary Dalits are completely different from those of Dalits in traditional India. This change is due to the difference in the vision perceived by the Untouchables of the past and of today. Visions set the agenda for both thought and action; philosophical, political, or social theories are built on them. Believers in one vision will view themselves in a very different moral role from the followers of another. The ramifications of such conflicting visions extend into economic, judicial, military, philosophical and political spheres. This is made clear in the case of Untouchables in the history of India.

Increased intellectual activism has marked Dalit–Bahujan cultural life at both the national and the regional levels in recent years. An interesting feature of this development is that the growth is well outside the formal educational sites that are supposed to be the normal locations for such a flourish (Guru and Geetha, 1997). This new trend of Dalit intellectual activism need to be understood sociologically.

The Dalit intellectual, social and cultural activism in contemporary India, thus, represents a very interesting scenario in which an urgent need is felt to make sense of Dalit reality at an abstract theoretical level. These intellectual efforts also show that Dalit theory might acquire a critical mass in the future.

All the same, it is well known that there is an intellectual critique and challenge to the very term 'Dalit' especially from the post-modernist and post-structuralist scholars. Some intellectuals and activists are of the view that the term 'Dalit' is hostile to the ex-Untouchables of today and this term has no ontological abilities and hermeneutic capacities of its own to help the ex-Untouchables in their total emancipation. Thus, the category Dalit faces violent rejection both from the Dalits and from the non-Dalits.

There are two sets of arguments that have been put forward by scholars while responding to this theoretical construct of the category Dalit. Professor Romila Thapar believes that there is a notion of 'out of date history' and in this notion of history, certain categories lose their significance, for example, the Arya–Anarya category. By the same logic, one can also argue that categories like Shudra, Adi-dhamma, etc., have also become part of the 'out of date history'. She, however, maintains that Dalit is a specific category and that there is a political necessity to hold on to it. Satyanarayana, another scholar, says that it is important to look at the category Dalit as a construct achieved through recruiting and restoring the hidden culture and textual history of Dalits. Without understanding this cultural and historical rootedness of the category Dalit, it is not possible to understand the complex and pluralistic culture of India (Guru and Geetha, 1997).

Thus, it is true that the subject 'Dalit' is under continuous scrutiny and critical examination. However, many scholars and activists feel that the category Dalit has had a promising start and will have a better future and thus are not ready to give up claims to this category that easily (see ibid.: 18–19). However, we need to be open to theoretical arguments in favour of the redefinition of this category and the possibility of more rigorous arguments. For this there is an urgent need for Dalit epistemology and Dalit knowledge systems.

Dalit sociology aims at knowing what the Dalit knowledge systems are and to what extent they are useful in recovery for a contemporary project of Dalit emanicipation. This need is best explained as an impassioned search for a way of knowing that will recover Dalit lives and agencies from the frozen times of the past. Knowledge and epistemologies thus assume a centrality in these resolutions of Dalit questions (see ibid.).

UNTOUCHABLES BY VARIOUS NAMES

To be an Untouchable in the Indian caste system is to be very low in, and partially excluded from, an elaborate hierarchical social order. Untouchables are persons of a discrete set of low castes, excluded on account of their extreme collective impurity from particular relations with higher beings (both human and divine). They make up about 16 per cent of the Indian population and number about 138 million. They have been called by various names such as 'Untouchables', 'Harijans' (a glorified term, coined by Narasimha Mehta and adopted and popularised by Mahatma Gandhi), 'Exterior Castes' (a term used by J.H. Hutton), 'Depressed Classes' (a term used by British officials), 'Outcastes', 'Pariahs' (commonly, but undoubtedly derived from the Tamil word *para* or *parai*, the drum, see Deliege, 1997). In more ancient times, the terms 'Mlechha', 'Chandala' (terms used by Manu), also Panchama (the fifth class), Avarna (that is, outside the four varnas), Nishada, Paulkasa, Antyaja, Atishudra, etc., were used.

The term 'Scheduled Castes' appeared for the first time in April 1935, when the British Government issued the Government of India (Scheduled Caste) Order 1936, specifying certain castes, races and tribes as Scheduled Castes. Prior to that these population groups were generally known as 'Depressed Classes'. The term 'Dalit', first used in journalistic writings as far back as 1931 to connote the Untouchables, gained currency only in the early 1970s with the Dalit Panther Movement in Maharashtra. As now used, it implies a condition of being underprivileged and deprived of basic rights and refers to people who are suppressed on account of their lowly birth.

THE ORIGINS OF CASTE AND UNTOUCHABILITY

The origins of caste and of untouchability lie deep in India's ancient past and the evidence of those origins provided by the archaeological and literary sources now available is, at best, circumstantial. Consequently, scholars have been forced to engage in considerable speculation in their efforts to reconstruct the past history of untouchability. What we now have are not hard and clear facts but a variety of competing theories, all of which have proved difficult to substantiate in a convincing manner.

The dominant view traces the origins of caste and untouchability to the Aryans themselves and to their ways of relating to the people of India with whom they came into contact. The Aryans, a set of related and highly self-conscious tribes sharing a common language and religion, began their invasions of India from the northwest around 1500 BC. For centuries they remained in seemingly constant conflict with the indigenous peoples, whom they looked down upon as culturally inferior and shunned as ritually unclean. Once conquered by superior military technology, some of these people withdrew into regions as yet unoccupied by the Aryans, while others were incorporated as separate and inferior castes within Aryan-dominated society. In post *Rig Vedic* literature, there are more frequent references to primitive forest-dwellers who were kept on the fringes of Aryan society in the conquered regions. Among these were the Chandala.

Although the Chandala were severely stigmatised in the later Vedic age, it was only in the period between 600 BC and AD 200 that untouchability appeared as such (Webster, 1994: 2). In the *Dharmasutra*s and in Kautilya's *Arthasastra*, the Chandala are treated as Untouchable and the 'mixed caste theory' of the origins of untouchability is enunciated. However, it is in the Manusmriti that this theory as well as the varna theory and the classification of castes in a hierarchy based on occupation and degree of pollution, receives its classic statement.

According to Manu, the ancient Indian lawgiver, untouchability is the punishment for miscegenation between a member of a high caste and that of a low caste or an outcaste. The children of such an unequal pair become Untouchables and the greater the social gap between the two parents, the lower the status of their children. The consequences are also more severe if the mother is of a superior caste. Thus, the offspring of a Brahmin father and a Shudra mother is called Nishada; the child becomes a fisherman. The offspring of a Shudra father and a Brahmin mother is called Chandala; he is the most degraded of all mortals. To Manu, a degraded occupation is not the cause of untouchability, rather untouchability condemns a person to a low and impure occupation. In later times, racial mixture was added as a factor of impurity. In the period after Manu, increasing numbers of the members of the lower castes belonged to different races and cultures. The practice of untouchability was intensified and applied to more groups in the years following AD 200, while Chandala became a label not simply for a tribe but for all whom the Aryans considered to be at the very bottom of society.

What has been described thus far relates to north India. The literature from south India suggests that the people whom the Aryans conquered were the Dravidians, who subsequently moved south subjugating the indigenous people. It was only later, when Aryan influence spread to the south, that the varna system and untouchability came into being there.

The eminent anthropologist J.H. Hutton, author of the best book on caste, *Caste in India* (1963), locates the origins of caste in the taboos and divisions of labour in the pre-Aryan tribes of India as well as in their efforts at self-preservation in the face of invasion. In his opinion, untouchability is the consequence of ritual impurity. He says: 'The origin of the position of the exterior castes is partly racial, partly religious, and partly a matter of social custom. There can be little doubt but the idea of untouchability originates in taboo' (ibid.: 207).

Christoph von Fürer-Haimendorf, another eminent anthropologist, believes that untouchability is an urban development and is the result of an unclean and ritually impure occupation (see the Foreword in *The Children of Hari*, Fuchs, 1950). Once untouchability had developed in urban or semi-urban settlements, its gradual spread to the villages was inevitable for it is everywhere the towns which set the standard.

Dr Ambedkar's thesis on the origin of untouchability, as expounded in his book *The Untouchables* (1948) is an altogether novel one. The distinction between the Hindus and the Untouchables in its original form, before the advent of untouchability, was the distinction between tribesmen and 'broken men' from alien tribes. It is the broken men who subsequently came to be treated as Untouchable. There are two roots from which untouchability has sprung: (*i*) contempt and hatred for the broken men, as for Buddhism by the Brahmins, (*ii*) continuation of beef-eating by the broken men after it had been given up by the others.

Dr Ambedkar tries to explain what he means by broken men. He proposes an ingenious hypothesis: When primitive society began to settle down and to cultivate, certain tribes remained nomadic and warlike. They began to attack the settled tribes as the latter were wealthier. In addition, they had grain, which the nomads wanted but did not possess. The settled men needed defenders as they had lost their warlike spirit. They employed 'broken men'—defeated nomads—and stray individuals who needed protection and shelter. These individuals became mercenaries, but were not allowed to stay within the settlement. They were kept at a distance, as they belonged to a different tribe. They were treated with disrespect, as 'broken men' and as mercenaries. Dr Ambedkar provided supporting evidence for such a process from Ireland and Wales. The difference was that in those countries, the outsiders were after nine generations absorbed into the settled community. This did not happen in India, for the Hindus had contempt for the broken men who were Buddhists and beef-eaters.

At first sight this theory may seem rather far-fetched. However, agreeing with the views of Dr Ambedkar, Dr Stephen Fuchs says: 'It is a well-known fact that the nomadic animal breeders of Inner Asia, for example, enjoyed nothing more than raiding and fighting. When a tribe was defeated and routed, the survivors often used to be sold into slavery by their conquerors. Those who managed to escape had to seek the protection of another tribe. Being powerless they had often to content themselves with menial jobs, tending horses and cattle, making and repairing saddles and other leather-work, such as tongs and bridles, making and cleaning weapons, etc. As these animal breeding nomads generally despised menial and manual work, this contempt was also extended to those who had to perform it' (1981: 13). There was thus, a deep social cleavage between the masters and their servant class. Dr Ambedkar believes that the root cause of untouchability lies in a pronounced cultural or racial difference of contempt and hatred coupled with a close economic dependence of the inferior society on the superior one.

Dr Stephen Fuchs proposes a new theory regarding the origin of untouchability (1981: 15ff). According to him, the theories proposed earlier as well as various others presented by a number of Indologists seem to suffer from one great defect: they do not penetrate deeply enough into the past of the dominant Indian peoples.

They restrict themselves unduly to happenings in India. It is true that the caste system and untouchability developed after the arrival of the Aryans and, most probably, of the Dravidians in India, that the caste system, as it has grown in India, is unique and not found elsewhere in the world, and that nowhere in the world are Untouchables found in such vast numbers—138 million! Yet, the roots must be sought in an age when both population groups lived on the steppes of Inner Asia. Here the animal breeding societies developed a pronounced hierarchical structure. These animal breeders gave up cultivation completely and regarded manual work of any kind as unworthy of a shepherd and a warrior. They also developed a social structure of their own: an extended joint family system with a patriarch at its head in whom all power was vested.

According to Dr Stephen Fuchs, there is sufficient evidence to prove that the Aryans as well as the Dravidians on their arrival in India still belonged to such an animal breeding culture. They must have brought along also their aversion to manual work and to foreign people. The Aryans, on their slow advance through northern India, and the Dravidians wandering down along the west coast into south India, encountered on their way a multitude of earlier settlers who either submitted passively to their conquest or were defeated in fierce battles. As conquerors they managed to impose many of their cultural values and prejudices on the subject peoples of India. Adding to their inherited attitude to manual work and racial purity a new dimension, namely, that of ritual purity, they gradually developed a unique Hindu caste system which was intimately connected ideologically with the concept of untouchability.

None of these explanations about the origin of untouchability are conclusively proved facts. As happens so often with human institutions, no single cause can explain untouchability. It is deeply rooted in Indian history, in the agrarian social order that dominated the Indian economy until the advent of the British, and which remains today India's largest economic sector. Though the relation of India's rural Untouchables to this social order has shifted in subtle ways in the past two centuries, there remain pervasive continuities, especially of meaning and of cultural construction, with this deeply-rooted past.

IMAGES OF INDIAN UNTOUCHABILITY
DURING COLONIAL RULE

Abbe Dubois

Perhaps the earliest and simplest Western image of untouchability is embodied in the term 'outcaste'. In this view, to be an Untouchable is to be beyond the reach of Hindu culture and society, to be almost cultureless. The stress in the outcaste image is on the Brahmins possessing culture and the Untouchables lacking it. Thus, the Abbe Dubois, a remarkable French missionary with first-hand knowledge of village India between 1792 and 1823, contrasts the Untouchable 'pariahs' with those higher-caste Hindus on whom the system has had its beneficent moral effect: 'We can picture what would become of the Hindus if they were not kept within the bounds of duty by the rules and penalties of caste, by looking at the position of the Pariahs, or outcastes of India, who, checked by no moral restraints, abandon themselves to their natural propensities' (1959: 29). The word 'pariah', which derives from the Tamil name of an Untouchable caste, has accordingly moved into the English language as a synonym for the socially ostracised and the morally depraved (see Deliege, 1997).

The Untouchables described by Dubois accept their status and believe in the legitimacy of the system so that there is no thought of equality in their mind: 'The idea that he (untouchable) was born to be in subjection to the other castes is so ingrained in his mind that it never occurs to the Pariah to think that his fate is anything but irrevocable. Nothing will ever persuade him that men are all made of the same clay' (Dubois, 1959: 50, quoted in Moffatt, 1979: 7).

The early outcaste image, as it was articulated by Dubois, implies a major disjunction between the higher 'caste Hindus' and the lowermost Untouchables, or outcastes. The very terms express the disjunction. The main body of the Hindu population 'has caste' and is regulated by its social and cultural conventions, while the Untouchables are outside the system.

Dr Frances Buchanan

Another Western observer of the same period as Abbe Dubois, who surveyed newly acquired territories in Mysore for the British in 1799,

describes the Untouchable Madiga as follows: '[The Madiga] are
divided into small tribes of ten or twelve houses, and intermarry
with the daughters of these houses only, in order to be certain of
the purity of their race; of which they seem to be as fond, as those
castes that are esteemed infinitely superior in rank' (Buchanan, 1807:
640, quoted in Moffatt, 1979: 8).

These two views of Untouchables and caste, the outcaste image
and the simple consensus image, dominated Western thinking through
the British period. This approach considered that, 'To be an Untouchable is not to be excluded from the culture of caste, but it is to possess
this culture in a thinner and less convincing form' (Moffatt, 1979: 8).

CONTEMPORARY ANTHROPOLOGICAL AND SOCIOLOGICAL PERSPECTIVES

In recent years, social anthropologists and ethnographers of South
Asia have been preoccupied with the subject of hierarchy in the
Hindu social system. Definitions of the caste system have been
advanced in which the authors have sought to isolate the code which
differentiates Hindus into exclusive social groups and ranks them in
a hierarchical relationship with one another. Two authors in particular, F.G. Bailey and Louis Dumont, have written on this subject and
other social anthropologists have aligned themselves with one or the
other theory (Dumont, 1957, 1960, 1966, 1970; Dumont and
Pocock, 1957; Bailey, 1959, 1963).

System of Ranking Related to Productive Resources

For Bailey, 'caste is a system of ranks which is related to differential control over the productive resources' (1957: 266). Each person
in the caste system performs economic, political and ritual roles and
except for certain anomalies, there is a 'high degree of coincidence
between politico-economic rank and the ritual ranking of caste'
(ibid.). The anomalies are mainly apparent at the uppermost and
lowermost ranks of the ritual system. A Brahmin of scant economic
means does not fall to a low ritual rank nor can a wealthy Untouchable
attain high ritual rank. For caste groups between these two extremes

'their ritual rank tends to follow their economic rank in the village community' (Bailey, 1957: 266–67).

Ritual Purity as the Basis of Hierarchy

Dumont, however, has criticised Bailey's interpretation of the caste system. For Dumont, ritual purity, not differential control over productive resources, is the code of the caste hierarchy. 'Perhaps as early as the eighth century before Christ tradition has distinguished absolutely between hierarchical status and power' (1966: 56). According to Dumont, the hierarchical caste system is founded on two basic ideological principles: first, the opposition between ritual purity and pollution, which defines the hierarchical relationship between the pure Brahmins and the polluted Untouchables, and second, the absolute separation of religious status, personified by the Brahmins, from politico-economic power, which is ideally concentrated in the hands of Kshatriya kings (see Burghart, 1996: 35–42).

In spite of their differences of opinion, Bailey and Dumont share an underlying assumption in their analyses of Hindu social relations. They assume that caste hierarchy was the exclusive and exhaustive order of social relations in the traditional Hindu social system. Their differences of opinion relate mainly to the nature of the code of that hierarchy. Bailey's theory of closed social stratification and Dumont's theory of hierarchy are seen to be applicable to the traditional Hindu social system (see Bailey, 1963).

Dumont's Structuralist Approach

Dumont (1966) postulated that caste is the most fundamental and most specifically Hindu institution of Hindu society. He calls his approach 'structuralist', for the oppositional structure of pure/impure governs the operation of the caste system. These principles are found universally within India, but they are also unique to India. According to Dumont, caste represents the institutionalisation of hierarchical values. In his holistic conception of caste, hierarchy is expressed in an Indian cultural code of relative purity and impurity,

in a continuously graded status order whose extremes are the
Brahmin at the top—the most pure of men—and the Untouchables
at the bottom—the least pure of men. Brahmin and Untouchables are
conceptually opposed in a number of ways that contribute to their
archetypal purity and impurity, according to Dumont. The Brahmin
lives in the centre of the village and is a 'god on earth', while the
Untouchable lives outside the village and is apparently excluded
from religious life. The murder of a Brahmin is as heinous a crime
as the murder of a cow, while the Untouchable is a scavenger
and the eater of dead cows. The Brahmin purifies himself in order
to approach the gods and thus mediates between man and
god. The Untouchable makes personal purity possible by removing
the strongest sources of organic impurity and mediates between man
and the maleficent 'demons'.

For Dumont, however, this opposition of Brahmin and Untouchable is also complementary—the completion of a 'whole' by two
equally necessary but unequally ranked parts. 'The impurity of the
Untouchable is conceptually inseparable from the purity of the
Brahmin.' Since 'the execution of impure tasks by some is necessary
to the maintenance of purity for others ... society is a totality made
up of two unequal but complementary parts' (Dumont, 1970: 92, 93).

The universe of caste is structured by dharma in the sense of
the ever-present order of the universe. Here dharma is an absolute
concept; all sentient beings including gods are subject to its laws.
In the classic Brahmanical formulation, the social universe is taken
to be a manifestation in time and space of the ever-present Brahma.
From the cosmic body of Brahma at the dawn of time issued forth the
four main castes (strictly speaking, varna), each endowed with a
particular quality necessary to enact the sacrifices necessary to sustain
the universe. The first-born were the Brahmins who emerged from
the mouth of Brahma. They were possessed of the power of speech
and were entitled to effectuate a sacrifice by means of their knowledge of ritual formulae. The warriors, who emerged from the arms
of Brahma, were born next. They were endowed with the martial
qualities necessary to protect the universal order. It was their task to
offer the oblation at the sacrifice. The third-born were the Vaishyas,
or herders and tillers (in some regions of India they are said
to be merchants) who emerged from the thighs of Brahma. They

produced the material wealth of the universe and were charged with providing the oblation for the sacrifice. The last born were the servants, who sprang from the feet of Brahma. It was their duty to serve the other three castes outside the sacrificial arena.

The four castes were ranked, both in their order of birth and the excellence of their sacrificial function. The Brahmins were the first born and they performed the most excellent function at the sacrifice. Virtue in this system, however, is not defined in terms of emulating the functions of the higher castes; rather it lies in the performance of one's own caste's duties; it is more virtuous for the cobbler to tan his polluting hides and to beat the drum at the village temple than to imitate the superior ways of the Brahmin scholar. In this way, by each caste observing its particular duties, the universe survives as a whole.

Separation pervades the entire caste system. Servants cannot enter the sacrificial arena, for they lack the sacred thread of the upper three castes. The most notorious separation is that of untouchability. The members of the four main castes, which constitute the mouth, arms, thighs and feet of Brahma, do not accept water, which has been handled by those castes that are outside Brahma's auspicious body.

Each person is said to have a certain amount of spiritual energy, or *samskara*, which he has accumulated by performing acts of self-sacrifice in previous lives. Unequal birth and unequal achievement in any particular lifetime are attributed to an unequal accumulation of spiritual energy. This energy also determines one's entitlement to follow a particular path of personal salvation. Untouchable castes are not admitted because the bodies and minds of such persons are considered to be impure, dull or otherwise unfit for initiation. Had such persons more spiritual energy, they would have been born into a higher station in life and would have been fit receptacles of religious knowledge (see Fuller and Spencer, 1996: 35–42).

Critics of Dumont's Approach

Dumont's understanding of Indian society seems to be situated at the confluence of sociology and Indology. His position has been severely criticised by several anthropologists and sociologists like Gerald Berreman (1971), Kathleen Gough (1973) and Joan Mencher (1974). It is a common criticism of Dumont that his use of Brahmanical sources in understanding Hindu society commits him to a Brahmanical view of society and that Untouchables may conceive of society differently (Freeman, 1979; see also Barnett et al., 1976; Burghart, 1983; Lynch, 1977). In the last two decades or so, many anthropological writings have been devoted to the cultural traditions of low caste groups; and they have emphasised the differences between the socio-religious ideology of upper castes and lower castes, especially Untouchables, who have traditionally been kept outside the varna hierarchy (see Appadurai, 1986; Burghart, 1983: 281; Deliege, 1992; Juergensmeyer, 1982; Khare, 1984). Had Dumont seen Hindu society from 'below', that is, taken a 'the bottom-up' view, his picture would have been different.

Untouchables Having a Distinctive Culture of Their Own

In her approach, Kathleen Gough points out that cultural differences between the high and low castes are due to political and economic variables generated by the upper castes. Gough has analysed the Untouchable Pallans of south India. Unlike most modern ethnographers of Indian Untouchables, she is emphatically on the side of the low castes and against what she sees as the hierarchical, etiquette-bound high castes. If some of the early observers on caste and untouchability like Dubois viewed the 'nature' of the Untouchables as uncivilised and degraded, Gough reverses the evaluation and sets up tacit oppositions between the inhibiting 'culture' of the Brahmins and the freer 'nature' of the Untouchables. She discerns in the Pallans (Untouchables) a looser, more psychologically healthy, approach to life. In their relation to sexuality and aggression, for example, the Pallans are said to be less restricted than the Brahmins: 'The expression of aggression toward elders and peers (among the Pallans) is not strictly inhibited (as it is among the Brahmins)....Similarly, the lower castes do not favour ascetic control of sexuality in marital relationships.... The ascetic control of sexuality for its own sake does not increase a man's spiritual strength' (Gough, 1956: 847; see also Moffatt, 1979: 9–10).

The cultural dimension of Gough's approach is 'certain moral values deriving from the Sanskrit religious tradition, of which [the Brahmans] are the main carriers' (1956: 826). Since the Pallans are among the lowest castes, farthest spatially and socially from the Brahmins, they are of all castes in the village the most free of the restraints of this Sanskritic culture. Most of Gough's cultural typifications of the low castes are framed in opposition to negatively loaded Brahmanic traits: 'The low castes place much less emphasis than do Brahmins on other worldliness and on the fate of the soul after death. Engaged in the practical business of earning a living through manual labour, the low castes care more for health and prosperity in this life' (ibid.: 846). Gough's positive restatement of the outcaste image is stated psychologically, but it is set within a broader materialist analysis. The Untouchables' alternatives vary according to the image. For Dubois, Untouchables are in a state of unbridled license, while for Gough, they are in a state of psychologically healthy removal from an obsessive high-caste culture (Moffatt, 1979: 13).

According to Kathleen Gough, the Untouchable Pallans have a distinctive social and cultural subsystem. Gough sums up these contrasts in a personal statement about the ethos of the Pallan life: 'Pallans show an almost fanatical passion for equality within their caste group. In fact, I found the equal and comradely style of life in the Palla street a great relief from the obsessive ritualism, hierarchy, and envy in the Brahmin street.... [The Pallans] react to their poverty [of which they are well aware] with a combination of anger, resignation, wryness and humor' (Gough, 1973: 232, 233–34). Though Gough does not make the point explicitly, the distinctive features that she discerns in the Pallans—solidarity, egalitarianism and the weakness of traditional kinship authority, might be expected to help them to radical anti-caste political action (Moffatt, 1979: 18).

Similar views of Untouchables having their own distinctive culture are found in the works of Joan Mencher (1974), Bernard Cohn (1955), Robert Miller (1966) and Gerald Berreman (1971). According to their approach, Untouchables are seen to have demystified caste and its accompanying ideology, seeing the caste system in an objective and culture-free way for what it really is—a system of oppression. Thus Joan Mencher feels that Paraiyans in south India have a more 'explicitly materialistic' view of the system and their place in it than do those at the top and that 'those at the bottom of the hierarchy have less need to rationalise its inequities' (Mencher, 1974: 476).

Bernard Cohn also regards the Untouchables as the bearers of an alternate social and cultural system, different from the upper-caste culture and adapted to the needs and experiences of those at the very bottom of the system. In his analysis of the Untouchable Chamars of north India, Cohn sees the Chamars as differing from the high castes for the same reason that Gough's Pallans differ from the Brahmins, that is, the social and spatial separation between Untouchables and higher castes. Because Untouchables cannot hear the Vedas, or be served by Brahmins, or enter high-caste temples, they suffer from a kind of communication block. The result of this block, however, is not a form of culturelessness, but the retention of a historically prior pre-Aryan little tradition. Unlike the great tradition of the higher castes and of the Brahmins in particular, the little tradition of the Chamars contains a 'pre-Aryan and non-Brahmanic' religion, which emphasises the propitiation of the goddesses of disease and the use of mediums and exorcists (Cohn, 1955: 58). Cohn has to qualify these disjunctive contrasts considerably, however: 'It is almost impossible to sort out those traits which are Sanskritic and those which are non-Sanskritic ... and ... what is idiosyncratic to the Chamars as a group and what is a common body of ritual and belief held by other low castes and high castes as well' (Cohn, 1954: 175). Given this qualification, then, Cohn's analysis amounts to a set of tentatively specified contrasts within an unanalysed framework of cultural continuities.

Robert Miller has studied the Untouchable Mahars of central India. Unlike Cohn's Chamars, who are attempting to diminish the despised cultural disjunction between themselves and the higher castes, to be in a sense revaluing their little tradition, the Mahars, Miller writes, 'have been building a tradition which can hardly be called "a distinctive variant of the Great Tradition cognate to those of the four major *varnas* of Hindu society"' (quoting Singer, 1958: 194). In fact, the Mahars are building on a counter-great tradition which has always existed in India, as an antithesis to the Brahmanic great tradition. In this counter tradition, 'equality is opposed to inequality;

individual ability is opposed to merger of the individual in the group; emotionalism is opposed to ritualism; escape *from* the system is opposed to movement *within* the system.' Miller's discussion amounts to an assertion that Bhakti devotionalism, Mahar militance and the eventual emergence of neo-Buddhism from the Mahar caste, attest the strength of these alternate values (see Miller, 1966: 26–28).

Recently, Kancha Ilaiah (1996a, 1996b) has asserted the distinctive culture of the Dalitbahujan (lower Shudras and Atishudras) in Indian society. He distinguishes and contrasts the cultural differences between the upper caste Brahmin, Baniya or Kshatriya with that of the Dalitbahujans. According to him, 'Mainstream historiography has done nothing to incorporate the Dalitbahujan perspective in the writing of Indian history.... To make matters worse, recent Hindu politics—and its historiography—has sought to wipe out the possibility of Dalitbahujan perspective and a Dalitbahujan history by simply declaring that the Dalitbahujan are (fallen) Hindus. This essay seeks to challenge that Brahmanical historiography by pointing to the contrariness—and differentness—of Dalitbahujan perspective and history' (1996b: 165).

Gerald Berreman's 'Caste School of Race'

Gerald Berreman has studied the rural Untouchables of a Himalayan village in north India. In a short critique of Louis Dumont's structural theory of caste, Berreman claims that when he presented his version of the Dumontian model to rural Untouchables, 'they laughed, and one of them said, "you have been talking with Brahmins"' (1971: 16–23). Like Mencher, Berreman maintains that Untouchables in some way reject a high-caste model of the system. The Untouchables act in accordance with the system of caste because they are forced to so act, but they cannot be forced to believe.

Berreman's interpretation of Indian untouchability is part of an explicit defence of the 'caste school of race' in American Sociology founded on the work of W. Lloyd Warner (1936), John Dollard (1937), Gunnar Myrdal (1944, 1967) and others (see Béteille, 1992: 15–56). In its original form, this school constructed a comparative analogy between the racial system of the American south in the 1930s and 1940s and the Indian caste system. In both systems, there are said to be two or more rigidly ranked groups between which individual mobility is impossible. Membership in each group is permanent and defined at birth (or 'birth ascribed'); each group is endogamous; and each system is maintained by prohibitions on inter-group contacts, especially on sexual ones between males of the low groups and females of the high groups. Ultimately, each system is maintained by the power of the high groups—by coercion rather than consensus.

Berreman's position on Untouchables is a return to the function-alist comparison of the 'caste school of race', adding insights from the more detailed anthropological fieldwork on caste carried out in the 1950s in India. Berreman compares the relationship between 'touchable' and 'untouchable' castes in India with the relationship between African–Americans and white Americans in the south of the United States.

Not all anthropologists or social scientists agree with Berreman's conclusion that 'race relations' in southern United States constitute a caste system. The work, however, is important because it illustrates the value and the necessity of cross-cultural comparisons of 'invidi-ous distinctions' (Cole, 1988: 467). Yet, Berreman points out that the power of high-caste Indians does have a role in maintaining the caste system and that caste is rife with manipulation and conflict. Thus, it does not differ from race in terms of these sociological abstrac-tions. He brings race and caste together as sociological equivalents (see Berreman, 1960, 1972, 1988). Berreman says, 'In the caste system, "Because intensive and status equal interaction is limited to the caste, a common and distinctive culture is assured. This is a function of the quality and density of communication within the group, for culture is learned, shared and transmitted"' (quoting Berreman, 1967: 51; 1972: 400). From this he concludes that each social unit (each caste) is imagined as a tightly-bound cultural unit (a 'distinctive culture') and proceeds to the following generalisation: 'Caste, race and ethnic stratification, like all plural systems therefore, are systems of social separation and cultural heterogeneity, main-tained by common or overriding economic and political institutions rather than by agreement or consensus regarding the stratification system and its rationale' (Berreman, 1972: 400).

Berreman's main point is that power alone, and consensus about power, determines caste and all other systems of structural social inequality. This position is admittedly extreme, but some of its comparative assumptions are shared by other anthropologists who have analysed Indian Untouchables disjunctively. Gough (1973), Mencher (1974) and Miller (1966), in particular, make very clear their personal distaste for caste, in all its social inequities and its oppression.

In contrast to this approach, Dumont does not see caste as an inexplicably 'unequal' system that requires an explanation because of the way in which it violates the more fundamentally egalitarian 'nature' of man. Rather, Dumont reverses the comparative question and suggests that it is Western egalitarian ideology that is the socio-scientific puzzle and that rank or hierarchy is more trans-humanly comprehensible: 'man does not only think, acts [sic].... To adopt a value is to introduce hierarchy, and a certain consensus of values, a certain hierarchy of ideas, things and people, is indispensable to social life.... In relation to these more or less necessary requirements of social life, the idea of equality, even if it is thought superior, is artificial' (Dumont, 1970: 54–55). Caste represents the institution-alisation of hierarchical values, the most elaborate known working out of a set of values that the West has been systematically denying for the last 300 years. To understand fully the egalitarian effort in the West, Dumont says, the West must confront its polar opposite in India, hierarchy.

In this comparative epistemology, Dumont differs radically from Berreman and from other conflict theorists and functionalists. For Dumont, to compare is not to dismiss ideological specificities as unimportant detail and to search for abstract, ahistorical essence common to caste, race and ethnic stratification. To compare is to construct a structural analysis of each ideological and social forma-tion, and then to confront these fully and specifically analysed formations with one another (see Barnett et al., 1976: 627–28). Dumont's comparative analyses contain a number of simple logical oppositions, but they are nevertheless interesting. Caste, Dumont says, is a homogeneous moral system that values hierarchy and does not isolate and value the individual as the 'measure of all things'. Racism, on the other hand, is ideologically linked to egalitarianism, individualism and to the Western denial of hierarchy. According to Dumont, in denying hierarchy in the social realm as a legitimate innate quality of the relations between humans, Western ideology must resituate it in a rigorously differentiated natural realm as racism, referred exclusively to natural difference (see Dumont, 1960; 1970: 35–55). Thus, for Dumont, Indian Untouchables are not the abstract sociological equivalent of racially subordinate groups in Western society.

Untouchability is a Fall from the Upper-Caste Status

Pauline Kolenda has studied the Untouchable Sweepers in north India. Kolenda begins her analysis by demonstrating that the basic themes in the Sweepers' religion are common not only to higher-caste religion but to themes found in the ancient Sanskritic texts. She then deals with a single disjunction—with the question of how the Sweepers deal with one unpleasant implication of the linked doctrines of karma, dharma and transmigration. According to these doctrines, which the Sweepers understand in abstract form, one's caste status in a given birth is the result of the total score of one's good or bad karma ('action' in accord with one's dharma, 'duty', as defined in a given caste) in past lives (Kolenda, 1964).

If the Untouchable Sweepers were to apply the karmic explanation to their present low status, they would be admitting that they deserved such a status—that they had been unusually wicked in past rebirths. This admission, according to Kolenda, would cause them 'religious anxiety'. Hence, the Sweepers refuse to apply the karma doctrine to their own low status. Instead, they refer their present status to collective myths which state that they were once of much higher caste and fell due to a terrible accident motivated by the best of intentions. According to one myth, for example, the original Untouchable was a Brahmin who came upon a cow mired in the mud. Intending to help the cow (a meritorious intent), he pulled on its tail. But the cow died and since he had been in contact with a dead cow—a polluting contact—his older brothers outcast him and he became the first Untouchable (Cohn, 1954: 113). Not only do myths like this protect Untouchables from the 'anxiety' of karmic explanation, according to Kolenda, but they provide them with a positive sense of having once been much higher in the social order (see Kolenda, 1964: 74–76).

UNTOUCHABILITY TO DALIT MOVEMENT

'Dalit', which, as shown earlier, means ground down, downtrodden, oppressed, is now being used by the low castes in a spirit of pride and militancy. The term began to be used by politically-awakened ex-Untouchables in the early 1970s when the Dalit Panthers, a youthful group of activists and writers in Bombay, came on the scene to protest injustice. The Dalit Panther organisation is now scattered and important only in a few places, but the pride and militancy that accompanied the name has created a new category of culture in India (see Zelliot, 1996: 1–4). The name has achieved widespread use in book titles and in newspaper reports on both violence against Dalits and accomplishments among them. The term Dalit is not merely a rejection of the very idea of pollution or impurity or 'Untouchability', it reveals a sense of a unified class, of a movement toward equality. It speaks of a new stage in the movement of India's Untouchables which is now a century old. Dalit self-assertion manifests itself today in a debate on several contrapositions: Gandhi vs Ambedkar, Harijan vs Dalit, Varna vs Jati, Manuwad vs casteless society.

In view of the social location of the Dalits, it should occasion no surprise that they were the last community in colonial India to be influenced by those liberal notions, which reached out to the country as a part of the cultural hegemony of the West. Perhaps the first modern Dalit voice was that of Jotiba Phule, a powerful advocate of social and gender equality based in Maharashtra. Another Dalit deeply influenced by liberal values was the Ezhava leader of Kerala, Narayana Guru, who attacked the institution of caste in a regional society where the Adi Shankara had argued, long centuries ago, of the essential oneness of things in his metaphysical formulation of *advaita* (non-dualism) as the true basis of reality. There was a fair sprinkling of Dalit leaders elsewhere holding out identical messages. Their principal argument was loud and clear. Humankind was made up of a vast community of individuals all of whom, in principle, were entitled to the same social status and economic and cultural dignity.

Though the Dalit voice expressed itself eloquently from the outset, it was left to B.R. Ambedkar, a second generation Dalit leader, to articulate the abject condition of his community in the idiom of modern politics. Ambedkar also spelt out why Hindu discourse offered no route to liberation for the oppressed classes located within the Hindu social matrix. The Dalit communities, Ambedkar argued, were not stratified constituents of an associational social order. Instead, they constituted the nethermost stratum of an organically integrated social body, held together somewhat tightly by the world view of Brahmanical Hinduism. The only way to liberation for the Dalits, therefore, was to opt out of the Hindu fold.

In the course of empowering his Dalit caste fellows, Ambedkar was drawn into an epic conflict with Gandhi, on the critical question of the Dalit location within the Hindu social order. Ambedkar felt that once India got freedom, his people, the Untouchables, would once again be subjected to the hegemony of caste Hindus and be forced to scavenge and sweep for them. To safeguard their interests, he proposed that there should be a number of special seats in Parliament for the depressed classes which would be filled through elections from special constituencies. While drafting a new Consti-tution for India in the 1930s, the British extended to the Dalit communities the privilege of voting as a separate electoral constitu-ency. Gandhi opposed this constitutional provision with all the strength at his command, since (so he believed) a separate Harijan electorate would damage Hindu society beyond repair. Instead, he offered the Dalits reserved seats in the central and provincial legislatures on a scale more generous than promised by the British. The so-called Poona Pact of 1932 was a triumph for the Mahatma because it ensured the social cohesion of Hindu society.

According to Gandhi, 'the most effective, quickest and the most unobtrusive way to destroy caste is for reformers to begin the practice with themselves.... The reform will not come by reviling the orthodox. The so-called higher classes will have to descend from their pedestal before they can make impression upon the so-called lower classes.' Ambedkar, on the other hand, believed that India required a cultural revolution to destroy the caste system and his call to his followers was: 'educate, organise and agitate'. Thus, Ambedkar's project rested on questioning the traditional social order in order to build a just and an equalitarian society, while Gandhi's interest was to preserve the traditional social equilibrium. In addition to providing leadership, Ambedkar engendered among the Depressed Classes the vital element of self-respect without which the Untouchables movement probably could not have arisen. Under his leadership they realised that it was possible for them to organise, resist and challenge the injustice they were suffering.

Dr Ambedkar's followers formed the Republican Party of India immediately after his death, mainly for representing the interests of the Scheduled Castes and other weaker sections. But the leadership crisis in the Republican Party and the growing attacks on the Dalits made the Dalit youth reject their leadership and adopt a militant method. These Dalits, especially the educated Dalits in Maharashtra, came forward and took up the task of bringing all the Scheduled Castes onto one platform and mobilising them in the struggle for their rights and justice. The caste stigma, which remained even after its legal abolition, was deeply painful to these sensitive youths. They firmly believed in what Fanon said: 'Hunger with dignity was preferable to bread eaten in slavery' (1965: 143). They struggled at various levels in villages, cities, educational institutions and working organisations by means of a number of political and social organisations like the Dalit Panther, mass movements, Dalit Liberation Army, Youth Republican, Dalit Sangharsha Samiti and through Dalit theatre, Dalit art, Dalit literature and among Christians, Dalit theology, etc. These organisations, dominated mostly by youth wings of the Dalit force, worked as pressure groups for educating and mobilising the Dalits and demonstrating in order to get their problems resolved. Dalit consciousness was also expressed in the formation of the Bhim Sena, Dalit Sena, Dalit Sahitya Movement, the emergence of Dalit Rangbhoomi (Dalit theatre) BAMCEF (The All India Backward SC, ST, OBC and Minority Communities Employees Federation), the Bahujan Samaj Party (BSP) and the Bharatiya Republican Party (BRP).

Thus, with the growth of democratic institutions and the 'politics of number' the Dalits began to assume some importance in national politics in independent India. The leaders among the Untouchables, in order to take due advantage of the situation and bring about their liberation, started to mobilise forces in their favour. Today the Dalit voters have successfully undercut the dominance of the upper caste and intermediate castes; and have thrown up a new leadership reflecting a social resurgence from below that provides, contemporaneously, an altogether novel complexion to democratic functioning. They are involved in mass social awakenings, providing a share in power, not only in government jobs but in all sectors. Their politics is aimed at a cultural revolution with a belief that unless there is a cultural and social revolution there cannot be a political revolution (Paswan, 1996: 7). This novel politics, which is Ambedkarite in inspiration, rests on a grand strategy that seeks to turn the Indian world 'upside down'; and shape an order of things wherein the hitherto deprived shall not only inherit the earth, literally and metaphorically, but also shape the principles of governance which mould the entire polity. In its strategic design, therefore, the Dalit upsurge of our times is a development of the highest significance, potentially speaking.

The current political initiative by the Dalit leaders only marks the beginning of a new era of democratic politics. In spite of its ups and downs with leadership crisis and demoralisation, Dalit liberation movements have become a force to be reckoned with today. More and more Dalits have begun to speak out openly and courageously and nobody can set their voice aside. They are actively participating in political alliances with other influential political parties in the country.

The chapters in this volume represent the major concerns of the Dalits. The book is divided into four parts. The first part deals with historical material on the origin and development of untouchability in Indian civilisation. Shrirama, after going through the traditional Sanskrit texts right from the *Rig Veda* to the later Smritis, comes to the conclusion that the foundations of untouchability are laid in the Hindu scriptures. This is followed by the chapter by John C.B. Webster that broadly deals with the genesis of the term 'Dalit'. After a historical search on the problem of who is a Dalit, he comes to the understanding that caste alone, not class or religion determines who is a Dalit.

The Dalit vision of Indian society is not the same as the upper-caste Hindu vision. The second section is concerned with this. Mahesh Gavaskar's chapter sets out to study the contributions of

Jotirao Phule, who laid the foundation for the contemporary Dalit movement and who is also known as the father of the Indian social revolution (see Keer, 1964). This is followed by S.M. Michael's chapter, which outlines the main ideas developed by eminent social philosophers like Jotirao Phule, E.V. Ramaswamy Periyar and Babasaheb Ambedkar, whose influence is very strong in the Dalit movement today. The next chapter by Timothy Fitzgerald further develops the social implications of the ideas of Ambedkar on Indian society. Gopal Guru takes up the question of the Dalit movement in mainstream sociology. According to him, the ideological position of scholars will shape their approach to a Dalit sociology. If some scholars believe that the Dalit movement is limited to achieving partial changes in the existing social order, then their view of Dalit sociology will be different from that of those scholars who believe in the total transformation of Indian society. A comparative study of liberation movements will be of great value in Dalit sociology. This is undertaken by K.P. Singh, who compares two underprivileged communities in two different cultural setups, namely, India and USA. Essentially, the social movements launched by Dalits and African-Americans are based on the ethos of protest directed against their socio-economic, religious-cultural and legal oppression and exploitation. The author is convinced that the emergence of a 'Dalit consciousness' and a 'Black consciousness' has dignified the Dalits and made the African-Americans more respected in their respective communities.

The third section deals with methodological and processual aspects of Dalits in Indian society. S. Selvam critiques traditional Indian sociology which looks at Indian society mainly from a Sanskritic perspective. In the course of this critique, he also makes an attempt to propose a method for the study of the complex nature of Hinduism and Indian society. He is also of the opinion that Brahmanical ideology, in a relatively peaceful and subtle manner, swayed the lower caste mind/attitude so that subordination in the Brahmanical ideological domain was accepted. He proposes that in order to unravel the ways in which first the Dalits, and now the tribals, have been incorporated into the Brahmanical social organisation, studies should be undertaken at the micro, regional and macro levels. The next chapter in this volume, by Arjun Patel, is in the spirit of this proposal.

Patel studies the Hinduisation of Adivasis in south Gujarat and shows how the tribals have been brought into a Sanskritic way of life at the expense of the tribal culture. The problems of Dalit women are dealt with in the chapter by Traude Pillai-Vetschera. Using information from her fieldwork on the Mahar women in Ahmednagar district of Maharashtra, Traude Pillai-Vetschera discusses the impact of patriarchy on Dalit women. Even though many Dalits nowadays say that they do not believe in 'Sanskritisation', they have nevertheless adopted from the high castes those behavioural patterns which are oppressive to Dalit women. A Dalit patriarchy has developed, in which Dalit men use the same mechanisms to subjugate their women as those used by high caste men for ages to subjugate women and also Dalits. The next chapter deals on the emerging power dimension of Dalits in contemporary India. Dalit politics has seen trajectories of various kinds in different parts of India. Christophe Jaffrelot in his insightful chapter analyses the power politics of the Bahujan Samaj Party (BSP) in Uttar Pradesh. The BSP's ambition for competitive electoral and party politics makes it to go beyond the Dalit threshold by reaching out to new caste groups. What this mean for the empowerment of Dalits needs to be watched very carefully as the Dalit movement progresses.

The fourth and last part concentrates on the economic conditions of the Dalits. Sukhadeo Thorat in his chapter on 'Ambedkar's Interpretation of the Caste System, its Economic Consequences and Suggested Remedies' points out that unlike other human societies, the Hindu social order in its classical form does not recognise the individual and his distinctiveness as the centre of social purpose. In this context, Thorat argues that Ambedkar's view of equal rights would provide the legal framework against violation of laws against discrimination in public and private spheres. Gail Omvedt discusses Dalits and economic policy, taking inspiration from the contributions of Ambedkar. At present there is a lot of discussion on the impact of the new economic policy on the Dalits. This is the concern of the next chapter by P.G. Jogdand. Dealing with the subject of the reservation policy and the empowerment of Dalits, Jogdand argues that the aim of establishing job reservations or quotas in government service and public sector undertakings has been to create a just society by providing a helping hand to disadvantaged sections of

Indian society. All the same, he laments that the government and its implementing agencies are playing politics over the job reservation issue. Hence, he stresses the need to conscientise and politicise the underprivileged to fight back against the unjust system in India. Dealing on the same subject, Richard Pais has done fieldwork on employment and social mobility among the SCs of Mangalore in Karnataka. He is interested in knowing whether or not the different government protective policies have helped the SCs towards upward mobility. He finds a positive correlation between protective measures of employment (reservation policy) and social mobility among the Dalits.

Dr Stephen Fuchs, our esteemed teacher and guide has contributed pioneering works to Dalit sociology. *The Children of Hari, At the Bottom of Indian Society* and several articles on Dalit castes are sufficient proof of his continuous interest in them. *The Children of Hari*, a monograph on the Nimar Balahis in Madhya Pradesh, published in 1950, is one of the first comprehensive scientific studies of a Dalit caste in India. This volume, *Dalit Sociology*, is a token tribute to a teacher from whom I have learned the craft of sociological and anthropological analysis and understanding.

REFERENCES AND SELECT BIBLIOGRAPHY

Ambedkar, B.R. (1948) *The Untouchables*. Bangalore: Dalit Sahitya Akademy.

Appadurai, Arjun (1986) 'Is Homo Hierarchicus?', *American Ethnologist*, 13(4): 745–61.

Bailey, F.G. (1957) *Caste and Economic Frontier*. Manchester: Manchester University Press.

———. (1959) 'For a Sociology of India?', *Contribution to Indian Sociology,* 3: 88–101.

———. (1963) 'Closed Stratification in India', *European Journal of Sociology*, 4: 107–24.

Barnett, Steven A., Lina Fruzzetti and Akos Ostor (1976) 'Hierarchy Purified: Notes on Dumont and His Critics', *Journal of Asian Studies*, 35(4): 627–46.

Berreman, Gerald (1960) 'Caste in India and the United States', *American Journal of Sociology*, 66: 120–27.

———. (1967) 'Stratification, Pluralism and Interaction: A Comparative Analysis of Caste', in A. de Reuck and J. Knight (eds), *Caste and Race: Comparative Approaches*, pp. 165–78. London: Churchill.

———. (1971) 'The Brahmanical View of Caste', *Contributions to Indian Sociology* (N.S.) 5: 16–23.

———. (1972) 'Race, Caste and Other Invidious Distinctions in Social Stratification', *Race*, 13(4): 385–414.

Berreman, Gerald (1988) 'Race, Caste, and Other Invidious Distinctions in Social Stratification', in Johnnetta B. Cole (ed.), *Anthropology for the Nineties: Introductory Readings*, pp. 484–521. New York: The Free Press.

Béteille, André (1992) *Society and Politics in India: Essays in a Comparative Perspective*. New Delhi: Oxford University Press.

Buchanan, F. (1807) 'Buchanan's Journey through Mysore, Canara, and Malabar', in F. Pinkerton (ed.), *Voyages and Travels to All Parts of the World*, Vol. 8. London: Longman, Hurst, Reese, Orme and Brown.

Burghart, Richard (1983) 'For a Sociology of Indias: An Intracultural Approach to the study of "Hindu Society"', *Contributions to Indian Sociology* (N.S.) 17: 275–99.

———. (1996) *The Conditions of Listening: Essays on Religion, History and Politics in South Asia*, in C.J. Fuller and Jonathan Spencer (eds), pp. 35–42. New Delhi: Oxford University Press.

Cole, B. Johnnetta (1988) 'Toward a New Anthropology: On Systems of Inequality', in Johnnetta B. Cole (ed.), *Anthropology for the Nineties: Introductory Readings,* pp. 463–69. New York: The Free Press.

Cohn, Bernard (1954) 'The Camars of Senapur: A Study of the Changing Status of a Depressed Caste', Ph.D. dissertation, Cornell University.

———. (1955) 'The Changing Status of a Depressed Caste', in McKim Marriott (ed.), *Village India*. Chicago: The University of Chicago Press.

Deliege, Robert (1992) 'Replication and Consensus: Untouchability, Caste and Ideology in India', *Man* (N.S.) 27: 155–73.

———. (1997) *The World of the 'Untouchables': Paraiyars of Tamil Nadu*. New Delhi: Oxford University Press.

Dollard, John (1937) *Caste and Class in a Southern Town*. New York: Doubleday.

Dubois, Abbe J.A. (1959 [1815]) *Hindu Manners, Customs and Ceremonies*. Oxford: Clarendon.

Dumont, Louis (1957) 'For a Sociology of India', *Contributions to Indian Sociology*, 1: 1–22.

———. (1960) 'A Rejoinder to Dr. Bailey', *Contributions to Indian Sociology*, 4: 82–89.

———. (1966) *Homo Hierarchicus: Essai sur le Systeme des Castes*. Paris: Gallimard.

———. (1970) *Religion, Politics and History in India*. Paris: Mouton

Dumont, L. and D. Pocock (1957) 'For a Sociology of India', *Contributions to Indian Sociology*, 1: 7–22.

Fanon, Frantz (1965) *Wretched of the Earth*. UK: Macgibbon and Kee, Penguin Books.

Freeman, J. (1979) *Untouchable: An Indian Life History*. London: Allen & Unwin.

Fuchs, Stephen (1950) *The Children of Hari: A Study of the Nimar Balahis in the Central Provinces of India*. Vienna: Verlag Herold.

———. (1981) *At the Bottom of Indian Society: The Harijan and Other Low Castes*. New Delhi: Munshiram Manoharlal.

Fuller, C.J. and Jonathan Spencer (eds) (1996) *The Conditions of Listening: Essays on Religion, History and Politics in South Asia* by Richard Burghart. New Delhi: Oxford University Press.

Fürer-Haimendorf, Christoph von (1950) 'Foreword', in *Children of Hari: A Study of the Nimar Balahis in the Central Provinces of India* by Stephen Fuchs. Vienna: Verlag Herold.

Gough, Kathleen (1956) 'Brahmin Kinship in a Tamil Village', *American Anthropologist*, 58: 826–53.

———. (1973) 'Harijans in Thanjavur', in K. Gough and H.P. Sharma (eds), *Imperialism and Revolution in South Asia*. New York: Monthly Review Press.

Guru, Gopal and V. Geetha (1997) *Dalit Intellectual Activism: Recent Trends*. Mumbai: VAK Publication.

Hutton, J.H. (1963) *Caste in India*. Oxford: Oxford University Press.

Ilaiah, Kancha (1996a) *Why I am not a Hindu: A Sudra Critique of Hindutva Philosophy, Culture and Political Economy*. Calcutta: Samya.

———. (1996b) 'Productive Labour, Consciousness and History: The Dalitbahujan Alternative', in Shahid Amin and Dipesh Chakrabarty (eds), *Subaltern Studies IX: Writings on South Asian History and Society*, pp. 165–200. New Delhi: Oxford University Press.

Juergensmeyer, Mark (1982) *Religion as Social Vision, the Movement against Untouchability in Twentieth Century Punjab*. Berkeley: University of California Press.

Keer, Dhananjay (1964) *Mahatma Jotirao Phooley: Father of Indian Social Revolution*. Bombay: Popular Prakashan.

Khare, R.S. (1984) *The Untouchable as Himself: Ideology, Identity and Pragmatism among the Lucknow Chamars*. Cambridge: Cambridge University Press.

Kolenda, Pauline (1964) 'Religious Anxiety and Hindu Fate', in E.B. Harper (ed.), *Religion in South Asia*, pp. 158–95. Berkeley and Los Angeles: University of California Press.

Lynch, Owen M. (1977) 'Method and Theory in the Sociology of Louis Dumont: A Reply', in Kenneth David (ed.), *The New Wind, Changing Identities in South Asia*, pp. 82–96. Paris: Mouton Publishers.

Mencher, Joan P. (1974) 'The Caste System Upside Down, or the Not-So-Mysterious East', *Current Anthropology*, 15: 469–93.

Miller, Robert (1966) 'Button, Button ... Great Tradition, Little Tradition, Whose Tradition?', *Anthropological Quarterly*, 39: 26–42.

Moffatt, Michael (1979) *An Untouchable Community in South India*. Princeton: Princeton University Press.

Myrdal, Gunnar (1944) *An American Dilemma: The Negro Problem in Modern Democracy*. New York: Harper and Row.

———. (1967) 'Chairman's Introduction', in A.de Reuck and J. Knight (eds), *Caste and Race*. London: J&A Churchill.

Paswan, Ram Vilas (1996) 'Dalit Political Figures', *Dalit International Newsletter*. Waterford, USA, February, p. 7.

Singer, Milton (1958) 'Traditional India: Structure and Change', *Journal of American Folklore*, 71: 191–205.

Sowell, Thomas (1987) *A Conflict of Visions: Ideological Origins of Political Struggles*. New York: Quill William Morrow.

Warner, W. Lloyd (1936) 'American Caste and Class', *American Journal of Sociology*, 42 (1): 234–37.

Webster, John C.B. (1994) *The Dalit Christians: A History*. New Delhi: ISPCK.

Zelliot, Eleanor (1996) ' "Dalit Movement",' in *Dalit International Newsletter*, 1(1): 1–4. No. 1, February, pp. 1–4.

PART

I

1

Untouchability and Stratification in Indian Civilisation

SHRIRAMA

In order to lay bare the roots of untouchability in Indian society, this chapter highlights, in its opening portion, the emergence of untouchability in traditional Sanskrit texts right from the *Rig Veda* to the later Smritis. In order to understand the nature of the forces that led to the emergence of this practice, it is necessary to analyse in proper perspective the shaping of the entire pattern of social stratification. This is done in the second part of this chapter. (For an earlier exposition of this perspective, see Indradeva, 1985.)

FOUNDATIONS OF UNTOUCHABILITY IN HINDU SCRIPTURES

The foundations of untouchability were laid in ancient times. The immigrant Aryans were very different from the non-Aryan dark-skinned people whom they found living in India. The Aryans considered themselves superior and were proud of their race, language and religion. They considered non-Aryans to be non-humans or *amanushya* (Deodhar, 1981: X.22.9). The non-Aryans were described as *krishna varna* (ibid.: IX.41.1) or dark-skinned, *anasa* or without nose (snub-nosed), those who speak softly and worship the phallus. In the seventh *mandal* of the *Rig Veda*, Vasishtha says, 'The worshippers of Phallus should not come near Rita' (ibid.: VII.XXI.5). Thus, the Aryans maintained a distance from the earlier settlers or *dasa*s. These *dasa*s were declared to have been created as the 'lowest of all' (ibid.: II.12.4).

In the *Vajasaneyi Samhita* (composed around the tenth century BC), the words *Chandala* and *Paulkasa* occur, but there is no indication that they were Untouchables. In the *Chhandogya Upanishad* (composed around the eighth century BC), it is clearly said that 'those persons whose actions were low, will quickly attain an evil birth, the birth of a dog, or a hog or a *Chandala*' (Swami Swahananda, 1975: V.10.7).

The *Gautama Dharma Sutra* for the first time tries to explain the origin of the Chandalas. It says that the Chandala is the offspring of a male Shudra and a Brahmin woman and is the most reprehensible among those born in the indirect order or *pratiloma* (Pandey, 1966: IV.15.23). Gautama calls *pratiloma* castes *dharmahina* or without religion (ibid.: IV.20). The *Apastamba Dharma Sutra* says that after touching a Chandala, one should plunge into water, on talking to him one should converse with a Brahmin, and on seeing him one should look at the luminaries of the sky such as the sun, the moon, or the stars (Srinivasaraghavacharya, 1960: II.1.2 8–9). The Sutras were composed around sixth century BC. Manu rules that the Chandalas and Shvapakas should live outside the village (Doniger and Smith, 1992: X.51). (The *Manusmriti* was composed between second century BC and AD second century.) Manu also provides that an *antyavasayin* should be employed in a cemetery (ibid.: X.39). Apararka's commentary on *Yajnavalkya Smriti* quotes a verse of Vriddha-Yajnavalkya in which it is laid down that on touching Chandalas, Pukkasas, Mlechhas, Bhillas and Parasikas and persons guilty of *mahapataka*s or grave sins, one should bathe with one's clothes on (quoted in Apararka, 1966: 923). It is interesting to note that even Parasikas or Iranians were considered outcastes by the Indian elites (Indradeva, 1980). Samvarta, quoted by Apararka, the well-known law-giver, provides that 'on touching a fisherman, a deer-hunter, a hunter, a butcher, a bird-catcher and a washer-man one must first bathe and then take one's meals' (1966: 1196). Atri provides that if a *dvija* or a person of the first three varnas touches a Chandala, he should take a bath; in case he touches him while eating his food, then he should reject that food and bathe (Desai, 1991: 267–69). Parashara says that if a Chandala or a dog touches a twice-born person while he is eating, he should forgo the rest of his food (Tarkalankara, 1973: VI.66).

Narada mentions Shvapaka, Meda and Chandala. He calls them *mala* or the refuse of human society. He rules that they should always be punished with corporal punishment. A fine from them is unacceptable because their wealth is also impure. The king should, therefore, never impose a fine on them (Tagara, 1980: XV.13).

Following Apastamba, Parashara says that on talking with a Chandala, one should talk to a Brahman, take a bath and recite the *Savitri mantra* once; for then he becomes pure. On touching a Chandala one should take a bath and look at the luminaries of the sky: either the sun, the moon, or the stars (Tarkalankara, 1973: IV.22.24). If a Brahmin drinks water from a well touched by a Chandala, he should consume barley water prepared in the urine of a cow for three days (ibid.: VI.26).

Parashara prescribes elaborate proceedings if a house is polluted by a Chandala. If a Chandala enters a house, the whole house should be washed with water mixed with cow-dung, and the earthenware in the house should be thrown away. The householder with all the family members and servants should bathe three times a day and consume curds with cow urine for three days; barley water with cow urine for the next three days, milk with cow urine for the next three days, and finally he should again consume all these things for one day each. Thus, in 12 days he becomes pure. Household utensils of bronze and bell-metal should be cleaned with ash. *Kusunbha, guda,* cotton, salt, oil and ghee should be burnt outside the house. After that, the householder should feed 21 Brahmins and make a gift of 20 cows and one bull to them (ibid.: VI. 411–12). A similar atonement has been prescribed if a washer-woman, a shoemaker's wife, a hunter's wife or a bamboo-worker's wife lives in the house (ibid.: VI.43–45). All these castes are considered Untouchable and impure and cause pollution according to Parashara. Parashara prescribes that a Brahmin should keep a Chandala at a distance of 16 cubits.

The Chandala has been declared the lowest of all men. He has been assigned the work of removing unclaimed bodies. Chandalas are called *nirvasita*, or exiled and they have to live outside the village.

Such untouchability has been built into the sociocultural structure of Hindu society. Hence, in order to understand the full ramifications of untouchability as it has developed in the course of Indian history, one should study it as a part of the social structure of the caste system in India. The following part of this chapter concentrates on the very formation of the Hindu social stratification in India and its implication for the Untouchables. This is expected to help in placing the phenomenon of untouchability in a sufficiently wide historical perspective.

SOCIAL STRATIFICATION IN TRADITIONAL INDIA

Stratification, that is, the structuring of society on the basis of differential social status of various groups, is a common feature of human societies. But the traditional pattern of social stratification in India has certain characteristics which are rather unique, and these have attracted and intrigued many scholars all over the world. The structural and cultural characteristics of the traditional pattern of stratification in India have deep roots in the past. They have stemmed from certain peculiar ethnic constellations that came into being some 3,000 years ago, and they have been given twists and turns by numerous sociocultural currents through all these millennia.

The roots of the varna system (varna literally means colour) lie in the clash of races. Fair-complexioned Aryan hordes that started pouring into India through the north-west around 1500 BC vanquished and subjugated the dark-complexioned earlier settlers; and thus foundations were laid for a class system based on birth. To begin with, the Aryans regarded the non-Aryans as non-human (Deodhar, 1981: X.228) and beyond the pale of human society. But it soon became clear to the Aryans that it was more advantageous to assign them a low position within society and exploit them on a permanent basis. This was achieved through myths and metaphysics. The primeval myth is that of the Purushasukta (ibid.: X.XC.12) in which the four orders of society emerge from four parts of the great sacrificed *Purusha*.

But the original dispensation based solely on race could not continue for all time. The Aryans like all invading hordes were short of women and they had to marry women of the dark-complexioned earlier settlers. Thus, their racial features were compromised. At the same time, new hordes were coming from the north-west intermittently and they had a fair skin and more pronounced Nordic features than the earlier Aryans who had already established themselves as the dominant elites. These ruling elites, therefore, had to play down the importance of physical features in determining social status. To take the place of racial characteristics, elaborate scruples of ritual purity were introduced. The in-coming hordes such as the Shaka, Huna and Yavana or Greeks, were declared to be low for being devoid of ritual and the vast masses of pre-Aryan settlers were condemned to a low social status by being given no right to undertake rituals. This important part that ritual played in establishing and sustaining the social order perhaps explains the unique and excessive elaboration and importance of ritual in India, which has intrigued many a scholar.

The metaphysical doctrine of karma has provided a powerful rationalisation for inequality based on birth and made it acceptable to the wide masses. According to the karma doctrine, this life is just one link in the infinite chain of births and rebirths and each being is born in a specific position according to his own deeds in past lives. He can improve the prospects for his later births only by adhering to, and performing well, the role proper to the stratum in which he is born. Paradoxically, the doctrine of karma—and that of moksha, that is, salvation from the cycle of births and rebirths—arose in the process of protest against Brahmanic supremacy and its extravagant ritualism. The doctrine of karma was systematically articulated for the first time in the Upanishads, which marked a challenge to the supremacy of the Brahmins and excessive ritualism. The Upanishads were composed around the eighth century BC.

Interesting, light is thrown on the circumstances and processes that have shaped the complex features of traditional stratification of Indian society when we analyse texts like the *Rig Veda*, the Brahmin Granthas, the Buddhist works and the Smritis. This is attempted in the following part of this chapter.

RIG VEDA: THE ESTABLISHMENT OF ARYAN SUPREMACY

In the *Rig Veda*, the word 'varna' clearly refers to the colour of skin and hair of the people of two different races, the Aryan varna and the krshna varna. Nowhere in the *Rig Veda* is the word varna used for the fourfold stratification of society. Though the two classes, Brahmin and Kshatriya are mentioned often, the word varna is not used to denote them. Even in the Purushasukta, where the origin of the four classes is described, the word varna does not occur.

The Aryan hordes were quite conscious of their cultural and ethnic identity and looked down upon the dark-complexioned earlier settlers. The latter people are referred to in the *Rig Veda* as Dasas and Panis. Both of these are described as dark complexioned (krshna varna). The word Dasa seems to be connected with the Iranian word 'Dahae', which means 'countryman'.

In the beginning, Aryans hunted and looted the non-Aryans. The poet Vishvamitra prays to Indra to destroy the black people through his brilliance (Deodhar, 1981: III.XXII.21). At one place, a poet says that Indra has destroyed black armies (ibid.: II.XX.7). At another place, we find that Indra has killed 50,000 black people (ibid.: VJ.XVI.13). It appears that Dasas were a militant people. They gave a tough fight to the Aryans. A poet praises Indra for killing Dasa Shambara, a dweller of the mountains in the fortieth autumn (ibid.: II.XII.II). Finally, they were vanquished and were either absorbed in the lower rungs of society or driven away from their dwellings and had to take shelter in dense forests and other inhospitable regions. A poet says: 'Indra kills Dasas and increases the might of the Aryans' (ibid.: I.CIII.3).

Some of the pre-Aryan people were city dwellers and traders rather than warriors. The Aryans were militant and well-armed and they massacred these peace-loving people at will. The Aryan god-hero Indra is credited with the demolition of 99 cities of the Dasa king Shambara: 'And Indra for the sake of king Divodasa demolished Shambara's ninety-nine cities' (ibid.: II.19.6).

Due to different racial features, the disdain of the Aryans towards the Dasas was so great that they looked down upon the Dasas as 'non-human'. And since the Dasas were considered non-human, all inhuman behaviour towards them was justified in the eyes of the Aryans. In a hymn of the *Rig Veda* we find: 'You [Indra] subdued Pipru and powerful Mrigayu for Rjishvan, the son of Vidathin, you smote down fifty thousand dark ones, you shattered cities as old age shatters good looks' (ibid.: IV.XVI. 13). Fire was the most effective and powerful weapon of the Aryans. They used it liberally against the Dasas:

O Fire due to thy fear fled the dark races, Scattered adobe, deserting their possessions, Glowing Vaishvanara, when for Puru, You burn up and rend their cities. (ibid.: VII.V.3)

Thus, the Dasas had to flee, leaving behind their settlements in utter despair. Similarly, at another place, it is asserted that 'fire drove Dasas and brought light to Aryans' (Deodhar, 1981: VIII.V.6).

From about 1500 BC onwards, the Aryans acquired the vast fertile lands of north-western India. They badly needed manpower. For them the Dasas were the most suitable source of labour. The Dasas were captured and compelled to work for them. The *Rig Veda* says: 'Indra binds a hundred and ten Dasas' (ibid.: II.XIII.9). Many Dasas accepted the slavery of Aryans. In a hymn in the *Rig Veda* it is said: 'An Aryan leads away a Dasa at will' (ibid.: V.XXXIV.6). Aryans hounded them from place to place: 'The dark coloured Dasas were driven away by Indra from place to place' (ibid.: IV.XI.VII.21). Such hymns indicate that the settlements of the Dasas were demolished more than once. Ultimately, the Dasas took shelter in dark caves and dense forests: 'Indra made *Dasa Varna* low and dweller of caves' (ibid.: II.XX.7). It is stated that 'Dasas lived in darkness' (ibid.: II.XX.7). The word Dasa is used for slaves even in the *Rig Veda*. In later times also Dasa has been the most common word for slave.

PANIS: THE PRE-ARYAN CITY PEOPLE

Another people mentioned in the *Rig Veda* are the Panis. Probably these were a commercial people and were later absorbed in the class of traders in the fourfold varna hierarchy. The Panis are often connected with the ancient Phoenicians. Phoenicia is the ancient name of the coastal part of Syria. These Panis are portrayed as rich cattle-breeders and traders. Culturally, the Panis seem to be akin to the civilised Mediterraneans, but by the time of the Aryan invasion, in terms of race they seem to have become predominantly proto-Australoid. This is, by and large, true also of the people of the Indus Valley civilisation, who probably belonged to the category of the 'Panis' of the *Rig Veda*. The wealth of the Panis lured the Aryans greatly. The Panis did not want to share their wealth with the Aryans. The tendency of the Panis to expect something in exchange for anything that they gave seemed absurd to the pastoral Aryans. Commercial values do not seem to have taken root by that time among the Aryans and they considered this tendency reprehensible.

In the tenth mandal of the *Rig Veda* we find a whole *sukta* in which the she-dog of the god-hero Indra came to find the hidden treasure of the Panis. In the dialogue, the Panis assert that their treasure comprising cows, horses and riches is well stored in the mountain castle and those Panis who are excellent guards protect it well (Deodhar, 1981: X.198). But, the Aryans found the concealed treasure of the Panis and appropriated it. 'Searching out everywhere, they have obtained the great treasure of the Panis hidden in the cave' (ibid.: II.XXIV.6). Fire was employed by the Aryans against the Panis also:

> Agni, the hero, kills his enemy;
> The poet takes away the riches of Panis. (ibid.: VI.13.3)

The poet here refers to the eminent Aryans who composed the Vedic hymns. Fire is praised because through its help the Aryans were able to open the doors of the Panis: 'The fire is the wisest god who opens the doors of Panis forcefully' (ibid.: VII.IX.2). It appears that before going on plundering expeditions, the Aryans used to drink *soma*. Therefore, it was quite natural for them to praise Soma too, along with Agni (fire), for the success they achieved in plundering the Panis: 'O Soma and Agni, your valour is famous through which you snatched the kine and food of Panis' (ibid.: 1.XCIII.4).

The Panis did not perform the Aryan sacrifices. Therefore, they seemed foolish and faithless to the Aryans. The Panis spoke softly or indistinctly (in the judgement of the Aryans). They did not worship the Aryans' gods and were, therefore, declared godless. The robust Aryans found no justification for allowing Panis to occupy the lands in which they were settled: 'They chased the Panis to the east and turned the godless westwards' (ibid.: VII.VI.3). Some of the Panis gave resistance to the Aryan hordes:

> With loud voice the people invoke thee, Indra,
> To aid them in the battlefield.
> Thou with the singers, has pierced through the Panis;
> The charger whom thou aidest wins the booty. (ibid.: VI.XXXIII.2)

The hoarded wealth of the Panis held great attraction for the Aryans: 'The men together found the Panis' hoarded wealth, the cattle, horses and kine' (Deodhar, 1981: I.LXXII.4). Sometimes the Aryans avoided direct confrontation and stole the wealth of the Panis: 'O wealthy dawn; may Panis sleep without awakening. Make us wealthy, we the rich people' (ibid.: 1.CXXIV.10). Similarly, at another place we find, 'They go to steal the food of Panis' (ibid.: V.XXIV.7). All those Panis who did not want to part with their wealth were looked upon as enemies by the Aryans: 'O king, you yoke the ruddy horse for Agastya's nephews and defeat all the Panis who do not give' (ibid.: X.LX.6). Soma helped in finding out the wealth of the Panis: 'O Soma you found out the wealth of Panis' (ibid.: IX.CXI.2). After consuming *soma*, plundering was easier:

O Soma you looted the wealth consisting of cows (make your presence felt by) making noise in the sacrifice. (ibid.: IX.XXII.7)

Similarly:

O Soma our crushing stones aspire
for your friendship.
Destroy the greedy Pani for he is a wolf. (ibid.: VI.LI.14)

The avariciousness of the Panis seemed reprehensible to the Aryans. They exhort their god Indra not to acquire this vice of the Panis:

O noble elderly Indra, while gathering great riches, Do not be a Pani to us. (ibid.: XLV.31–33)

In course of time, the Aryans settled down on the land and developed cordial relations with the Panis and Dasas. A poet prays to the god Pushan: 'O Pushan, one who does not want to give make him liberal and soften the heart of Panis' (ibid.: VI.53.3). And we find some hymns in praise of Bribu, a leader of the Panis:

Among Panis, Bribu is the greatest;
His heart is as large as the plains of Ganga;
He who is ready to give immediately;
His thousand noble gifts of cows are running like wind,

Therefore all our poets praise the noble prince, the giver of thousands. (Deodhar, 1981: XLV.31–33)

In due course it seems that the Panis were absorbed among the Vish or the Aryan countrymen. The commercial terminology in Sanskrit owes a great deal to the Panis. Among such terms are *apana* or market, *panana* or to sell, *panya* or commodity, *pana* or coin and *vanik* or the trader. In the word vanik the sound of 'pa' has changed to 'va', which is not uncommon in the evolution of languages. It is common to add the letter 'ka' for making diminutives in the Avesta as well as in the Sanskrit language. The word *vanijya* or trade is derived from the word vanik.

In the Indo-Aryan social structure, this whole class was given the third position; lower than that of the priests and the warriors. In the Purushasukta this class is called Vaisbya or 'the sons of Vish'. In the *Rig Veda*, the word 'vish' is used for people. In the Zend-Avesta the word vish means many families or a village.

We also find Dasas named Balabutha and Taruksha who made gifts to an Aryan poet:

I received a hundred (cows) from Dasa Balabutha and Taruksha. Vayu, these are thy people protected by Indra, protected by gods thy rejoice. (ibid.: VIII.XLVI.32)

PRIESTS, WARRIORS AND COMMONERS

In the *Rig Veda* we find a society in which any individual of Aryan origin had the right to choose his profession according to his ability and achievements. He could become a priest or a warrior, or an ordinary man. The word 'Brahma' means hymn and also the power inherent in the hymn. Thus, a Brahmin is one who is the repository of hymns. Like all ancient civilisations, in the ancient *Rig Vedic* civilisation too, priesthood was considered the highest profession. A priest had precedence even over the king. But becoming a successful priest was not easy. The priest was expected to compose such hymns that would lull wealthy enemies to sleep and lead swollen rivers to lower their level so that armies could cross them without difficulty.

But the priest also had to be a master strategist and excellent warrior himself. Naturally, there was competition among various priests for the patronage of powerful kings. King Sudasa replaced Vasishtha by Vishvamitra as his priest. Many of the composers of hymns seem to be priests of one king or another. Some of their sons became composers of hymns while some others found the profession of warriors more suitable. A poet vividly describes that everybody has to do some work or other to earn his livelihood:

> I am a poet, my father is a physician,
> My mother grinds corn with stone;
> Striving for wealth,
> We follow different occupations. (Deodhar, 1981: IX.CXIII.3)

Since the professions of priest and warrior were considered nobler, it is not surprising that many people aspired to these. A poet prays to Lord Indra:

> O Indra, fond of Soma, make me a guardian of people;
> Or either make me a king;
> Would you make me a Rshi drunk with Soma?
> Would you not impart to me wealth that lasts forever? (ibid.: III.XLIII.5)

It appears that only those persons among the Aryans who were able to compose hymns were called Brahmins:

> Brahmanas, the drinkers of Soma,
> Making hymns set their voices at a high pitch. (ibid.: VII.CIII)

Composing hymns was not an easy task. Mere knowledge of language was not considered enough to become a good poet. A poet compares speech with a fond wife who exposes her charms only to her husband:

> A man though knows speech, does not know her;
> Though he hears her yet not hears.
> Like a fond well-groomed wife,
> She exposes her beauty to her master. (ibid.: X.LXXI.4)

Not everyone could be a composer of hymns. The difficult process
of composing a hymn is well described by a poet:

> The heart woven with mental brilliance,
> When friendly Brahmanas sacrifice together,
> Through their attainment they leave far behind,
> Those who count themselves as Brahmanas but are preparers of
> libations,
> Using Vak (language) in a wrongful manner they spin out bad
> threads in ignorance, and
> Have to take ploughshares and engage in (agricultural) operations.
> (Deodhar, 1981: XLXXI.8–9)

Thus, if a person could neither compose hymns nor become a
warrior, the only profession left for him was that of the agriculturist.
The profession of an agriculturist was considered lower than that
of the priest and warrior. These norms of assigning a low status to
agriculturists and to all those who earn their living by physical labour,
have been inherited by the later tradition. The whole structure of
the varna hierarchy is based on such norms.

Entry into the rank of warrior was also quite difficult. One who
failed to be a good poet could hardly be a success on the battlefield:

> Wandering in illusion gainlessly;
> The speech heard by him bears neither blossom nor fruit.
> Dull in friendship he is called a laggard;
> Nobody expects him to perform deeds of valour. (ibid.: X.LXXI.5)

From this description it becomes quite clear that the heroes of war
often composed the hymns themselves.

Vish was the third rank. Nowhere in the *Rig Veda* do we find a
hymn in which a poet aspires to be a Vish or a common man.
Obviously those who could not get entry into the two higher
professions remained Vish. The Vish are described as those who give
taxes to the king (ibid.: X.CLXXIII.6). They were cattle-breeders and
agriculturists. Perhaps agriculture became a common occupation
later than that of tending cattle. The poet compares the earth with
a cow from whom he milks a rich harvest year after year:

May Indra press the furrow down,
May Pushan guide its course aright,
May she be rich in milk,
For milking year by year. (Deodhar, 1981: IV.LVII.78)

THE FOURFOLD HIERARCHY: ORGANISMIC ANALOGY

In the *Rig Veda* we do not find the mention of the Shudra except in the Purushasukta, which is considered to be of a later origin. The Purushasukta contains a myth about the origin of the fourfold social structure. Here all the four ranks are mentioned together. In this hymn it is asserted that all four ranks originated from the great sacrificed Purusha. The occupations of the four ranks are related symbolically to the parts of the body of the Purusha. Obviously, it is an organismic analogy between man and society, legitimising the varying ranks and functions of different groups. As far as the *Rig Veda*, the oldest scripture, is concerned, the words Rajanya, Vaishya and Shudra occur only in the Purushasukta:

The Brahmana was his mouth,
The Rajanya was made of his two arms;
His thighs became the Vaishya,
From his feet was produced the Shudra. (Deodhar, 1981: X.XC.12)

The Brahmin has been called the mouth of the Purusha and is placed highest in society. His special function pertains to speech. Being a priest, invoking gods is his privilege. The second rank, Rajanya, is born of the arms of the Purusha and has the privilege of wielding arms. The thighs of the Purusha became the Vaishya. The occupation of Vaishya is agriculture and trade. From his feet were produced the Shudra. Just as the feet are the lowest in the body, Shudras are the lowest in society.

The Purushasukta appears to be the composition of an era when the Aryans had already settled down in the Indian subcontinent around 1200–1000 BC. The Vish or the commoners among Aryans required agricultural labour. They employed Dasas. Gradually the Dasas were given the generic name of Shudra. Both these words are of Iranian origin. The word Dasa is the transformed Iranian word Dahae or common man (Indradeva, 1980).

In the *Rig Veda* itself we find the tendency of considering the profession of the priest and warrior higher and the profession of the agriculturist lower. The people who were employed as agricultural labourers or slaves had naturally to occupy the lowest position in society.

The composition of the Purushasukta and its inclusion in the *Rig Veda* was probably the first attempt to systematise, justify and legitimise the exploitation of the non-Aryan masses by Aryans. The easiest way was to find some supernatural basis. This tendency of imputing divine sanction is a characteristic of the period of later Samhitas and Brahmanas. We do not find this tendency in the earlier parts of the *Rig Veda*. In those parts of the *Rig Veda*, the non-Aryans were considered amanushya or non-humans as mentioned earlier and not the descendants of Manu, the primogenitor. Their subjugation was considered natural. The Vish or the agriculturists employed non-Aryan labour. In an agricultural society, labour force is always needed. Later, through their shrewd farsightedness, the Aryan elites made an institutionalised arrangement that made cheap labour available as a matter of course. Shudras formed the lowest class of the Aryan society. The inclusion of the Purushasukta hymn in the *Rig Veda* sanctified this arrangement as natural and god-given. Society was conceived as an organic whole and all the classes formed its parts. Afterwards, in order to preserve the privileges enjoyed by the upper classes, and to avoid further racial admixture, it was necessary to give a more clear-cut character to various classes. Considerations of birth replaced those of individual achievement and the classes crystallised into castes.

In the Avesta, the land of seven rivers is mentioned as one of the settlements of the Aryans. In this land the leader of Aryan migration, Yim, married a 'demoness' and gave his sister, Yimuk, to a demon. The issues born of these unions have been referred to as 'abnormal' in the Avesta and 'monkeys and bears' in the Pahlavi texts. These descriptions allude to the racial admixture that took place in the early era. To avoid deformity, Yim married his sister Yimuk and thus preserved racial purity. From this myth it is quite clear that during the earliest era of settlement, the Aryans married indigenous women; but when the children born of such unions had dark complexions, snub noses and other non-Aryan features, such marriages were avoided. In ancient Iran, where the racial features of victorious Aryans and the subjugated people were not so different, ranks did not crystallise into endogamous groups, which is what happened in India (Indradeva, 1980). In Iran, the rank of priest was hereditary but not endogamous. In India, too, caste became hereditary first. Marriages in direct order were permissible. But in the course of time, castes crystallised into endogamous as well as hereditary groups.

LATER SAMHITAS AND BRAHMANAS: LOW STATUS OF THE SHUDRA INSTITUTIONALISED

In the later Samhitas, hypergamy is permissible. Thus, the Aryans or men of the upper varnas could have Shudra wives. It can also be seen in the *Taittiriya Samhita* that the Aryans used to establish illicit relations with Shudra women: 'If a Shudra woman has an Aryan paramour she does not expect wealth for maintenance' (Keith, 1967: VII.4.19.3). A Shudra could never think of marrying an Aryan woman legally. The later Samhitas and Brahmanas give a number of justifications for the low status of Shudras. In the *Taittiriya Samhita* of the black *Yajur Veda*, we find: 'Among men, Shudra has the same position as are conveyances of the beings [Aryans]: therefore the Shudras could not participate in a sacrifice' (ibid.: VII.I.I.6).

On the basis of the Purushasukta, the Tandyamaha Brahmana propounds: 'Therefore even if a Shudra has a lot of cattle, he is not entitled to perform a sacrifice, as he is without god, no god was created after him, since he was created from the feet, he should not do anything but wash the feet (of the three higher varnas)' (Godbole, 1979: VI.I.II). The *Aitareya Brahmana* puts forth another mythical justification: 'He created the Brahmana with Gayatri, the Rajanya with Tristubh and the Vaishya with Jagati, but he did not create the Shudra with any metre' (Agashe, 1930–31: V.II). In the *Shatpatha Brahmana* a Shudra is simply declared: 'toil' (Eggeling, 1894: V.XIII.6.2.10). These Brahmana Granthas were composed around 1000 BC.

At another place, Shudras, women, dogs and crows are called the untruth itself, that is, the personification of falsehood, and it is suggested that a teacher while teaching should not look at them (Eggeling, 1894: V.XIV. 1.2.31). The *Aitareya Brahmana* ordains that the Shudra is to be ordered about by the other (three varnas), he can be made to rise at will, he can be executed at will (Agashe, 1930–31: XXXV.3). Thus, the Shudras were given the lowest position in society. The elites of society maintained a strict vigil to ensure that though the Shudras have been assigned a place in society they should not be considered as belonging to the Aryans. Their inclusion in the fourfold hierarchy was meant only for the service that they performed for the higher varnas. They could in no way be counted among them. To serve the three higher varnas was the sole duty of the Shudra class. This relationship is asserted again and again in all the works of the later periods also.

CHANGE IN THE ROLE OF THE PRIEST

By the time of the later Samhitas and Brahmanas, the doctrine of the four varnas was broadly accepted by all members of society as god-given. We can perceive the change in the ethos of this period from the period when the hymns of the *Rig Veda* were composed. In the later Samhitas, the struggle with non-Aryans no longer existed. The non-Aryans, now the Shudras, accepted the superiority of the Aryans and considered serving the latter as their sacred duty. (This continued in traditional Indian society till the advent of modern times, as is amply shown by the content of traditional literature and also by field studies.) Consequently, the old militant spirit of the Aryans declined. For acquiring the comforts of life, they no longer had to fight. Since priesthood was the most remunerative and respected occupation, a good many Aryans became Brahmanas or priests. The simple sacrifices were made elaborate and expensive.

The priest now was neither a military strategist nor a poet; his sole job was to preserve the hymns and employ them in various complicated sacrifices, which were to be performed for the fulfilment of different wishes. The character of the gods, too, changed. The militant gods lost their heroic spirit and vigour. Around 1200–1000 BC, the Aryans had settled down in the Indo-Gangetic plains. For the settled agricultural way of life such gods were no longer needed. The gods were now expected to fulfil their mundane wishes and solve their day-to-day problems. The centres of civilisation shifted farther east. The land of the seven rivers finds mention no longer. The land of

Kuru and Panchala now became the seat of Aryan culture. The river Sarasvati in the west and the river Drasadvati in the east formed its boundaries. Broadly speaking, this land comprised the modern states of Haryana and Uttar Pradesh. The secure and comfortable life of the plains made the priests self-assured and complacent.

The priestly elites preserved the highest position for themselves. There are many assertions in the later Samhitas that are meant to establish their supreme position. It appears that the priestly elites themselves were not quite sure of their superiority. Therefore, it became necessary for them to assert it repeatedly. In all the texts of the later Vedic era, we find glorification of the priestly elites. The *Taittiriya Samhita* declares them 'the gods on earth' (Keith, 1967: 1.7.3.1).

The sacrament of initiation, *yajnopavita*, played an important part in rationalising and strengthening the system of varna. The first three varnas acquired a privileged position for themselves. Though studentship is mentioned in the *Rig Veda*, we do not find any mention of initiation rites. In the *Atharva Veda*, for the first time, we get the description of initiation. The poet conceives the sun as the child who is to be initiated into studentship by his teacher. This seems to be a forced analogy and there remain a number of incongruities. In this hymn studentship is called a second birth.

Gradually, the sacrament of initiation became much more elaborate. The *Taittiriya Aranyaka* (composed around 800 BC) prescribes that a Brahmin should wear an *ayajnopavita* of antelope skin or of cloth. It asserts that the sacrifice that is performed while wearing an *ayajnopavita* is spread out, or becomes successful, whereas the sacrifices of he who does not wear an *ayajnopavita* would not spread (Desai, 1971: II.1). In the Dharma Sutras, which were composed a couple of centuries later, we find that the sacred cord is introduced as an option. The *Apastamba Dharma Sutra* prescribes that a householder should always wear an upper garment, or in its place he may wear the sacred thread (Srinivasaraghavacharya, 1960: II.2.4.22–24).

In the *Shatpatha Brahmana*, the Brahmin and Kshatriya varnas are identified with the twin gods Mitra and Varuna: 'Mitra is priesthood and Varuna is nobility; and the priesthood is the conceiver, and the nobility is the doer.' It is asserted that Mitra or the priest could stand without Varuna, the nobility; but Varuna, the nobility, could not without Mitra, the priest. It is concluded, 'therefore a Kshatriya who wants to do something should seek guidance from a Brahmana, for he verily succeeds only when he is guided by a Brahmana' (Eggeling, 1894: IV.1.4.1–6).

UPANISHADS: REVOLT AGAINST RITUALISM AND BRAHMANIC SUPREMACY

Gradually (around the eighth century BC), the three varnas other than the Brahmin developed a kind of apathy for the ritualistic way of life and a new school of thought appeared in the Aranyakas and Upanishads. In these texts it is asserted that expansive, cumbersome and prolonged sacrifices do not lead to real knowledge. It was a challenge against the supremacy of the Brahmins, and signified loss of faith in the sacerdotal science inherent in it. People began to doubt the efficacy of these sacrifices. Another interesting feature of the Upanishads is that, contrary to tradition, the newer thought was marked by contributions primarily from Kshatriyas, lower varnas and women.

The Upanishadic thought is quite different in its spirit from the Vedas. As a matter of fact, there was implicit in it a revolt against the varna hierarchy. The teachings of the Upanishads are in a simple language, therefore, they earned great popularity among the people. The younger generation of the priestly class took an active interest in it. In this era, the importance of family and varna also diminished. The Upanishads contain the seeds of the systems of metaphysics which evolved a couple of centuries later, that is, around sixth century BC. We come across many instances where Brahmin teachers went to learn the ultimate truth from Kshatriyas. 'Brahma', which means only prayer in the *Rig Veda* assumed a new mystical meaning in the Upanishads. Since then this term stands for the Ultimate Reality.

In the era of the Upanishads, the supremacy of the Brahmins was challenged in various overt and covert ways. In the *Chhandogya Upanishad* we find a story in which a procession of white dogs is pictured like the Brahmins. Each dog holds the tail of the preceding dog in his mouth. This is very similar to the ceremony associated with the singing of the vahishapavamana hymn. In this ceremony, priests have to walk in a procession, each priest holding the gown of the preceding priest. According to the story in the *Chhandogya Upanishad*, when all the dogs settled down, they began to recite, 'Om, let us eat; Om, let us drink; Om, may the divine Varuna, Prajapati, Savitri bring us food; Lord of food, bring hither food, bring it, Om!' (Swami Swahananda, 1975: 1.12.1–5).

Many established teachers (Brahmins) approached kings (Kshatriyas) to acquire ultimate knowledge. Pravahana Jaivali, king of Pancala, instructed Gautama and claimed that 'Brahmanas do not have this knowledge, only the Ksatriyas possess it' (ibid.: V. 3.7). We find glorification of Kshatriyas in the *Brahadaranyka Upanishad* also: 'The Brahmana being not strong enough, the most excellent power or Kshatriyas was created. Therefore [at the Rajasuya sacrifice the] Brahmana sits down below the Kshatriya. He confers that glory on the Kshatriya along' (Sri Ramakrishna Math, 1951: 1.4.41.11). At another place we find that 'five great householders and theologians approached king Ashvapati of Kekaya carrying fuel in their hands like students to get the knowledge of Self' (Swami Swahananda, 1975: V.U.7).

Even the kings sometimes approached persons of lower classes to get knowledge of self. In a famous Upanishadic story, a king, Jansruti Pautrayana, approached a cartman named Raikva for instruction.

Before the Upanishads were composed, a great deal of racial admixture must have taken place. Whereas in the Vedic tradition, persons of dark complexion were considered subhuman and the birth of a daughter was considered a misfortune, in the Upanishads we perceive, in both these respects, a distinctive world view that is astonishingly literal and is totally absent in the literature composed both before and after the Upanishads. In the Upanishadic literature, a dark complexion is not considered necessarily bad. The *Brahadaranyka Upanishad* mentions rituals for having a dark-complexioned son together with that for a blond son. We find a ritual even for the birth of a daughter, which is very uncommon in the Indian elite tradition (Sri Ramakrishna Math, 1951: VI.4.14–17).

The Upanishads mark a new epoch in the history of Indian thought. The ideas found in the Upanishads are in marked contrast to the traditional way of thinking which always looks back to the golden past. The Upanishads are refreshingly forward looking.

Instead of expecting people to stick to the beaten path of the past, they exhort them to move on. They expect the new generation to be better than the older ones. In the *Brahadaranyka Upanishad*, the father blesses his newborn son to be more accomplished than his father and his grandfather.

In the Upanishads, for the first time, the concept of rebirth is introduced. As a matter of fact, it is not in consonance with the Aryan tradition. In the *Rig Veda*, as well as the Avesta, the dead go to live with their forefathers in heaven. This idea of transmigration of soul was developed in the classical Indian systems of metaphysics specially in Samkhya, Yoga and Vedanta from the sixth century BC onwards. It crystallised into the theory of karma, which rationalised and provided the rock-bed to the system of varna hierarchy for thousands of years.

The Upanishads marked a revolt against Brahmanic supremacy. This wave of liberalisation must have led to the adoption of ideas from non-Aryan sources; and the notion of transmigration of the soul and rebirth seems to be one of these (Indradeva, 1990). However, it is ironic that this very idea was turned into the most effective instrument to justify inequality based on birth. The doctrine is that one is born as a Brahmin or a Shudra entirely on the basis of his own deeds in the earlier lives; in his present life he should pursue steadfastly the duties of his own varna in order to better his prospects in subsequent lives. Not only was this doctrine propagated by the Brahmins as self-evident truth, but it was accepted and internalised by the most underprivileged and exploited sections also. The doctrine provided a perfect justification for gross inequality based on birth.

SUTRAS: THE REASSERTION OF VARNA HIERARCHY

During the Upanishadic era, the varna hierarchy and the strong patriarchal order that constituted the foundation of the ancient Indian social structure were badly undermined. The Grihya Sutras (which were composed around the sixth century BC) seem to mark the systematic and concerted efforts on the part of the priestly elites to re-establish their supremacy and resuscitate the social order in which they would have an unrivalled position (Indradeva, 1973). The hierarchy could not be established on the basis of race as there had already been a great deal of racial admixture. Because of this, it seems that criteria of ritual purity were introduced by the Grihya Sutras to take the place of racial purity.

In the Grihya Sutras, for the first time, a number of *sanskaras* or sacraments were explicitly codified. These *sanskaras* are to begin before the birth of a child and this process of performing *sanskaras* lasts for many generations even after the death of an individual. It is expected that each individual offers oblations to his father, grandfather and great-grandfather. A professional priest has to officiate at these sacraments. Members of the higher varnas, who wanted to establish themselves as respectable members of the elite, had to get these sacraments performed. Non-performance of these sacraments could even result in their excommunication from the community.

During the era of Aryan invasion and colonisation, the victorious Aryans had to marry women belonging to the subjugated people; but there is no evidence that they gave their own women in marriage to the non-Aryans. Thus, a sort of hypergamy was established. However, during the Upanishadic period, some kings gave their daughters in marriage to persons belonging to a lower order in gratitude for the esoteric knowledge received from them. An example of this is that of King Janashuti Pautrayana who gave his daughter in marriage to the cartman Raikva, from whom, as mentioned earlier, he sought knowledge. It seems that the Brahmanical revival marked by the Sutras sought to revive this trend. The Grihya Sutras laid down that marriages should be hypergamous, that is, in the direct order of the varnas.

As far as the varna of the progeny is concerned, there seem to be two types of traditions which are divergent. According to one, the progeny belongs to the varna of its father irrespective of the varna of the mother. This seems to have been the practice in the early period when the Aryans had no option but to marry women from amongst the non-Aryan people. The other set of norms, which is already in evidence in the Sutras, and is vigorously asserted in the Smritis, insists that both the parents should belong to the same varna. This is in sharp contrast to the practice of bestowing sonhood on the children acquired in various ways. The *Gautama Dharma Sutra* recognises 12 types of sons, which include besides real sons even sons who had no biological relationship with the father or the mother. Even those whose parents are unknown have been included. The sons of all these types were given the class name, which would imply also their inclusion in the varna of their social father. It would be reasonable to surmise that such a son had to be of fair complexion.

The Dharma Sutras introduced many new rules about not accepting food from the house of persons of lower varnas. In the early Vedic texts, we do not find such rules. The *Baudhayana Dharma Sutra*, which, because of its archaic language seems to be the earliest among the Dharma Sutras, does not contain any rules prohibiting the eating of food in the house of the lower varnas. Gautama introduced such restrictions in a liberal way. It is interesting to note that Gautama allows a Brahmin student to accept food from the house of all the three higher varnas (Pandey, 1966: XVII.1), but after completing his studentship he should not take food from the house of a member of the Kshatriya and Vaishya varnas. He was expected to eat food only at the house of a Brahmin householder. Apastamba further propounds that even among Brahmin householders, one should eat only in the house of a true Brahmin (Srinivasaraghavacharya, 1960: 1.6.18.9–10).

It appears that society was not prepared for the imposition of such rigid norms and many among the elites took objection to this. Apastamba refers to the opinions of 'some who allow a Brahmana to take food in the houses of Kshatriya and Vaishya householders'. In times of distress, a Brahmin could eat food prepared in the house of a Shudra who was under his protection for the sake of spiritual merit. Gautama says that during distress, a Brahmin may take food from a Shudra (Srinivasaraghavacharya, 1960: 1.6; Pandey, 1966: XVII.5).

In the Upanishadic era, Kshatriyas enjoyed a position at least equal if not higher than that of Brahmins. But in the Dharma Sutras, the priestly elites made it a point to assign a lower position to Kshatriyas. It is provided that even a king should make way for a Brahmin on the road. The gap between the two higher varnas definitely widened. 'A Brahmana of ten years and a Kshatriya of a hundred years stand to each other in the relation of father and son; of the two the Brahmana is the father' (Srinivasaraghavacharya, 1960: II.5.11.5–6, 1.4.14.25).

Shudras constituted the fourth varna. Apastamba and Vasishtha refer to the Shudras and outcastes as burial-grounds (Srinivasa-raghavacharya, 1960: 1.3.9.9). Apastamba, Gautama and Vasishtha provide that serving the three higher varnas is the sole occupation of the Shudra. The higher the varna he serves, the greater the merit he earns (Caland, 1925: II.20; Pandey, 1966: X.56; Srinivasa-raghavacharya, 1960: i.i.i.7–8). Gautama provided that for serving the three higher varnas, the Shudra would get remnants of their food, cast-off shoes, umbrellas, garments and mats. When a Shudra servant was unable to serve his Aryan employer due to old age or illness, the Aryan employer was expected to support him. Similarly, if the employer fell into distress, the servant was expected to look after his master. It is ordained that the savings of the servant could be used by the master.

Baudhayana and Apastamba both provide that a Shudra can cook under the superintendence of the first three varnas. The cooks should have their hair cut, shave their beards and cut their nails daily before cooking (Srinivasaraghavacharya, 1960: II. 10–27.15). Though it is provided in the Sutras that a Shudra can cook the food of a Brahmin, Apastamba and Baudhayana provide that food brought by an impure Shudra must not be eaten (Shastri, 1934: II.2.1; Srinivasaraghavacharya, 1960: I.5.16–22). This suggests that the distinction between 'pure' and 'impure' Shudras existed since the sixth century BC.

During the Upanishadic era, Shudras too participated in meta-physical discussions. In the revivalist era, the priestly elites scrupulously forbade the Shudra from listening to a recitation of the Vedas—if a Shudra were to intentionally listen to the recitation of the Vedas, his ears were to be filled with molten lead or lac. If he recited the Vedic texts, his tongue was to be cut off; if he remembered them, his body was to be split into two (Pandey, 1966: XII.7). Apastamba and Gautama provide that if a Shudra tries to converse with an Aryan on an equal footing, walks on the road side-by-side with him or sits on the same couch, he should be given corporal punishment. The tongue of a Shudra who speaks evil of a virtuous person belonging to one of the first three varnas should be cut out (Pandey, 1966: XII.I; Srinivasaraghavacharya, 1960: II.10.27.14). It is provided that if a Shudra commits homicide or theft, appropriates land, or commits similar crimes, his property should be confiscated and he himself should suffer capital punishment (Shastri, 1934:

II.2.1; Srinivasaraghavacharya, 1960: 1.5.16.22). It seems that the priestly elites were quite aware that the Shudras were as capable of learning and propagating knowledge as any member of the three higher varnas. They did not want to share the privileged position that they enjoyed on the grounds of possessing sacred knowledge even with the Kshatriya and Vaishya varnas, and not at all with the Shudras. All the members of the Brahmin varna were expected to maintain a close vigil over the Shudras to prevent them even from listening to a Vedic recitation. Any kind of self-assertion on the part of a Shudra amounted to a crime according to the Dharma Sutras.

The value of the life of a Shudra is assessed to be quite low. Apastamba provides the same penance for killing a Shudra as he provides for killing a crow, chameleon, a peacock, Brahmani duck, a swan, a frog, a mongoose, a muskrat, or a dog (Srinivasa-raghavacharya, 1960: 1.9.25.13).

BUDDHISM: A CHALLENGE TO THE BRAHMANICAL ORDER

In the eastern parts of India, however, there developed a parallel non-orthodox stream of thought—the emergence of the Upanishads and Buddhist literature. Gradually this became a challenge to the Vedic-Brahmanical tradition—in the beginning rather covertly, but later on openly.

In these philosophical and religious movements we find a unique synthesis of different ethno-cultural streams. Because of the complex interweaving of the varied strands, it is not easy to identify and isolate the contribution made by various cultures. Among the prominent ethno-cultural strains are the Aryan, the civilised Mediterranean, the Australoid, and the Mongoloid. In the early *Rig Vedic* times, though there existed the notion of superiority based on race, the division of society was not as rigid and elaborate as found in the post-*Rig Vedic* treatises. In Buddhist literature, the people described are highly commercial, liberal, affluent and happy. It appears that in the north-eastern parts of India, which became the seat of the Upanishads and Buddhism, trade and commerce flourished extensively and liberal ideas developed among the elites of that region. Perhaps it was these ideas that found expression in the two revolts (Upanishadic and Buddhist) against Brahmanical orthodoxy. A strong plea was made for equality and fraternity in that early era of civilisation, both in the monarchical and republican states of that region. The predominant position of Brahmans, on the basis of birth, was challenged. This, in a way, was also a challenge to Aryan supremacy.

Though the Upanishads picture many respectable teachers as belonging to the lower varnas, they do not directly criticise the varna hierarchy. On the other hand, the Buddha openly declared the varna system unreasonable and reprehensible, as all human beings belong to a common human species, whatever be the colour of their skin. He refuted the Vedic myth of the origin of the varna hierarchy and declared it to be false.

The social structure depicted in the Buddhist texts, like the Jatakas, is not very different from the structure that actually existed in recent pre-modern times. We find in the Buddhist texts proud kings and warriors, Brahmins who were well-versed in the Vedas, Vaishyas or rich Sreshthis, who liberally made gifts to the new religion, and skilful craftsmen.

In the Buddhist texts, the supremacy of the Brahmins was openly challenged. The Buddha declared that one cannot be considered superior just by virtue of birth. He declares:

By mere birth no one becomes a Brahmana,
By mere birth no one becomes an outcaste.
By deeds one becomes a Brahmana,
By deeds one becomes an outcaste. (Anderson and Smith, 1913: 135)

During a discussion with a young Brahmin, Buddha systematically argued that all the varnas, whether white or black, belong to one human race.

In Buddhist literature we can witness the earlier phases of industrial and commercial society in India. Various beautiful things were produced by artisans. The artisans were organised into strong guilds. There were traders who used to take long sea voyages to sell silks, muslins, brocades, drugs, ivory and ivory work, perfumes, jewellery and gold (Cowell, 1979: 1.108). Thus came into existence a rich, liberal middle class mainly comprising artisans and Vaishyas. It is remarkable that in the Buddhist texts we find norms and values

of the rising puritanical middle class. These values promoted activism
and the formation of capital. The advice given to traders in the *Digha
Nikaya* brings out the commercial spirit of the Buddhist era:

> Making money like the bee,
> Who does not hurt the flower;
> Such a man makes his pile,
> As an ant-hill gradually;
> The man grown wealthy,
> Thus, can help his family,
> And firmly bind his friends to himself.
> He should divide his money into four parts,
> On one part he should live,
> With two expand his trade,
> And the fourth he should save
> Against a rainy day. (Carpenter, 1911: 3.180.ff)

These values promoted accumulation of capital, which was necessary
for industry and commerce. It appears that the revolt of Buddhism
against the Brahmanical system of stratification, which was based on
birth, had much to do with the rise of the commercial class in the
times of the Buddha.

SMRITIS AND THE BRAHMANICAL REVIVAL

Buddhism was the greatest challenge to the priestly elites, for it gained
great popularity among the masses. Many kings and Sreshthis found
Buddhism more suitable and they contributed to its spread in India
and abroad. The religion of the pre-Aryans, too, reasserted itself
among the people. The priestly elites were quite conscious of all these
forces. It was clear to them that the ancient Vedic religion could not
be revived in its earlier form. Many old Aryan practices had,
therefore, to be rejected and non-Aryan customs found entry into
the revived religion. For restoring the varna hierarchy, the backbone
of the traditional Indian social structure, the Smritis came into
existence. The *Manusmriti* was composed sometime between second
century BC to AD second century. During the first revival of the Sutra
period, many ancient Indo-European rituals and customs were

consolidated into aphorisms or Sutras. We do not find much about the *sanskaras* (Indian *rites de passage*) in the *Rig Veda*. The *sanskaras* were introduced in an effective manner primarily by the Sutras. It seems that when racial purity was compromised beyond the point of retrieval, ritual purity was substituted for it. And ritual purity itself became the hallmark of the higher varnas. It was all the more necessary because during the Buddhist era, marriages with persons of the lower varnas was no longer prohibited. In the Jatakas we find mention of many such marriages.

Since the Smritis belong to the revivalist era, all the authors of Smritis adopted the names of Vedic seers to get authority for what they said. *Manusmriti* is the first attempt of the priestly elites in this direction. Therefore, it was perhaps natural to attribute this Smriti to the primogenitor, Manu. Armed with the ancient myth of creation and various sacraments, together with the doctrine of karma, Manu tried to revive the bygone golden age by re-establishing the ancient system of varna hierarchy. In this process, women and Shudras were the greatest losers. The social justice they had got during the Buddhist period was taken away with a vengeance. Manu tried to assign each and every ethnic group, whether Indian or foreign, a specific place in the varna system according to his own criteria. Manu generally followed the guidelines laid down by the Dharma Sutras. The Smritis attributed to Yajnavalkya, Brihaspati, Narada and Katyayana followed the institutes of Manu.

Broadly speaking, those ethnic groups and lineages which were to be given a higher place in the social hierarchy were described to be the offspring of hypergamous unions between two varnas, and those that were to be assigned a low status were declared to be the progeny of hypogamous unions. The social entities of various kinds (tribes, craftsmen of different kinds and even hordes which came from outside) were assigned a high or low position in the social hierarchy in this way. Through the myths of the origin of various castes as a result of hypergamous and hypogamous unions between men and women of different varnas, a way was found to explain the existence of a multiplicity of castes (not just the four varnas) and each was assigned a specific status in the system of stratification. This, in fact, was a device to bring social reality in tune with the fourfold varna system, which was put forth as an ideal.

The *Manusmriti* reflects the strong resentment of the Brahmanical elites against the Buddhist levelling influence. It has been categorically asserted in the *Manusmriti* that the dominance of priestly elites and the hierarchy based on varna was to be re-established not only through religious prescriptions but by the full might of the king and the state. The use of arms to restore their supremacy was commended openly. Manu calls punishment, 'the son of the creator'. The king was enjoined to establish varna hierarchy through the power of punishment. Other twice-born people, too, were exhorted to resort to arms if they were in any way hindered in carrying out the duties prescribed for their particular varna (Doniger and Smith, 1992: VII.4, VIII.346). It is obvious from these ardent exhortations and ruthless prescriptions that Manu was conscious that re-establishing the supremacy of the Brahmins was no easy task—its attainment required all the power at their command, physical as well as moral.

In the Smriti era, once again the Brahmins ensured unquestionably the supreme position for themselves. Manu declares that 'the Brahmana from the very birth is an eternal incarnation of the sacred law'. Manu calls the Brahmin a great god just like fire, be he ignorant or learned. Just as the fire does not get contaminated, so also a Brahmana, although he may follow even a low occupation, should always be honoured and should be considered a great deity (ibid.: I.98).

This is in marked contrast to the theory of equality proclaimed by the Buddha. Birth in a particular varna was considered enough for securing all sorts of privileges. It appears that by the time the *Manusmriti* was composed, norms of ritual purity had substituted those of racial purity. Manu declared that the Brahmin is the lord of all varnas because of his superiority of birth and observance of rituals and sacraments (ibid.: X.3). He says that a non-Aryan may have Aryan appearance, therefore one must judge a person by his acts, not by his physical appearance.

The Shudras are considered lowest of all varnas because no sacrament is prescribed for them. Following Apastamba and Baudhayana, Manu too, justified the low status of the Shudras. The sacrament of initiation is not permissible for the Shudras. Initiation is like a second birth because through initiation a boy becomes a full member of Aryan society. Since the Shudras are not entitled to the initiation, they have only one birth. Manu has emphasised that their sole occupation is to serve the twice-born. Brahmins belong to the highest varna; serving them would be most meritorious for the Shudras. Manu took no cognisance of the doctrine forwarded by Buddha that the people of all the varnas belong to one human species as all of them are biologically similar. To justify the low position of the Shudras, Manu refers to the ancient divine myth of the self-existent Brahman: since the mouth is the purest part of the body, the Brahmins are the lords of this whole creation (Doniger and Smith, 1992: I.92–94). The Shudras were produced from the feet of the self-existent; the service of a Brahmin alone is declared to be an excellent occupation for the Shudras. In return, the Shudras are entitled to receive the leftover food, old clothes, the refuse of grain and old household furniture. Since the Shudra has only one birth (he is not a twice-born) no sin would cause loss of varna (ibid.: X.123–25) to him. Brihaspati provides that if a Shudra cannot serve the twice-born, he may pursue the artisan's occupations and handicrafts (Doniger and Smith, 1992: X.99–100; Upadhyaya, 1982: Sanskara Kanda, I.530). In any case, a Shudra must not be allowed to possess wealth. Obviously, if a Shudra became rich he would no longer serve a Brahmana or any other twice-born. Manu explicitly declares that the existence of a wealthy Shudra is painful for the Brahmins (Doniger and Smith, 1992: X.129). According to commentators, this is so because by accumulating wealth Shudras become proud and do not want to serve members of the higher varnas. In the Buddhist era, people of all the varnas were free to follow the occupations that they liked without attracting any social disapproval.

The fact that Manu assigns low position to the Vaishyas and Shudras does not mean that he was not aware of their functional utility. In fact, he enjoins the king to ensure that the people of the Vaishya and Shudra varnas continue to perform the work prescribed for them because if these castes 'swerved from their duties, the world would be thrown into confusion' (ibid.: VIII.417–18).

The varna hierarchy influenced the legal system a great deal. Since the Brahmins are placed highest in the social structure they enjoyed the highest privileges. The life of a Brahmin is given the highest esteem while that of the Shudras the lowest. The provisions are not based on any faith in equality before law for all. The traditional Indian legal system clearly discriminates between persons belonging to different varnas. It is particularly harsh towards the Shudras. This system of law seems to have its roots in the ancient confrontation between the fair-complexioned Aryan hordes and the dark-skinned, snub-nosed, earlier settlers whom they vanquished and subjugated. In the course of time, the criteria of racial purity had to be substituted by those of ritual purity, but the attitude of disdain persisted. Though this traditional system of law may not be enforced by the state today, its norms even now underlie the patterns of behaviour and attitudes of a large portion of the people of India (Indradeva, 1980). For instance, inheritance among the Hindus was governed largely by the principles of *mitakshara* and *dayabhaga* propounded by the Smritis and their commentaries till the enactment of the Hindu Succession Act in 1956. The dicta of the Dharma Sutras and Smritis still form the basis of traditional institutions and values.

REFERENCES AND SELECT BIBLIOGRAPHY

Agashe, Kashinath Shastri (ed.) (1930–31) *Aitareya Brahmana*. Poona: Anandashram Sanskrit Series.

Apararka (1966) Commentary of Nyayamuktavali of Apararkadeva and Nyayakalanidhi of Anandanubhavacarya. Edited by S. Subramanya Sastri and V. Subramanya Sastri. New Delhi: Indian Institute of Sanskrit Research.

Andersen, Dines and Helmer Smith (trans.) (1913) *Sutra Nipata*. London: Published for the Pali Text Society by Henry Frowda, Oxford University Press.

Caland, Willem (ed.) (1925) *Vasishtha Dharma Sutra*. Lahore: The Research Department, DAV College.

Carpenter, J. Estlin (ed.) (1911) *Digha Nikaya*. London: Published for the Pali Text Society, Oxford University Press.

Cowell, E.B. (ed.) (1979) *The Jatakas*. New Delhi: Cosmo Publications.

Deodhar, S.K. (trans.) (1981) *Rig Veda*. Pune: Prasad Prakashan.

Desai, M.R. (1971) *Taittiriya Aranyaka*. Kolhapur: Susheela Prakashan.

———. (1991) *Atri Smriti*. Kolhapur: Prin. M.R. Desai Publication Trust.

Deva, Indradeva and Shrirama (1980) *Growth of Legal System in Indian Society*. New Delhi: ICSSR/Allied Publishers.

Doniger, Wendy and Brian K. Smith (trans.) (1992) *Manusmriti*. New Delhi: Penguin.

Eggeling, J. (trans.) (1894) *Shatpatha Brahmana*. Oxford: Sacred Books of the East Series.

Godbole, N.S. (ed.) (1979) *Tandyamaha Brahmana*. Poona: Anandashram Sanskrit Series 37.

Indradeva, Shrirama (1973). 'Genesis of Indian Civilisation: The Evidence of Grhya Sutras', *Diogenes*, 84. Paris: UNESCO.

Indradeva, Shrirama (1980) 'Cultural Interaction between Ancient Civilisations: A Study of Indo-Iranian Relations', *Diogenes*, 3. Paris: UNESCO.

———. (1985) 'Shaping of the Traditional Pattern of Stratification in India: An Analysis of Processes through the Ages', *Diogenes*, 130. Paris: UNESCO.

———. (1987) 'The Doctrine of Karma: Towards a Sociological Perspective', *Diogenes* 140. Paris: UNESCO.

———. (1990) 'Reassertion by Subjugated Cultures: The Case of Religion in India', *Diogenes*, 150. Paris: UNESCO.

Keith, Arthur Berriedale (trans.) (1967) *Taittiriya Samhita*. Delhi: Motilal Banarsidass.

Pandey, Umesh Chandra (trans.) (1966) *Gautama Dharma Sutra*. Varanasi: The Chowkhamba Sanskrit Series Publications. The Kashi Sanskrit Series No. 172.

Panshikar, Wasudev Laxmansastri (1926) *Vriddha-Yajnavalkya*. Bombay: Nirnaya-Sagar Press.

Shastri, Chinnaswami (ed.) (1934) *Baudhayana Dharma Sutra*. Varanasi: Chowkhamba Sanskrit Series Office.

Srinivasaraghavacharya, A. (trans.) (1960) *Apastamba Dharma Sutra*. Mysore: Mysore University Oriental Institute.

Sri Ramakrishna Math (trans. and notes) (1951) *Brahadaranyka Upanishad*. Mylapore: Sri Ramakrishna Math Publications.

Swami Swahananda (trans.) (1975) *Chhandogya Upanishad*. Madras: Sri Ramakrishna Math.

Tagara, Ganesh Vasudeo (1980) *Narada Smriti*. Delhi: Motilal Banarasidass.

Tarkalankara, Mahamahopadhyaya Chandrakanta (ed.) (1973) *Parashara Smriti*. Calcutta: The Asiatic Society.

Upadhyaya, Vachaspati (ed.) (1982) *Brihaspati Smriti*. New Delhi: Navarang Publications.

caste-based use

2

Who is a Dalit?[1]

JOHN C.B. WEBSTER

I

Dalit ('oppressed' or 'broken') is not a new word. Apparently it was used in the 1930s as a Hindi and Marathi translation of 'Depressed Classes', the term the British used for what are now called the Scheduled Castes. In 1930, there was a Depressed Classes newspaper published in Pune called *Dalit Bandu* ('Friend of Dalits') (Pradhan, 1986: 125). The word was also used by B.R. Ambedkar in his Marathi speeches. In *The Untouchables*, published in 1948, Ambedkar chose the term 'broken men', an English translation of 'Dalit', to refer to the original ancestors of the Untouchables for reasons which must have been self-evident because he did not explain them. The Dalit Panthers revived the term and in their 1973 manifesto expanded its referents to include the Scheduled Tribes, 'neo-Buddhists, the working people, the landless and poor peasants, women, and all those who are being exploited politically, economically and in the name of religion' (Omvedt, 1995: 72). There has thus been a narrow definition, based on the criterion of caste alone, and a broader one to encompass all those considered to be either similarly placed or natural allies. Since the early 1970s, the word has come into increasingly wider usage in the press and in common parlance where it is normally used in the original, narrower, caste-based sense.

Scholars have also written about Dalits in different ways. Two views predominate. Those using a class analysis of Indian society subsume Dalits within such class or occupational categories as peasants, agricultural labour, factory workers, students and the like. This can be seen in most Marxist historical writings, in subaltern studies and, to a lesser degree, in the Dalit Panther manifesto. To those using a communal analysis of caste, Dalits are the people within Hindu society who belong to those castes which Hindu religion considers to be polluting by virtue of hereditary occupation. The histories of the Dalit movement by Kamble (1979), Gupta (1985), Pradhan (1986) and Nath (1987) are based on this premise. Both views require critical re-examination.

The analytical framework within which the Census of India set its descriptions and enumerations of Dalits provide a useful starting point for such a re-examination. On the one hand, the census-takers sought to depict Indian social reality as they found it; on the other, what they depicted was not always accurate and, such was its power, the Census of India could play an important role in shaping that reality. Dalits were listed in the chapters of the census devoted to castes and tribes. The 1881 Census simply described and enumerated castes in the various provinces and states. Varna categories were often used to group them and so the Dalit jatis generally appeared at or near the end of the lists. The 1891 Census, on the other hand, adopted a standard classification of castes according to the occupation assigned to each by tradition. Dalit castes were thus included within such occupational categories as field labourers, leather-workers, scavengers, watchmen and village menials. The 1901 Census classified Hindu castes in order of social precedence 'as recognized by native public opinion' (Pradhan, 1986: 197). The 1911 Census provided a separate enumeration of those castes and tribes which either did not conform to or were excluded from certain aspects of what was considered to be generic Hindu religion.[2] Ten criteria were used to determine whether a caste or tribe was, to quote Ambedkar, 'one hundred percent Hindu' or not (Ambedkar, 1969: 92). The five which applied to Dalits pertained to the denial both of various services by Brahmin priests and access to the interior of temples, to causing pollution by proximity or contact, as well as to the Dalit practice of eating beef and not revering the cow (Pradhan, 1986: 197).

However, under special instructions from the Government of India, which wanted more information about them, an entire appendix of 30 pages in the 1931 Census was devoted to what J.H. Hutton, the census commissioner, chose to call the 'exterior castes'. Hutton's instructions to the various superintendents of census operations was to develop their own criteria in determining which castes should or should not be included, since such criteria might vary across India.

Nevertheless, he did point out subsequently that the defining characteristic of the exterior castes was that contact with them entailed
purification on the part of high-caste Hindus. 'It is not intended that
the term should have any reference to occupation as such but to those
castes which by reason of their traditional position in Hindu society
are denied access to temples, for instance, or have to use separate
wells or are not allowed to sit inside a school house but have to remain
outside or which suffer similar social disabilities' (Hutton, 1933:
417).[3]

Later in his report, Hutton did ponder two criteria which would
indicate that pollution, and hence interaction with high-caste Hindus,
might be a consequence of a caste's socio-economic position (ignorance, illiteracy, poverty) or occupation, both of which are changeable,
rather than of its traditional position *in* Hindu society, which was not,
but he did not consider those criteria to be functionally operative
(ibid.: 472–73). In the end, he stayed with an inherited pollution
inherent in one's caste, which seriously affects interaction with those
belonging to other castes as the distinguishing characteristic that made
these castes 'exterior'. He placed their disabilities into three categories:

> Firstly, that under which they are barred from public utilities, such
> as, the use of roads and tanks, and secondly, their religious
> disabilities which debar them from the use of temples, burning
> grounds, *mat*s and some other institutions. In addition to the above,
> but arising out of the second of these, there are the disabilities
> involved in relation with private individuals, such as the services
> of barbers and the admission to tea-shops, hotels or theatres
> owned by private individuals. (ibid.: 482)

This analysis was largely supported by contemporary witnesses. On
the one hand, Dr Ambedkar had testified before the Simon Commission in 1928 that the Bombay labour unions wished to preserve
caste distinctions, while at a Bihar Depressed Classes Conference in
1937, Jagjivan Ram said that members of the Kisan Sabha were
exploiters of the Dalits (Webster, 1994: 127). From their Dalit perspective, caste was much more powerful than class. On the other hand, not
only Gandhi's anti-untouchability and Harijan uplift campaigns,

which sought to remove the stigma of inherited pollution and change patterns of social interaction, but also the opposition which his campaigns aroused bore eloquent testimony to Hutton's understanding of what set Dalits apart from other Indians of the same social class.

A number of recent sociological studies indicate that, despite all the changes which have occurred in the past 60 years, this continues to be what sets Dalits apart. The assumption underlying the Government of India's constitutionally mandated compensatory discrimination policy has been that if Dalits can raise their class status through the educational, employment and political opportunities opened up to them, then their caste status, defined in terms of interaction with people belonging to other castes, will also be raised. This assumption has, however, proven to be only partially true. Even the integration of the middle-class Dalits into wider middle-class society was only partial and incomplete at best, more obvious in public than in private settings.[4]

Class analysis, thus, not only fails to take account of the basic contradiction and oppression which Dalits face, but also hides these by using categories which divert attention away from them. It is, therefore, no accident that historians using class analysis have largely ignored the Dalits, while those who have written histories of the Dalits do not make class analysis the basic framework of their histories.[5]

II

The census also provides a useful entry point into the communal analysis of caste in Indian society. As noted earlier, the Census of India saw caste as a religiously sanctioned Hindu pattern of social organisation. The Muslim pattern was seen as primarily tribal, at least at its upper levels. At the same time, the census reports often provided statistics on the religious affiliations of members of various castes, thus opening up the possibility that caste might not be a strictly Hindu phenomenon. When the 1911 Census had to determine which Hindu castes and tribes had to be enumerated separately for reasons of non-conformity or exclusion, religious criteria were used.

The 1931 Census treated the 'exterior castes' as Hindu castes occupying a 'degraded position in the Hindu social scheme' (Hutton, 1933: 473). They were Hindus because 'they worship the same deities and, though refused entry to the temples, boxes are placed outside, at the limits to which they can approach, to receive their offerings' (ibid.: 484). Thus, Hutton's entire appendix is devoted first to those disabilities which high-caste Hindus impose upon their co-religionists that define the latter as 'exterior castes' and then to naming the castes so defined. It is significant that 'it was decided that Muslims and Christians should be excluded from the term "depressed class"'. The reason for the decision may have been practical,[6] but the decision had a very definite ideological dimension. It was in keeping with that kind of thinking which the British government used when introducing separate electorates for Muslims in the 1909 Constitution, extending them to Sikhs in Punjab and Indian Christians in the Madras Presidency in the 1919 Constitution, and continuing them in the 1935 Constitution. The fundamental divisions within Indian society are religious; each religious community constitutes a water-tight compartment; each has its own distinct social patterns, religious beliefs and political interests, which require that each community be represented by co-religionists of its own choosing. Thus, despite evidence to the contrary (ibid.), the stigma of untouchability and its accompanying disabilities were seen as affecting relationships only among Hindus. The Order in Council specifying the SCs referred to in the 1935 Constitution, turned this communal view of caste into law by specifically stating that 'no Indian Christian shall be deemed to be a member of any Scheduled Caste'.[7] Gandhi was also wedded to this communal view of caste; not only his fast in response to the Communal Award but also his scrupulousness in having the Harijan Sevak Sangh confine its uplift activities to Hindu Harijans was based on this premise. Ambedkar, on the other hand, came to the opposite conclusion; while agreeing that Hindu religion was clearly a, if not *the*, major source of Dalit oppression, he did not consider the Dalits themselves to be Hindus. The same communal view of caste, which initially defined the SCs in 1936, was stated even more strongly in the President's Constitution (Scheduled Castes) Order No. 19 of 1950, which designated these castes to be considered SCs in the constitution of independent India. It stated that 'no person who professes a religion different from the Hindu religion shall be deemed to be a member of a Scheduled Caste'. This was amended in 1956 to include the Sikhs and in 1990 to include the Buddhists. Moreover, in 1985, this religious criterion for determining caste membership was upheld by the Supreme Court, which argued that caste was a peculiarly Hindu phenomenon. According to the constitution, when one moves out of the Hindu community into the Christian community, then one must show equal disabilities and backwardness *within the Christian community* in order to be considered a member of the Scheduled Castes.[8] The assumption here is that Indian society is divided into totally separate compartments according to religion and that an Indian lives *exclusively* within one community or another and is affected *only* by his/her own community's norms.

Historians as well as social scientists have also based their work on this set of assumptions by consciously or unconsciously applying a religious criterion in addition to caste to determine whether or not a person is a Dalit. This is understandable. The colonial government, through the provision of separate electorates as well as in its census procedures and categories, had shaped the history about which historians now write in those terms and the government of independent India, while dropping communal electorates, continues to use the old categories in areas of 'social policy'. Kamble, Gupta, Pradhan and Trilok Nath in their histories of the pre-Independence Dalit movement treated those Dalits who converted to other religions as no longer Dalits and, therefore, no longer part of the history of the Dalit movement, whereas Mark Juergensmeyer (1982) included Christian Dalits in his history of the movement against untouchability in Punjab.[9] Most sociologists and political scientists in studying Dalits since Independence confine their samples to 'Hindus'[10] and, where relevant, Buddhist Dalits. Suma Chitnis, however, included Christians and Sikhs in her national survey on the grounds that conversion had not changed their situation and that several state governments had recognised this (Chitnis, 1981: 20–22).

Research on the history of the Dalit Christians indicates that this 'communal' framework of analysis does not do justice to the complexity of either Dalit social reality or the modern Dalit movement. In fact, it breaks down at three crucial points. The first is in its assumption that the social consequences of conversion to

Christianity were the same for Dalits as for members of higher castes. In fact, they were quite different. In the last quarter of the nineteenth century and the first quarter of this century, when most of the Dalit mass conversions occurred, high-caste people were completely cut off from their family and jati upon conversion to Christianity. For them, the Supreme Court's assumption proved to be substantially correct; they moved out of their jati community into the Christian community and were to be governed only by the latter's norms.[11] However, this did not happen to Dalit converts. They were not made outcasts but almost always continued to live with their caste fellows on the periphery of the village, or, in the south, in the *cheri* outside the village. They also continued to marry within their *own* jatis, preferably with co-religionists. Moreover, their place in the village economy and social system was not altered by conversion, as immediate persecution was designed to point out! This is not to suggest that conversion produced no strains in self-understanding and social relationships or no alterations in the lifestyles and attitudes of the converts. It is to say that these strains and alterations occurred without totally changing the converts' social identity and relationships within the village. These could change only if the converts left the village, which the vast majority of them could not and did not do.[12]

A second point where the communal framework of analysis breaks down is in its assumptions about Dalit Christian political activity during the 1920s and 1930s. In 1919, Christians in the Madras Presidency, where the vast majority of Dalit Christians lived, were granted separate electorates. Dalit Christians there were placed in the Christian rather than in the general constituency. (Elsewhere in India, all Christians were part of the general constituency until 1935.) There is not much evidence of Dalit Christian political activism during this period; Ambedkar was right about that (Ambedkar, 1989: 472). However, what evidence there is indicates that they were more active as Dalits on Dalit issues than as 'Christians' on general 'Christian' issues. They had no voice in the All-India Conference of Indian Christians or other Christian political organisations and these bodies were as guilty of patronising neglect as were the Congress, other non-Dalit political parties and the government. Where Dalit Christians were politically active was in Dalit caste associations[13] and in protesting against caste discrimination within the churches.[14] In fact, in 1929, a deputation of Dalit Christians gave evidence before the Simon Commission in Madras, arguing that they should be put in the general constituency where they expected fairer treatment than they had received in the Christian constituency (Indian Statutory Commission oral evidence, 1929: 14–20). It would seem, therefore, that the modern Dalit movement was not just a movement within the Hindu community alone, but, like the nationalist movement, it included people on all sides of the neat communal boundaries which the British had built up.

Finally, the communal framework of the analysis breaks down because it accepts as exclusively valid the 'sacral view' of caste according to which castes are treated as 'components in an overarching sacral order of Hindu society' and does not include the more secular associational and organic views of caste,[15] which can be equally oppressive to Dalits (Ambedkar, 1946; Joshi, 1982). Here too, research on caste in the Christian community and churches since Independence, while of uneven quality, is nonetheless instructive. Caste exists in and affects the Christian community today, even though castes are rarely part of the 'Christian sacral order'. Moreover, caste does not function within the Christian community in the same way throughout India. Three variables account for virtually all the differences: location (rural versus urban), region (north versus south) and denomination (Protestant, Roman Catholic or Syrian Orthodox).

Denomination is a significant variable because historically these different branches of the Christian Church have viewed caste differently. The Protestants have been the most consistent in attacking it as part of the Hindu sacral order and in trying to establish among Christians a community without caste. The Roman Catholics adopted an organic view of caste, treating it as simply the Indian system of social stratification and, until recently, have chosen to work within its constraints. The same can also be said of the Syrian Orthodox churches which have tended to function as one caste among many in Kerala society rather than as a multi-caste community (Koshi, 1968). Region is an important variable because the patterns of conversion have not been the same in the north as in the south. Whereas in the north a small number of converts from miscellaneous castes as well as from Islam combined with large numbers of converts from only one Dalit caste (for example, the Chuhras in Punjab and the Bhangis in Uttar Pradesh) to form the Christian community (Webster, 1976: 46–53, 227–34), in the south, large numbers of several castes of differing status converted to form the Christian community.[16] Thus, it has been possible in the south, as it has not been in the north, for two, three or four castes to carry on within the churches the same competition for status and precedence as their Hindu caste fellows were carrying on in other arenas. Location is also a variable because it is generally recognised that caste sanctions are more strictly enforced in rural than in urban settings. Given these variables, one would expect to find caste weakest in urban Protestant congregations in the north and strongest in rural Roman Catholic or Syrian congregations in the south. One simply cannot generalise for India as a whole.

Given these variations, it is possible to make a few additional generalisations about caste in the Christian community and its impact upon Christian Dalits. First, the Christian population, like the Indian population as a whole, is predominantly rural.[17] In the overwhelming majority of villages where Dalit Christians live, the dominant castes are Hindu and so social identity and social relationships are determined by Hindu rather than by Christian norms and values. There the sacral view of caste still generally prevails; Christian Dalits are simply categorised with other Dalits and treated accordingly. Second, within the urban Christian community, caste seems to have been replaced by class in the north (Alter and Singh, 1961: 87–115), whereas the associational view of caste prevails in the south. There, caste often provides the social networks necessary for getting jobs or winning elections to positions of leadership within the churches. Because Dalit caste networks are less effective than those of the higher castes, Dalits often lose out in the competition (Caplan, 1987: 152–63). Third, studies of south Indian villages, where both the dominant castes and the Dalits are Christians, not only indicate that the distinctions of status and precedence on the basis of caste exist, but also suggest that considerations of purity and pollution still affect relations between Christians of differing castes (Fuller, 1976: 63–65; Japhet, 1987: 59–87; Koilparampil, 1982: 154–68; Mosse, 1986: 264–80), even though, as Mosse (1986) has pointed out, both Hindus and Christians alike recognise that Christian deities are less concerned about purity and pollution than are Hindu deities (Mosse, 1986: 276). Thus, in Christian rituals Dalits play subordinate roles.

In the face of this body of evidence it is difficult to retain a basically communal view of caste when writing the history of the modern Dalits. They did not automatically cease to be Dalits upon conversion to Christianity and the vast majority of them remain victims of the very disabilities that Hutton had listed back in 1931. Instead, the evidence points to the conclusion that, at least for Dalits, the stigma of untouchability and its accompanying disabilities based on caste are an Indian, rather exclusively, Hindu phenomenon. A communal view of caste imposes a framework for studying the history of the modern Dalit movement, which seriously distorts the empirical realities of the Dalit situation and Dalit movement. A more inclusive framework is thus required.

A historian, when using concepts and labels, is under obligation to be as faithful to the complexities of past empirical reality as possible. Concepts and labels carried over from the colonial past, even when enshrined in law, cannot be utilised without testing their ideological biases, particularly with regard to what they leave out. The same would be true of those brought to study the past from present-day political struggles and controversies. This critical examination of alternate referents for the label, Dalit, indicates that the original definition of who is a Dalit is empirically the soundest one for the historian to work with. Caste alone has determined who is a Dalit, not class or religion. Social stigma and a variety of disabilities were based on caste; these were and, to a significant degree, still are the defining characteristics of a Dalit, even if a Dalit moves up in social class or changes religion.

NOTES

1. This chapter is a revision of a paper first presented at the Indian Institute of Advanced Study, Shimla, in October 1995. The author wishes to express his thanks to the director, Professor Mrinal Miri, and Fellows of the Institute for their comments and suggestions.
2. The use of 'Hinduism' in modern times has come in for serious review. For two examples, see Romila Thapar (1985: 14–22) and Robert Eric Frykenberg (1989).

3. See Gail Omvedt (1995: 77). The 1931 Census made reference to the possibility that in Punjab, members of the 'exterior castes' would list themselves in the census returns as Dalits (Hutton, 1933: 488).

4. For a summary of some of these findings of Nandu Ram and other studies, see Nandu Ram (1988) and John C.B. Webster (1994: 153–54).

5. Gail Omvedt's critique in the first chapter of her *Dalits and the Democratic Revolution: Dr. Ambedkar and the Dalit Movement in Colonial India* (1994) is relevant at this point.

6. See the comments from the Madras Report referred to in Hutton (1933: 499).

7. Cited in Pradhan (1986: 339). The same also applied to Buddhists in Bengal.

8. The 1985 judgement is published in full in Jose Kananaikil (1986: 43–50). The anomaly of including Sikh Dalits among the SCs was first accepted on the basis that they were originally SC Hindus who had recently been converted to the Sikh faith and 'had the same disabilities as the Hindu Scheduled Castes' (ibid.: 48). This was taken as proven in the case of the Sikh Dalits but not in the case of Christian Dalits.

9. Mark Juergensmeyer (1982). See also Joseph Mathew's treatment of the Pulayas in *Ideology, Protest and Social Mobility: Case Study of Mahars and Pulayas* (1986).

10. 'Hindu' is often used as a residual category for those Dalits who are neither Muslims, Buddhists, Christians nor Sikhs.

11. The only exceptions to this were those high-caste people who converted to Christianity in large groups rather than as individuals or nuclear families. They tended to carry their old norms over into the Christian community.

12. Discussion of the issues presented in this paragraph may be found in John C.B. Webster (1976: 65–72; 1994: 63–70), James P. Alter and Herbert Jai Singh (1961: 24–36), Duncan B. Forrester (1979: 69–96), Dick Kooiman (n.d.: 168–96) and G.A. Oddie (1969: 259–91; 1975: 61–79).

13. This was particularly true of the Pulayas in Travancore. See J.W. Gladstone, (1984: 343) and Census of India (1933)

14. Evidence for this is given in John C.B. Webster (1994: 88–89, 105–6, 115–16).

15. This typology, which also includes the sectarian view of caste, is that of Marc Galanter (1968: 300–301).

16. In Kerala they were the Syrian Christians (who either migrated to India or converted to Christianity well before the sixteenth century and were about equal to the Nairs in status), the Izhavas and the Pulayas; in Tamil Nadu they were the Vellaias, the Nadars and the Adi Dravidas; in Andhra Pradesh they were the Kammas, Reddys, Malas and Madigas.

17. In the 1971 Census, 74.8 per cent of the Christians were rural, as compared to 80 per cent for the population as a whole. In the 1981

WHO IS A DALIT?WHO IS A DALIT? 87

Census these figures were 70.8 and 76.3 per cent respectively; in 1991 they were 68.7 and 74.3 per cent. Thus Christians, while slightly more urban than the population as a whole, remain predominantly rural.

REFERENCES AND SELECT BIBLIOGRAPHY

Alter, James P. and Herbert Jai Singh (1961). *The Church in Delhi*. Lucknow: National Christian Council of India.

Ambedkar, B.R. (1946) *What Congress and Gandhi Have Done to the Untouchables* (second edition). Bombay: Thacker & Co.

———. (1969) *The Untouchables* (second edition). Balrampur: Jelavan Manavir.

———. (1989) 'The Condition of the Convert', in Vasant Moon (compiler), *Dr. Babasaheb Ambedkar, Writings and Speeches*. Bombay: Education Department, Government of Maharashtra.

Caplan, Lionel (1987) *Class and Culture in Urban India: Fundamentalism in a Christian Community*. Oxford: Oxford University Press.

Census of India (1933). *Census of India 1931. Volume XXVIII, Travancore Part I: Report*, p. 439. Delhi: Manager of Publications, Government Press.

Chitnis, Suma (1981). *A Long Way to Go: Report on a Survey of Scheduled Caste High School and College Students in Fifteen States of India*. New Delhi: Allied Publishers.

Forrester, Duncan B. (1979) *Caste and Christianity*. London: Curzon Press.

Frykenberg, Robert Eric (1989) 'The Emergence of Modern "Hinduism" as a Concept and as an Institution: A Reappraisal with Special Reference to South India', in Gunther D. Sontheimer and Hermann Kulke (eds), *Hinduism Reconsidered*, pp. 263–87. New Delhi: Manohar.

Fuller, C.J. (1976). 'Kerala Christians and the Caste System', *Man*, 11: 63–65.

Galanter, Marc (1968) 'Changing Legal Conceptions of Caste', in Milton Singer and S. Bernard (eds), *Structure and Change in Indian Society*. Chicago: Aldine Publishing Co.

Gladstone, J.W. (1984). *Protestant Christianity and People's Movements in Kerala 1850–1936*. Trivandrum: Seminary Publications.

Gupta, S.K. (1985) *The Scheduled Castes in Modern Indian Politics: Their Emergence as a Political Power*. New Delhi: Munshiram Manoharlal.

Hutton, J.H. (1933) *Census of India, 1931*, Vol. I, *India: Part I—Report*. Delhi: Manager of Publications, Government Press, Indian Statutory Commission Oral Evidence. 1929. Fourteenth Meeting, Madras. 1 March.

Japhet, S. (1987). 'Christian Dalits: A Sociological Study on the Problem of Gaining a New Identity', *Religion and Society*, 34, September: 59–87.

Joshi, Barbara R. (1982) *Democracy in Search of Equality: Untouchable Politics and Indian Social Change*. New Delhi: Hindustan Publishing Corporation.

Juergensmeyer, Mark (1982) *Religion as Social Vision: The Movement against Untouchability in 20th-century Punjab*. Berkeley: University of California Press.

Kamble, J.R. (1979) *Rise and Awakening of Depressed Classes in India*. New Delhi: National Publishing House.

Kananaikil, Jose (1986) *Scheduled Castes in Search of Justice. Part II: The Verdict of the Supreme Court.* New Delhi: Indian Social Institute.

Koilparampil, George (1982) *Caste in the Catholic Community in Kerala.* Cochin: CISR.

Kooiman, Dick (n.d.) *Conversion and Social Equality in India.* Columbia: South Asian Publications.

Koshi, Ninan (1968) *Caste in Kerala Churches.* Bangalore: CISR.

Mathew, Joseph (1986) *Ideology, Protest and Social Mobility: Case Study of Mahars and Pulayas.* New Delhi: Inter-India Publications.

Mosse, C.D.F. (1986) 'Caste, Christianity and Hinduism: A Study of Social Organisation and Religion in Rural Ramnad', D.Phil. thesis, Oxford University.

Nath, Trilok (1987) *Politics of the Depressed Classes.* New Delhi: Deputy Publications.

Oddie, G.A. (1969) 'Protestant Missions, Caste and Social Change in India', *Indian Economic and Social History Review*, 6, September: 259–91.

———. (1975). 'Christian Conversions in the Telugu Country 1860–1900: A Case Study of One Protestant Indian Movement in the Godavery-Krishna Delta', *Indian Economic and Social History Review*, 12, January–March: 61–69.

Omvedt, Gail (1994) *Dalits and the Democratic Revolution: Dr. Ambedkar and the Dalit Movement in Colonial India.* New Delhi: Sage Publications.

———. (1995) *Dalit Visions: The Anti-Caste Movement and the Construction of an Indian Identity.* Hyderabad: Orient Longman.

Pradhan, Atul Chandra (1986) *The Emergence of the Depressed Classes.* Bhubaneshwar: Bookland International.

Ram, Nandu (1988). *The Mobile Scheduled Castes: Rise of a New Middle Class.* New Delhi: Hindustan Publishing Corporation.

Thapar, Romila (1985) 'Syndicated Moksha', *Seminar*, 313, September: 14–22.

Webster, John C.B. (1976) *The Christian Community and Change in Nineteenth Century North India.* New Delhi: Macmillan.

———. (1994) *The Dalit Christians: A History* (second edition). New Delhi: ISPCK.

PART

II

PART

II

3

Colonialism within Colonialism: Phule's Critique of Brahmin Power[1]

MAHESH GAVASKAR

Nowadays British colonialism is loaded with every positive sin. The cause of every 'malaise' in contemporary post-colonial India is sought in the policies initiated by the British. So much so that the 'malaise' of caste reservation and its recent manifestation in the form of the Mandal Commission is also traced to the colonial method of mapping the Indian populace according to their caste identities in the government censuses and gazetteers. That such a codification had a role to play in the emergence of various caste associations and caste-based politics in the early decades of this century is not to be denied. But to emphasise the colonial authorities' ascribing rigidity to caste identities, while overlooking the denial of basic civil rights in pre-colonial times on the basis of those very identities is lopsided. If it were not, there would have been no need for Jotiba Phule to throw open the well in his courtyard to the Shudras and Atishudras in 1869.

The Phule-Ambedkarian discourse draws attention to the fact that just as India went through a phase of British colonialism, it had previously passed, at various stages of its history, through 'Brahmanical colonialism' and that British colonialism inadvertently made available certain normative and cognitive tools with which to fight Brahmanical colonialism.

Brahmanical colonialism has its roots in certain Hindu scriptures that provide divine justification for caste-based discrimination and domination. In times of resurgence of orthodoxy, in the pre-British days, caste-based communitarian rules strictly guided the daily life of the populace. Economic exploitation was implicit in caste communities but was legitimised on extra-economic grounds. British colonialism, in contrast, was a child of capitalist global expansion.

Yet, the epoch-making contributions of the Enlightenment had given
birth to the notion of civil society, though the colonial state was often
to violate the norms of civil society during its hold over India.
Nevertheless, civil society was the contradiction of the colonial state
at an ideational level and led to the latter's ultimate demise. Phule
locates himself in this space of civil society to develop a critique of
Brahmanical colonialism, which apparently was devoid of such a
notion.

   This chapter is a textual reading of Phule's corpus and attempts
to argue that the normative ground for Phule's favourable attitude
towards British rule stems from his identification of the British with
the forces of Enlightenment, which aimed to reconstitute intra-
human and human–divinity relationships on a higher level of egalitarianism.

SITUATING PHULE

The political economy of pre-British days granted many bodies,
extending from the tillers of the land to the topmost political
authority, rights to the agricultural produce. The produce was
expropriated by power holders beyond the ambit of the village while
within the confines of the village the produce was distributed
according to the customary practice of *balutedari* prevalent in
Maharashtra in those days. Thus, an interlinked two-tier structure
reigned before the advent of the British—first, a hierarchy which
included *deshmukh*s, *mansabdar*s, *jagirdar*s, the Mughal emperor (or the
peshwa, the regional ruler of the Deccan), standing above the village
system and second, the balutedari pattern determining the intra-
village relationships. In a long process spanning the latter half of the
eighteenth century to the first half of the nineteenth century, the
British knocked off the top half of this two-tier structure and in
its place either institutionalised the zamindari system to collect land
revenue, or, as in the Deccan, inaugurated the *ryotwari* system,
wherein the cultivator paid revenue directly to the state (Fuller, 1989).
The ryotwari system, besides doing away with a host of intermediaries
between the state and the cultivator,[2] introduced private ownership
of land into the village economy. Land was no longer owned by the
village community as a whole but by individual *meerasdar*s. Firmly tied

to their piece of land and with no obligations to the village community, they were bound to develop a world view that saw previous inter-dependencies of the balutedari as parasitical upon agricultural produce.

The new bureaucratic setup of the British administration, accompanied by the development of communication infrastructure, opened up new avenues of employment in the colonial period. This resulted in increased labour migration between cities and their hinterlands. A handful rising from the lower sections of semi-rural society took advantage of the various schemes of development initiated by the British and in the process came in contact with the urban environment.

> The process of 'development', i.e., of building the roads, railroads and buildings that linked Maharashtrian agriculture to the world economy, also required labour and its organisation. The business of contracting for these development projects which grew in importance after 1850, was an important source of wealth ... at lower levels of the contracting process many non-brahmans would rise to a fair degree of wealth; these were not usually old aristocratic landlords or wealthier peasants. But often poor and rising men. (Omvedt, 1976: 75)[3]

But this social mobility also made these upcoming men from the lower strata painfully aware of the need for acquisition of literacy skills to secure employment. Since, within Hindu society, the Brahmins traditionally enjoyed the privilege of learning, they were able, in spite of the downfall of the *peshwai*, to make a smooth transition to the new order and corner almost all the job opportunities. At the village level, because of the introduction of a new legal system, the traditional role of the *patil* (village headman) as maintainer of law and order became redundant and it was the Brahmin *kulkarni* (village accountant) who gained in importance. Thus, the colonial transition brought the Brahmin to the forefront in two ways. The gradual demise of the balutedar and the increasing penetration of a monetary economy brought to the forefront the *joshi* (village priest and astrologer) at his unproductive parasitical best. Second, in the new expanding economy too, the Brahmins, with a virtual monopoly over jobs, were an overwhelming presence.

REALITY REDEFINED

Jotiba Phule, who was born in Pune into a Mali (gardener) household of comparative stability a decade after the collapse of peshwa rule was to occupy in his later years the strategic socio-economic position of a member of the rising, independent yeomanry which placed him at the centre of the changing times. Besides his exposure to new intellectual currents after coming in contact with Christian missionaries in his early formative years, Jotiba's agricultural activities drew him into a widening market circuit of rural–urban interlinkages. Govind Ganapat Kale, a younger contemporary of Phule, recalls that in the 1870s, Phule owned 60 acres of land at Manjri on the outskirts of Pune.

> Besides the farm at Manjri, the main income earning activities of Jotirao were contracts of construction works, a shop vending *Mushi* and an agency to sell vegetables.... The tunnel at Katraj on Pune–Satara road was completed shortly before my birth. Jotirao had taken sub-contract for this scheme. Further, he had taken a sub-contract of supplying stones, cement for the construction of a dam on Mula-Mutha and a bridge Yervada. (Kale, n.d.: 12)

Transactions at these sites provided Phule with first-hand experience of Brahmin nepotism and corruption at the lower and intermediate rungs of the colonial bureaucracy. The recent past of peshwai where the Brahmins (especially, the Chitpawan or Kokanastha Brahmin, whom Phule consistently addresses in his writings as 'Bhat'), controlled economic, administrative and cultural functions, raised for Phule an ominous spectre of the persistence of Brahmin domination into the future. Thus, when Phule launched a scathing attack on Brahmins for their privileged positions in both the decaying and the emerging economies, the particular historical background of peshwai together with a couple of significant events in his life were crucial in formulating his critique.

The rule of Bajirao II (1796–1818), the last peshwa, besides being a period of sheer wastage of wealth on decadent practices and utter chaos in administration, was a period when Brahmanical orthodoxy attained its zenith. As Narayan Vishnu Joshi notes:

In those days the brahmins of Poona had grown supercilious and purity pollution was strictly observed. Mahars, mangs, chambhars, bhangi, dheds were not even allowed to spit on roads. They should walk with earthern pots tied to their waists. If a brahmin is noticed on the road [they] should immediately sit down for the shadow not to fall [on the Brahmins]. Such was their misery. (1868: 61)

The amount of money that was distributed as *dakshina* for the Brahmins got enormously inflated in the regime of Bajirao II and a five-day spectacle of Ramana used to be held annually in Pune. Brahmins, all and sundry from Kashi in the north to Kumbhakonam in the south, used to flock to attend the 'Ramana'. This dependence on dakshina made them lazy, ignorant and greedy. They were chiefly interested in 'Brahmin-Bhojan' and considered the British to be residents of an island named Calcutta (ibid.: 69). The Brahmins of the late peshwai boasted of their superiority, recounting that only two varnas—Brahmins and Shudras—remained in the kalyug after Parashuram completely annihilated the Kshatriyas. Such being the common notion of those days, it is not surprising to read that when Govindrao Phule sent his son Jotiba to a village school near Pune, a Brahmin clerk insisted that Govindrao withdraw his son from the school since learning was not the dharma of a Shudra. It was later, after a Muslim teacher, Gaffar Beg Munshi, and a British admin-istrator, Liggit, prevailed upon Govindrao, that Jotiba was admitted to a Scottish Mission school run by Murray Mitchell.[4]

Another incident occurred when Phule was 20 years of age. He was upbraided for joining the marriage procession of his Brahmin friend and thus considering himself equal to the Brahmins. In those days, Phule and his Brahmin friends used to take lessons in *dandapatta* under the tutelage of Lahuji Mang. The body-building exercises and training in martial skills were aimed at accumulating strength to drive away the British.[5] But Phule's experiences of discrimination in his life convinced him that far more important than fomenting anti-British hatred was the need to cleanse the minds of his fellow men and women of the outdated belief system that denied equal status to all human beings. It was this conviction that prompted Phule to extend normative support to British rule which, Phule expected, would unleash the forces of enlightenment to root out the Brahmanical religion that legitimised evil customs and practices.

(RE)ENTRY INTO HISTORY

Phule locates the beginnings of Brahmanical tyranny in the usurpation by the Brahmins of a privileged position for themselves in the form of Bhudev. This not only helped them justify asymmetrical application of justice in mundane matters, but also let them appropriate a position more exalted than that of a god. The following conversation between a Brahmin priest and an illiterate Kunbi woman from *Tritya Ratna*, a play Phule wrote for the Dakshina Prize Committee in 1855, brings out the Brahman's claim to omnipotence. Here the joshi explains to the Kunbi woman why her neighbour's child died:

> Joshi: ... had she satisfied me [by giving ample bhiksha] then certainly I would have removed all the evils [pidda] on her son and she would have bore a son, isn't so? ...
>
> Bai: I can't understand what evils prevailed over her son, why don't you tell me?
>
> Joshi: Don't you know the evil forces of planet? O, where a god like Mahadev had to hide under waters fearing him and who has escaped from his clutches? (Phule, 1991: 6)

It is because of his sway over destiny, his power of making and breaking others' futures that he should be fed properly, claims the Brahmin. Phule denounces this parasitical livelihood.

> To ashes go your living
> Fresh food without toil. (ibid.: 97)

With the use of well-chosen phrases like '*arranging* the horoscope' (*rashichakra manduri*), '*laying out the planets*' (*grihayojuniya*), '*plotting* in mind, *inventing* planets' (*mani yojun, graha dhundun*), Phule unveils the concocted world of the Brahmin. The Brahmins make merry by defrauding ignorant folk who, on the other hand, sink into absolute misery. Phule argues that the labouring masses by being trapped in notions of *daiva* (fate), *sanchit* (accumulated demerits of previous births), *prarabdha* (predestination) have lost their dialectical relationship with the world and have become *dasa* (serf) to external forces. Hence, Phule exhorts that British rule is the appropriate moment to recollect their glorious heritage and liberate themselves from the tyranny of the Brahmins.

> It is god's grace that the British have come and denounced the bhats totally. How Aryas became masters, Shudras slave. This is the time to inquire into the fraud. (Phule, 1991: 557)

> Narratives are always told from someone's point of view.... Narrative does not therefore aspire to be a universal form of discourse. It draws lines, distributes people .... Narratives are not for all to hear, for all to participate in to an equal degree. It has a self in which it originates a self which tells the story. (Kaviraj, 1992: 44, 59)

To grasp the narrative structure of *Gulamgiri*, especially Phule's vituperation of some Hindu myths, the theological underpinnings of Phule's vision needs to be understood first. Keeping company with Christian missionaries, Phule came to accept the deist conception of the universe wherein God—Phule calls him *Nirmik*, the creator— after creating the world, no longer intervenes, allowing the world to operate according to the laws of reason. Says Phule:

> The creator has produced all things. After working day and night by contemplating on where and how to utilise each object [one will realise] the *unfathomable power, unfathomable skill and unfathomable splendour* of the creator. (1991: 445; emphasis in the original)

This implies a radical transcendentalisation of God, a separation of the superhuman from the human world, of myth from history. From this perspective, Hindu myths, which display the imminence of supernatural forces in the human world, are rendered highly problematic. *Gulamgiri*, by situating itself in chronological time as against mythical time, narrates a sequence of dramatic events, a history of conflict extending to 3,000 years between the alien Arya invaders and the indigenous Shudras and Atishudras. It dispels the sacred aura bestowed by Hindu myths on its deities of great and little traditions and reveals them in human form. Thus, Narasimha, Vaman, Parashuram and others no longer appear as incarnations of the same 'Lord' Vishnu, but as successive chiefs of an army waging war against the aborigines. Similarly, on the indigenous side, Khandoba, Jotiba, Mhasoba and others are no longer 'deities' of a little tradition in the Hindu pantheon, but regional chiefs in the regime of King Bali. Phule coins his own etymology to explain the origins of their names. For instance, 'Khandoba' emerged because Bali made his lieutenant chief of nine provinces (*khand*s) of his kingdom, while 'Mhasoba' is a corruption of the original 'Mahasuba' (large province) (Phule, 1991: 150–51).

Phule's construction of the 'Aryabhats' as satanical forces[6] has its roots in his acceptance of Christian theology. Christian theology, which conceived of God, the creator of the universe, as essentially good, attributed the sufferings in the mundane realm to the evils inherent in man himself. Thus:

> The implicit accusation against God is turned around to become an explicit accusation against man. In this curious reversal the problem of theodicy is made to disappear and in its turn appears a problem of anthropodicy. (Berger, 1969: 74)

Employing 'the form of a catechism', Jotiba informs his pupil, Dhondiba, about the essential evil nature of the Aryabhats:

Dhondiba: How was Narasimha by nature?

Jotiba: Narasimha was greedy, deceiving, treacherous, cunning, heartless and cruel.... (Phule, 1991: 160)

Dhondiba: How was Parashuram by nature?

Jotiba: Parashuram was reckless, adventurous, wicked, pitiless, stupid and mean.... (ibid.: 160)

Thus, Phule's historiography presents a Manichean world with a ceaseless battle between the forces of good and evil. If in the ancient times the opposite camp had villains ranging from Matsyas and Varahas to Narasimha and Parashuram, on his side, Phule narrates, were heroes like Shankhasur, Hiranyakashapu and Bali. It was in this period that the most savage violence, aggression, loot and plunder took place. It was after Parashuram annihilated the Kshatriyas that the age of coercion ended and the age of domination started. Smritis, Samhitas and Shastras were compiled to establish hegemony; diacritical markers like the Gayatri mantra and the sacred thread[7] were invented to legitimise superiority; Shankaracharya, Mukundraj, Dnyaneshwar and Ramdas philosophised to reinforce the Brahmanical view of the world (Phule, 1991: 156–67). In recent times, according to the divine plan, the Muslims were entrusted with the mission of freeing the lame Shudras and Atishudras from the slavery of crafty Aryabhats but they failed to execute their task as they became engrossed in aristocratic pleasures (ibid.: 457).[8] Now it was upon the British to rescue the subject populace from Brahmanical oppression. Phule reorients the cyclical notion of *yuga* to suit his eschatology. If the orthodox Brahmins of his times were lamenting, '*Kalyug aale, vidya shudraghari geli*' (Kalyug has descended, knowledge has been passed on to the Shudras), Phule inversely hails the coming of the British as *satyayug*:

With the dawn of truth, wisdom of Vedas stunts....
By giving knowledge to Shudra, Bhudev is put to shame. (ibid.: 422–23)

Yet, the struggle against the evil forces is not over, cautions Phule. Brahmins in the new incarnation of kulkarnis and *bhatkamagar*s were maintaining day-and-night vigil over their interests in villages and urban centres and poisoning the minds of the British against the Shudras. In *Brahmananche Kasab* (Priestcraft Exposed), Phule, by depicting the omnipresence of Brahmins in the roles of a priest, a schoolteacher, a kulkarni, a *mamlatdar*, a reformer, a clerk in the public works, a reporter in the vernacular press builds a demonology of *gramraksha*s (village demons) and *kalamkasai*s (wielders of the pen) who are out to gobble up the ignorant Shudras. Behind this demonology lay Phule's sharp grasp of power relations that made him boldly state:

We know perfectly well that the Brahmin will not descend from his self-raised high pedestal and meet his Coonbee [*sic*] and low caste brethren on an equal footing without a struggle. (ibid.: 125)

It was this acumen that drove him to search for an anchorage in an alternative centre of power that would overthrow the inegalitarian social setup of his times.

RECUPERATING 'BALISTAN'

Phule also discerned that power had been transferred from the sword to the pen and hence, any transformation in power relations meant establishing command over the new skill. Convinced that the Brahmin *pantoji* (schoolteacher) will never step forward to disseminate knowledge among the lower orders, Phule beseeches, pleads, advises and warns the British to exert their state apparatus to educate the downtrodden. Yet, to his chagrin, Phule notices that the colonial education system instead of addressing the needs of the downtrodden is bent upon prioritising higher education, which ultimately serves the interests of the upper castes. Phule graphically depicts the drain of wealth within the country wherein the taxes paid by the labouring classes go into educating the sons of Brahmins:

> He who owns goods suffers the most
> goes the Pathan saying,
> Children of queer people study;
> Mali, Kunbi slog in the fields to pay taxes,
> don't have enough to clothe. (Phule, 1991: 77)

He demands, 'how long should the Shudras pay funds, to feed Aryas, says Joti' (ibid.: 568). What most alarms Phule is that although times have changed, the Brahmins still continue to function as middlemen, albeit in a different way. If in pre-British days the *purohit* used to withhold knowledge from the masses, in contemporary times, the pantojis deny access to education to the downtrodden. Hence, it is with great apprehension that Phule observes the political developments of the later years of his life. The formation of the Sarvajanik Sabha in 1870 and the Indian National Congress in 1885[9] were seen as Brahmin ploys to oust the British. These Brahmanical moves, intended to give them a decisive role in politics, provoked Phule to question their claim to represent the whole of India. Phule debunks the absolutist claim of the 'nationalists' by reminding them of their culture based on *bhed*:

Listen, crafty Aryabhat Brahmins following the mischievous, self-serving religion of the Aryas consider the Shudras inferior.... Moreover, besides themselves, crafty, excessively puritan Aryabhats imposed a ban on inter-marriage and inter-dining amongst all Shudra-Atishudra because of which their different lifestyles, habits, customs do not merge. How is it possible [to accept] that the crisp 'kadbole' born out of a unity of such eighteen varieties be a 'ekmaya lok', a 'Nation' [*sic*]? (Phule, 1991: 494)

It is against this *bhedniti* (ethic of discrimination) of the Aryabhats, which ghettoises communities into programmed behaviour, that Phule posits his Satyashodhak Samaj based on universal brotherhood. Phule stresses fraternity as a distinctive characteristic of his future society so as to sharply distinguish its *jagbhandu* (universal pattern) from the *jatbhau* (kinship pattern) of the Aryabhats. Further, even though the relationship between the Nirmik and earthly creatures is that of a parent and a child (not a blood relationship but one based on faith), the transcendentalisation of God makes 'Him' remote and in a way foregrounds the fraternal aspect between the residents of earth. Says Phule, 'Hug brotherly Christians, Muslims, Mangs, Brahmans' (ibid.: 537). Nonetheless, Phule's Nirmik being transcendental and unitary, like the sun, the moon and the wind, is equally available to all (ibid.: 536). It is in this sense of empirical confirmation that Phule's Nirmik is *sarvojanik* and not esoteric and hidden as the gods of the Aryabhats are in the Vedas. Moreover, Phule's Nirmik, by being non-exclusive, that is, by being accessible to all at any particular moment, does not have any chosen people and chosen language through which to reveal Himself. In fact, Phule views Brahmanical mystification as an outcome of the withdrawal of the Brahmins—either in the form of renunciation or of purity–pollution—from any engagement with the empirical world. This has goaded them to despise natural functions of human organs and deluded them into believing that self-mortification will reveal 'Brahma' (ibid.: 564–65). Nowhere does Phule's eulogisation of labour as value come out as strongly as in his 13-stanza poem on a Kunbi woman entitled, *Kulumbin*. If early Phule predominantly portrays the reified labour of toiling masses as a tool of Brahmin exploitation, the later Phule, by attaching positive value to productive labour symbolically undermines[10] the Brahmin lifestyle by speaking about it consistently in negative terms. Thus, in *Kulumbin*, the labour of the Kunbi woman, near the hearth and in the fields, becomes the point of reference. While her labour nourishes and sustains the whole of humankind, including the 'Brahmin beggar', the *bhatin* (Brahmin woman) 'doesn't look after Shudra children, doesn't kiss them....' (Phule, 1991: 485).

Like labour, reciprocity is another normative site defining human relations in Phule's schemata, opposed to the hierarchical notions of the Aryas.[11] The myth of the dispossession of Baliraja by Vaman is read politically by Phule as the destruction of the egalitarian, agrarian community of Bali and the establishment of a hierarchical society of the Aryabhats. Phule, by identifying the present-day Shudras and Atishudras as descendants of Bali, legitimises the claim that they are the primordial inhabitants of this land.[12] Thus, by providing a contesting renditions of history, education, politics and religion and morals, Phule re-politicised diverse arenas of public discourse. In a combative mood, he challenges, '*Brahmananache Ved maidani aanand*' (bring the Vedas of the Brahmins out into the open).

'PRODUCTIVE' POWER

There is, however, a theological inconsistency in Phule's world view. If Phule maintains his Nirmik to be transcendental, devoid of human attributes, then it is surprising to find him saying that the Nirmik was enraged at the intemperance of the Muslims and dispossessed them of their glory. Thereafter:

> ... he raised the Englishmen in an extremely barbarous country, and making them brave, *deliberately* sent them *to this country to liberate* the lame Shudras-Atishudras from the *slavery* of crafty Aryabhats. (Phule, 1991: 457, emphasis in the original)

Thus, Phule's 'God' reveals human passions and motivations. Yet, politically, Phule is consistent. Throughout his 'conjectural reconstruction of the past' Phule searches for those forces which at a normative level espoused the cause of egalitarianism. Seen from this perspective, Phule's Nirmik is his imagining of an absolutist power centre that works in his favour.[13] In a way, Phule recognises that even to establish egalitarianism, power is essential.[14]

Though Phule's attribution of egalitarian purpose to pre-British state(s) is open to question, his similar expectation from the British colonial state is not exaggerated. For the first time in the history of India, the state, as established by the British colonialists, was poised to do away with its 'traditional marginality'[15] that had inhibited it from restructuring social relations on a large scale. The British colonial state in the first half of the nineteenth century, buoyed by the evangelical and utilitarian zeal[16] of a 'civilising mission', certainly articulated such ambitions. But the resistance of traditional, entrenched power centres in India forced the British colonial administrators to take a negotiating stand (a position which made Phule impatient with British rule) and, later, as the exploitative political economy of colonialism became all too evident, to abandon its self-imposed role altogether. If Phule's acuteness is seen in his excavating of the Brahmanical self-interest in the maintainance of a hierarchical society, its shortcoming is that he overlooked the vested interests of the British as a colonial power. Though it is true that he severely admonished the British rulers for neglecting the welfare of the downtrodden and, in his later years, for formulating policies that were detrimental to the interests of the toiling mass,[17] it was always from the point of view of reminding them of their historic duty and cautioning them against succumbing to the guile of the Brahmins. Phule's understanding missed the point that there might be—in fact, was—a need on the part of the British rulers themselves to enter into a nexus with the Brahmins (and other power-wielding sections of society) so as to legitimise their entry into the political domain of India. The complete deletion of the conquestorial intent of the colonial rulers is a serious lacuna in Phule's historiography.[18] Yet, given the powerless site from which Phule was articulating his radical critique of inegalitarian society, it was inescapable for him to side with one of the two power centres—the British or the burgeoning nationalist assertion of the Brahmans[19]—to render his reality meaningful.[20] Earnest Gellner, commenting on the dilemma of diaspora nationalism, says:

Those [entropy inhibitions] which are not due to mere communication failures and are remedial neither by assimilation into the dominant pool, nor by the creation of a new independent pool using the native medium of the entrants, are correspondingly more tragic. (Gellner, 1983: 67)

Phule's case in his times exemplifies this predicament, though Phule attempted vigorously to create 'a new independent pool using the native medium....' (Omvedt, 1976: 189).

NOTES

1. This chapter was first presented as a paper at the Cultural Studies Workshop jointly organised by the Centre for Studies in Social Sciences, Kolkata, and International Development Studies, Roskilde University, Denmark, on 19–23 November 1995 in Mysore. I thank all the participants present at the workshop for their comments on the paper. The translations of Phule's writings into English in this text are mine.

2. The removal of intermediaries between the state and the cultivator under the ryotwari system runs parallel to Phule's insistence of removal of middlemen between God and the laity. Phule also looked upon the British state as '*maibaap*' and directly addressed his grievances to it, without recourse to the Brahmans.

3. A large number of the early members of the Satya Shodhak Samaj belonged to this upcoming economic stratum:

   A high proportion of the most prominent members were engaged in commerce as merchants and contractors, and often formed business connections in addition to their ideological commitments. A considerable number were also employed in local government administration, or had a profession. (O'Hanlon, 1985: 246)

4. The central characters—the *padri*, the husband of the Kunbi woman and the *vidhushak*—in Phule's first literary production, *Tritya Ratna*, seemed to have evolved from a mix of the real life personalities of Murray Mitchell, Gaffar Beg Munshi and himself.

5. It is interesting that the Rashtriya Swayamsevak Sangh (RSS) was formed in 1925 with similar emphasis on martial skills 'to organise Hindus'.

6. At one place Phule clearly addresses the Brahmins in these terms: '[Brahmin] is the true descendant of demon brahma, a son of devil, says Joti' (Phule, 1991: 558).

7. Phule on other occasions mockingly calls the sacred thread as the '*pandhra dora*' (white thread) to contrast with the black thread that the Untouchables

were forced to wear during the Peshwa regime. Significantly, unlike the Arya Samaj, which sought to make the Vedas accessible to Hindu women and Shudras, Phule does not seek democratisation of the Brahmanical marks of difference. He insists on the overthrow of the Brahmanical framework and instead demands democratisation of the British educational system.

8. If Phule considers that aggression, violence and annihilation by the Aryabhats ultimately led to the subjugation of the Shudra and Atishudras, he also blames the excessive indulgence of the native chiefs as leading to the downfall. His disdain for the 'hollow splendour' of the aristocratic sardars of his times emerges from his appreciation of a life of honest labour as an antidote against sloth.

9. Phule derisively calls the National Sabha as 'Naradachi Subha', province of Narad, the Brahmin emissary from the heavens.

10. Cohen (1985) talks about 'tactical and symbolic reverses', a recent strategy among the disadvantaged groups, to render positive their very stigma and thus de-stigmatise it. The most eloquent example being the 'Black is Beautiful' movement that swept the US in the late 1960s.

11. Phule is radically egalitarian in gender relations too. In the context of sati, Phule asks, 'Has anyone heard of a man having done "sata" out of sorrow for her [deceased wife]?' (Phule, 1991: 447). Phule wrote *Satsaar* in defence of Pandita Ramabai when the latter was reviled for conversion to Christianity. Tarabai Shinde who wrote *Stree-Purush Tulna* in the 1880s found inspiration in Phule's work.

12. Smith (1986) considers 'association with specific territories' as one of the dimensions of ethnic claim. The others are: a collective name, a common myth of descent, a shared history, a distinctive shared culture, and a sense of solidarity (ibid.: 23–31).

13. Chatterjee (1994) labels the form of history writing of Mrityunjay Vidyalankar, the early nineteenth century Brahmin scholar of Bengal, as 'puranic history' wherein the divine element plays the omnipotent role of directing the course of history. It would not be out of place to characterise Phule's history writing too as 'puranic history', only with the difference that while Phule saw the advent of the British as a transition from kalyug to satyayug, Vidyalankar saw it otherwise.

14. See Dirks et al. (1994), especially the 'Introduction', for a recent commentary on the Foucauldian concept of power.

15. See Kaviraj (1991) for his two notions, 'ceremonial eminence' and 'traditional marginality', describing the place of the state in traditional Indian society.

16. See Stokes (1989) for an account of the mental make-up of the British colonial administrators in the early nineteenth century.

17. In *Shetkaryacha Asud*, Phule sarcastically comments:

While assessing after every thirty years land of such ignorant farmers, the European servants who pray, keeping our pious government in darkness, do not get up saying 'Amen' [sic] unless they have slightly raised the burden of taxes on the farmers. (1991: 275)

18. In the present context, Sharad Joshi of Shetkari Sanghatana whole-heartedly welcomes the globalisation process, calling Dunkel the *muktidata* (liberator) of Indian farmers. Though Sharad Joshi may position himself as a modern-day Phule, contemporary geopolitics is vastly different from Phule's times.

19. Besides the Indian National Congress, Phule was equally harsh towards the attempts made by some contemporary Brahmans, especially people like Vasudev Balwant Phadke, to stage a revolt against British rule by recruiting youth from the Bhil, Ramoshi and other communities. Phule advises 'our righteous government ... to finalise a reasonable tax on the lands of the illiterate farmers [and] to educate them in agricultural matters so that they won't lose life by following treacherous rebellious Brahmins like the Peshwa, Tope, Khajgiwale, Patwardhan, Phadke and others (1991: 293).

20. Later on, Ambedkar too, took a collaborationist stand vis-à-vis the British, though on pragmatic rather than normative grounds. That is, giving topmost priority to the welfare of the Dalits, Ambedkar extended his cooperation to the British after taking due cognisance of the prevalent balance of power. Nevertheless, he never lost sight of the exploitative nature of British colonialism and its lack of seriousness towards the abolition of untouchability.

REFERENCES AND SELECT BIBLIOGRAPHY

Berger, Peter L. (1969) *The Sacred Canopy: Elements of a Sociological Theory of Religion.* New York: Anchor Books, Double Day and Company.

Chatterjee, Partha (1994) 'History and Nationalisation of Hinduism', in Preben Kaarsholm and Jan Hultin (eds), *Inventions and Boundaries: Historical and Anthropological Approaches to the Study of Ethnicity and Nationalism,* pp. 176–92. Roskilde: International Development Studies, Roskilde University.

Cohen, Anthony P. (1985) *The Symbolic Construction of Community.* London: Tavistock Publications.

Dirks, Nicholas, Geoff Eley and Sherry B. Ortnor (eds) (1994) *Culture/Power/History: A Reader in Contemporary Social Theory.* New Jersey: Princeton University Press.

Fuller, Chris (1989) 'British India or Traditional India? Land, Caste and Power', in Hamza Alavi and John Harriss (eds), *Sociology of Developing Societies: South Asia,* pp. 112–43. London: Macmillan Press.

Gellner, Ernest (1983) *Nations and Nationalism.* Oxford: Basil Blackwell Publishers Ltd.

Joshi, Narayan Vishnu (1868) *Pune Shaharache Varnan*. Mumbai: Sahitya Shahakar Sangha Prakashan.

Kale, Govind Ganapat (n.d.) *Mahatma Phuleyanchya Aprakashit Athavani*. Pune: Raghuvanshi Prakashan.

Kaviraj, Sudipta (1991) 'On State, Society and Discourse in India', in James Manor (ed.), *Rethinking Third World Politics*, pp. 83–101. London: Longman Group UK Ltd.

——. (1992) 'The Imaginary Institution of India', in Preben Kaarsholm (ed.), *Modernisation of Culture and the Development of Political Discourse in the Third World*. Denmark: International Development Studies, Roskilde University.

O'Hanlon, Rosalind (1985) *Caste, Conflict and Ideology: Mahatma Jotirao Phule and the Low Caste Protest in Nineteenth Century Western India*. Hyderabad: Cambridge University Press in association with Orient Longman Ltd.

Omvedt, Gail (1976) *Cultural Revolt in a Colonial Society: The Non-Brahman Movement in Western India—1873 to 1930*. Mumbai: Scientific Socialist Education Trust.

Phule, Jotiba (1991) *Mahatma Phule Samagra Vangmaya (MPSV)*, edited by Yeshwant Dinaker Phadke. Mumbai: Maharashtra Rajya Sahitya ani Sanskriti Mandal.

Smith, Anthony D. (1986) *Ethnic Origins of Nations*. New York: Basil Blackwell.

Stokes, Eric (1989) *The English Utilitarians and India*. New Delhi: Oxford University Press.

4

Dalit Vision of a Just Society in India

S.M. MICHAEL

The word 'Dalit' in Sanskrit means 'broken' and 'downtrodden'. Dr Babasaheb Bhimrao Ramji Ambedkar often described the 'Untouchables' as broken people. The Dalits are socially weak, economically needy and politically powerless, despite the protective policies followed by the government under the provisions of the constitution (guaranteeing them educational concessions and scholarships, employment and political reservations and socio-economic welfare benefits). The term 'Dalit' thus describes a condition of being underprivileged and deprived of basic rights and refers to people who are suppressed on the ground of their lowly birth. The word 'Dalit' is a descriptive word evocative of bondage and agony, the anguish and frustrated aspirations of a vast victimised section of the Indian population right down the ages.

The word 'Dalit' as such was first used as far back as 1931 in journalistic writings. Following this, the Dalit Panther Movement of Maharashtra in the early 1970s, gave currency to the concept and word 'Dalit' to highlight the sufferings and struggles of the Untouchables. Later, they extended their movement to include all oppressed groups, namely the SCs, the STs, workers, landless labourers, small farmers and other poor people and also the neo-Buddhist converts. However, nowadays, the SCs (earlier called Depressed Classes under the British and Harijans by Gandhiji) prefer calling themselves 'Dalits' or 'the oppressed', while the tribals prefer to call themselves 'soshits' or the exploited. Both the words are evocative of the anguish and frustrated aspirations of these people who have been the victims of social injustice for several thousand years. The word 'Dalit' particularly emphasises the dehumanising 'caste oppression' that makes them outcastes and Untouchables (a degradation not shared by the tribals or soshits), within the context of the Hindu caste system with its religio-social organising principle of 'purity and pollution' (see Irudayaraj, 1990; Massey, 1990: 40–41; Prabhakar, 1990: 24–25; Zelliot, 1992).

Though some scholars belonging to this socially and culturally oppressed community themselves do not like the term 'Dalit' to designate them and their community, yet they still have not found a better word to replace it. While the search for an appropriate term is still on, the word 'Dalit' continues to designate them and express their anguish and fight for justice in the social and political life of India.

The foundation of the Dalit ideology for a just society was mainly laid by eminent personalities like Mahatma Jotirao Phule (1826–90), E.V. Ramaswamy Periyar (1879–1973) and Babasaheb Ambedkar (1891–1956), with many others throughout India (Narayanswami Guru in Kerala, Acchutanand in Uttar Pradesh and Mangoo Ram in Punjab) (see Omvedt, 1996). They attacked the system of exploitation at all levels, cultural, economical and political. They developed their vision of Indian society as an alternative to the upper caste understanding of India. Hence, it is important to pay some attention to this historical context in which the Dalit ideology has been developed.

TWO VISIONS OF INDIAN NATIONHOOD

Indian civilisation is the outcome of a confluence of various cultural, religious, linguistic and ethnic traditions. Years of mutual fecundation, synthesis and challenge have led Indian civilisation to be characterised by diversity of culture, religion, language, race and caste groups. According to Kothari, 'in the absence of a centralized political authority it was "the Indian civilizational enterprise" which "over the centuries achieved a remarkable degree of cohesion and held together different sub-systems in a continental-size society"' (Kothari, 1988: 2223). Thus, the unifying force of Indian civilisation was the acceptance of multiculturalism and linguistic diversity rather than a political ideology of regimentation.

The Age of Nationalism in the modern sense of the word is a recent phenomenon. It developed in the eighteenth century in the West and emerged at a later period as a universal political concept.

According to Kohn, it was only between 1815 and 1920, that the political map of Europe was redrawn, while the political map of Asia and Africa changed between 1945 and 1965 (Kohn, 1956: 63). Before this period, nationalism with its present implications did not exist; there were city-states, tribal groups and dynastic states and empires (Gellner, 1994: 62).

Nationalism presupposes the existence, in fact or as an ideal, of a centralised form of government over a large and distinct territory (Kohn, 1956: 4). In India, nationalism emerged in the context of colonialism (see Oommen, 1997; Singh, 1997: 117–30). It can be traced to the political and administrative unification of India by the British followed by its economic unification. Politically speaking, there was no India at the beginning of the nineteenth century, and for at least a century before that India did not possess any knowledge of its own past and its ancient history (Majumdar, 1965: 4). The introduction of English education, European science and philosophy, as well as the pride in India as a nation and her past culture, emerged at this historical turning point.

In its early manifestation, the struggle for nationalism, anti-colonial consciousness and the need for independence were not in the realm of politics but in the realm of ideology and culture (Pannikar, 1995: 57). The first expression of this consciousness was in the form of social and religious reform movements. The important question then was—what is the cultural foundation of Indian society and how are we to reconstruct it as a modern nation on a par with other modern nation states?

 Two strands of thought emerged from upper-caste Hindus: one led to an attempt at reconstructing Indian society on the basis of Western ideas originating in the age of Enlightenment and Liberalism, and the other wanted the reconstruction to take place on the basis of ancient Hindu traditions. These two visions of India developed their own ideology, leadership and organisation in the course of the freedom struggle in India. A third vision was voiced by the oppressed and marginalised people of India. These three visions of modern India shaped the course of dialogue in India at the birth of the Indian nation and the framing of her constitution. They are also influential in the current political debates of today. Let us concentrate on these strands of thought.

INDIAN NATION BUILT ON A RATIONAL
APPROACH TO CULTURE

The Enlightenment philosophy of the West began to have its impact on the newly Western-educated Indians during the colonial period. It gave rise to the 'Indian Renaissance'. The spirit that was promoted by English education was usually that of British liberalism, rationalism and utilitarianism, a spirit that challenged many of the presuppositions on which the orthodox Brahmanic Hindu world outlook was based. With ruthless self-criticism, the new Western-educated elites sought to lay the basis for a total social transformation, to weld science and rationality to recreate India.

The beginnings of this social revolt can be easily identified in the thoughts of Raja Rammohun Roy (1772–1833). Roy vividly described the degraded state of society and acknowledged without embarrassment the virtues of Western learning, liberal legal and social institutions and Western social ethics (see Damle and Aikara, 1982: 77). With a view to cleansing Hindu culture and society of its weakness and incongruities, he founded the Brahmo Samaj in 1828 in Calcutta. Its main ideological thrust was to transform Hinduism in the mould of Christianity. The assumption was that Hindu society could only be healed of its social evils if it adopted the Christian rejection of polytheism and idolatry.

The purpose of the Brahmo Samaj was to restructure Hindu culture in terms of modernity. Roy campaigned for the prohibition of sati until Governor-General Lord William Bentinck enacted a ban in 1829. His revolt against Hindu society and his appeal to Indians to purify their religion and reform their social institutions echoed throughout the century after his death. The Brahmo ideologues imbibed quite a bit of Christianity along with some deism of European Enlightenment. The third-generation Samaj leader, Keshub Chandra Sen (1838–84) professed a Christian-like veneration of Jesus of Nazareth and interiorised the Christian concept of man's basic sinfulness.

The massive all-India impact of such reform measures led to a widespread reaction to restrain its further diffusion and subsequent erosion of traditional Hindu values.

INDIAN NATION BUILT ON ARYAN VEDIC CULTURE

While Rammohun Roy cherished a vision of an Indian society rejuvenated by centuries of exposure to Western science and Christian morality, Dayananda Saraswati (1824–83) urged a regeneration of Hinduism through adherence to a purified 'Vedic faith'. Dayananda praised the Vedic Aryans as the primordial and elect people to whom the Veda was revealed by God and whose language (Sanskrit) is said to be the 'Mother of all languages' (Dayananda, 1981: 249). According to Dayananda, the Vedic Aryans migrated at the beginning of history from Tibet—the first land to emerge from the ocean— towards the Aryavarta. Their territory, the original homeland of the Vedic civilisation, covered Punjab, the Doab and the Ganges basin. From there the Aryans were in a position to dominate the whole world till the war of the Mahabharata, a historic watershed that inaugurated a phase of decadence. National renaissance for Dayanda implied a return of the Vedic Golden Age.

The chief object of the Arya Samaj, which he founded in 1875 in Bombay, was to bring about social and religious reform through a renaissance of early Hindu doctrines. The popular slogans of the Arya Samaj were 'Back to the Vedas' and 'Aryavarta for the Aryans' (Smith, 1938: 57). It is in the context of the upper-caste Hindus identifying the 'nation' and 'national culture' as basically Hindu, as deriving from Vedic times and as fundamentally a creation of the Aryan people, that we should view the alternative vision provided by Jotirao Phule who was born a Shudra.

JOTIRAO PHULE'S VISION OF A JUST SOCIETY

Jotirao Phule (1826–90) was the first Indian to proclaim in modern India the dawn of a new age for the common man, the downtrodden, the underdog and for Indian women. It was his aim to reconstruct the social order on the basis of social equality, justice and reason. As discussed earlier, the 'Aryan theory of race' constituted the most influential common discourse for discussing caste and society in Phule's time. European 'Orientalists' like William Jones, Charles Wilkins, James Prinsep and others (see Marshall, 1970: 1–44) conveniently used it to assert an ethnic kinship between Europeans and the ancient Vedic peoples (see O'Hanlon, 1985: 57–59). The constant interest of European scholars like H.H. Wilson, C. Lassen, H.T. Colebrooke, Monier Williams, Max Mueller and others (see Kejariwal, 1988) in ancient Aryan society and their appreciation and praise of this society provided an important moral boost to high-caste Indians. Thus, Indian civilisation was seen as primarily a derivative of Aryan civilisation and the caste system was lauded as a means by which people of diverse racial and cultural backgrounds were brought together and subjected to the civilising influence of the Aryans (Omvedt, 1976: 103).

At one level, Phule simply reversed this notion, arguing that the low castes, whom he sometimes called 'Shudras and Atishudras' and were simply listed as 'Kunbis, Malis, Dhangars ... Bhils, Kolis, Mahars and Mangs', were the original inhabitants of the country, enslaved and exploited by conquering Aryans, who had formulated a caste-based Hinduism as a means of deceiving the teeming masses and legitimising their own power. It was the confirmed and sincere view of Jotirao that the ancient history of India was nothing but the struggle between Brahmins and non-Brahmins (Keer, 1964: 120). Hence, Phule consciously sought to bring together the major peasant castes (these were, besides the Kunbis or cultivators, the Malis or 'garden' cultivators and Dhangars or shepherds) along with the large Untouchable castes of Mahars and Mangs in a common 'front' against Brahmin domination (see O'Hanlon, 1985: 131).

Jotirao's attack on Brahmanism was uncompromising. He realised that the seeds of the Brahmins' power, supremacy and privileges lay in their scriptures and Puranas; and these works and the caste system were created to exploit the lower classes (see ibid.: 122–32). Phule also reinterpreted sacred religious literature. To give an example, Phule did so by reading the nine avatars of Vishnu as stages of Aryan conquest and used King Bali as a counter symbol to the elite's use of Ram, Ganapati and Kali (see Keer, 1964: 90-125; O' Hanlon, 1985: 137). Thus, Jotirao attacked the Brahmanical scriptures and Puranas, revolted against priest craft and the caste system and set on foot a social movement for the liberation of the Shudras, Atishudras (Untouchables) and women.

Phule realised that the strongest hold of religious tradition on the people derived from the extensive integration of Hindu religious literature into the popular culture and oral traditions. Phule's answer to this was to provide alternative accounts of the texts, myths and stories most common in popular Hinduism. He linked these with important symbols and structures from contemporary Maharashtrian society in order to convey the real community of culture and interest that united all lower castes against their historical and cultural adversaries: the Brahmans.

To fulfil his life's ambition to establish a casteless society, Phule founded the Satya Shodhak Samaj (Truth Seeking Society) on 24 September 1873. The Samaj set up the first school for girls and Untouchables. Phule also organised marriages without Brahmin priests, widow remarriage, etc. According to Phule, the performance of any religious ceremony by a Brahmin priest for a member of another caste, expresses in a concrete form the relations of purity between them which make up the basis for Hindu religious hierarchy. It is the Brahmin priest alone who, in his ritual purity, has the power to mediate between the human world and that of the high gods, and so it is he who controls the entry of divine power into the world (see Babb, 1975: 31–67). For this reason, Phule felt that the employment of Brahmin priests negated the very principle upon which he hoped a community of the lower castes would be based. The Satya Shodhak Samaj actively encouraged marriages without Brahmin priests. Thus, the Satya Shodhak Samaj assumed a vital role as the ideological conscience for all those who identified themselves with the lower castes, whether they belonged to the Samaj or to one of the numerous other groups working for the uplift of the lower castes.

A fundamental difference between the 'historical' religions, Christianity and Islam, and Hinduism, consists in their attitudes to history. While the latter conceives of human history as the eternal recurrence of illusion, historical religions work out their destiny within those very processes, organised around the Church, the visible body of the faithful, the Book and the incarnated Saviour. All human history takes its meaning from the struggle (Weber, 1958: 167). As we have seen, one of Phule's main concerns was to locate the struggle of the lower castes within history, to transform myth into history and establish a diachronic relation between present and past oppression. King Bali had stood as the symbol and mainstay of the pre-Aryan realm. Here, it is possible to see how Phule's perception of human history strengthened his scheme more generally. On the mass level, history became purposive (see O'Hanlon, 1985: 203–5).

Thus, the nineteenth century saw the beginning of a violent and controversial movement of protest amongst western India's low and Untouchable castes, aimed at the effects of their lowly position within the Hindu caste hierarchy (see ibid.).

CULTURAL CONTROVERSIES IN THE NATIONAL CONGRESS

A second stage in the modern development of Indian nationalism emerged in 1885 with the foundation of the Indian National Congress by an Englishman, Allan Octavian Hume. The Indian National Congress tried to define a new India in terms of ideas borrowed from European political experience and Western social ethics (see Smith, 1963: 88). All the same, by the end of the nineteenth century, there was a mighty struggle for the control of the Congress. The two factions, namely, the moderates and the extremists, held radically different views about the proper ends and means of the nationalist movement. While the moderates in the National Congress like Dadabhai Naoroji, Madhava Govinda Ranade and Gopal Krishna Gokhale stood up for reforms in Hindu culture, the extremists like B.G. Tilak glorified Hindu culture and opposed any kind of reform. While the moderates or liberals envisioned a modernisation of India through the adoption of the Western parameters of justice, order, rationality and the secular state, Tilak glorified the deeds of Vedic civilisation (Parvate, 1959: 463). Tilak's overall consideration was the promotion of solidarity and unity among the Hindus and hence he emphasised the superiority of their religion, encouraged revivalism, polticised the Ganapati festival and converted Shivaji into a cult figure, thus serving both religious and political objectives (Michael, 1986: 91–116). The style of the revivalists was aggressive and tended to reflect a Kshatriya (warrior) world view.

When Mohandas Gandhi publicly emerged on the Indian political scene after World War I as the Mahatma, he received widespread revivalist support. Indeed, many believed him to be one of themselves. While Gandhi had much in common with the revivalists, many came to oppose him as they gradually became better acquainted with his ideas. Gandhi declared that his Hinduism included all that he knew to be best in Islam, Christianity, Buddhism and Zoroastrianism. Gandhi strove unceasingly for Hindu–Muslim unity, convinced that ultimately both religions were true and valid (see Gandhi, 1949). His deepest conviction was that God, truth and *ahimsa* (non-violence) were all one and the same. Satyagraha (truth-force, non-violent resistance) was thus based on Gandhi's personal religious faith and outlook.

The revivalists were disturbed by Gandhi's ascetic non-Kshatriya style of leadership, his definition of dharma as the non-violent pursuit of 'truth' and his assimilationist conception of the Indian nation, which he saw as a brotherhood or a confederation of communities. Dr Kurtakoti, sankaracharya (a Hindu spiritual guide) of the Karvir Peeth implored Hindus to return to the militancy advocated by Tilak, Vivekananda and Gose (Anderson and Damle, 1987: 20).

THE QUESTION OF EQUALITY AMONG THE REVIVALIST

As a result of the intensification of Hindu–Muslim tension between 1921 and 1923, the dormant Hindu Mahasabha, formed in 1915 as a forum for a variety of Hindu interests (for example, protection of cows, the writing of Hindi in the Devanagari script, caste reforms, etc.), was revitalised. It is in this setting of 'Hinduism in danger' that a new, more influential Hindu militant organisation, known as the Rashtriya Swayamsevak Sangh (RSS) was established in 1925 by Dr Keshab Baliram Hedgewar, who was deeply influenced by Tilak.

The RSS claims to defend Hinduism against its so-called antagonists. Its avowed objective is the unification of the Hindu community and the inculcation of a militant awareness of its common heritage and destiny. One of the most influential books in the development of Hindu nationalist ideology was the treatise on Hindutva by V.D. Savarkar, a close associate of Tilak. 'Hindutva' refers to a people united by a common country, blood, history, religion, culture and language. This idea became the foundation and basis of the RSS's activities. Members of all castes are welcomed into the RSS if they conform to behavioural standards considered proper by the RSS leaders. Those standards continue to reflect, to a larger extent, the Maharashtrian Brahmin cultural values of the founders of the RSS.

According to M.R. Golwalkar, who succeeded Dr Hedgewar as the chief of the RSS, at the heart of Hindu culture is Hindu religion, and at the heart of the Hindu religion are the noble ideas of the Vedas. He also asserted that the diverse languages of India are the offshoots of Sanskrit, the dialect of the gods and the enlightened Aryans (Golwalkar, 1947).

Golwalkar regretted the fall of the Brahmins in Hindu society, which, according to him, was deliberately brought about by the British. Thus, he presents what may be called the 'Golwalkar notion of social structure' in these terms:

> The unique feature of our society is its diverse functional groups (castes). The present-day mind accustomed to viewing through foreign 'isms' and their high-sounding slogans of equality, has failed to grasp this unique feature and talks of classless society. The glorious main feature which once distinguished our society, was the Varna Vyavastha. But it is being dubbed as casteism and scoffed at. There are some who never tired of propagating the idea that the caste system was responsible for our downfall. This is not true, the so-called caste-ridden society has remained intact and firm and alive and unconquerable whereas the so-called 'casteless' societies crumbled at the very outset before foreign conquests. (Golwalkar, 1968: 89–120)

GANDHIAN APPROACH TO CASTE AND VARNA

Hindu reformers, including Gandhi, were of the opinion that the Untouchables could maintain a Hindu as well as a Vankar or Malliga identity without the stigma of being Untouchables. The Hindu reformers delinked the problem of untouchability from the caste system. Untouchability, according to them, was not an essential part of Hinduism or, for that matter, of the caste system. It resulted from a violation of the basic spirit of Hinduism. 'Varnashram, Gandhi asserted, was for the preservation of harmony and growth of soul' (Shah, 1995: 28). Gandhi repeatedly harped on the evils of untouchability. He himself adopted a Dalit girl as his daughter. He voluntarily decided to live with the Untouchabes to become one with them. He symbolically called Untouchables Harijans, that is, people of God. He started the Harijan Sevak Sangh to launch programmes to remove untouchability and improve the economic conditions of the Untouchables (ibid.: 28–29).

It is in this context of Hindu revivalism and the Gandhian approach to caste and varna that one has to view the ideas and visions of non-Brahmin leaders like Periyar and Ambedkar.

PERIYAR'S VISION FOR JUSTICE

E.V. Ramaswamy Naicker (1879–1973), known as Periyar (great sage), was born in 1879 in Erode into a respectable middle-class family of artisans. He married at the age of 13, but after six years he became a sanyasi, travelling as a religious mendicant all over India. During his travels to places of pilgrimage, he gained an intimate knowledge of the evils of popular Hinduism and also of the exploitation of the masses by Brahmin priests.

Periyar became convinced that casteism and Hinduism were one and the same. He wanted Hinduism, as he saw it, to go altogether. His movement took a turn towards racial consciousness and became a 'Dravidian' movement, seeking to defend the rights of the Dravidians against Aryan domination. It blamed the Aryans for introducing an unjust and oppressive social system in the country (see Hardgrave, 1965: 17). Periyar realised that the important feature of all new ideologies of the elites was the 'Aryan view of race'. The 'Aryan view' was adopted enthusiastically by the Indian elites as a new model for understanding caste. That is, Brahmins, Kshatriyas and Vaishyas were believed, almost as a matter of definition, to be the descendants of the invading Aryans, while Shudras and Untouchables were believed to be the descendents of the native conquered inhabitants. In this new language of caste and race, to claim 'Aryan' descent was equivalent to claiming 'twice-born' status, and to claim 'Dravidian' or 'non-Aryan' descent was almost equivalent to saying that one was a 'Shudra'.

The high caste elites of India began to take Aryan and Sanskritic culture as the basis of 'Indian nationality', but in so doing they were, in fact, taking a part—the culture of the upper castes and roughly more northern groups—for the whole. Periyar's movement sought to defend the rights of the Dravidians against Aryan domination. He saw the Brahmins as the representatives of Hindu arrogance and the stronghold of social injustice (see Devanandan, 1960).

Naicker quit the Congress and attacked it as a tool of Brahmin domination. In 1925, he organised the 'Self-Respect Movement', designed as a movement of Dravidian uplift, seeking to expose Brahmin tyranny and the deceptive methods by which they controlled all spheres of Hindu life. Naicker publicly ridiculed the Puranas as fairy tales, not only imaginary and irrational, but grossly immoral as well. Naicker attacked the Hindu religion as the tool of Brahmin domination.

Under the Congress ministry of C. Rajagopalachari in 1937, Hindi was introduced in the south as a compulsory subject in schools. Taking this as an affront to Tamil culture and its rich literary tradition, Tamil patriots like Annadurai, Karunanithi and others under the leadership of Naicker reacted with violent protest. Naicker saw the imposition of Hindi as a step towards the subjugation of the Tamil people by the north Indian Aryans.

Hindu religion was denounced as an opiate by which the Brahmins had dulled and controlled the masses. 'A Hindu in the present concept may be a Dravidian, but a Dravidian in the real sense of the term cannot and shall not be a Hindu' (A.S. Venu, cited in Harrison, 1960: 127). Images of Hindu deities such as Rama and Ganesha were destroyed. According to Periyar, 'Rama and Sita are despicable characters, not worthy of imitation or admiration even by the lowest of fourth-rate humans.' Ravana, on the other hand, is depicted as a Dravidian of 'excellent character'. In his preface to *The Ramayana: A True Reading*, Naicker states that 'the veneration of the story any longer in Tamil Nadu is injurious and ignominious to the self-respect of the community and of the country' (Naicker, 1959: iii–iv).

On the eve of Independence, Naicker called upon the Dravidian people of south India 'to guard against the transfer of power from the British to the Aryans' (*The Hindu*, 11 February 1946). Fearing Brahmin dominance under Aryan 'imperialism', Naicker called for the formation of a separate south Indian state of Dravidasthan. Today, several Dravidian political parties in Tamil Nadu trace back their inspiration to Periyar in their programme to build a Dravidian civilisation in the Indian subcontinent.

AMBEDKAR—A REVOLUTIONARY

It is indeed impossible to understand the contemporary Dalit revolt without understanding the ideas of Dr Bhimrao Ramji Ambedkar

(1891–1956). For a growing number of young Dalits across India, many born after his death in 1956, he has become a symbol of a vision that can be achieved, a vision of freedom from social and economic injustice. Ambedkar attacked two central features of the Indian order: culturally enforced inequality and economic inequality. Throughout his writings and actions there is one common thread, namely, that socio-economic transformation in India requires a cultural revolution, one that will not only destroy the culture of the past but also build something of value in its place.

Ambedkar was inspired and guided by the noble example set by Mahatma Jotiba Phule. Phule was no longer there to guide Ambedkar. Nevertheless, his example had left an indelible imprint on Ambedkar's mind. He was determined to complete the work started by Jotiba and it is not surprising that it became his life's mission (Rajasekhariah, 1971: 18–19; also seen Keer, 1974: vii).

Ambedkar was a revolutionary. He led the fight against untouchability, Hinduism and the Brahmin caste. He was convinced that the caste system was not only unjust but also immoral. He established a new dispensation, a new religion (neo-Buddhism) whose foundation is its unequivocal rejection of Hinduism. Ambedkar criticised the caste system vehemently. For him, the fight against casteism and untouchability was central to his agenda. Hence, he was very critical of the two contemporary approaches to the reform of the caste system, namely, those of Dayananda Saraswati and Gandhi (see Baxi, 1994). According to him neither could bring about a real solution to casteism. He held that society should be based on the three fundamental principles of liberty, equality and fraternity.

If caste was to be destroyed, he said, then its religious foundation in the Vedas and Shastras also needed to be destroyed. Faith in these scriptures was nothing more than a legalised class ethic favouring the Brahmans. 'If you wish to bring about a breach in the system, then you have got to apply the dynamite to the Vedas and the Shastras, which deny any part to reason, to the Vedas and Shastras, which deny any part to morality. You must destroy the Religion of the Smritis' (Ambedkar, 1945a: 70). Hinduism, he declared, had neither morality, nor revolutionary force, nor social utility; instead, it promoted the interests of a particular class.

Ambedkar, for his part, saw clearly that Brahmanical Hinduism had to be fought directly with religious symbolism if his struggle was to succeed. Without religious symbolism, the case of the Dalits would be forever lost in the logic of a new nationalism led by the upper castes. It was this realisation that led him to reject a Marxian materialistic solution to the problem of untouchability. Because caste distinctions went beyond the purely economic, they could not be resolved by an economic argument alone.

Ambedkar also rejected the position of Gandhi with regard to caste and its reform. Gandhi felt that the ancient Hindus had already achieved an ideal social system with varna vyavastha. According to Gandhi, 'The law of *varna* means that everyone will follow as a matter of *dharma*-duty the hereditary calling of his forefathers ... he will earn his livelihood by following that calling' (Zelliot, 1992: 154). In contrast, Ambedkar believed that an ideal society had yet to be achieved in India. For him, the priority was not making 'Hinduism' or Hindu society 'shine forth' but building a new, equal, free, open, non-hierarchical, modern India.

According to Ambedkar 'It is wrong to say that the problem of the Untouchables is a social problem ... the problem of the Untouchables is fundamentally a political problem (of minority versus majority groups)' (Ambedkar, 1945b: 190). Hence, Ambedkar launched his revolutionary movement for the liberation and advancement of the Dalits. On 20 July 1942, he declared at Nagpur:

With justice on our side, I do not see how we can lose our battle. The battle to me is a matter of full joy. The battle is in the fullest sense spiritual. There is nothing material or sordid in it. For our struggle is our freedom. It is a battle for the reclamation of human respectability which has been suppressed and mutilated by the Hindu social system and will continue to be suppressed and mutilated if in the political struggle the Hindus win and we lose. My final word of advice to you is, 'educate, organise and agitate'; have faith in yourselves and never lose hope. (see Das and Massey, 1995: viii)

Thus, Ambedkar was able to put the untouchability issue at the centre stage of Indian politics (see Shashi, 1992).

Ambedkar painfully realised that within Hinduism the Untouchables would never be able to get equal status and receive just treatment. He was also convinced that individual and group mobility was difficult for the Untouchables within the Hindu social system. In this context, he saw two possibilities for social emancipation: the political unity of Untouchables and an *en masse* conversion. Hence, in 1936 he talked of conversion to another religion: 'Though I have been born a Hindu, I shall not die as a Hindu' (31 May 1936, Bombay). He had already made mention of conversion at the Yeola Conference of 1935.

The call for conversion by Ambedkar disturbed the Hindu leadership very much. Several leaders tried to persuade him not to go ahead with his plan. Ambedkar expressed surprise that the caste Hindus, who had never shown any fellow-feelings for the Untouchables were suddenly beseeching them to stay within the fold of Hinduism. Since the Untouchables had been for centuries ill-treated and humiliated by caste Hindus, why did they now suddenly take such an interest in keeping them within the Hindu fold?

On 14 October 1956, after long deliberation and a conscious choice in favour of Buddhism, Ambedkar took his *diksha* at Nagpur at 9.30 AM. Assembled were about 500,000 Mahars, who all converted to Buddhism on that day. Ambedkar's embracing of Buddhism was a strong protest against all that the Hindus had failed to do. For him *swaraj* did not mean anything if it did not also put an end to the slavery of the Untouchables (Gore, 1993: 144).

Ambedkar's legacy at the time of his death was a large body of writings; a political party for all oppressed Indians—the Republican Party; a nascent Buddhist conversion movement; a system of higher education that began with Siddharth College in Bombay and spread to other cities; a host of reserved places for SCs in education, administration and legislative bodies; and a critical mass of awakened ex-Untouchables (Zelliot, 1996: 12).

The tradition established by Phule, Periyar and Ambedkar represents the effort to construct an alternative identity of the people, based on non-Aryan and low-caste perspectives, that was critical not only of the oppressiveness of the dominant Hindu caste society but also of its claims to antiquity and of being the dominant Indian tradition (see Omvedt, 1994, 1996).

THE POLITICS OF NUMBERS IN INDEPENDENT INDIA

With the growth of democratic institutions and the emergence of the 'politics of numbers' in contemporary India, the Dalits began to assume some importance in national politics. Dalit leaders in different political parties, in order to take advantage of the situation and bring about their liberation, began to mobilise forces.

To fight untouchability, which was spread throughout the country and was deeply rooted in the minds of the people, was not a simple task. First, the Dalit leaders had to lift their brothers and sisters from their ignorance, teach them to agitate against injustice and to organise them into a pulsating force. The response was at first weak, clumsy and slow, but later it became positive and healthy. Second, the leaders had to face and stand up against the reactionary caste Hindus. Every step towards the liberation of the Dalits was followed by sharp reaction from the caste Hindus in the form of boycotts, atrocities, arson and other crimes. In all such critical situations, the Dalit leaders had to stand by their poor brethren, raise their morale and help them wage a peaceful and legal battle against the forces of the reactionaries. Third, the Dalit leadership had to convince the government to accept their demands of human rights.

AN UNFINISHED REVOLUTION

All these things, certainly, have had an impact on the socio-economic and cultural life of the Dalits. Economic development in general as well as the reservation policy and the special component plan have led to some improvement in the educational and economic status of the Dalits. Their literacy rate has increased from 10.2 per cent in 1961 to 37.41 per cent in 1991 and their enrolment in schools doubled between 1981 and 1991.[1] The reservation policy has also had a positive impact. The number of Dalit employees in government service has risen from 212,000 in 1956 to 604,000 in 1992. The number of Dalit employees in public sector undertakings increased from 40,000 in 1970 to 369,000 in 1992 (see Thorat, 1996: 1). These and other positive trends have led to some decline in the percentage of poor Dalits. In rural areas, the percentage of the poor among Dalits declined from 58.07 per cent in 1983–84 to 50 per cent in

1987–88, while in urban areas, that percentage went down from 56.52 per cent to 46.95 per cent during the same period (see Thorat, 1996: 1).

Despite these improvements, Dalits still lag far behind other groups in Indian society. While their literacy rate is now 37 per cent, that of non-Dalits is 57 per cent. In rural areas, where most Dalits live, their economic base continues to be weak. In the late 1980s, 63 per cent of Dalit households were landless or near-landless wage labourers, but only 31 per cent of non-Dalit households were landless or near-landless wage labourers. Only a fraction of Dalits owned land and 73 per cent of those who did were marginal farmers with too little to live on. The cumulative result has been a high incidence of poverty among Dalits, 50 per cent as compared with 37 per cent among non-Dalits in 1987–88. Meanwhile, civil rights violations and atrocities against Dalits continue to increase. Between 1966 and 1976, 40,000 cases of atrocity against Dalit were registered, which works out to an average of 4,000 cases per year. Between 1976 and 1987, there were 17,000 such cases or an average of 8,500 cases per year. Between 1981 and 1986, there were 91,097 cases or an average of 18,000 cases per year! (ibid.: 4). The government admitted in Parliament on 22 April 1994 that there were 62,113 cases of atrocities against Dalits and tribals were registered between 1991 and 1993. The annual report of the ministry of welfare for 1995–96 shows that the number of cases of crimes against SCs and STs committed by members of non-SCs and non-STs has shown a continuous increase with the number of cases going up from 25,352 in 1992 to 38,926 in 1994. The increase in crimes against SCs and STs in 1994, as compared with crimes in the preceding year, was as high as 36 per cent and 27.4 per cent respectively (Godbole, 1997: 14). Studies indicate that these atrocities were committed over land disputes and minimum wages as well as to prevent Dalits from securing justice under civil rights laws.

With regard to Dalit women, in all respects, they are at the lowest level of the socio-economic and educational hierarchy. Dalit women tend to be concentrated in areas of work in which wages are lowest and regular employment least certain. In 1991, about 71 per cent of them were agricultural labourers, whereas only 43 per cent of non-Dalit women were agricultural labourers. Even in urban areas,

28 per cent of Dalit women were employed as agricultural labour, as compared to only 5 per cent in the case of non-Dalit women (Thorat, 1997: 1).

The new economic policy also affects the Dalits adversely. After the new reforms were implemented in 1990, both unemployment and poverty levels increased. The poverty ratio increased from 38 per cent in 1989 to 48 per cent in 1992. Since the Dalits constitute the bulk of the poor and unemployed, they have suffered the most. The number of Dalit employees in government service declined from 628,000 in 1991 to 604,000 in 1992, while the number of those employed in the public sector dropped from 432,000 in 1990 to 369,000 in 1992 (see Thorat, 1996: 4). What is most disturbing is that most of this decline has occurred in the lower-level posts. Thus, the burden of the new economic policy has fallen most heavily upon the poor.

The persistence of poverty and caste injustice remains a shameful blot on Indian society. Over the past 10 years, an emerging Dalit identity and social consciousness has created a new political consciousness among poor rural Dalits. Dalit consciousness is by no means limited to the SCs. It has begun to symbolise a much broader sector of the oppressed and hitherto excluded social strata. It is based on an attempted, though by no means realised, solidarity of the poor and the discriminated classes of the people.

Today's political scene in India cannot be understood without taking into consideration the phenomenon of the upsurge of Dalit-OBC self-consciousness that has spread from the south and the west to the north. Among the northern states, the meteoric rise of the Bahujan Samaj Party (BSP) in Uttar Pradesh since the 1980s is almost unprecedented. Of late, the BSP has also made significant inroads in Punjab and Madhya Pradesh. Dalit consciousness has made a political assertion. The most startling feature is the emergence of other political groups like the Dalit Sena and the Backward and Minority Communities Employees' Federation (BAMCEF), linked directly to political parties controlled by the Dalits themselves. Javed Alam observes that the oppressed castes have begun to realise their power (2001: 105). This new spirit of independence among Dalits is not confined only to the economically-developed western states of India, but is a country-wide phenomenon. This together with the logic

of fresh realignments of political parties has made the Dalits the new
pivotal players in Indian politics. The Dalits and the Backward Castes
hold immense political potential, if only they can be brought together
as a powerful force. They would be able to bring about a true social
revolution for equality and justice.

There are some signs of this today. The Dalits are asserting
themselves much more than before (Vanaik, 1997: 323–26). They
have decided that they will not call themselves 'Harijans' simply
because it is a paternalistic expression. There are numerous small and
large organisations of Dalits all over the country such as the Dalit
Sangharsh Samiti in Karnataka, the Indian Dalit Federation in Kerala,
the Dalit Maha Sabha in Andhra Pradesh, the BSP in Uttar Pradesh,
Bihar and other northern states, the Dalit Sena consisting of Dalits
of several states, etc. The Dalits are trying to get organised into a
well-coordinated political movement with an all-India organisation and
all-India leadership that can challenge the established socio-political
order. This became very clear in the way the Dalits worked towards
including caste on the agenda of the Durban Conference on Race.
This aim was inspired by their resentment against the existing social
system which expresses itself through various forms of agitation and
struggle and is bound to acquire the momentum of a national
movement in the years to come (Ayrookuzhiel, 1990: 14–23).

However, the movement has always been opposed by external and
sometimes by internal forces. Every move of Dalit mobilisation has
been virtually followed by a counter upper-caste assemblage. The on-
going controversy centred around Ambedkar and his detractors is
one of such kind (see Shourie, 1997). While there is a concerted
attempt by the Brahmanical forces to co-opt Jotiba Phule and
Ambedkar as 'Hindu reformers', a sustained attack has been launched
by Hindutva/Brahmanical ideologues like Arun Shourie to denigrate
and malign these great Dalit-Bahujan personalities. In reality this
controversy centred around Ambedkar and his detractors should be
analysed in the broader perspective of the emerging socio-political
trends in the country. As shown earlier, the social justice movement
has been one of the most remarkable and relevant socio-political
movements of modern India. In fact, it is evolving into a democratic,
empowering and assertive mass movement against the Brahmanical
social order.

Ambedkar is of central relevance to the growing human rights movement and is fast emerging as the pan-Indian leader, a symbol of the Dalits and other oppressed masses. The trajectory of Ambedkar's life, starting as a poor Dalit and culminating as the architect and framer of the nation's constitution, stands as the supreme example of a struggle successfully waged and won. His resolute war with Hinduism, and conversion to Buddhism, his differences with Gandhi over separate electorates for Dalits, the formation of his Republican Party of India, his many speeches and public utterances all taken together comprise a distinct ideology of Dalit rights. Ambedkar's thoughts and example have provided Dalits with a vision that no one can ignore, motivating them to speak the language of rights, self-respect and dignity. By leaning towards a historical explanation of Shudras and former 'Untouchables' as originally being warriors displaced by threatened Brahmins, he gave to Dalits a conflictual model of resistance and a right to reclaim their lost status.

Precisely because of this, Ambedkar has been chosen by some like Shourie and others as their prime target since he best symbolises the aspirations of the Dalit-Bahujan masses. The Phule–Ambedkar ideology has challenged the very legitimacy of Hindutva/Brahmanism as a social order or religion. Ambedkar's decision to embrace Buddhism stands today as one of the most serious attempts to find a new meaning and relevant cultural strategy to empower the Dalit community.

Unfortunately, Dalits are also divided among themselves and their leadership too is rife with both confusion and schism. The Dalit movement is beset by the virus of endemic co-option—from the old days of the Scheduled Caste Federation and the Republican Party to the Dalit Panthers to the various anti-reservation movements to the recent controversy on Arun Shourie's book on Ambedkar (Shourie, 1997).

Modern Dalit movements following Ambedkar's ideology face two stumbling blocks: first, the pervasiveness of Brahmanical control over social norms governing inter- and intra-jati behaviour and, second, the profound appeal of popular (non-Brahmanical) Hindu religious practices to a large rural mass of Dalits. The old Brahmanic hegemony reiterates itself through popular Hinduism. Buddhism on which Ambedkarism ostensibly rests has not quite managed to make a sharp enough break with popular Hindu beliefs. Jati identities among Dalits have remained firm through jati endogamy and political parties too have played a reinforcing role by forming alliances based on jati. To speak of a unified Dalit identity would be to simplify a complex situation to the point of falsification. Among Ambedkarites the lack of sharp differentiation between Buddhism and Hinduism has created a greater ambivalence.

In spite of this experience of continuing let downs, reactions and co-options, there are also signs of new hope emerging, namely the Bahujan alliance of SCs and OBCs, couched not only in terms of achieving social justice but also capturing political power (see Kothari, 1997: 439–58). The human right approach with regard to the Dalit problem has definitely opened a new door, basing the Dalit struggle on the understanding of Dalits, first and foremost, as human beings and citizens, and carriers of inviolable rights to be granted by national and international communities. The approach clearly moves beyond religious, jati and caste affiliations and claims to have set the foundations for a more broad-based approach. There is also no shortage of sensitive and committed people in the Dalit movement to take forward the vision of Phule, Periyar and Ambedkar. Hence, what is required is a strong unity among the poor, the marginalised and the outcastes. This will not be an easy task because they are internally divided into several castes and sub-castes, externally scattered almost throughout the vast country and prone to be a prey to divisive forces. Therefore, the Dalit leadership has to strive constantly for bringing about unity among the Dalits and other oppressed groups to fight against their common foes and enemies (see Kshirsagar, 1994).

CONCLUSION

The pioneers who worked for the liberation of the Dalits and OBCs, like Phule, Periyar and Ambedkar, propagated the idea of the need for a cultural revolution or a total transformation of Indian society. They rejected the vision of the upper castes which identified the Indian nation as basically Hindu, deriving from Vedic times and fundamentally a creation of the Aryan people. While rejecting the ideals of the upper-caste notion of Indian society based on the ideas and values of Manu and varna vyavastha, they propagated the principles of equality, justice, liberty and rationality. This broad-based standpoint is widely accepted among the Dalits.

There is, however, much discussion and dispute on the means of attaining these ideals of social justice. This problem is worsened by the multiple divisions existing in the Dalit ranks; for example, the Dalits are divided among themselves along sub-caste lines and like the proverbial crabs, keep clawing at each other, pulling down those who move up, so that all of them remain in their lowly position. They are also hindered by the present political climate where the upper castes are trying to establish a unified Hindu cultural nationalism.

All the same, it is true that if the goals of a movement are clearly outlined and well defined, and if it finds active support, first in its own ranks and, second, in those of others likely to be sympathetic to their cause, the movement will become an organically living one. What is needed is good and able leadership. If the cause is right and the leadership is good, then the movement will certainly grow even if faced with antagonism and hostility. Every step ahead will encourage the Dalits to move forward towards final victory.

NOTE

1. For updated information on this subject, see the chapter by P.G. Jogdand (Chapter 14) in this volume.

REFERENCES AND SELECT BIBLIOGRAPHY

Alam, Javed (2001) 'Is Caste Appeal Casteism?: Oppressed Castes in Politics', in Surinder Jodhka (ed.), *Communities and Identities*. New Delhi: Sage Publications.

Ambedkar, B.R. (1945a) *Annihilation of Caste*. Bangalore: Dalit Sahitya Akademy.

———. (1945b) *What Congress and Gandhi have done to the Untouchables*. Bombay: Thacker and Co.

Anderson, W.K. and S.D. Damle (1987) *The Brotherhood in Saffron: The Rashtriya Swayamsevak Sangh and Hindu Revivalism*. New Delhi: Vistaar.

Ayrookuzhiel, Abraham, A.M. (1990) 'The Ideological Nature of the Emerging Dalit Consciousness', *Religion and Society*, 37(3), September: 14–23.

Babb, Lawrence A. (1975) *The Divine Hierarchy: Popular Hinduism in Central India*. New York: Columbia University Press.

Baxi, Upendra (1994) 'Emancipation as Justice: Babasaheb Ambedkar's Legacy and Vision', in *Ambedkar and Social Justice*, Vol. 1. Ministry of Information and Broadcasting, Government of India.

Damle, Y.B. and Jacob Aikara (1982) *Caste, Religion and Politics in India*. New Delhi: Oxford University Press & IBH Publishing Co.

Das, Bhagwan and James Massey (1995) *Dalit Solidarity*. New Delhi: The Indian Society for Promoting Christian Knowledge (ISPCK).

Dayananda, Swami (1981) *The Light of Truth* (translated and introduced by Ganga Prasad Upadhyaya). Allahabad: Upadhyaya Press.

Devanandan, P.D. (1960) *The Dravida Kazagham: A Revolt against Brahmanism*. Bangalore: Christian Institute for the Study of Religion and Society.

Gandhi, M.K. (1949) *Communal Unity*. Ahmedabad: Navajivan.

Gellner, E. (1994) *Encounters with Nationalism*. Oxford: Blackwell.

Godbole, Madhav (1997) 'Crime and Punishment: Trying Times for Tribal Peoples', *The Times of India*, 14 February, p. 14 (Mumbai).

Golwalkar, M.S. (1947) *We or Our Nationhood Defined* (fourth edn). Nagpur: Bharat Prakashan.

———. (1968) *Bunch of Thoughts*. Bangalore: Bharat Prakashan.

Gore, M.S. (1993) *The Social Context of an Ideology: Ambedkar's Political and Social Thought*. New Delhi: Sage Publications.

Hardgrave, Jr. Robert L. (1965) *The Dravidian Movement*. Bombay: Popular Prakashan.

Harrison, Seling (1960) *India: The Most Dangerous Decades*. Princeton: Princeton University Press.

Irudayaraj, Xavier (ed.) (1990) *Emerging Dalit Theology*. Madras: Jesuit Theological Secretariat.

Keer, Dhananjay (1964) *Mahatma Jotirao Phooley: Father of Indian Social Revolution*. Bombay: Popular Prakashan.

———. (1974) *Dr. Ambedkar: Life and Mission*. Bombay: Popular Prakashan.

Kejariwal, O.P. (1988) *The Asiatic Society of Bengal and the Discovery of India's Past*. New Delhi: Oxford University Press.

Kohn, H. (1956) 'Nationalism', *International Encyclopedia of Social Sciences, Vol. II*. The Macmillan Co. and The Free Press.

Kothari, Rajni (1988) 'Integration and Exclusion in Indian Politics', *Economic and Political Weekly*, 22 October: 2223–29.

———. (1997) 'Rise of the Dalits and the Renewed Debate on Caste', in Partha Chatterjee (ed.), *State and Politics in India*. New Delhi: Oxford University Press.

Kshirsagar, R.K. (1994) *Dalit Movement in India and Its Leaders*. New Delhi: M.D. Publications.

Majumdar, R.C. (1965) *The History and Culture of the Indian People: British Paramountcy and Indian Renaissance II*. Bombay: Bharatiya Vidya Bhavan.

Marshall, P.J. (1970) *The British Discovery of Hinduism in the Eighteenth Century*. Cambridge: Cambridge University Press.

Massey, James (1990) 'Christian Dalits in India: An Analysis', *Religion and Society*, 37(3), September: 40–53.

Michael, S.M. (1986) 'Politicization of Ganapathi Festival', *Social Compass*, 33(2–3): 185–97.

Naicker, Ramaswamy, E.V. (1959) *The Ramayana: A True Reading*. Madras: Rationalist Publications.

O'Hanlon, Rosalind (1985) *Caste, Conflict and Ideology. Mahatma Jotirao Phule and Low Caste Protest in Nineteenth-Century Western India.* Cambridge: Cambridge University Press.

Omvedt, Gail (1976) *Cultural Revolt in a Colonial Society: The Non-Brahmin Movement in Western India, 1873 to 1930.* Poona: Scientific Socialist Education Trust.

———. (1994) *Dalit and Democratic Revolution.* New Delhi: Sage Publications.

———. (1996) *Dalit Visions. The Anti-caste Movement and the Construction of an Indian Identity.* New Delhi: Orient Longman, Tracts for the Times/8.

Oommen, T.K. (1997) *Citizenship, Nationality and Ethnicity: Reconciling Competing Identities.* Cambridge: Polity Press.

Pannikar, K.N. (1995) *Culture, Ideology and Hegemony: Intellectuals and Social Consciousness in Colonial India.* New Delhi: Tulika.

Parvate, T.V. (1959) *Gopal Krishna Gokhale.* Ahmedabad: Navjivan Publishing House.

Prabhakar, M.E. (1990) 'Developing a Common Ideology for Dalits of Christian and Other Faiths', *Religion and Society*, 37(3), September: 24–39.

Rajasekhariah, A.M. (1971) *B.R. Ambedkar: The Politics of Emancipation.* Bombay: Sindhu Publications.

Shah, Ghanshyam (1995) 'Dalit Movements and Search for Identity', in Manorama Savur and Indra Munshi (eds), *Contradictions in Indian Society*, pp. 23–45. Jaipur: Rawat Publications..

Shashi, S.S. (ed.) (1992) *Ambedkar and Social Justice.* New Delhi: Government of India.

Singh, Yogendra (1997) 'Social Processes and Dimensions of Indian Nationalism', in Ghanshyam Shah (ed.), *Social Transformation in India.* Jaipur: Rawat Publications.

Shourie, Arun (1997) *Worshipping False Gods: Ambedkar and the Facts which have been Erased.* New Delhi: ASA Publications.

Smith, William Roy (1938) *Nationalism and Reform in India.* London: Yale University Press.

Smith, Donald Eugene (1963) *India as a Secular State.* London: Princeton University Press.

Thorat, S.K. (1996) 'Dalits and the New Economic Policy', *Dalit International Newsletter*, 1(2).

Thorat, Vimal (1997) 'Dalit Women', *Dalit International Newsletter*, 2(1).

Vanaik, Achin (1997) *Communalism Contested: Religion, Modernity and Secularisation.* New Delhi: Vistaar.

Weber, Max (1958) *The Religion of India* (edited and translated by Hans H. Gerth and Don Martindale). New York: Free Press.

Zelliot, Eleanor (1992) *From Untouchable to Dalit: Essays on the Ambedkar Movement.* New Delhi: Manohar.

———. (1996) 'The Dalit Movement', *Dalit International Newsletter*, 1(1).

5

Ambedkar, Buddhism and the Concept of Religion

TIMOTHY FITZGERALD

INTRODUCTION

The leader of the Untouchable movement from the 1920s until his death in 1956 was not Gandhi but Ambedkar, himself an Untouchable and one of the great men of modern world history, though one would rarely find his name mentioned in religious studies books. It is notable that in books published within the 'religion' genre one rarely, if ever, finds any analysis of the rituals of untouchability or bonded labour. Instead, one finds idealised accounts of gods and goddesses, *varnasramadharma*, the various theological schools, the great high-caste Hindu reformers, and of course the satyagraha and vegetarianism of Gandhi. I have never seen a religious studies book that gave a proper account of why Untouchables generally despise the paternalistic Gandhian word 'Harijan', or an account of Ambedkar's detailed critique of Gandhi's high-caste reformism. Generally speaking, religious books give the high-caste view of the ecumenical construct of Hinduism, and it is a view which facilitates a rapprochement between the elites of the colonisers and the colonised.

In this chapter I have two aims. The first is to discuss the different concepts of religion found in Ambedkar's writings. The second is to suggest why, for the researcher, 'religion' has become a fairly useless concept. These aims are connected. Ambedkar was a highly educated and intellectually brilliant man, who mastered the law to such an extent that he was able to chair the constitutional committee of the new republic. He was also able to write penetrating analyses of Indian society that reflected a sophisticated anthropological understanding. But the centre of his life was his devotion to the liberation of the

Backward Classes, and he struggled to find a satisfactory ideological expression for that liberation. Though he talked a great deal about 'religion', I believe he really went beyond that concept (see Ambedkar, 1957: 225). His evolving ideas about religion suggested to me why we could abandon the word without any real loss.

I will try to place different concepts of religion found in Ambedkar's writings in a theoretical context, which illustrates wider social and cultural issues affecting the SCs. I have in mind particularly the modern coexistence in India of an egalitarian constitution (for which Ambedkar was largely responsible) and caste hierarchy. Ambedkar himself offers a striking example of the subjective aspect of this institutional dichotomy by his identity as a middle-class barrister and political activist on the one hand, and a member of an Untouchable caste, on the other. We seem to have a direct conflict of fundamental principles or values, and passages in the *Annihilation of Caste* (Ambedkar, 1936: 123–28) suggest that for Ambedkar this conflict could be expressed as being between different 'religions'. He referred to these respectively as 'the Religion of Rules' (by which he meant essentially caste hierarchy) and 'the Religion of Principles' (by which he meant essentially democratic egalitarianism, though not the extreme individualism of the West). Ambedkar has the insight here that principles or values which are normally referred to as 'secular' are as sacred as those conventionally referred to as 'religious', for example, those found in Hindu texts like the *Manusmriti*. Furthermore, the so-called 'secular' values—unlike those found in the *Manusmriti*—are universal, and thus make possible what he calls a 'True Religion' (1936: 126). But I will show that in other texts such as *The Buddha and the Future of His Religion* (Ambedkar, 1950) his concept of 'religion' changes again, until eventually in *The Buddha and His Dhamma* he concludes that it is 'an indefinite word with no fixed meaning' (Ambedkar, 1957: 225).

Though Ambedkar certainly believed in the liberation of the individual, he saw clearly that in the modern world the priority must be *institutional* liberation. The struggle for liberation, traditionally symbolised by the solitary renouncer in the forest, or by Gautama Buddha sitting alone beneath the bodhi tree, had to be transformed into a struggle against *institutionalised* bondage. I use the word 'bondage' here deliberately, because even today there is bonded labour in parts of Maharashtra such as Marathwada (Fitzgerald, 1994; Pandit, 1990). Thus, for Ambedkar, 'fetters' were not only those karmic hindrances that conditioned the individual's conscious- ness from one lifetime to another. They were also institutionalised realities that required a political solution.[1]

Ambedkar studied anthropology at Columbia University in New York, where he received a Ph.D in 1916. He also qualified as a barrister at the Inns of Court in London. But though a great scholar, his main goal in life was to help create a peaceful revolution in India that would liberate the Untouchables and the Backward Classes generally from caste oppression. Much of his writing is, therefore, polemical. It is not surprising, therefore, if his uses of the word 'religion' should be as varied and imprecise as that of many other scholars. But, in fact, as with so much in his writing, Ambedkar had insights into the nature of 'religion' which help us to disentangle some of the different meanings which make it an inherently confused concept. In his desire to formulate a new consciousness for people who are now called Dalits and Buddhists, he raised many important issues, which we can try to develop.

THE 'RELIGION OF RULES' AND THE 'RELIGION OF PRINCIPLES'

In some of his most famous writings, such as *Annihilation of Caste* (1936), *The Buddha and the Future of His Religion* (1950) and *The Buddha and His Dhamma* (1957), Ambedkar tried to develop a coherent account of the nature of religion and its relation to politics and power. In *Annihilation of Caste*, he argues that Hinduism is a religion of rules, a compendium of ritual regulations which are based on the caste ideology of hierarchy and untouchability. For him, caste is the central fact of Hinduism and untouchability is a defining characteristic of caste. He argues that you cannot reform caste because untouchability is an inherent feature. This was one fundamental reason why he strongly opposed Gandhi's reformism. *Annihilation of Caste* was originally written as a speech that he had been invited to deliver by the Jat Pat Todak Mandal of Lahore, a high-caste reform group. When they read it they found it too dangerous so they cancelled the speech. Consequently, Ambedkar published it as a pamphlet instead.

The second edition includes a preface, a prologue including the correspondence between him and the Jat Pat Todak Mandal and two appendices, which include Gandhi's review and Ambedkar's reply to Gandhi.

The published correspondence makes it clear that the reason the Jat Pat Todak Mandal cancelled the speech was that Ambedkar refused to cut what he considered to be the essential point of his argument, but which the Jat Pat Todak Mandal variously found to be either irrelevant or too dangerous. The point of contention was Ambedkar's belief that 'the real method of breaking up the Caste System was not to bring about inter-caste dinners and inter-caste marriages but to destroy the religious notions on which caste is founded' (1936: 49).

The 'religious' notions he was referring to was of course the traditional Hindu ideology of rank based on purity and untouchability, which manifested itself in caste, in ritualism and in the suppression of autonomous individuality. He was not thinking primarily of the tradition of renunciation, of *sannyas*. On the contrary, in a footnote he suggested that the Upanishads contain ideas about equality and freedom.[2] At this stage, Ambedkar's focus was the pervasive hierarchical ritualism which was given its most potent codification in the 'religious' principles in the *Manusmriti*, a text of fundamental importance in orthodox thinking, which he burnt in public protest at the Mahad Satyagraha of 25 December 1927 (see Ahir, 1990: 15).

A SUMMARY OF AMBEDKAR'S ARGUMENT

Political and constitutional reform cannot succeed unless it is preceded by social reform aimed at the eradication of untouchability. But social reform can only mean abolition of caste, because untouchability is a *defining feature* of caste. In reality, caste cannot be *reformed* (contrary to Gandhi's hope) only annihilated. And the annihilation of caste implies the abolition of Hindu ideology particularly as it is formulated in the Shastras and Smritis. Caste is fundamentally 'a state of mind' (he meant this both collectively and individually), which is systematised in these scriptures; and while endogamy is what he calls the 'mechanism' of caste, it is religious dogma that prohibits intermarriage and therefore ultimately it is the religious values that must be destroyed: '... it must be recognised that the Hindus observe caste not because they are inhuman or wrong-headed. They observe caste because they are deeply religious ... the enemy you must grapple with is not the people who observe caste, but the Shastras that teach them this religion of caste' (Ambedkar, 1936: 111).

Ambedkar's insistence that political reform could not succeed unless preceded by social reform (and therefore by a revolution in the sphere of values) may, in retrospect, appear to contradict his own achievement as India's first law minister in piloting through the constitution which made untouchability illegal. More likely though, it will prove his point, since making untouchability unconstitutional has not in fact abolished it. This demonstrated something that Ambedkar was painfully aware of: that modern law (which implies equality and which was introduced by the British) is subordinated in fact to ritual hierarchy.[3] In contrast, at around this time, Gandhi did not want to abolish caste as such, but to reform it according to an ideal model. True, his views changed over the years (Zelliot, 1972: 6ff). But Ambedkar severely criticised Gandhi for his view that caste was essentially a division of labour and that inequality and untouch-ability were extraneous distortions.

Ambedkar wished to replace the religion of rules with true religion, the religion of principles, which is the basis for civic government. These principles, liberty, equality and fraternity (1936: 9, 128) are true religion. He says, 'True Religion is the foundation of society.' For Ambedkar, these principles were religious principles. He was perfectly well aware that these were the principles of the American and French revolutions. However, he wanted to bring this alternative (non-Indian) tradition into line with traditional Indian ways of thinking, which in effect meant identifying a strand of his own indigenous culture, which could legitimately be presented as a critique of Hindu ritual orthodoxy. This was the connection with the *sannyasi* tradition mentioned before; near the end of the *Annihilation of Caste* he suggested in a footnote that this ideology of liberty, equality and fraternity could be found in the Upanishads, though he does not pursue this tantalising statement. Later, he found it in Buddhism. In both cases, it is the religion of the renouncer where he identifies the universal values which can replace the Hindu ritual system. However, though there is a sense in which renunciation remained important in Ambedkar's thinking about religion, his modernising tendency transformed the renouncer into a socially engaged and politically committed individual. I return to this point later.

Putting the issue of renunciation on one side for the moment, so far we have identified two concepts of religion, one, a religion essentially characterised by caste hierarchy and the other a religion essentially characterised by individual freedom and equality. The religion of caste hierarchy described by Ambedkar reveals an opposition between Brahmin purity and dominance, on the one hand, and Untouchable impurity and subservience on the other. These ritual values permeate traditional Hindu society and are most clearly codified in texts such as the *Manusmriti*. The other concept of religion is similar to, and perhaps initially derived from, Western democratic principles and institutions, based on the belief in the formal equality of all individuals, equal rights under the law, the abolition of hereditary status, personal freedom to choose one's own occupation and to develop one's own individual talents. These were the principles that he was to build into the constitution. These sacred principles are what Westerners generally like to think of as the secular, the non-religious, but which Ambedkar suggests are the basis for a concept of 'True Religion' (1936: 126). This is one reason why Ambedkar's view of religion is interesting. For him, the bases of religion are *values*, the values that hold a society together. Concepts of the supernatural were not the essentially important point for Ambedkar. Indeed, he came to see supernaturalism as irrational and irrelevant to true religion.

Thus, the concept of religion implied in this kind of analysis is not essentially about supernatural beings, transcendental worlds or spiritual salvation in a life after death. It is about the fundamental values that make possible different kinds of social institutions, in one case the institution of caste, which is based on the sacred Brahmanical principles codified in the Smritis, and in the other case the institutions of democracy, which are based on the sacred principles of liberty, equality and fraternity.

However, one significant way in which these sets of values differ from each other is that for Ambedkar the democratic values are universal in the sense that they apply equally to everyone in principle, for all humans are individuals and all humans have equal rights and obligations and all humans deserve the opportunity to discover their own true talents. In contrast, the Hindu values are particularistic. There is one set of rules for Brahmins, one for Marathas, one for Mahars and one for Mangs. In a democratic world, anybody can, in principle, become president, get a good education, marry the partner of their choice regardless of caste (and presumably of nationality), live in their preferred neighbourhood, be respected for what they are or do rather than for their inherited status. But in the case of the caste system in India, rules apply to particular people in particular situations. Different categories of people must marry only into a specific sub-caste, must have different occupations, must live in different parts of the village, must wear different clothes and so on.

In a democratic kind of society, freedom of the individual implies a new kind of freedom, the freedom to choose one's religion. But here we have a different concept of religion emerging. Here religion is conceived as a body of doctrines about salvation, which the individual can choose to adhere to because he finds it the best, the most rational, the most suitable for his or her personal needs. The religious principles of equality, liberty and fraternity make possible (paradoxically) a 'secular' society in which religion becomes a matter of personal commitment and choice. This different concept of religion is implied in Ambedkar's *The Buddha and the Future of His Religion*, where he provides a comparative analysis of the rationality and ethical principles of Buddhism, Christianity, Islam and Hinduism and concludes in favour of Buddhism. I do not want to claim that the distinction between these different concepts of religion is clearly and consciously demarcated, but I believe it is there. Indeed, I would argue that it is inevitably there, because the emergence of what in the West and elsewhere is referred to as secular society, but which Ambedkar (in my view very perceptively) calls a religion, has historically also produced a concept of religion which is a private affair, a matter of personal choice and commitment, something one gets converted to. In a caste society, you do not get converted to Brahmanical hierarchy. It is not something which anybody chooses.

According to Ambedkar's understanding, Buddha dhamma is essentially *morality*. By morality he means compassion, caring for one's fellow human being and for the natural world, feeling a sense of responsibility and commitment, being actively committed to the well-being of the world. Morality, unlike ritual obligation, springs from the heart of the individual and is based on a sense of brotherhood and sisterhood. Thus, Buddhism, on this line of reasoning becomes the basis of the new egalitarian society, the structural equivalent of hierarchy as the basis of Hindu society. For this is not a traditional sectarian dispute about which is the true path to liberation—a disputation which takes for granted a whole structure of shared assumptions. This is a questioning of the basis of the structure itself.

On the other hand, this very notion that one can change one's religion, that one can move from one religion to another, that one can look around for a more suitable religion than the one which one has at present, is itself a modern idea. On this concept, Buddhism is one of a number of religions that, in *Buddha and the Future of His Religion*, Ambedkar compares with Christianity, Islam and Hinduism. Buddhism is the best of these because it is the most rational, the most scientific in its principles, the most moral. It is, therefore, the religion that Ambedkar advocates and that he seeks to persuade others to adopt.

But this concept of religion as being a matter of private choice itself involves another political principle, the freedom of religion, which is guaranteed by the Indian Constitution. Buddhism is thus intended both as the fundamental basis of the new social order and as the most rational choice for the individual. So his Buddhism is a highly rational blend of individualism with socio-political commitment, a Buddhist modernism with a crucial element of liberation theology, but intended to be the basis of the new social order.

Ambedkar's own analysis of Hindu ideology sometimes sounds more like a kind of Marxist revolutionary sociology when he says 'The problem of Untouchability is a matter of class struggle' (B.R. Ambedkar, quoted in Ahir, 1990: 21). But this surely is as much an appeal for class-consciousness as an analysis, a revolutionary desire to transform the traditional inertia of untouchability into a politically-conscious movement cutting across caste lines. In fact, Ambedkar was not a Marxist in one sense because he did not believe in violent revolution. But he seems to have believed that the emergence of politically-conscious classes might act as an agent for fundamental change in Indian society. He was also a socialist in the sense that he believed that the redistribution of wealth and opportunity in a society

needed some direct government intervention, such as the nationalisation
of key industries. He also wanted separate electorates as a way around
the problem of electoral intimidation and a guaranteed number of
seats for Backward Classes; and he wanted an employment and
educational policy that actively countered the discriminatory tendencies of traditional caste loyalties. But his long-term aim was the
creation of a society of morally free and responsible individuals.

From as early as 1935, Ambedkar indicated the fundamental
importance of religion by publicly declaring untouchability to be an
inseparable part of Hinduism and his own intention to convert to
Buddhism (Ahir, 1990: 20ff). There is no doubt that Ambedkar was
an intensely religious man, in the sense of a deep commitment to
values and principles such as compassion, justice and equality. But
he needed a religion that made a difference in this world, a religion
that could change society and empower the Backward Classes.
Therefore, his interpretation of Buddhism has some modernist
features. As a soteriology (doctrine of salvation), Buddhism has
always been concerned with the fate of the individual, but in the sense
of release (nirvana) from this world (samsara) through the self-
discipline of the four noble truths and the eightfold path. Ambedkar
was critical of the Theravada Sangha of South and South East Asia
for its tendency towards detachment from the world. For Ambedkar,
soteriology has a strong social and political component. *Bhikshu*s
should be socially and politically committed to justice. He was more
attracted by the Mahayana concept of the Bodhisattva, who delays
his own liberation out of compassion for less fortunate or less
advanced beings. Furthermore, the Bodhisattva ideal lends itself
more easily to modern concepts of democracy, human rights and
social justice, for it can easily be seen as a compassionate activity in
favour of the oppressed and the fight against social and political
injustice. Salvation is conceived in terms of the struggle for emancipation and dignity of the oppressed classes of Hindu society. And
the individual is in *some* respects more like the autonomous individual
of Protestant Christianity, committed to rational action in this world,
than the renouncer who turns his back on the world.

In this sense, I find it illuminating that in all Buddhist shrines in
Maharashtra, one finds two pictures. One is of the Buddha sitting
cross-legged in the rags of the renouncer meditating beneath the

bodhi tree and achieving enlightenment. In the other one sees Ambedkar, dressed in a modern blue business suit, wearing heavy-rimmed glasses and holding a large book, which represents literacy, education and also perhaps the egalitarian Constitution of India, which he wrote and which is reputed to be one of the most advanced constitutions in the world. These are the ancient and modern conceptions of liberation side-by-side (see Tartakov, 1990).

In his posthumously published *The Buddha and His Dhamma* (1957), Ambedkar wanted to revive what he took to be the main principles of original Buddhism. In this book he says that 'dharma' and 'religion' are entirely different (1957: 225), which is another shift of meaning. His interpretation of Buddhism here is strongly flavoured with 'scientific' materialism. It has to be remembered that this book was not completed before he died, he had written some notes while he was ill and the editors had the task of putting it together afterwards. The end result is a book which tends to emphasise an interpretation of Buddhist liberation as a social and political liberation, rather than as traditional enlightenment. For example, he equates nirvana (the Buddhist concept of the transcendent) to the eightfold path (which in traditional Buddhism is the way, the practice, by which to obtain nirvana). He said 'Nibbana is naught but that 8-Fold Path' (1957: 288); and the eightfold path's most important aspect, 'right outlook', is in turn defined as the recognition of cause and effect (1957: 291). Logically, therefore, this is almost like saying that nirvana is equivalent to scientific rationality. In this way, Ambedkar attempts to present traditional Indian Buddhism as fully consistent with materialism, with scientific rationality, with parliamentary democracy, with the principles of equality, fraternity, liberty. To do this he asserts that Buddhism has no place for belief in the supernatural; that the doctrine of karma is a theory of causation only; that *prajna* (wisdom) means the ability to think rationally and without superstition; that *karuna* (compassion) means the ability to love one's fellow men and to work for social justice; that the bhikshu (monk) is not (or should not be) merely be an ascetic intent on his own enlightenment but a social worker dedicated to the betterment of his human beings. In his account, enlightenment seems much closer to the enlightenment of the French philosophies of the eighteenth century than to the nirvana of the Buddha. In short, he has almost nothing to say about the central Buddhist soteriology concerning nirvana, meditation, and the ending of karma and rebirth. This does not mean that he was not concerned about the traditional concept of *pratitya samutpada* (conditioned origination), only that his goal was conceived in terms of *institutional* liberation (liberation from the institution of untouchability and ritual pollution) as a necessary precondition to any personal freedom.

RITUAL, POLITICS AND SOTERIOLOGY

I have suggested that Ambedkar uses religion in different ways to mean (*i*) the system of caste hierarchy; (*ii*) traditional asceticism, that is, release from this world through meditation and self-discipline, as found in the Upanishads and traditional forms of Buddhism; (*iii*) democratic society (usually referred to as secular society in the West) based on the sacred values of liberty, equality and fraternity; (*iv*) the religions such as Christianity, Islam, Hinduism and Buddhism, which in a free society the individual should choose on a personal basis. One point to note is that so much is included in these different uses that one might as well abandon the word altogether and find different terms which make more precise distinctions.

This idea, in fact, coincides with my own research on Buddhism in Maharashtra. I have not found the concept of religion very useful as an analytical concept for understanding the situation of the Ambedkar Buddhists. If I were a 'comparative religionist', meaning someone who believes that there are many religions in the world, and all one has to do is go out and find them, probably the first thing I would notice if I visited the communities at all would be their temples and their *puja* performed to pictures of Gautama Buddha and Ambedkar side-by-side in the shrines. And there is no doubt that many Buddhists conceive Buddha and Ambedkar (who is considered a Bodhisattva) as supernatural beings who can bring benefits. In this sense they fulfil the same function as some Hindu deities.

The concept of Ambedkar as a Bodhisattva or enlightened being who brings liberation to all Backward Classes is widespread among Buddhists. However, Ambedkar himself was entirely against supernaturalism, seeing it as a form of dependency induced by the traditional oppression of Hindu caste culture. And the dominant understanding of present-day Buddhists, especially more educated Buddhists, is explicitly against the idea that Ambedkar is a supernatural being. Some Buddhists believe Ambedkar was enlightened or partially enlightened in a way similar to traditional Theravada interpretations of Gautama Buddha's enlightenment, which stresses his humanity and refrains from turning him into a god. Indeed, in the traditional stories the god Brahma is depicted as asking Buddha to show him the way to liberation. When such Buddhists perform puja, they are recalling Gautama Buddha's and Ambedkar's outstanding life and example. Many educated Buddhists interpret Ambedkar's enlightenment not in a transcendental way, but as the product of education and the full realisation of his potential as a human being.

The concept of religion either as a traditional soteriology or as interaction with superhuman beings is patently inadequate for dealing with the realities of the situation. This is true even though transcendentalist or supernaturalist aspects of the movement exist. And when one realises that the vast majority of Buddhists are members of the same Untouchable caste, then it becomes obvious that caste hierarchy must be a fundamental part of the analysis. This reflects Ambedkar's focus on liberation as an *institutional* problem in the first place.

I have developed a typology of ritual, politics and soteriology to make sense of my fieldwork. Here I can do no more than summarise my published research in order to clarify why the concept of 'religion' is in my view analytically redundant.

RITUAL

It seems to me that Ambedkar's analysis of Indian (Hindu) society was that it is fundamentally a ritualistic (rather than moral) system and that caste, untouchability and supernaturalism were its main institutional expressions. Though he did advocate some simple Buddhist rituals such as puja and simple Buddhist weddings and funeral rites, he believed that these should be cheap (to avoid dowry problems), transparent and non-mystifying. The *ritual* referred to in this category is the whole spectrum of ritualistic practices that Ambedkar condemned, ranging from worship of the supernatural, exorcism, possession states, caste ritualism such as endogamy and dowry and rituals of purity and pollution. This would include the ritual location of the Untouchable quarter in the villages (previously called Maharwada, now Buddhawada) and the ritually defined duties of scavenging and night-soil removal. As I have shown earlier, Ambedkar himself analysed 'Hinduism' as a ritual system encoded in texts such as the *Manusmriti*, which gave ideological justification for untouchability. Ideologically, when we identify the form of life indicated by ritual, we are not really talking about Buddhism here (certainly not Ambedkar's understanding of Buddhism), but about a de facto lifestyle that many people who are proud to identify themselves as Buddhists do (by default) practise. For example, sub-caste endogamy is widespread among all categories of Buddhists, at least in certain areas such as Nagpur and Marathwada,[4] including highly-educated academics with a sophisticated understanding of Ambedkar's teaching. It is therefore part and parcel of contemporary Buddhist identity, even though Buddhists themselves deplore it. Another example is that Buddhists who have proved their commitment and courage by exposing themselves to the dangers of high-caste anger by refusing to perform some ritual services such as scavenging may still be themselves practising untouchability against other Untouchable castes like Mangs and Holars, or be involved in the worship of the goddess Mariai, or may be worshipping Buddha and Ambedkar as though they were Hindu gods. The importance of this element of *ritual* is that, though logically it is incompatible with Ambedkar's teaching, it is to some variable degree part of the actual situation and identity of Buddhists and consequently has to be investigated as such.

POLITICS

It seems to me that 'secular' rationalism and social democracy are central to Ambedkar's understanding of Buddhism and that again this kind of interpretation is to some variable extent identifiable in the thinking of most Buddhist groups in Maharashtra, whether they be Dalits, academics, village teachers, community spokesmen, local urban activists who sometimes lead the puja in the local temple, or even monks and dharmacharis.[5] I believe that 'politics' in the sense of social activism directed towards the exercise of political power for the purpose of peaceful social revolution may be the best single word to encapsulate this element of Ambedkar's Buddhism. This notion of politics is not arbitrary, for it is closely linked with the fundamental principles of a democratic constitution (largely written by Ambedkar himself as India's first law minister, an astounding achievement for a man who carried the stigma of untouchability throughout his life), a modern judicial system based on the value of equality before the law and the legitimate pursuit of power through constitutional means.[6]

SOTERIOLOGY

Soteriology is traditionally a doctrine of spiritual salvation or liberation from the world of suffering and evil. Traditional Theravada Buddhism is a soteriology par excellence, for it provides the analysis of suffering, the means for its eradication and the transcendental goal. It is a doctrine particularly concerned with the individual, for it is the individual consciousness that is put together through the karmic factors of suffering and it is the individual who practises moral restraint, social concern and meditation along the path to enlightenment. However, in Ambedkar's writings, social concern is given a distinctively political emphasis. The institution of caste hierarchy and its ritualistic mechanism are particularly identified as major causes of suffering. The concept of individual liberation is very closely linked with socio-political liberation and the factors of suffering are identified more broadly with institutionalised exploitation, particularly caste and untouchability. Therefore, in Ambedkar's writings, soteriology and politics are closely identified, politics being understood as the pursuit of power within the jurisdiction of a democratic constitution and soteriology as liberation from inequality and exploitation.

Nevertheless, many Buddhists hold strongly that soteriology is not *only* political and social activism in Ambedkar's thinking, but has an important spiritual or transcendental element as well, which is pursued through reading Buddhist texts, practising meditation and going on retreats. Socio-political activism and a more 'spiritual' understanding of liberation are often (though not always)[7] seen as complementary and even dialectically implicated. One highly-organised expression of this idea of soteriology is the Trilokya Bauddha

Mahasangha (TBMSG), which has developed a sophisticated interpretation of Buddhist soteriological doctrine based on both Ambedkar's
teaching and the scholarly writing of the venerable Sangharakshita.
This teaching holds social revolutionary and transcendental goals as
complementary.

To what degree any particular Buddhist group in Maharashtra does
or does not exemplify these elements is an empirical issue. My point
is that, when we talk about Buddhism in Maharashtra, we are talking
about different combinations of, and oppositions between, these
qualities. Buddhists want liberation from their ritual status as Untouchables, but the dilemma is that they are defined by that status
in the predominant caste ideology. I suppose ritual, politics and
soteriology could all be defined as 'religion', but then I cannot see
that the word picks out anything distinctive.

My own ethnography of Buddhism is based on three broadly
distinctive categories within the Buddhist community: (*i*) Buddhists
living in villages, in this case in Marathwada, a remote and backward
area of Maharashtra; (*ii*) middle-class Buddhists, in this case academics living in Nagpur; and (*iii*) Buddhists who have actually renounced
ordinary lay life and become monks, or something equivalent,[8] in a
community that is explicitly concerned with traditional Buddhist
practices such as meditation, in this case the TBMSG in Pune, which
is arguably the most effective of the agencies for propagating
soteriological Buddhism of a transcendentalist kind. However, this
agency is deeply committed to social work and though it is non-
political, it certainly sees individual liberation as being strongly
connected with peaceful social revolution. It would not do justice to
the reality of the situation to present one of these emphases out of
context.

This is not an exhaustive classification of all the varied occupations and lifestyles of Buddhists. Many Buddhists are poor urban
factory workers. There is a strong element of political activism both
in the formal political parties such as the Republican Party (founded
by Ambedkar, but now factionalised) and also in the Dalit movement,
which is a generally Backward Classes militant movement dominated
by Buddhists. There are Buddhist novelists and poets writing in
Marathi (see Zelliot, 1992). Nevertheless, the groups that I have
interviewed do, in fact, tend to reveal the predominance in one way
or another of these different factors.

CONCLUSION: HIERARCHY AND EGALITARIANISM
AS VALUES

What is notable about all these different categories of Buddhists is the high degree of consciousness that exists of Ambedkar's writings, his political and soteriological goals, in short, of the meaning of Ambedkar's Buddhism. In my view, the fundamental value of Ambedkar's Buddhism is egalitarianism understood as the ethical autonomy of the individual but with the political realism to realise that dominant institutions such as caste can only be changed through the agency of alternative institutions, such as courts of law and anti-discrimination policies of governments. Ambedkar is sometimes described as a socialist and he certainly wanted to use the power of the state to bring about social reform and redistribute wealth, for example, through nationalisation. But his concept of liberation through social revolution is based, to a significant extent, on an appeal ultimately to the ethical autonomy of individuals and their ability to transform themselves and their society through collective action.

This understanding is widely understood among present-day Buddhists. This is true despite the fact that the Buddhist movement is almost completely confined to one Untouchable caste of about four million people.[9] Though Buddhists apparently continue to practise untouchability against other Untouchable castes,[10] there is also simultaneously, widespread conscious and bitter rejection of these notions. Buddhists are thus caught in a contradiction, much as a committed British communist is caught in a contradiction when he puts his house on the market and tries to get the best price. If one is living within a system, one is to some degree forced to conform to it unless alternative institutions grow strong enough to legitimate an alternative lifestyle. Not only is there no consensus[11] with the dominant ideology, but there is conflict within the minds of Buddhists when, for example, they simultaneously decry caste endogamy but, in fact, practise it.

NOTES

1. This raises an interesting philosophical problem of explanation in Buddhism. For it would be difficult to argue that institutionalised

inequalities can be adequately explained simply as the sum of individual karmas. For example, can one really explain the invasion of Tibet by the Chinese and the consequent creation of a Tibetan diaspora in terms of individual karmas?

2. He had not found Buddhism yet, though he was soon to develop an interest in it.
3. My own research on Buddhism in Pune, Nagpur and Marathwada suggests that this is still largely the case, though there is no space to present this ethnography here.
4. I am told by Eleanor Zelliot and Dharmachari Lokamitra that this is not the case in Pune.
5. Dharmacharis (and dharmacharinis) are fully committed members of the Buddhist organisation Trilokya Bauddha Mahasangha (TBMSG), which I discuss later in this chapter.
6. Ambedkar was himself a barrister (trained at the Inns of Court in London) and spent a great deal of his enormous energy defending the rights of Untouchables against the oppressive goals of high-caste Hindus during the British Raj.
7. There are committed Buddhists, especially some Dalits, who see the transcendental element as a form of mystification and alien to Ambedkar's revolutionary understanding of liberation (moksa). There is thus a split within the movement on this issue. See, for example, Guru (1991).
8. These are men and women called dharmacharis and dharmacharinis. They may marry, or they may make a vow of sexual abstention if they choose.
9. This is not entirely true, because some Buddhists come from other castes, though overall their numbers are small. There is also another Untouchable caste, the Chamars in Uttar Pradesh, who are Buddhists.
10. I found evidence of this in Parbhani district in Marathwada.
11. I dispute, for example, the claim by Michael Moffatt that Untouchables are in deep conformity with the caste system, even though it is true that high-caste notions of purity and pollution get replicated to some extent in the Untouchable subsector (Moffatt, 1979).

REFERENCES AND SELECT BIBLIOGRAPHY

Ahir, D.C. (1989) *The Pioneers of Buddhist Revival In India.* New Delhi: Sri Satguru Publications.
———. (1990) *Buddhism in Modern India.* New Delhi: Sri Satguru Publications.
———. (1991) *The Legacy of Dr. Ambedkar.* New Delhi: BR Publishing Corporation.
Ambedkar, B.R. (1916 [1936]). 'Castes in India: Their Mechanism, Genesis and Development', in B.R Ambedkar (ed.), *Annihilation of Caste*, pp. 32–46. Jallandhar: Bheema Patrika Publications.
———. (1936) *Annihilation of Caste.* Jallandhar: Bheema Patrika Publications.

Ambedkar, B.R. (1950) *Buddha and the Future of His Religion*. Jallandhar: Bheema Patrika Publication.

———. (1957) *The Buddha and His Dhamma*. Bombay: People's Education Society.

———. (1994) 'Sangha and Social Change. Lokamitra, Dhammachari', in A.K. Narain and D.C. Ahir (eds), *Dr Ambedkar, Buddhism and Social Change*, pp. 49–65. New Delhi: B.R Publishing Corporation.

Fitzgerald, T. (1994) 'Buddhism in Maharashtra: A Tripartite Analysis', in A.K. Narain and D.C. Ahir (eds), *Dr. Ambedkar, Buddhism and Social Change*, pp. 83–97. New Delhi: B.R. Publishing Corporation.

———. (1996) 'From Structure to Substance: Ambedkar, Dumont and Orientalism', *Contributions to Indian Sociology*, 30(2): 273–88.

Guru, Gopal (1991) 'The Hinduisation of Ambedkar', *Economic and Political Weekly*, 26(7): 339–41.

Moffatt, M. (1979) *An Untouchable Community in South India: Structure and Consensus*. Princeton: Princeton University Press.

Narain, A.K. and D.C. Ahir (eds) (1994) *Dr. Ambedkar, Buddhism and Social Change*. New Delhi: B.R. Publishing Corporation.

Pandit,Vivek (1990) *Report of the Campaign for Human Rights*. Bombay: Vidhayak Sansad.

Tartakov, G.M. (1990) 'Art and Identity: The Rise of a New Buddhist Imagery', *Art Journal*, Winter: 409–16.

Zelliot, E. (1972) 'Gandhi and Ambedkar: A Study in Leadership', in J.M. Mahar (ed.), *The Untouchables in Contemporary India*, pp. 69–96. Arizona: University of Arizona Press.

———. (1992) *From Untouchable to Dalit: Essays on Ambedkar Movement*. New Delhi: Manohar.

6

The Dalit Movement in Mainstream Sociology[1]

GOPAL GURU

The study of the Dalit movement has attracted some leading sociologists over the past two decades in India and abroad. The centenary year of B.R. Ambedkar has seen a plethora of publications, thus adding to the growing literature on Ambedkar, Dalit politics and the Dalit movement. Among sociologists it is possible to discern a dominant ideological current that has bearings on the study of the Dalit movement. There is a 'liberal' trend among a group of scholars, who believe that it is the ancient Hindu reactionary traditions and the deep-rooted prejudice of the upper castes against Dalits, which has led to the protest of the latter. Thus, this trend views Dalit protest as a necessary outcome of an obscurantist Hindu tradition. This liberal view also has a strong tendency to assume that the Dalit movement is limited to achieving a partial advance in the socio-economic, civic and political fields within the existing social order, thus hardly any thought is expended on radical transformation in other respects. It is due to this ideological position that concepts like 'social mobility', 'reference group' and 'relative deprivation' figure so prominently in their writings on the Dalit movement thus becoming a major frame of reference in studying the Dalit movement.

Among those notable scholars who fall into this liberal category is M.S.A. Rao, who has used similar concepts for understanding the emergence of the protest movement among the Backward Classes and the Dalits in India (Rao, 1982: 4). Rao, taking a cue from Merton and Runciman, has argued that social mobility forms the major basis of the theory of relative deprivation (ibid.). (Social conflict as a basis of relative deprivation finds mention in Rao's study but without much detailed discussion.) Rao further argues that the relative deprivation is connected with the moment of emulation of a positive reference group (1982: 194). Other scholars too have tried to link the emergence of the Dalit movement with the issue of relative deprivation, reference groups and social mobility (Bhat, 1971; Issac, 1964; Joshi, 1987; Lynch, 1974; Patwardhan, 1973; Ram, 1988; Sachchidananda, 1978; Silverberg, 1968; Singer and Cohen, 1968). It is obvious from the works of these scholars that terms like social mobility and relative deprivation form the major frame of reference in discussions of the emergence of reform, protest and movement among the Dalits.

In studying Dalit mobility, it has been suggested by some scholars that the process of Sanskritisation could be a model. Certain Dalit groups or individuals try to adopt either ritually or culturally higher groups or individuals in order to achieve a similar social position or to adopt the values that promote the aspirations of an atomised individual in a civil society. This is referred to as the process of Sanskritisation. According to some scholars, if the Dalits fail in their achievement of this imitation of the Sanskritisation model of upper mobility, they then suffer from relative deprivation. This is because at the social level, their attempt to overcome relative deprivation is restricted by the upper-caste group whom they cite as a reference group existing mostly in a pre-civil social situation, which is still dominant in some parts of the country. At another level, the articulation of relative deprivation among the educated Dalits might take place when compared to the Westernised high caste. Thus, in the Indian case, as Oommen has pointed out, the deprivation is multi-faceted (1990: 255).

However, studies establishing a link between the emergence of the Dalit movement and relative deprivation, social mobility and reference group theory, though inadequate in understanding the Dalit movement, need to be supported on the following theoretical and strategic grounds. Both historically and dialectically, this concept of relative deprivation could capture social reality at a particular historical juncture when Indian society was trying to release itself from the feudal ethos, which was facing an ever-increasing threat from the advancing civil society in India. In this transitional process, the Dalits, who were aspiring towards mobility of various kinds but were unable to achieve it due to the restrictions imposed by the feudal as well as colonial vested interests, felt deprived, a fact which time and again prompted the Dalit movement, for example in the 1930s in Maharashtra, to challenge feudal values through a process of emulation and Sanskritisation (see Omvedt, 1994). This attempt to imitate the upper-caste values particularly in the case of the Mahars of Maharashtra, certainly contributed to the development of a negative consciousness which according to Gramsci may not constitute a mature and fully evolved class consciousness, but certainly is the first glimmer of such consciousness constituting the basic negative, polemical attitude (see Guha, 1983: 20). Gramsci further argues that the lower classes, historically on the defensive, can only achieve self-awareness through the identity and class limits of their enemy (ibid.).

Taking a cue from Gramsci, Ranajit Guha tries to understand this consciousness of the insurgent peasantry in colonial India. He says, it was only by attacking the material symbols of authority of the government and the landlords that the insurgents upset the established order. They did so by undermining its dominant semi-feudal culture as well. Insofar as religion constituted the most expressive sign of this culture in many of its essential aspects, the peasants' defiance of the rural elites often involved an attempt to appropriate the dominant religion or to destroy it. To those who were high up in society, the emulation of their culture by the lower strata seemed always fraught with danger. There have been occasions when, thanks to the stimuli given to casteism by British colonial policy, Sanskritising movements among the lower castes to upgrade themselves by adopting the rituals and religious idioms of their superiors were resisted by the latter and generated much social tension and even some actual violence (ibid.: 20).[2]

In the same vein, the Dalit social protest of the 1930s, under the leadership of Ambedkar focused its attention on entering the *savarna* temples and tried to improve the status of Dalits through the imitation of Hindu lifestyle by adopting gods and rituals of the upper castes, that is, through the process of Sanskritisation (see Srinivas, 1962). Although the usual tendency is to view Sanskritisation as a cultural process aimed at bringing about changes in the lifestyle of Dalits, it had important structural ramifications in that the protest orientation and counter-mobilisation were necessary attributes of

Sanskritisation movements since the Dalits often did so in a spirit. of recalcitrance and the upper castes invariably opposed such attempts (see Oommen, 1990: 255).

Second, studies understanding the Dalit movement in terms of relative deprivation and social mobility helped to reveal the role of caste and inherited status that have for long influenced the monopolising of the available jobs by the upper castes, which viewed caste mobility as dangerous and disruptive to the social fabric. It is in this context that studies establishing a connection between the Dalit movement and the concepts discussed earlier bring out the latent contradictions of a socio-economic and political nature. Moreover, such studies also reveal that relative deprivation leading to socio-economic mobility has after all a democratising impact on the socio-economic, political and bureaucratic structure of India (Shah, 1991: 603).

Studies linking relative deprivation and social mobility with the Dalit movement assume importance at least for tactical and strategic reasons especially when the studies of these movements are denied their legitimate place in the academic world and are considered to be deviations from the mainstream and irrelevant in the Indian context (Oommen, 1990: 30). Oommen, while criticising this approach as historical and biased, has argued that an adequate framework for the study of social movements should take into account the historicity, the elements of social structure and the future vision of the society in which they originate and operate and it is the dialectics between these which provides the focal point for the analysis of social movements (ibid.).

However, the present scenario, highlighted by three major developments of the total marginalisation and annihilation of the rural Dalits, Hinduisation of the Dalit masses and the growing crisis of the Indian welfare state seems to be questioning the theoretical validity of relative deprivation both as a conceptualisation and as a form of consciousness. Concepts of relative deprivation and also social mobility are quite inadequate to capture this reality at the theoretical level. Given the happenings in the rural areas where the upper castes or class forces are committing brutal atrocities on the Dalits, and when the state's response is either callous or repressive, the Dalits do not feel a sense of relative deprivation so much as a total alienation and exclusion and the threat of physical liquidation. What one observes in rural Maharashtra and also in the rest of the country is the complete alienation of the Dalits from resources like land, water and agricultural implements. Thus, the Dalits do not find sufficient access to either natural or human resources and, therefore, feel completely marginalised in relation to the so-called decentralisation of political power in rural India. Such a situation where the Dalits are collectively and absolutely worse off, questions the validity of the concept of relative deprivation, which primarily presupposes the perception of contrasting one's situation, even at the most trivial level, with that of others worse off than oneself (Runciman, 1966: 9). Moreover, it is this perception of total exclusion from the developmental processes that forces the Dalits to protest in the most militant way, ranging from radical reaction to physical retaliation in self-defence. This militancy is evident among the Dalits of Andhra Pradesh, Bihar and Maharashtra.

However, in the urban setting in Maharashtra, the concept of relative deprivation and social mobility has some relevance to the new educated, employed Dalit class that is emerging from among the Mahars and Mangs. It is true that the Mahars do feel relative deprivation at two levels. First, at the vertical level, the Mahars feel relatively deprived both socially and materially in comparison with the upwardly-mobile upper castes. To assuage this feeling of deprivation, these Dalits, particularly officers, float some kind of welfare association to gain, among other things, more patronage from the system. This is to overcome their relative deprivation by raising the material and social status of the individual up to the level of those who are immediately above them. Thus, at the vertical level, the reference group for the Mahars is the upwardly-mobile upper castes.

However, at the horizontal level, for the Mahars and for the Mangs the reference group is the emerging Mahar elites. The Mahars and even the Mangs in the urban setting seem to have developed a sense of relative deprivation often reflecting the feeling of hatred, contempt and jealousy towards those Mahars who according to the group under reference are more fortunate in raising their material status. This feeling of relative deprivation among the less fortunate Mahars and Mangs is now being openly articulated—an articulation that can lead to the formation of a subgroup or a social category based on the region-specific identity of these Mahars. The

Marathwada Mitra Mandal (an organisation of Dalit teachers from Marathwada University) is a case in point. It is alleged that the members of this organisation feel relatively deprived in comparison with the Dalits of north Maharashtra and Vidarbha (see Jondhale, 1992). It is interesting to note here that this is true of the Dalits of Telangana who feel relatively deprived in comparison with the Dalits of coastal Andhra Pradesh, particularly of the Guntur region, who, according to the former, are far ahead in terms of socio-economic and educational achievements. Instead, it fetters itself to the narrow contours of envy, contempt and hatred against persons from the same social situation. For example, the Dalits (Mahars, Buddhists) of Marathwada who, in educational and material terms, are relatively backward as compared with the Dalits of Vidarbha consider this relative advance of their counterparts from Vidarbha as the major cause of their own backwardness. They, however, do not consider their backwardness as being a result of the feudal ethos that dominated the socio-economic life of Marathwada for 500 years, which eventually led to the late arrival of these Dalits in the main channels of advancement.

Similarly, the feeling of relative deprivation makes the Mangs (Dalit) overlook the connection between their backwardness and their traditional skilled occupation which had bound them to the feudal agrarian structure. Due to socio-economic and technological changes in Indian agriculture and state intervention in the condition of the Dalits in general, the Mangs are now being displaced from the agrarian economy and are compelled to get an education and subsequently look for jobs. This compulsion and displacement is a result of the replacement of old agricultural implements that were made by the Mangs by the more sophisticated implements manufactured by the Garwares. In this situation, the Mangs are lagging behind the Mahars owing to their late response to the state, which, as we will see, seems to have lost the capacity to accommodate these latecomers in its rather obsolete network of patronage. Why do the Mangs not question the capacity of the Indian state and find faults with the market society, which underlines and renews the structures of inequality? Why does their feeling of relative deprivation revolve around the relative advance of the microscopic section of Mahar elites? The answer to this question lies in the politicisation of relative deprivation.

The politics of relative deprivation finds expression among the Mang elites. These elites, though emerging on a very small scale, are now found vocalising the sense of relative deprivation of the common Mangs with the intention of sharing the spoils with the Mahars by forcing a bargain with the power centres.[3] This political expression of relative deprivation, aimed at creating a constituency among the ignorant but innocent Mangs, surfaced in one of the state-level conferences organised by the Mang elites in Maharashtra at Ichalkaranji in November 1991. It is interesting to note that in this particular conference, the feeling of relative deprivation with a negative reference to the Mahars, was articulated by the Mangs with the encouragement and patronage of the upper-caste political forces which are alleged to be instrumental in fanning hostilities between the two communities for the electoral politics of the former in the state.[4]

Needless to say, this feeling of relative deprivation, suspends, if not eliminates completely, the possibility of the development of a homogeneous Dalit unity cutting across castes as well as regions. Second, since relative deprivation underlines the quest for social mobility, this mobility syndrome of Dalits has the potential of diffusing the formation of social consciousness by promoting individual consciousness, which has atomising dimensions leading to the isolation and independence of the Dalits from their community. Thus, this feeling of deprivation and the element of mobility inherent in it pushes the Dalits away from the centre of collective struggles to the periphery (participating in the struggle by paying only lip sympathy to the Dalit cause), thus bypassing the assumption of the historical responsibility that Ambedkar had rested on their shoulders for their emancipation and that of the common Dalits from their dehumanising conditions. Therefore, while studying the Dalit movement in terms of relative deprivation or social mobility, one should not lose sight of the fact that social mobility has sustained the belief in functionalism, which has a stabilising influence on society and polity.

The real serious damage that the concept of relative deprivation can cause to the Dalit movement today is that it represents a negative Utopia in two major senses. First, this concept at the theoretical level attempts to describe 'what is' without linking it with the question 'what can be' and, thus, results in an adequate description of social phenomena. While it denies to sociology a critically subversive character, it also denies an emancipatory consciousness to the groups under reference. It impels the Dalit groups to organise their thought and action not in their own authentic terms but in terms of those privileged sections whose hegemonic world view underlines the structures of domination.

The state plays an extremely important role in keeping the sense of relative deprivation vital. This is done systematically and shrewdly by transferring resources from the more privileged sections to the underprivileged sections as a part of its welfare strategies. In doing so, the state not only weakens the critical consciousness that had begun to articulate itself against the structure of domination but as a corollary also discredits the movement by co-opting the most vocal and assertive elements into the pacification structures built around the welfare state.

For example, in the 1960s in Maharashtra, the state seems to have, time and again, effectively scattered Dalit consciousness which in the process of its development had opened up the possibility of reaching the level of a broad social consciousness. In Maharashtra this was exemplified by the Dalit movement led by Dadasaheb Gaikwad in the early 1960s. Later, there was an alliance of the Dalit Panthers with the Left and democratic forces. However, this integrating consciousness got dissolved into separating individual consciousness which brought about the fragmentation of the Dalits into at least a dozen small groups of the Republican Party of India (RPI) in Maharashtra. This diffusion was effected through the introduction of the Integrated Rural Development Programme (IRDP) and the National Rural Employment Programme (NREP) package and the discrediting was achieved through the co-option of important Dalit leaders, including Gaikwad, by the state.

But scholars studying the Dalit movement have not focused much attention on such a vital aspect of the movement, which involved the subversive role of the state. Oommen has tried to locate the state's response to the Dalit movement, but he seems to have given a more formal and legalistic explanation of the state's response to the Dalit movement and for other movements of the weaker sections of the population (Oommen, 1990: 187). For example, he tends to argue that the state becomes either repressive or it discredits the movement because the latter defies its authority (Oommen, 1990: 187). This, however, is not true. The emasculation of the Dalit movement in Maharashtra in the late 1960s and early 1970s in particular, was carried out by the state not only because the Dalit movement had undermined its authority, but largely because the movement in this phase focused only on the question of redistribution of land. The Dalit demand for government land, and land declared surplus under the ceiling law, had seriously threatened the material interests of the rural rich.

Though the concepts of relative deprivation and social mobility play a diffusionist role as they render the formation of an integral Dalit consciousness difficult in the urban setting, they were relevant inasmuch as they could capture the social reality, although fractionally. However, it seems now that the growing crisis of the Indian welfare state, the systematic attempt by the Hindutva forces to Hinduise the Dalits and the revitalising of Buddhist culture among the Dalits all seem to have rendered the concept of relative deprivation too fragile to lead to new initiatives.

The levels of the feeling relating to relative deprivation and social mobility are conditioned by the capacity of the state to intervene in the conditions of the population sections concerned. This can be corroborated by citing Runciman, who observes that in Europe, the welfare provisions of the inter-war period helped to keep the level of relative deprivation lower than the actual hardships imposed by the depression might have warranted (1966: 70). Moreover, in the Indian context, the experience is quite contrary to that stated by Runciman. This is because, in view of the absolute deprivation of the Dalits, it was politically imperative for the Indian state to nurture the feeling of relative deprivation among them by shifting resources (which should have included various constitutional provisions and different welfare programmes for the Dalits) from the more privileged sections thus reducing absolute deprivation to relative deprivation. And this tends towards atomisation, thus denying a collectively critical subversive consciousness to the community as a whole.

In the last few years—particularly in the urban setting—developments in Maharashtra in the sphere of state and religion are likely to conduce towards the initiation of the reverse process: a shift from relative to absolute deprivation. This is so because the current fiscal crisis of the Indian state renders it difficult to shift resources from the privileged to the under-privileged. This impels the state to withdraw largely from the social sphere. This withdrawal is evident from two facts. First, according to a rough estimate, the budgetary provision for social welfare is 1 per cent. In fact, the percentage outlay for the Scheduled Castes had increased only marginally from 0.35 per cent in the First Five-Year Plan to 0.84 per cent in the Fifth Five-Year Plan. Thus, we find that the Scheduled Castes, who constitute 15 per cent of India's population and a much greater proportion of the poor, have been provided a disproportionately low share of the plan resources. Second, the state's thrust towards privatisation means practically a total marginalisation of the Indian Dalits because the private sectors would hardly be interested in accommodating them. This growing privatisation and the resultant exclusion of the Dalits from the urban settings also is likely to lead towards an articulation of their critical consciousness as a collectivity. At any rate, this is a likely consequence when deprivation tends towards absolutisation under present circumstances. However, as of today, such an articulation of corporate Dalit consciousness has not found any organised expression among the urban Dalits. Unfortunately, the growing privatisation of the Indian economy and the crisis of the welfare state in India did not figure at all in the state conference organised by the Backward, Adivasi and Muslim Caste Federation (BAMCEF) at Nasik in 1992.

Moreover, the sense of relative deprivation that emanated as a reaction to upper-caste restrictions against Dalits adopting certain high-caste social norms had led the Dalits in the late 1930s to overcome it through collective mobilisation. But today, the Hindutva forces are taking the initiative in accommodating the Dalits in the savarna culture.[5] A notable example of this deceitful elevation of the Dalits was marked by the laying of bricks during the Ram Shilanyas at Ayodhya by two Dalits who were pressed into God Rama's service by the BJP–VHP combine a couple of years ago. In this particular case, it was certainly not a genuine desire to overcome the relative deprivation of the Dalits that led to their mobilisation. However, whatever the reasons, this certainly suspends the necessity for the Dalits to initiate movements towards Sanskritisation. Further, since this concept or relative deprivation has meaning only in the hierarchical socio-economic situation, it cannot explain the phenomenon of the Buddhist conversion movement in Maharashtra and of late in Andhra Pradesh.

By way of conclusion, it can be observed that if the critical function of the social sciences, and, therefore of sociology, consists of an attempt to question its own theoretical assumptions in relation to the changing socio-economic reality, then it becomes necessary to develop this critical function in order to understand any movement from below.

NOTES

1. This chapter is a revised version of an earlier draft presented in the seminar on 'Dalit Movement in India' organised by Vikas Adhayan Kendra, Bombay, August 1992 and subsequently appeared in *Economic and Political Weekly,* 3 April 1993, pp. 570–72.
2. This is also borne out by Ambedkar's Chowdar Tank movement at Mahad in 1927 and the temple entry movement in 1929 at Nasik.
3. This was evident at the state-level conference organised by one of the important Mang leaders at Tehalkaranji in November 1991.
4. During the Ichalkaranji Conference, the Congress leaders from the state tried to instigate the Mangs against the Mahars by projecting the latter as prospering at the cost of the former.
5. *Sugawa,* a special number on the theme 'Ambedkar and Hindutvavadi' was published by Sugawa Publications at Pune, 1991 (in Marathi).

REFERENCES AND SELECT BIBLIOGRAPHY

Bhat, Anil (1971) 'Politics and Social Mobility in India', *Contributions to Indian Sociology,* 105(3): 428–43.
Guha, Ranajit (1983) *Elementary Aspects of Peasant Insurgence in Colonial India.* London: Oxford University Press.
Issac, Harold (1964) *India's Ex-Untouchables.* Bombay: Asia Publishing House.
Jondhale, B.V. (1992) 'A Report on Milind College', *Maharashtra Times,* 6 July.
Joshi, Barbara (1987) 'Recent Developments in Inter-Regional Mobilisation of Dalit Protest in India', *South Asian Bulletin,* 7: 112–35.
Lynch, Owen (1974) *The Politics of Untouchability.* New Delhi: National Publications.
Omvedt, Gail (1994) *Dalits and the Democratic Revolution: Dr. Ambedkar and the Dalit Movement in Colonial India.* New Delhi: Sage Publications.
Oommen, T.K. (1990) *Protest and Change: Studies in Social Movements.* New Delhi: Sage Publications.

Patwardhan, Sunanda (1973) *Change among India's Harijans*. New Delhi: Orient Longman.
Ram, Nandu (1988) *The Mobile Scheduled Castes, Rise of a New Middle Class*. New Delhi: Hindustan Publishing Corporation.
Rao, M.S.A. (1982) *Social Movements in India* (Vol. 1). New Delhi: Manohar Publications.
Runciman, W. (1966) *Relative Deprivation*. London: Routledge and Kegan Paul.
Sachchidananda, S. (1978) *Harijan Elite*. Faridabad: Thomson Press.
Shah, Ghanshyam (1991) 'Social Backwardness and Politics of Reservation', *Economic and Political Weekly*, Annual Number, March: 603.
Silverberg, James (ed.) (1968) *Social Mobility in the Caste System in India*. The Hague: Mouten.
Singer, M. and Bernard Cohen (eds) (1968) *Structure and Change in Indian Society*. Chicago: Aldine.
Srinivas, M.N. (1962). 'A Note on Sanskritization and Westernization', in M.N. Srinivas (ed.), *Caste in Modern India and Other Essays*, pp. 5–32. London: Asia Publishing House.

7

Liberation Movements in Comparative Perspective: Dalit Indians and Black Americans

K.P. SINGH

The status of Dalits in India and blacks in America is characterised by their relative deprivations and disabilities. The blacks were first imported from Africa into Virginia in 1619 as plantation labour, though they have stressed for a long time that they are part and parcel of American society. Initially called 'negroes', they were enslaved by the whites. By about 1700, the growing demands of the expanding plantation economy of the new world attracted slave traders to bring increasingly large cargoes of black slaves from Africa. Soon after, slavery was institutionalised in American society. In this system, family members, even wives, husbands and their children could be separated easily. Negro children often derived their status from their mothers. Negroes were denied not only socio-economic, political and legal rights, but even minimum civil rights. The Dalits, on the other hand, are the original inhabitants of India though they have been treated as 'Untouchables' under the fourfold division of the varna system. It has generally been held that the Untouchables are outside the hierarchy of the varna system, though they are considered to be the lowest in the Hindu caste system.

Systems of slavery and serfdom also existed in India, for instance in the state of Kerala and some other parts of south India, but these were not as developed as in America. In Kerala, the Untouchable castes, especially the Pulayas, Cherumans and Panas (a tribe), were recruited as agricultural labour. They were considered to be the property of their high-caste Hindu masters and were sold and bought like a commodity in the market. But their family members could not be separated from them as in the case of the blacks in America.

Instead, these slaves were assigned to particular farm sites of their masters and were obliged to live there and work for them. They also suffered from social, cultural and religious disabilities and educational, economic and political deprivations. They were not allowed to worship at the Hindu temples or even read the sacred Hindu scriptures. They not only suffered from 'touch pollution' but also from an extreme form of 'distance pollution'. Untouchable women were obliged to leave their breasts uncovered and were even sexually exploited, the Yellamma cult in south India being one example of such exploitation. The numerous forms of exploitation, deprivation and disabilities were institutionalised and governed by certain rules and regulations, the violation of which was punished in various ways. Thus, both the Indian Untouchables or Dalits and the American blacks have suffered from cumulative deprivations and inequalities in their respective societies. The authority of castes and the supremacy of ascribed values as determinants of social status are highly typical characteristics of Indian society to which neither individuals nor social groups are exceptions. Dalits, as a distinct group in Indian society, by virtue of heritage could enjoy only the provision of the lowest rank of social status. As a consequence, they remained socially, economically, politically and culturally backward as compared to any other social category.

However, as a result of consistent efforts in several directions, the widening spread of education and consciousness of the rights enshrined in the Indian Constitution, there has been a great change in the position of Dalits. In this chapter, I intend to deal with the problem of social protest movements with special reference to the achievements of Dalit men and women in India and to compare them with those of blacks in the United States of America.

Comparing caste and race, Cox (1948: 438–39) emphasises that factors influencing the choice of occupation for both the races in the United States (blacks and whites) are fundamentally different from those which operate in the caste system in India. The questions asked by caste members in viewing the field of labour are different from those that confront whites and blacks. In estimating the possibility of an occupation, the caste-man wants to know primarily the altitude of his caste and the degree of purity of occupation in question for upward mobility. However, in both societies, the dominance of the subordinate groups is upheld by a social ideology to which the subordinate groups must seem to subscribe in face to face interaction, but which they may reject in backstage discourse among themselves, that is, both blacks and Dalits do not subscribe to the racial and caste inequalities, though they may be victims of their respective race and caste ideologies. On this point Berreman (1979) is in agreement with other sociologists such as Simpson and Yinger (1953) and Cox (1948) that in the Western forms of inequality, inegalitarian practice confronts egalitarian ideology.

THEORETICAL FRAMEWORK

Scholars in sociology and social anthropology adopted various theoretical approaches in studying issues related to caste, gender and social movements in India. However, some major theoretical concepts and approaches may be grouped as follows: (*i*) structural approaches grounded on functional and dialectical models; (*ii*) historical approach; and (*iii*) conflict approach. In this chapter, I do not intend to review all these, but attempt to find common grounds for an intersectional theoretical approach. I also intend to show the biases and limitations from which the different approaches suffer.

TOWARDS AN INTERSECTIONAL THEORETICAL APPROACH

In evaluating these theoretical approaches, I find that each has advantages of its own for the study of caste, gender and social movements in India, but that none of them provides a comprehensive enough perspective on these issues. Therefore, there is a need for a theoretical approach that reflects and focuses on all aspects.

An intersectional theoretical approach, in my view, interlocks various theoretical concepts in order to study a research problem. A series of concepts related to caste, gender and social movements in this approach, could be integrated into a viewpoint on the basis of theoretical formulations. It is my endeavour to find out the underlying theoretical and conceptual formulations of various approaches to study the issues of caste, gender and social movements, and then unite them into a viewpoint, which would achieve a fair degree of conceptual analysis of a particular problem. A comparison of the given situation of caste, class and gender in India with race, class and gender in the US, suggests that multiracial feminism provides similar integrated concepts in the study of all three. Multiracial feminism provides an analysis of these intersections and asserts that gender is constructed by a range of interlocking inequalities, what Patricia Hill calls 'a matrix of domination'. The idea of a matrix is of several fundamental systems interacting with and through each other. A person experiences race, class, gender and sexuality differently depending upon his social location in the structure of race, class, gender and sexuality (Zinn and Dill, 1996: 11). Multiracial feminism encapsulates all aspects of the problem under the intersectional theoretical approach. In the case of caste and gender in India, an individual or group may face a similar situation, and it might be very useful to adopt an intersectional approach in order to understand the crux of the issue. What is most important conceptually and analytically in this work is the articulation of multiple oppression (Brewer, 1993: 13). The intersectional theoretical approach is quite open to the development of a multidimensional paradigm and articulation of the basic issues from different dimensions. Further emphasising the importance of this approach, Brewer said that as theorists explicate the intersection of race, gender and class, our conceptualisation of racial inequality will change. The complexity of race, gender and class intersections suggests that scholarly work must accomplish a number of difficult theoretical tasks especially around interrelationship (ibid.: 18). Glenn stressed that 'a starting point for developing such a theory would appear to lie in those models which view race and gender stratification as a part of a larger system of institutionalized inequality' (1985: 87). Similarly, the intersectional theoretical understanding of caste and gender in India gives a more specific multidimensional picture of the problem. Understanding race and gender as a relational, interlocking, socially constructed system affects how we strategise for change and also alerts us to sources of inertia and resistance to change (Glenn, 1992: 35–36). In the case of India, the relationship between caste and gender depends upon the same situation as in the case of race and gender in the US.

LIBERATION MOVEMENTS IN COMPARATIVE PERSPECTIVE

In order to ameliorate their socio-economic condition, as well as their cultural, religious and other deprivations and disabilities, both the Dalits in India and blacks in the US have been engaged in struggles and protest movements of several types for a long time. For an adequate sociological analysis of these social protest movements for a new social identity based on de-stigmatised caste and racial considerations of their ideologies and their styles of assertion, it is essential to put both the Dalit and black protest movements together into a common theoretical framework.

There have been two types of ideology among the Dalits and blacks. The first is an *acquiescent* ideology in which one accepts his/her low status or position and avoids any confrontation with others, but may request the dominant group (oppressor) to allow access to education, employment, etc., in order to serve them better. Such a person is submissive and the dominant group grants him/her some of the facilities out of generosity. The other popular ideology is *protest* by the deprived sections of the society who organise themselves to resist innumerable types of exploitation and oppression by the dominant groups.

Both the Indian Dalits and American blacks have organised assertive efforts for their respective societies. Their protest ideology involves resistance, opposition, confrontation and conflict with the dominant groups (oppressors). Dalits and blacks alike have adapted these to achieve their desired goals of social equality, social dignity and de-stigmatised social identity.

Retrospectively, it can be seen that the identity achieved with the help of *acquiescent* ideology was a type of self-mortification since the identifier accepted the status of servitude. A movement based on such an ideology could hardly be called a movement to achieve social mobility that might lead to the formation of a new social identity. It was a situation *of sponsored mobility* where the dominant groups granted access to modern education and employment opportunities out of generosity. Under the rubric of an acquiescent ideology, there was no enhancement of self-image, honour, dignity and esteem, as patronage was received for being obedient, humble and submissive. Sponsored mobility merely buttressed the superordinate–subordinate relationship (Rao, 1984: 208). To support his argument, Rao has cited the movement of the Chambhars (Untouchables) in Maharashtra who did not challenge the superiority and hegemony of the caste-Hindus, accepting their status as leather-workers and following all the religious rituals and rites of caste-Hindus, as an example. The patronage given to them by the caste-Hindus enabled them to get modern education, which, however, resulted in individual rather than group mobility (Rao, 1984: 208).

Booker T. Washington in the US followed the same ideology (Wood, 1970: 88), asking his followers and supporters to accept their unequal status but to pursue business-oriented education so that they could serve their masters in a better way (Washington, 1915: 113–14). Since this meant accepting a position of servitude, this movement did not raise the honour and self-respect of the blacks. Gunnar Myrdal stressed that 'Washington was an all-out accommodationist leader because he never relinquished full equality as the ultimate goal. Washington's main motive was "accommodation for a price". He was prepared to give up social and political equality if the Blacks were allowed to work undisturbed with their White friends for education and business' (Myrdal, 1944: 210).

In contrast, the protest movements of Dalits and blacks asserted the demand for self-respect, social dignity and equity and gave a new direction to liberation struggles in their respective societies. These movements did not depend on any kind of patronage from the dominant groups; rather they sought confrontation. Basically, the protest ideology of both movements centred around socio-economic-cultural dimensions rather than economic and political disabilities.

Historically speaking, the Brahmanical orthodoxy and legitimacy of caste in India were first challenged in the sixth century BC by Buddhism, which preached equality, justice and the fraternity of all human beings. In the present century, the Untouchables have been drawn towards Buddhism ever since Dr Ambedkar revived it as an emancipatory religion for the oppressed. Some Indian Dalits and black Americans rejected their parental religions, that is, Hinduism and Christianity respectively, in order to escape from the trap of degraded social status. They either sought for reform in their parental religion or embraced another religion in protest. In either case, there were organised movements. In India, from the thirteenth century to the present day, reformist movements like the 'Bhakti movements', which attracted Dalits, were led by Kabir, Ravidas, Shivnarayan, Chaitanya, Chokhamela and others, who attacked the caste system and stressed equality of status. Oommen has emphasised that all the Bhakti movements shared the following characteristics: First, they were 'reformist' in that they only attempted to correct some of the evils of Hinduism, particularly the practice of untouchability, without questioning the caste system in general. Second, they were mostly initiated by caste Hindus. Third, once caste with differing ritual rank was associated with the movements, the participants developed a dual identity: a religious ideological identity with fellow participants of the movements and a sociocultural identity with social collectivities (caste) to which they traced their origin. Fourth, none of the Bhakti movements had a programme of socio-economic status; the equality professed by them remained a mirage (Oommen, 1990: 258).

A new style of protest was established by Swami Vivekananda and Dayananda Saraswati in the middle of the nineteenth century. Their movements, called the Neo-Vedantic movements, upheld the varna system as an occupational division of society, though they certainly called for the removal of the practice of untouchability in Hinduism. Thus, these movements were reinterpretationist, talking of equality, self-respect and the dignified social identity of all human beings but within the fold of the religion of their origin, that is, Hinduism.

Likewise, another important movement was the SNDP (Shree Narayana Dharma Paripalana) Movement of Kerala, led by Sri Narayana Guru Swami who established a new social identity for the Izhavas, a former Untouchable caste. This was based on the reinterpretation of orthodox Hinduism. The Izhavas constitute about 26 per cent of Kerala's population and have suffered from educational, religious, economic and political disabilities. Sri Narayana Guru Swami gave them a new religion of one God, one religion and one caste which changed their lifestyle and social outlook. He also established a set of religious institutions, like temples, priests, monks and monasteries that are parallel to that of Brahmanical Hinduism and facilitated their protest and challenge against the religious, economic, educational and political supremacy of the upper castes.

The same type of protest ideology of reinterpretation of faith was adopted by the blacks in the US. For instance, in the second and third decades of the twentieth century, Marcus Garvey launched such a movement to establish a new social identity of the blacks. He created a new religious faith, New Christianity, characterised by Christ as a god of the blacks only, since they considered themselves as oppressed and the oppressed are always blessed by God. Garvey also made a move to prepare a separate black Bible, which contained the pictures of their holy saints and angels. In addition, he established a black theology that emerged as the theology of liberation by identifying the blacks as the oppressed and the whites as the oppressors (Garvey, 1971: 90). According to Rao, black Christian theology, which ran parallel to white Christian theology, 'gave them a new basis of identity, legitimizing their efforts towards self-determination and their efforts to gain honour and prestige' (Rao, 1981: 210–11). Altogether, black theology was a package of revolt against the supremacy and hegemony of the whites in American society.

Another set of protest movements was launched on the basis of the ideology of rejection. This, for both the blacks and the Dalits, meant rejecting their parental religion and embracing another which advocated equality and self-respect and also satisfied their human dignity. The main pioneers of this ideology in India were Jotiba Phule (Satya Shodhak Samaj 1873), E.V. Ramaswami Naicker Periyar (Self Respect Movement 1930) and Dr B.R. Ambedkar (Religious Conversion Movement 1956). They not only rejected the Brahmanical supremacy of the Hindu caste system, but also advocated a new social order based on social justice. Ambedkar, who kindled this fire of 'social revolution' among the Dalit Indians, stated that 'religion must recognize the fundamental tenets of liberty, equality and fraternity. Unless a religion recognizes these three fundamental principles of social life, religion will be doomed' (see Ahir, 1991: 302). Certainly, Ambedkar was a Hindu till a few months before his death, but he was anguished at the iniquity of the caste system. 'To untouchables', he said, 'Hinduism is a veritable chamber of horrors. The iron law of caste, the heartless law of *Karma* and senseless law of status by birth are veritable instruments of torture which Hinduism has forged against the untouchable' (see ibid.: 293). Hence, in October 1956, he subsequently rejected Hinduism and embraced Buddhism, which satisfied his conscience and his understanding of the concepts of equality and justice.

Ambedkar's embracing of Buddhism, along with thousands of his followers in 1956 at Nagpur in Maharashtra has been popularly known as his religious conversion movement. However, Zelliot has pointed out that 'conversion as a way out of the untouchables' status was not new in India. Islam, and more especially Christianity, drew large numbers of their converts from the lower castes, and Sikhism in the twentieth century actively encouraged untouchables' conversion' (Zelliot, 1992: 191).

Similarly, in 1925, E.V. Periyar Ramaswami Naicker, the founder leader of the Dravida Kazhagam (DK Movement) in south India, and in 1873 Jotiba Phule in Maharashtra organised anti-Brahmin movements and emphasised the creation of a just social order without any caste hierarchy. Naicker rejected all types of myths of the Aryan religion and culture and organised his protest movements against the Sanskritic culture of the Brahmins and self-respect movements among the Dravidians. Phule too emphasised the building of a social system free from social inequalities, Brahmanical hegemony and orthodoxy and the caste system. Naicker's movement played an instrumental role in changing the political power structure in Tamil Nadu while the movements organised by Phule and Ambedkar played a powerful role towards changing the social system.

As stated earlier, the ideology of rejection was also adopted by the black Americans in several protest movements launched for evolving a just society and achieving a dignified social identity. Through such movements, a large number of black Americans rejected their parental religion and converted to another that preached equality, justice and fraternity for all. Though Christianity advocated brotherhood and equality in principle, the situation was one of utter frustration in which the blacks were given the impression of living in the same religion yet were denied equality and justice. They identified Christianity with the whites and, therefore, embraced Islam, thus protesting not only against multiple forms of oppression but also against the domination of the whites in American society. The first such black protest movement was launched by Elijah Muhammad who rejected Christianity and embraced Islam. He started the black Muslim protest movement in the US.

In 1960, the nationalist phenomenon in the US reasserted itself and the black protest movement ran parallel to the Civil Rights

Movement (Draper, 1969: 544–55). During this period, the important black leader was Malcolm X, who was also actively involved in the black Muslim protest movement. He linked the black Muslim ideology with African nationalism and black African civilisation and insisted on the rejection of the white Western civilisation. A new identity was formed on the basis of claims to an African heritage and civilisation. The ideology of an African heritage was also adopted by Marcus Garvey and Du Bois, both of whom emphasised the superiority of their race and culture. In fact, Garvey's protest movement may be seen as a synthesis of two ideologies of protest: (*i*) a re-interpretation of Christianity and (*ii*) a rejection of American cultural values.

Both Dalit Indians and black Americans strove to achieve their desired goals of equality and laid stress on the civil rights of the oppressed as a counter to atrocities perpetrated on them. In Maharashtra, the Mahar movement under the leadership of Ambedkar adopted the civil rights ideology while in Agra, a city in Uttar Pradesh, a self-respect movement was launched by some Jatav youths. These movements generated a sense of self-respect and an awareness of their basic rights as enshrined in the Constitution of India. From 'Mahad March in 1927 to Yeola Conference in 1936' Ambedkar adopted the ideology and means of civil rights to protest against the socio-economic, cultural-religious and political disabilities and oppression of the Dalits. He not only protested and fought against the practice of untouchability and the tenets of Hinduism but also demanded basic civil rights for Untouchables. However, recently, the social awareness among Dalits is being manifested in conflict, especially in rural areas where atrocities on Dalits have increased tremendously in comparison to the past. This indicates that there is a need to generate still more awareness among them of their legal and constitutional rights so that they can protect themselves under the law.

Inspired by Ambedkar's ideology, Ram Vilas Paswan, a Janata Dal member of Parliament, also launched a self-respect movement in December 1991. This movement was organised by the 'Dalit Sena', which he headed from Tusundur, Andhra Pradesh where 22 Dalits had been massacred by caste-Hindus. During the course of his movement between 6 December 1991 and 14 April 1992, Paswan highlighted the issues and problems faced by the Dalits and also drew the attention of the whole nation towards the increasing atrocities against them. By mobilising the Dalits to fight for their self-respect, honour and prestige in Indian society, he not only demanded protection for them from atrocities but also made them aware of their socio-economic, political and legal rights.

In the 1950s, a new chapter in the history of black protest movements was added in the US by Rev. Dr Martin Luther King Jr, who adopted the civil rights ideology as a strategy in the black movement and organised the Southern Christian Leadership Conference (SCLC) and by Du Bois, who established the National Association for the Advancement of Coloured People (NAACP). King practised non-violent direct action on the model established by M.K. Gandhi during India's Independence struggle with Britain. He moved the black struggle from the courtroom to the street and from law liberties to church pews. He also led several economic boycotts, desegregation and voter registration campaigns always adopting a non-violent ideology of civil rights. Similarly, Du Bois also organised movements demanding full civil rights, economic opportunities and education for all the black youth. He was influenced by Marxism and had developed an interest in pan-Americanism though he always maintained that race was stronger than class. Du Bois 'vacillated between Marxism and a middle class ideology and the latter eventually got the better of the former in him. This was the strategy that he adopted in fighting for basic civil rights, and he came to be regarded as the father of the civil rights movement' (Rao, 1984: 201). Thus, both Du Bois and Martin Luther King Jr protested against the whites' supremacy and the racial segregation which had subjected the blacks to multiple types of deprivation.

A new ideological phase started in the history of social protest movements with the formation of the Black Panther Party in the US and the Dalit Panther Movement in India. While the immediate cause of the formation of the Black Panthers was the increasing brutality by the white police, the increasing atrocities perpetrated by the caste-Hindus on the Dalits were responsible for the formation of the Dalit Panthers.

The Black Panther Party was organised in the US in October 1966, at Oakland in California, with the aim of protecting the blacks from police brutality and other harassment by the whites. Bobby Seal and Huey P. Newton organised this movement for self-defence by carrying arms. It was an extremist development in the protest movement of black Americans, which held that war could be stopped only by war and not by any soft means. The Panthers emphasised revolutionary nationalism rather than cultural nationalism (Jones, 1988: 416–41). They were very radical and militant and were able to penetrate into the poor working class of the urban ghettos in the US.

The Dalit Panthers in India, for their part, organised themselves to attack the upper-caste Hindu capitalists and those who committed atrocities on Dalits. On 9 July 1972, the Dalit Panther Movement was formed under the leadership of Raja Dhale as president, Namdev Dhasal as defence minister and J.V. Pavar as its general secretary. To protect their fellow Dalits from violence and atrocities, they were prepared, if necessary, to adopt violent strategies. Thus, both the Black Panthers and the Dalit Panthers accepted the ideology of class conflict and chose to directly confront the oppressors by adopting radical and violent means.

The Dalit Panthers, embellishing the concept of Dalits' emancipation in their 'manifesto' emphasised that a complete revolution was needed. 'We do not want a little place in the *Brahmin Alley*. We want the rule of the whole land, we are not looking at persons but at systems and change of heart ... liberal education etc. will not end our state of exploitation. When we gather a revolutionary mass, rouse the people, out of the struggle, the giant mass will become tidal wave of revolution' (Dhasal, 1974: 28). However, the Dalit Panthers recognised only the contributions of Jotiba Phule and Dr B.R. Ambedkar for their struggle. They drew the organisational structure and strategies from the Black Panther Party. They were also greatly influenced by black literature.

This resumé of the black protest movements brings out the similarities and differences in the sociocultural, political and economic aspects of their social life. American racism in many ways parallels Indian casteism and the condition of Dalits in India is very similar to that of blacks in America. Though untouchability is not practised against the blacks in the American social system, the practice of racial segregation is very much there. Historically, most of the blacks were both psychologically and materially deprived by the presumption that they were racially inferior to the whites. In a similar fashion, the Dalits were deprived by the caste system in India. They were denied educational, political, economic as well as other civil rights before the period of British rule in India. Thus, the major cause behind the social protest movements of both blacks and Dalits was their centuries-old exploitation, oppression and repression in their respective societies.

Yet, the sociocultural differences between India and America are so great that the various types of protest movements tend to be more different than alike. While the Dalits in India are the original inhabitants of the country, the blacks were migrant labourers in the US, which led to their enslavement by the whites. Whereas the discriminatory practices against the blacks are racial, based on the colour of their skin, the Dalits are the victims of religious discrimination based on the theory of *chaturvarna* of Hindu religion and suffer from ritual disabilities. The caste system has been prevalent for centuries in Indian society, while racism in the US is only 350 years old. The most important difference, sociologically speaking, between the blacks and the Dalits in the structural placement of their respective societies is that the blacks, though they have several political opinions or factions among them, are not segmentally divided into numerous endogamous groups like Dalits. The Dalit Indians are heterogeneous castes based on different cultural and linguistic divisions, while this is not the case of American blacks. Moreover, they also do not suffer from ritual disabilities, as do the Dalits.

Class-based divisions among the Dalits are not as sharp as in the case of blacks. It is only in urban society that a middle-class Dalit group has appeared in increasing numbers and their bourgeoisie is still comparatively radical in its thinking. In contrast to this, black capitalists have promoted a cultural and national integration approach, which is opposed to the revolutionary approach adopted by the lower strata among the blacks. Another important difference between the blacks and Dalits is that the latter are a social category that is broad enough to include even the poor and downtrodden of other sections of society while the blacks maintain a racial category, and can easily be distinguished physically from the whites and segregated because of their visible racial identity.

CONCLUSION

Any social movement is an organised effort by an individual, group, or community to achieve a particular goal. Essentially, the social movements launched by the blacks and the Dalits are based on the ethos of protest which has been directed against their socio-economic, religious-cultural and legal oppression and exploitation.

The status of the blacks in the US has changed drastically especially in the last two decades as a positive result of powerful and effective black protest movements. These movements broke down the barriers of institutionalised racial segregation. For the blacks, the social, cultural and psychological process that activated and main-tained these movements reinforced collective and political personal identities. Politically correct terms used in reference to blacks today are 'African-Americans' or 'black Americans' instead of 'negro' or 'coloured people'. Black pride is in vogue, in addition to the pursuance of the equality of rights and integration. As a result of these protest movements, the government was forced to adopt the policy of affirmative action and other measures which have done much to improve their socio-economic status in American society. The affir-mative action policy has helped in structural changes and in creating a new class of black bourgeoisie, even though others have remained in the lower class. However, the mass mobilisation of the blacks has led to the emergence of a new kind of consciousness. This particular black consciousness has helped them to form a special identity, which is recognised both by American society and by the rest of the world.

Similarly, the Dalits too have organised several protest movements and intensified their struggle against socio-economic, religious, cul-tural and political deprivation and oppression in Indian society. The caste system of today is not the same as it was a hundred years ago. These protest movements have brought about various structural-functional changes. And yet, though Dalits have achieved much in their struggle for socio-economic and political rights in the Indian social system, atrocities against them by caste-Hindus have increased rather than decreased. However, these atrocities may paradoxically be taken as a positive phenomenon in the social life of Dalits, for wherever and whenever they assert their legitimate rights, the result is confrontation and consequently atrocities. The Dalits are still socio-economically very poor and weak but psychologically and morally they have become very confident and strong and are able to raise their voice against any kind of exploitation and oppression at any level. The social consciousness generated by the Dalit protest movements has played a very effective and important rote in making them confident enough to gear up their struggle against age-old discrimination. This consciousness may be termed as Dalit conscious-ness, which, as in the case of the black Americans, reflects the consciousness of a collectivity or group.

It is very unfortunate, however, that the policy of protective discrimination or what is referred to as the reservation policy, a result of these decades-old social protest movements, has proved to be beneficial only to a limited section of the Dalits. The beneficiaries of this policy are very small in number in comparison to the percentage of their population and form a small segment of the middle class among Dalits, who may be termed as the Dalit bour-geoisie. The policy needs to be more effective in its implementation and more realistic in taking into account the Dalit population and position.

To sum up, it may be stated with full conviction that due to the emergence of Dalit consciousness and black consciousness, the Dalits have become dignified and the blacks have become beautiful for their respective communities. But it is essential to note that governmental policies in the US and India still need to be made more effective in their implementation process. In India, for example, the laws need to be made stricter in order to wipe out the practice of untouchability and caste-based discrimination. Only by such mea-sures can the Dalits and the blacks be fully integrated within their respective societies in a meaningful way.

REFERENCES AND SELECT BIBLIOGRAPHY

Ahir, D.C. (1991) *The Legacy of Dr. Ambedkar.* Delhi: B.R. Publishing Corp.

Anand, Mulk Raj (1970) *Untouchable.* London: The Bodly Head.

Balu, Peter M. (1977) *Inequality and Heterogeneity—A Primitive Theory of Social Structure.* New York: The Free Press.

Berreman, Gerald (1979) *Caste and Other Inequalities.* Meerut: Folklore Institute.

Béteille, André (1971) *Caste, Class, and Power. Changing Patterns of Stratification in a Tanjore Village.* Berkeley: The University of California Press.

Brewer, Rose M. (1993) 'Theorizing Race, Class, and Gender: The New Scholarship of Black Feminist Intellectuals and Black Labor Women', in Stalie M. James and Abena P.A. Busia (eds), *Theorizing Black Feminism*, pp. 173–96. London: Routledge.

Cohn, B.S. (1970) 'Changing Status of a Depressed Caste', in Mckim Marriott (ed.), *Village India*, pp. 38–53. Chicago: The University of Chicago Press.

Cox, Oliver C. (1948) *Caste, Class, and Race*. New York: Modern Reader.

David, Popenoe (1977) *Sociology*. Englewood Cliffs: Prentice-Hall, Inc.

Dhasal, Namdeo (1974) *Itihasachi Chakra Ulti Firvu Naka Nahitat Khaddyat Jal* (in Marathi). Bombay: Namdeo Dhasal.

Draper, Theodore (1969) *The Re-Discovery of Black Nationalism*. New York: Kegan Paul Ltd.

D'Souza, Victor S. (1969) *Changing Socio-Economic Conditions and Employment of Women in Transition*. Shimla: Indian Institute of Advanced Study.

Dube, S.C. (1978) *Indian Village*. London: Routledge & Kegan Paul Ltd.

Dumont, Louis (1979) *Homo Hierarchicus*. London: Weidenfield and Necolson.

Garvey, Marcus (1971) 'Arms and Objectives for the Evaluation of the Negro Problem', in Broderick Francis (ed.), *The Black Protest Thought in Twentieth Century*, pp. 218–37. NewYork: Routledge.

Glenn, Evelyn Nakano (1985) 'Racial Ethnic Women's Labor: The Intersections of Race, Gender and Class Oppression', *Review of Racial Political Economic*, 17(3): 86–106.

———. (1992) 'Race and Gender Stratification', *Review of Racial Political Economics*, 38(1): 36–49.

Gore, M.S. (1993) *The Social Context of an Ideology: Ambedkar's Political and Social Thoughts*. New Delhi: Sage Publications.

Haper, E.B. (1968) 'Social Consequences of an Unsuccessful Low Caste Movement', in Sivam James (ed.), *Social Mobility in the Caste System in India*. The Hague: Mouten.

Issac, Harold (1965) *India's Ex-Untouchables*. Bombay: Asia Publishing House.

Iyer, Justice V.R. Krishna (1990) *Dr. Ambedkar and the Dalit Future*. New Delhi: B.R. Publishing Corp.

Jones, Charles E. (1988) 'The Political Repression of the Black Panther Party', *Journal of Black Studies,* 18(4), June: 38–45.

Keer, Dhananjay (1962) *Dr. Ambedkar: Life and Mission*. Bombay: Popular Prakashan.

Laadry, Bart (1988) *The New Black Middle Class*. Berkeley: University of California Press.

Lynch, Owen M. (1969) *The Politics of Untouchability*. New York: Columbia University Press.

———. (1974) 'The Politics of Untouchability: A Case from Agra', in M.S.A. Rao (ed.), *Urban Sociology in India*. New Delhi: Orient Longman.

———. (1981) 'Rioting as Rational Action: An Interpretation of the April 1978 Riots in Agra', *Economic and Political Weekly*, 16(48), 28 November: 2797–801.

Majumdar, D.N. and T.N. Madan (1976) *An Introduction to Social Anthropology*. New Delhi: Asia Publishing House.

Malik, Suneila (1979). *Social Integration of Scheduled Castes*. New Delhi: Abhinav Publications.

Mead, Lawrence M. (1992) *The New Politic of Poverty—The Networking in Poor America*. New York: Basic Books.

Myrdal, Gunnar (1944) *An American Dilemma: The Negro Problem and Modern Democracy.* New York: Harper Brothers.

Omvedt, Gail (1994) *Dalits and the Democratic Revolution: Dr Ambedkar and the Dalit Movement in Colonial India.* New Delhi: Sage Publications.

Oommen, T.K. (1990) *Protest and Change: Studies in Social Movements.* New Delhi: Sage Publications.

Ram, Nandu (1981) *Mobile Scheduled Castes.* New Delhi: Hindustan Publications.

———. (1995) *Beyond Ambedkar: Essays on Dalits in India.* New Delhi: Har-Anand Publications.

Rao, M.S.A. (1981) *Social Movements and Social Transformation.* New Delhi: Manohar.

———. (1984) *Social Movements in India.* Vol. 2. New Delhi: Manohar.

Richard, H. Hall (1969) *Occupation and Social Structure.* New Jersey: Prentice-Hall, Inc.

Sertima, Ivan Van (ed.) (1995) 'Great Black Leaders', *Journal of African Civilization*, 9(2): 128–41.

Simpson, G.E. and J.M. Yinger (1953) *Racial and Cultural Minorities.* New York: Harper Brothers.

Singh, Yogendra (1988) *Modernization of Indian Traditions.* Jaipur: Rawat Publications.

Smith, Robert C. and R. Seltzer (1992) *Race, Class and Culture—A Study in Afro-American Mass Opinion.* New York: State University of New York Press.

Stevenson, H.N.C. (1954) 'Status Evaluation in Hindu Caste System', *Journal of Royal Anthropological Institute*, 62(3): 93–106.

Thorat, S.K. (1993a) *Ambedkar's Contribution to Water Resources Developement.* New Delhi: Water Commission, Government of India.

———. (1993b) 'Passage to Adulthood—Perception from Below', in Sudhir Kakkar (ed.), *Identity and Adulthood.* New Delhi: Oxford University Press.

Vasta, Rajendra Singh (1977) 'Introduction to Depressed Classes of India', in Krishna Sondhi (ed.), *Gitanjali.* New Delhi: Prakashan.

Washington, Booker T. (1915) 'My Views of Segregation Laws', *New Republic*, 5, 4 December: 22–23.

Wilson, William J. (1988) *The Declining Significance of Race.* Chicago: The University of Chicago Press.

Wood, C. Vann (1970) 'Folkway, Stateway, and Racism', in Allen Weinstein and Otto Gate II (eds), *The Segregation Era, 1863–1954*, pp. 87–102. New York: Harper Brothers.

Zelliot, Eleanor (1992) *From Untouchable to Dalit: Essays on Ambedkar Movement.* New Delhi: Manohar Publications.

Zinn, Maxine Baca and Bonnie Thornton Dill (1996) 'Theorizing Difference from Multiracial Feminism', *Feminist Studies*, 1(1): 1–23.

PART

III

III

8

Sociology of India and Hinduism: Towards a Method

S. SELVAM

Hindu society has historically been marked by a rigid form of social stratification based on the varna-jati model of social organisation in which the Brahmanical religious principle, namely purity and pollution, played a central role in defining social hierarchy and separation. This led to a variety of social inequalities characterised by social oppression and economic exploitation. However, caste as a social fact is now fast losing its significance in many areas of social life. Traditional meanings, especially, are slowly changing. The association of individual castes with specific occupations has, to a great extent, broken down. Significantly, the system of production and structures of authority and power have detached themselves from the ideology of caste under which they were for centuries subsumed. In other words, the individual's position in the system of production and structures of power is no longer tied to caste as in the past. A steadily rising awareness among the members of lower castes, especially the Dalits, and their aspiration for equality in every sphere of social life has led to a continued questioning of the fundamental principles of the caste system and its practices. The idiom of caste is invoked today by the oppressed for the purpose of political and social mobilisation to challenge the traditional oppressive institutions and oppressors. But, in spite of these changes in the public domain, the idea of caste continues to be an important factor in Indian private and domestic life.

Against this backdrop, this chapter attempts a critique on two important and dominant trends in the study of India and Hinduism, set in motion by two eminent sociologists: M.N. Srinivas and Louis Dumont. Although their scholarship has made insightful contributions to the understanding of the Hindu society and Hinduism, their concepts and theoretical formulations solicit reconsideration. This chapter is a preliminary effort towards this end. The focus of this chapter is only on their key concepts and general theoretical formulation for it is not possible to cover all their writings and the entire ground. It is also important to state at the outset that the discussion here confines itself to Hinduism and Hindu society since it is beyond the scope of this chapter to consider all religions and the whole of India. In the course of this critique, an attempt is also made to propose a method for the study of the complex nature of Hinduism and society in India.

SOCIETY AND RELIGION

Religion, as a system of beliefs and practices, is eminently social and its representations are collective. Worship signifies specific human behaviour that arises in the context of religiously linked social groups forming a community of worshippers. Acts of worship 'excite, maintain and recreate certain mental states in these groups' (Durkheim, 1964: 10). Religion unites the worshippers into 'one single moral community called a church, all those who adhere to them' (ibid.: 47). It is important to note that places of worship like temples, churches and mosques bring worshippers into some kind of solidarity, which may vary from religion to religion.

Another aspect of religion, which is a subject of much controversy, is its relationship with economic factors. A much-debated question has been whether and to what extent religion is shaped by these factors. In the Marxist scheme, the economic base in the ultimate analysis determines various components of the superstructure including religion. Without entering into a debate over this issue, we state that religion has a relative autonomy that may be located in the link between religion and social structures. It is important to stress that economic factors certainly influence religious institutions and sometimes do so substantially. In other words, religious institutions have an economic function too. Weber combines both the material circumstances that entail interest and the guiding power of ideas in governing individual and group actions. Weber states: 'Not ideas, but material and ideal interests, directly govern men's conduct' (1965a: 34).

It is shown later in this section that in India, religious institutions like temples had, in the past, an active role in the structures of authority and power. This was facilitated, though not in a strict sense, not only by economic factors but also by the ideas governing the notions of caste, God and salvation. A religion that lays emphasis on salvation might have its origin within socially privileged groups. However, in the course of time, as the relationship of such a religion with privileged groups changes, the underprivileged are also incorporated to become a part of it. This transformation in the religion of the privileged with an intellectual leadership has to accommodate the lay groups for whom 'intellectualism is both economically and socially inaccessible' (Weber, 1965b: 102).

Religion also constitutes, among other things, an elaborate system of symbols and myths that capture the popular imagination and keep worshippers under its spell. Religion thus viewed is 'a system of symbols which acts to establish powerful, pervasive and long lasting moods and motivations in men by formulating conceptions of a general order of existence and clothing these conceptions with such an aura of factuality that the moods and motivations are seen uniquely realistic' (Geertz, 1973: 90). Let us now look at Hinduism in this light.

Hinduism, unlike Islam or Christianity, is a religion that comprises many traditions, denominations, gods and temples. Central to Hinduism is the Vedic-Brahmanic religious tradition, which was for centuries, a hegemonic religious system incorporating and, at times, influencing or adjusting to and coexisting with local and regional traditions. We shall return to the hegemonic nature of Brahmanic Hinduism later. (Hereafter the Vedic-Brahmanic religious tradition is referred to as Brahmanic Hinduism.) The structural basis of Hinduism and traditional Hindu society was the caste system as prescribed by the Brahmanas. But the caste system, besides its religious and ideological dimensions, has an important material basis in the economic and social division of functions. The varna-jati model of social organisation prescribed by Brahmanic Hinduism incorporated various occupational groups into its fold with hierarchy and separation based on the notions of purity and pollution as organising principles. The entire internal coherence of Hindu social organisation is sustained by the ideology governing the caste system.

According to Brahmanic Hinduism, the idea of dharma is '*the* socio-cosmic order which organises the empirical world' (Biardeau, 1989: 41). 'Dharma is therefore that all encompassing order that goes so far as to include even that which denies it (and) which consists in the well-balanced hierarchy of the four goals of man as well as in a respect for the hierarchy and proper definition of the four varnas' (ibid.: 42).

The three cardinal components of Brahmanical ideology are samsara, the belief in the transmigration of souls, the karma doctrine of compensation and the varna-jati model of society. It is the doctrine of karma that transforms the empirical world into a strictly rational and ethically-determined cosmos. In this doctrine, order and rank of the varna-jati model are eternal. The karma doctrine and the varna-jati system together place the individual within a clear circle of duties. They also offer him a well-shaped, metaphysically-satisfying conception of the world and the self. It is indeed the ideological basis of Brahmanical Hinduism that made order and rank into something divine and permanent, for membership is by birth.

FUNCTIONALIST METHOD

Studies that provide insight into various aspects of religion and society in India are diverse, covering both indological as well as social anthropological studies. While the former attempt to construct Indian society or an aspect of it through the exposition of Sanskrit textual sources (Biardeau, 1989; Karve, 1953; Singer, 1959; Singer and Cohn, 1968), the latter place the fieldwork orientation and participant-observation as central to their method (Béteille, 1965; Fuller, 1984; Gough, 1961; Marriott, 1955; Moffatt, 1979; Srinivas, 1952, 1955). It is to his credit that it was Srinivas who brought the anthropological approach to the forefront to challenge the Indological construction of Indian society.

Srinivas (1952), by placing religious beliefs and practices in their social context, presents a sociological insight into Hindu religion and society. In his efforts to explore the nature of diversity and uniformity in Hinduism, he follows Radcliffe-Brown's holistic structural-functionalism which considers that every part of society is functionally integrated in order to maintain the solidarity of the society. Based on the extent to which Sanskrit elements are present, Srinivas divides Hinduism into four levels, namely, all-India Hinduism, peninsular Hinduism, regional Hinduism and local Hinduism (1952: 213). He identifies all-India and local Hinduism with Sanskritic and non-Sanskritic Hinduism while granting some amount of intermixing of these two levels in peninsular and regional Hinduism.

He states that 'Regional Hinduism often contains some Sanskritic elements in which case it directly stresses Regional ties and indirectly all-India ties' (ibid.: 217–18). However, he underplays facts such as that there are traditions like Bhakti Hinduism of Tamil Nadu that have their own characteristics.

Srinivas uses the concept of Sanskritisation to explain the four levels of Hinduism and its unity and diversity. For Srinivas, 'All India Hinduism is Hinduism with an all India spread and this is chiefly Sanskritic in character' (ibid.: 213). The term 'spread' used by Srinivas to indicate the extent of the influence of Sanskritisation that had taken place both vertically and horizontally suggests that the process is automatic and desired by everybody. It does not provide a coherent picture of the historical and social change that he attempts to unravel. To what extent the cultural process has been harmonious and conflict-free is a question that remains to be probed. It is, however, important to mention that the process of Sanskritisation has now been largely rejected by the members of the lower castes as the process of Dalitisation, a counter force, has in recent times been on a constant rise. It has lead to increasing self-awareness, self-confidence and sense of dignity among the people of lower castes and has also led to the emergence of a new assertive identity as Dalits.

For Srinivas, all-India Hinduism had been spread all over India by the upper-caste people, particularly the Brahmans. He describes the other levels of Hinduism in terms of geographical area and the extent of Sanskritic elements found in the ritual and cultural life of the people. Srinivas' approach locates the unity of Hinduism, 'in a set of normative standards in belief and ritual and suggests a process whereby these standards have been adopted by an ever increasing number of groups' (Singer, 1972: 44). Therefore, by constructing all-India Hinduism, which is based on a body of Sanskrit scriptures, and identifying it mainly with the ritual practices prescribed by Brahmanic Hinduism, one of the traditions in Hinduism, Srinivas offers the Brahmanic tradition as an ideal standard bearer for personal and social life. In other words, the Brahmanic tradition is privileged above other traditions. This is an ideological construct that needs to be decoded and decanonised.

Because of his Brahmano-centric approach, Srinivas is unable to explore and explain convincingly the ways by which people were made to worship the 'Sanskritic deities' with ritual practices. Nor does he provide a clear picture of the process of the 'greater Sanskritisation' of the rituals and beliefs of various groups that together form Hinduism.

Changes and intermixing of beliefs and practices over a long period of time make it difficult to categorise present-day Hindu religious practices either as Sanskritic Hinduism or non-Sanskritic Hinduism. This is particularly true of religion in Tamil Nadu. The Brahmanical temples in Tamil Nadu are, in fact, Brahmanised temples in which a synthesis of both 'native' Bhakti and Brahmanical idea and practices was in existence for centuries.

Srinivas states that 'every caste tended to imitate the customs and rituals of the top most caste and this was responsible for the spread of Sanskritisation. When the process is viewed on a continental scale over a period of at least 2,500 years, it is easy to see how Sanskritic ideas and beliefs penetrated the remotest hill tribes in such a manner as not to do violence to their traditional beliefs' (1952: 31). He uses this notion of Sanskritisation to study the cultural processes that took place ever since the Vedic Aryans established their supremacy in India (Srinivas, 1989: 56). Srinivas' analysis indeed lacks historical insight. Though it advances, to some extent, our understanding of the fluid nature of the social hierarchy among the Hindus, Srinivas does not explain how the fluidity existed in spite of the rigid social order. He considers it in terms of status arising out of the caste to which an individual or a group of persons belonged. Though he admits in a later study that economic or political conditions should be taken into consideration (Srinivas, 1962: 56–57), his analysis is based mainly on cultural elements and does not provide an insight into the origin, sustenance and hegemony of this specific cultural process that placed a group of castes above the rest and made their cultural practices influential. In fact, Srinivas does not fully recognise the political function of the Brahmanical rituals and ideology (Hardiman, 1984:

212–14), and though he has attempted to combine history, his analysis makes this cultural process appear as though it takes place outside the realm of ideology, politics and economy. One is made to believe that the goal towards which everyone is expected to strive is that of Brahmanical purity (Hardiman, 1984: 214). This is obviously not always true. However, the cultural process Srinivas designates as Sanskritisation is indeed an important hegemonic process, which requires a deeper study.

Srinivas subsequently expands the scope of his concept of 'Sanskritisation' by redefining it as: 'a process by which a low Hindu caste or tribal or other group changes its customs, ritual, ideology and way of life in the direction of a high, frequently twice born caste. Generally such changes are followed by a claim to a higher position in the caste hierarchy than that traditionally conceded to the claimant caste by the local community' (Srinivas, 1966: 6).

This leads him to offer three models of Sanskritisation, namely, the Brahmanic, Kshatriya and Vaishya models. It is also important to state that the texts written in Sanskrit to which Srinivas refers, embody a tradition providing a social, religious and cosmic framework, a tradition to which a Brahmana, considered to be the universal self, and Brahmanism as an ideology, are central. These Sanskritic texts advocate and support specific social, religious and cosmic orders. Srinivas does not take this ideological dimension seriously since he takes the pre-eminence of Brahmanical beliefs and practices for granted. However, the reality is very different.

As Staal puts it: 'the material to which sanskritisation is applied consists of non-Sanskritic deities' and 'non-Sanskritic rituals and beliefs—for example, the worship of village deities, ancestors, trees, rivers and mountains and local cults in general. Sanskritisation takes place "at the expense" of these non-Sanskritic elements' (1963: 262). Staal stresses the point that the Sanskritic tradition itself is not as monolithic either in the use of language or in the matter of culture as made out by Srinivas. In Staal's view, the Sanskrit language and Sanskritic culture owe much to the vernacular languages and native non-Sanskritic cultural traditions. In his own words: 'There is much evidence to show that origins of the great tradition in India lie often in little traditions and that these origins generally remain visible in the later stages. The new does not replace the old but the old continues to exist side by side with the new' (Staal, 1963: 269). Staal suggests that the process could only add Sanskritic elements to non-Sanskritic ones. We are in agreement with Staal's position that one tradition does not, in fact, replace the other. It coexists or influences and modifies the other to some extent. The process is certainly complex, creating conditions for the rise of a hegemony, which has, among others, political and ideological dimensions.

Rao rightly points out that the emphasis on imitative processes of change does not take into account the aspects of alienation and conflict resulting at times in protest movements:

> The ideology of these movements based on relative deprivation conceived both religious and secular axes of mobility on the same structural (conceptual) level. Both were expressions of egalitarianism and the language of mobility was protest, confrontation, agitation, aggression, conflict and in some cases violence. The basic spirit behind articulating the demands was to attack the monopolistic rights, privileges and possessions of high status, symbols, goods and services of Brahmins and other upper castes. (Rao, 1979: 235–36)

Both the Bhakti Movement led by Basavanna (1106–68) in Karnataka (Ramanujam, 1972) and the recent Self-Respect Movement led by E.V. Ramaswamy Naicker (1879–1973) in Tamil Nadu (Barnett, 1976; Ryerson, 1988) questioned the Brahmanic monopoly in various aspects of social life. Therefore, in making emulation by choice the mode of Sanskritisation, Srinivas fails to take into consideration conflicts among various caste groups, making it seem instead that Sanskritisation is an inbuilt, self-propelling process (see Hardiman, 1984: 214).

This view of Sanskritisation is due to the presumption that emulation gives status and that therefore every group undergoes the process willingly; second, the concept itself has its own limitations. As a result, Srinivas ignores the role of various other institutions and values and overlooks the role of Brahmanic ideology, politics and economy in shaping and hegemonising the specific cultural process he designated as Sanskritisation.

For Srinivas, 'Brahmanisation is subsumed in the wider process of sanskritisation though at some points Brahmanisation and sanskritisation are at variance with each other' (1989: 42). Srinivas prefers the term Sanskritisation to Brahmanisation as certain Vedic rites are confined to the Brahmanas (Srinivas, 1952: 30). Since he derives the concept of Brahmanisation from the top category of the varna-jati model, namely, the Brahmins, he finds the term narrow and, therefore, uses a common term to cover other categories of the twice-born, namely, the Kshatriyas and the Vaishyas. He takes the Sanskrit language and texts written in it as the basis for designating the process in question. In this way, he is able to present an innocuous term and a picture of a conflict-free process.

However, we derive the concept of Brahmanisation not from the category of Brahmins but from the ideology of Brahmanism, which, as stated earlier, prescribes models for social and religious/cosmic orders. Since it is Brahmanical ideology that determines the position of each caste category in the social hierarchy and their respective duties, we give primacy to the ideology rather than to the Brahmins themselves though their role as carriers of this ideology is important.

Srinivas notes the transmission of theological ideas embodied in the Sanskritic texts. In his words: 'sanskritisation means not only the adoption of new customs and habits but also exposure to new ideas and values which have found frequent expression in the vast body of Sanskritic literature, sacred as well as secular. '*Karma, dharma, papa, maya, samsara* and *moksha* are examples of some of the most common theological ideas and when people become sanskritised these words occur frequently in their talk' (Srinivas, 1989: 48). In fact, these ideas are part of the ideology of Brahmanism. Hence, all three models of Sanskritisation offered by Srinivas are squarely Brahmanism-centred since the reference groups he identifies for emulation are the castes grouped only under the first three 'twice-born' varnas. For us, Brahmanisation is a process by which the Brahmanical ideology and practices effect and influence the 'native' social institutions such as religion, caste, politics and economy. By this process, people are made to adopt ideas embodied in the Vedic-Brahmanic scriptures as the basis for organising their social and religious life.

In his attempt to explain the ways by which a village is articulated with the universe of Indian civilisation, Marriott (1955) argues that the village extends itself to form part of a wider society and system of relationship. His concepts of parochialisation and universalisation provide insight into historical transformation and the ways by which transmission of religious values and practices takes place from one tradition to another (Marriott, 1955: 211–18). Marriott provides illuminating evidence to show that 'Sanskritisation' has not replaced any aspect of the 'little tradition' by the 'great tradition'. According to Marriott, 'while elements of the great tradition have become parts of local festivals, they do not appear to have entered village festival custom at the expense of much that is or was the little tradition' (ibid.: 208). Thus, instead of one replacing the other, Sanskritic elements coexisted with native, vernacular elements to a large extent. This view indeed contradicts Srinivas' view.

STRUCTURALIST HOLISM

Dumont's (1988) holistic view seeks to place the system of Brahmanic Hindu beliefs and practices as central to his analysis of religion and society in India. His structuralist approach is shaped by his emphasis on religious beliefs and values. For Dumont (1970, 1986, 1988), the basic institution of Indian society is caste. He constructs the caste system in terms of values of hierarchy and separation based on the ideology of purity and pollution. The level of purity is the sole criterion for ranking of occupations and caste groups.

For Dumont's structural model what matters most is the extent or degree to which a particular caste occupation is pure and not the wealth or income it yields. As a result, for him, the politico-economic dimensions are unimportant or secondary aspects of the caste system. This is amply exhibited in his remark that, 'just as a religion in a way encompasses politics, so politics encompasses economics within itself. The difference is that the politico-economic domain is separated, named in a subordinate position as against religion whilst economics remain undifferentiated within politics' (1988: 165).

In his efforts to conceptualise the caste system from Indian sources and ideas, Dumont has failed to consider diverse textual sources and sociological and anthropological studies. As a consequence, for Dumont's holistic view a specific set of religious beliefs and values becomes central as a source and ideology. What Dumont calls the ideology of purity and pollution or impurity is nothing but the criteria set out by an ideology based on a body of beliefs and values embodied in the classical Sanskrit texts. We agree with Berreman's critique that apart from its being a distorted version of the caste system, Dumont's conception of caste is based upon 'the limited, biased, albeit scholarly sources of evidence' (Berreman, 1979: 162).

We do not underestimate the role of the system of ideas constituting purity and impurity in sustaining the caste system. But it is not realistic to reduce the perpetuation of the caste system to these ideas alone by giving them a central place, without being aware of the institutional framework within which such ideas and practices flourish. It is important to place the caste system in a wider socio-economic and political context than the narrow religious ideas of purity and impurity in order to reveal the ramifications of the whole system.

Dumont is not convincing as to how those numerous castes in the middle rung of the hierarchy occupy a specific rank while the lower castes, considered permanently polluted and hence impure, are destined to remove the temporary pollution of higher castes. He, in fact, avoids the problem by stating that caste as an institution, by encompassing power within status, accommodates itself to power. Thus, Dumont overlooks other essentials of the caste system, which are mainly shaped and sustained by politico-economic factors (Tanaka, 1991: 6).

Dumont regards Sanskrit texts as sources embodying the indigenous ideas concerning the caste system. Though we do not dispute the fact that the dichotomous notion of purity and impurity is derived from indigenous ideas, it is pertinent to ask whose ideas these are: and how they are produced, sustained and reproduced in society throughout history. Since the indigenous ideas Dumont refers to and relies on are mainly drawn from Sanskrit sources, his conception of the caste system restricts the scope of his sociological-anthropological method to a segment of ideas that lead him to perceive a large number of castes as well as gods as merely adjuncts, which are, in fact, essential to the formation and functioning of the whole system.

The argument that impurity is an essential element to maintain purity in society is basically a specific religious view. This view, to our mind, inherits a bias and takes the social processes as given. Further, it blinds Dumont to the other essential aspects of the caste system including the interplay of politico-economic factors.

For us, caste ranking is a function of power relations and is a form of social inequality. Interdependence among various caste groups cannot be seen as a harmonious condition free of the conflicts prevailing in society. We consider the 'harmony' among people of a village to be a consequence of the control of upper caste(s) over the economy and economic activities. It is the control over resources, not just the caste strictures, which plays a crucial role in ranking and maintaining the caste system (Gough, 1961). It is, in fact, the access to resource that provided power and maintained it in favour of those who controlled the economy. Lewis states that 'In the past the potential contradictions between the interests of the farm and non-farm populations in the village were held in check by the power of the landholders and by lack of alternatives for the untouchable and other low caste people' (1955: 151).

If we place the caste system in an economic context as opposed to Dumont's religious interpretation, we arrive at a different conclusion. As Habib puts it:

> ... the menial castes were deprived of any pretension to setting up as tillers of land themselves, they could, therefore, form a vast reservoir of landless labour with exceptionally depressed wages. This would in turn correspondingly enlarge the surplus that the ruling class could derive from the peasant. At the same time that share in the surplus could obtain for the ruling class a larger return in terms of goods and services because of the larger productivity form 'special skill' transmitted through the system of hereditary occupation while wages could be further depressed owing to the low station assigned to artisan castes. (1986: 38–39)

Beidelman argues that the caste system entails inequality in the distribution of power. He too considers land as the major integrative factor around which the caste and village system operate. 'Although castes are separated, dependence upon land unites castes about *jajmans* by means of this coerced dependence. Such coercive integration is supported and reaffirmed by ritual and ceremonies which *jajmans* hold both to emphasise the *jajman–kamin* relationship and to enhance or affirm their status' (Beidelman, 1959: 75).

Dumont argues that Beidelman confuses inequality with exploitation, stating that Beidelman 'failed to see that the system assures subsistence to each proportionately to his status' (1988: 32). This assertion of Dumont is derived from the theory of compensation known as karma prescribed by the ideology of Brahmanism. We entirely agree with Berreman's criticism of Dumont on this count:

> It also assures life, comfort, health, self-respect, food, shelter, learning, pleasure, society, education, legal redress, rewards in the next life and all of the other necessary and valued things proportionately to status. And that is what exploitation is, that is what oppression is: providing for those at the top 'proportionately to status' and at the expense of those at the bottom. This does not distinguish inequality from exploitation, it identifies the common characteristics, and caste systems in India and elsewhere epitomises this relationship. That the relationship is described as paternalism, that it is rationalised as being for the benefit of all—is universal and hardly surprising since such descriptions are purveyed by the beneficiaries of the system who arrogate to themselves the role of spokesmen for it. (Berreman, 1979: 159–60)

Dumont (1986: 349–448) observes that deities in the Hindu temples are divided into two groups, namely, pure vegetarian deities and impure carnivorous deities. For Dumont, the principle that activates the caste system is identical with the principle that gives the religious pantheon its structure. Therefore, the existence of impure deities becomes essential for the maintenance of pure vegetarian deities. The carnivorous impure deities are made to perform the duties of doorkeepers and guardians and are made into an 'indispensable adjunct to the worship of pure deities—an inseparable part of the same system of activity' (Sharma, 1970: 7). A parallel hierarchy as in the caste system is thus established by the application of the same principle of purity and impurity, a principle that Dumont makes central to the study of both religion and society, for, to him 'the religious order (ideas of the gods and their relationships with man) and the ideology of the caste system are inseparable' (Tanaka, 1991: 15).

Thus, though the Brahmins and Brahmanic traditions played a central role in shaping Hinduism, it is important to place it in a wider context. As Biardeau put it: 'Orthodox Brahmanism, which is closer to the Revelation is not the ancestor of modern Hinduism: it is its permanent heart, the implicit model for or/and against which Bhakti, Tantric and all their sects have been constituted' (1989: 15). In our view, it is the hegemonic nature of orthodox Brahmanic ideology that holds the key to understanding social and cultural processes in India. It cannot be fully understood without taking into account its inter-dependent relationship with other aspects of society. For us, religion is a part of society and it can only be understood in a wider socio-economic and political context. We consider that the ideology of purity and pollution is a device by which social inequality by caste is defined and legitimised in terms of hierarchy and separation. As mentioned earlier, the source of the ideas of purity and pollution is to be found in the Brahmanical values and beliefs embodied in the classical Sanskritic texts.

TOWARDS A MARXIAN METHOD: THE CONCEPT OF HEGEMONY

The Marxist formulation in general regards the reality of base, primarily economic relations, as being reflected or reproduced directly in the superstructure, which is considered to be the realm of all ideological and cultural activities. We regard this as inadequate to explain the complex nature of Indian social and cultural realities and processes, which are not a mere reflection of primary economic activities. It is very important for us to recognise the relative autonomy of the various components of the superstructure. This autonomy is not a mere separation from the base but a fluid dynamic condition in which 'homologous structures' are in existence. Gramsci's (1975) concept of hegemony would help us understand the role of Brahmanic ideology in influencing and shaping various sociocultural processes in India. The concept of hegemony refers to an active and continuing process, not to a static condition. Gramsci points out that a class sustains its dominance not just by an organisation of force but with a moral and intellectual leadership. He also lays emphasis on the fact that compromises are made with a variety of allies who are unified as a social bloc of forces. This bloc manifests and articulates a basis of consent for a certain social order. It is in this social order that the hegemony of a dominant class is created, sustained and recreated in the web of various institutions and social relations. The implied consent is not always achieved through force, but by various other means, like ideology and religion, which have a capacity to influence people towards a specific world view.

The concept of hegemony postulates the existence of something that is truly total and not merely secondary or superstructural like the weak sense of ideology, something lived at such a depth as to saturate society to the extent that it constitutes the substance and limit of common sense for most people under its influence (Williams, 1980: 37). It is also important to state that the notion of hegemony implies and emphasises the element of domination. Hegemony, in fact, contains highly complex internal structures. These are renewed, recreated, defended, continuously challenged and to some extent modified (ibid.: 37–38). Therefore, hegemony, with dominance as an integral part, constitutes variations and contradictions, besides, to some extent, sets of alternatives.

In any given society at a particular period, there are certain systems of practices, meanings and values that are central and dominant. They are well organised and persist as they are influential and effective. They not only exist in the realm of abstract ideas, but are practised everyday in concrete situations.

Therefore, hegemony is not 'mere opinion' or 'mere manipulation'. In fact hegemony is a whole body of practices and expectations: our assignments of energy, our ordinary understanding of the nature of man and of his world. It is a set of meanings and values, which as they are experienced as practices appear as reciprocally confirming. It thus constitutes a sense of reality for most people in the society, a sense of the absolute, an experienced reality beyond which it is very difficult for most members of the society to move in most areas of their lives. (ibid.: 38)

If we look at Hinduism and Hindu society in this light, it becomes very clear that the Brahmanic tradition had a hegemonic role, which resulted in Brahmins acquiring supremacy in the social hierarchy and monopoly in religious affairs. This evolved over time through a complex process in which politics and economy played an important role. In other words, the relationship between the Brahmanic tradition

and the structures of power and authority in the past would throw
some light on the emergence of dominance within the socio-religious
sphere. Patronage of the temples and Brahmins by the king and the
spiritual authority of the Brahmins to legitimise political authority
articulate the evolution of a process in which the Brahmanic tradition
had a central place with a political function. It is, therefore, important
to situate the study of society and religion in India in a wider context
in which institutions are developed or modified or transformed into
something different and new.

Religion in Tamil Nadu, for example, is a distinct variant of
Hinduism in which both the Bhakti and Brahmanical traditions are
present. This religious synthesis can be termed Bhakti Hinduism, for
which the Agamas and Saiva Siddantha form a scriptural basis. Bhakti
Hinduism evolved and was shaped throughout the medieval period.
It emerged in a context in which an active alliance between the kings,
Brahmins and upper-caste non-Brahmans existed. It has historically
been centred around what are now known as Brahmanical temples
devoted to Lord Siva and Lord Vishnu. Hence, these 'Brahmanical'
temples display a very strong regional character with vernacular and
regional traditions. It is very evident that the evolution of the
synthesis comprising mythological elements from the classical Puranas
and epics such as the *Mahabharata* and *Ramayana* and local/native
materials with Tamil origin, orientation and experiences provided the
ideological foundation for the temples in Tamil Nadu. For instance,
sthalapuranam of the 'Brahmanical' temples reveal the process of
localisation of the universal deities such as Lord Siva. This process
of localisation, which took place at the time of the Bhakti Movement
with the active support of the dominant sections of society during
that period, fashioned the evolution of religion and society in Tamil-
speaking areas (Shulman, 1980: 3–7). The Brahmanical temples
indeed grew into an institution with a specialised priestly community
during and after the Bhakti Movement (sixth to ninth century) when
the huge temples were established and Agamas, the scriptural base
of the 'Brahmanical' temples were introduced. The scriptural and
mythical base not only supported the temples as institutions but also
sustained the dominant social groups, which enjoyed a privileged
status and complete access to the temples and their endowments. This
is how the Brahmanical temples as an ideological institution legitimised

the then social structure, which was marked by a rigid social hierarchy, oppression and exploitation.

A brief consideration of the evolution of Bhakti Hinduism centred round the Brahmanical temples in Tamil Nadu will reveal the manner in which the Brahmanical tradition attained dominance by incorporating the Bhakti traditions. The historical context, the establishment of the dominance of the peasantry of the plains and their culture against that of the non-peasant warrior tribes of the hills and forests, between the sixth and ninth centuries, created a need for a cohesive ideology. This was provided by the long associated Brahmin groups. Brahmins were able to offer an ideology because of their monopoly over the maintenance, development and transmission of Sanskritic religious knowledge. The ideology was, however, a unique one. It was the ideology of Bhakti schools, which accorded a legitimate and high place in the Brahmanical religion to the non-Brahmins as well as to popular folk traditions. It indeed facilitated the Brahmins receiving extensive material support and enjoying some measure of autonomy from state control in return for according a high status to the dominant non-Brahmin peasantry. The Brahmins were motivated to enter into this 'alliance' by the great strides Buddhism and Jainism had made in south India around this period which seriously threatened their position and privilege (Stein, 1980: 72–89).

This alliance between the Brahmins and the dominant peasantry continued till about the twelfth century, by which time a new social base of power comprising a combination of the dominant peasantry and local traditional artisan groups began to develop. Concomitant with this were other developments like the growth of towns, increased Brahmanisation of the non-Brahmin population and its participation in the Brahmanical religious institutions such as temples and monasteries. The Bhakti religion undoubtedly contributed to these developments since it opened the doors of the classical Brahmanical religion to the large non-Brahmin householder population, especially its upper stratum. Stein vividly demonstrates that for a period spanning the sixth and the sixteenth centuries, groups and classes rising to economic and political dominance acquired higher status by making gifts like land to Brahmins and temples. Brahmins in return legitimised the claims of these classes. This 'alliance' between Brahmins, upper non-Brahmin castes and kings at the macro level existed throughout medieval south India. Brahmins and sectarian leaders helped to legitimise the political authority of kings and dominance of the upper castes who in turn extended material support and respect to the Brahmins (Stein, 1980).

It may be stressed that during the medieval period, temples functioned as a principal power centre along with the palaces from where the kings reigned. The state and the temples reinforced each other, with temples legitimising political authority while the state or the kings supported the temples and their functionaries with land grants and other resources, the kings and the local rich thus acting as protectors and patrons of the temples. The relationship of the temples with structures of power was unambiguous. It was regarded as a shared sovereignty between the gods and man.

In spite of the absence of any centralised authority to link the temples of all denominations during the pre-British period, the way in which the medieval state exercised its control over numerous temples demonstrates the close association which existed between the temples, denominations (or sects) and kings. Appadurai's model provides an insight into the process by which the king, through endowments, placed himself in an active relationship with the deity, who was contextualised in a distributive system. This enabled the king to receive the honours as well as perform his 'dharmic' duty as protector of his subjects and various institutions including the temples. The king as an administrator, not as a legislator, exercised his royal commands to maintain his control over the temples. The king's mandatory function in resolving conflicts by arbitration had wide acceptance. The affiliation or association of the king with his agents (or ministers), local assemblies, 'sectarian' groups and leaders, temple functionaries and worshippers was not established and sustained in the line of the Weberian model of bureaucracy based on legal-rational principles (Weber, 1965a). Instead, this association articulated through power relations, provided a human framework which was sustained by the king. In turn, the king received active support from the former. It may be added here that the human framework or social base of these temples including the 'sectarian' (or denominational) groups and their leaders formed the immediate support base of the king's authority (Appadurai, 1977: 50– 55; 1981: 68–74).

Throughout the medieval period, the alliance forming a social bloc continued to be dominant in exercising religious, intellectual and political authority and leadership. Acceptance by the majority of the lower caste status governed by the principle of ritual pollution was achieved not by coercion but by the process of hegemony in which consent was secured through the ideology of Brahmanism. It was not simply political force that succeeded in making people believe in the institution of caste but the theory of karma and of the cycle of rebirth. In the process, hierarchy and separation became important organising principles. Ideas of karma and dharma brought about a passive endorsement of the religious principle of pollution governing certain forms of social inequalities in India. It was this social and political milieu in which the Dalits were ideologically separated as Untouchables and excluded from certain social as well as religious spheres.

The social bloc, which had exclusive rights over the temples for centuries, began to disintegrate slowly with British intervention in temple affairs. The efforts of the British government to root out corruption among the traditional trustees and other administrators of the temples were resisted. The temple entry proclamation in 1930 was opposed vehemently.

Opening of temples to Untouchables and other lower non-Brahman castes was contested on the ground that their entry would destroy the sanctity of the holy temples. An enormous amount of conflict arose between the state and various groups and individuals involved in temple affairs. This conflict arising out of changes brought about by governments both before and after Independence demonstrates the extent of opposition from those who enjoyed power and status derived from their traditional monopoly over the affairs of temples. The temple priests and traditional trustees especially, challenged various reform measures in courts of law (Appadurai, 1981; Fuller, 1984; Good, 1989). The arbitration of conflicts by courts of law, especially after Independence, meant that the secular constitution and other modern laws, not the religious texts, became the basis of the interpretation of certain practices in the realm of temples (Baird, 1976). This led to certain aspects of the temples being seen by the courts of law as secular while the basic character of the temple was accepted as religious.

It may be stressed that the principal purpose of state intervention in the affairs of the temples both before and after Independence was to remove corruption amongst trustees and mismanagement of resources including temple funds and endowments attached to temples in the form of large estates. The alleged extortion and lack of Agamic knowledge of the priests and their consequent incompetence in organisation and performance of worship accentuated the demands of the reformists and the efforts of successive governments since Independence in Tamil Nadu (Fuller, 1984; Kennedy, 1974; Mudaliar, 1975). It is adequate to state here that the British government had established the foundation for the bureaucratic control of the temples by instituting the Hindu Religious Endowment Board in 1925. With subsequent modifications in the relevant Act, which legalised bureaucratic control, the department of Hindu Religious and Charitable Endowments (HRCE) was established on a firm footing during the post-Independence period. In the light of the growing influence of the Dravidian ideology and its political success in 1967, when the DMK formed its government in Tamil Nadu, the pace of change was accelerated. It may be stated here that the mutually complementary functioning of temples and the state during the pre-British period has now been reversed by the modern state by universalising Hindu temples. There is indeed a process of de-hegemonisation of the temples at one level and of society at another, for upper-caste monopoly in various areas of social life is also in constant decline.

Thus, the concept of hegemony would help to reveal the diverse nature of Indian society and religion. It would certainly explain the process by which modes of dominance and subordination unfolded over time in India: the manner in which caste—class relations, centred around the ownership of the means of production such as land existed in the past; the way human labour was tapped with the ideology of caste determining the social hierarchy and legitimising oppression and exploitation.

That the principle of purity and pollution and social hierarchy existed even among the members of lower castes indicates the powerful influence of Brahmanical ideology, on the one hand, and the acceptance of the caste ideology by the lower castes, on the other. The Brahmanical ideology in a relatively peaceful manner swayed the lower-caste people so that subordination and incorporation into the Brahmanical ideological domain was accepted. The theory of karma and the belief in fatalism made these people endure inequality and oppression. To unravel the ways in which first the Dalits and now the tribals have been incorporated into the Brahmanical social organisation and religious pantheon now termed as Hinduism, studies will have to be undertaken at micro, regional and macro levels. Reinterpretation of cultural symbols, which embody the ideological elements drawn from Brahmanism is most important. For a large section of Dalits, caste and the principle of purity and pollution are a reality offered by God from which one cannot escape. A change in this belief system of the Dalits, which is modelled on the Brahmanical ideology holds the key to a major social transformation bringing about social equality. Change also needs to come from within.

REFERENCES AND SELECT BIBLIOGRAPHY

Appadurai, A. (1977) 'Kings, Sects and Temples in South India, 1350–1700 AD', *Indian Economic and Social History Review*, 14(1): 47–73.

———. (1981) *Worship and Conflict under Colonial Rule: A South Indian Case*. Cambridge: University Press.

Baird, R.D. (1976) 'Religion and the Secular: Categories for Religious Conflict and Religious Change in Independent India', in B.L. Smith (ed.), *Religion and Social Conflict in South Asia*, pp. 87–103. Leiden: E.J. Brill.

Baker, C.J. (1976) *The Politics of South India 1920–1937*. Cambridge: Cambridge University Press.

Baker, C.J. and D.A. Washbrook (1975) *South India: Political Institutions and Political Change 1880–1940*. New Delhi: Vikas.

Barnett, M.R. (1976) *The Politics of Cultural Nationalism in South India*. Princeton: Princeton University Press.

Beidelman, T.O. (1959) *A Comparative Analysis of the Jajmani System*. New York: J.J. Augusun.

Berreman, G.D. (1979) *Caste and Other Inequities: Essays on Inequality*. Meerut: Folklore Institute.

Béteille, André (1965) *Caste, Class and Power: Changing Patterns of Stratification in a Tanjore Village*. Berkeley: University of California Press.

Biardeau, M. (1989) *Hinduism*. New Delhi: Oxford University Press.

Dumont, L. (1970) *Religion, Politics and History in India*. Paris: Mouton.

———. (1986) *A South Indian Subcaste: Social Organisation and Religion of the Pramalai Kallar*. New Delhi: Oxford University Press.

———. (1988) *Homo Hierarchicus: The Caste System and Its Implications*. New Delhi: Oxford University Press.

Durkheim, Emile (1964) *Elementary Forms of the Religious Life*. London: Allen & Unwin.

Fuller, C.J. (1984) *Servants of the Goddess: The Priests of a South Indian Temple*. Cambridge: Cambridge University Press.

———. (1988) 'The Hindu Temple and Indian Society', in M.V. Fox (ed.), *Temple in Society*. Winona Lake: Eisenbrauns.

Geertz, C. (1973) *The Interpretation of Cultures*. New York: Basic Books.

Good, A. (1989) 'Law, Legitimacy, and the Hereditary Rights of Tamil Temple Priests', *Modern Asian Studies*, 23: 233–57.

Gopalkrishnan, S. (1981) *Political Movements in South India. 1914–1929*. Madras: New Era Publications.

Gough, K. (1961) 'The Social Structure of a Tanjore Village', in M. Marriott (ed.), *Village India: Studies in Little Community*, pp. 46–62. Bombay: Asia Publishing House.

Gramsci, A. (1975) *Selections from the Prison Note Books*. New York: International Publishers.

Habib, I. (1986) 'Theories of Social Change in South Asia', *The Journal of Social Studies*, 33: 34–54.

Hardiman, D. (1984) 'Adivasi Assertion in South Gujarat: The Devi Movement of 1922–3', in Ranajit Guha (ed.), *Subaltern Studies III: Writings on South Asian History and Society*, pp. 134–51. New Delhi: Oxford University Press.

Karve, I. (1953) *Kinship Organisation in India*. Poona: Deccan College.

Kennedy, R. (1974) 'Status and Control of Temples in Tamil Nadu', *Indian Economic and Social History Review*, 11(4): 260–90.

Leavitt, J. (1992) 'Cultural Holism in the Anthropology of South Asia: The Challenge of Regional Traditions', *Contributions to Indian Sociology*, (n.s.) 26: 13–49.

Lewis, Oscar (1955) *Village Life in Northern India*. New York: Vintage Books.

Marriott, M. (1955) 'Little Communities in an Indigenous Civilisation', in M. Marriott (ed.), *Village India: Studies in Little Community*, pp. 12–31. Bombay: Asia Publishing House.

Moffatt, M. (1979) *An Untouchable Community in South India: Structure and Consensus*. Princeton: Princeton University Press.

Mudaliar, Chandra (1975) *State and Religious Endowments in Madras*. Madras: University Press.

Ramanujam, A.K. (1972). *Speaking of Siva*. Harmondsworth: Penguin Books.

Rao, M.S.A. (1979) *Social Movements and Social Transformation: A Study of Two Backward Classes Movements in India*. New Delhi: Macmillan.

Ryerson, C. (1988) *Regionalism and Religion: The Tamil Renaissance and Popular Hinduism*. Bangalore: The Christian Literature Society.

Sastri, K.A.N. (1955) *History of South India*. London: Oxford University Press.

———. (1963) *Development of Religion in South India*. Bombay: Orient Longman.

Sharma, U. (1970) 'The Problem of Village Hinduism: Fragmentation and Integration', *Contributions to Indian Sociology*, (n.s.) 4: 1–21.

Shulman, D.D. (1980) *Tamil Temple Myths: Sacrifice and Divine Marriage in the South Indian Saiva Tradition*. Princeton: Princeton University Press.

Singer, M. (1959) *Traditional India: Structure and Change*. Philadelphia: American Folklore Society.

———. (1972) *When a Great Tradition Modernizes*. New Delhi: Vikas Publishing House.

Singer, M. and B.S. Cohn (eds) (1968) *Structure and Change in Indian Society*. Chicago: Aldine Publishing Company.

Srinivas, M.N. (1952) *Religion and Society among the Coorgs of South India*. Oxford: Clarendon Press.

———. (1955) 'The Social System of a Mysore Village', in M. Marriott (ed.), *Village India*, pp. 32–45. Chicago: Chicago University Press.

———. (1962) *Caste in Modern India and Other Essays*. Bombay: Asia Publishing House.

———. (1966) *Social Change in Modern India*. Bombay: Allied Publishers.

———. (1984) 'Some Reflections on the Nature of Caste Hierarchy', *Contributions to Indian Sociology*, (n.s.) 18: 151–67.

———. (1989) *The Cohesive Role of Sanskritization and Other Essays*. New Delhi: Oxford University Press.

Staal, T.F. (1963) 'Sanskrit and Sanskritization', *Journal of Asian Studies*, 22: 261–75.

Stein, Burton (1980) *Peasant State and Society in Medieval South India*. New Delhi: Oxford University Press.

Tanaka, M. (1991) *Patrons, Devotees and Goddesses: Ritual and Power among the Tamil Fishermen of Sri Lanka*. Kyoto: Institute for Research in Humanities.

Weber, Max (1965a) *The Theory of Social and Economic Organisation*. New York: Free Press.

———. (1965b) *The Sociology of Religion*. London: Methuen and Co. Ltd.

Williams, R. (1980) *Problems in Materialism and Culture*. London: Verso.

9

Hinduisation of Adivasis: A Case Study from South Gujarat

ARJUN PATEL

THE PROBLEM

Culture plays an important social role in every community so also among the Adivasis.[1]Attempts have been made to understand this assumption. The changing social and cultural life of the Adivasis has been the subject matter of studies done by some anthropologists and sociologists. J. Troisi (1979) has classified the study of Adivasi religion into two major trends: evolutionist and functionalist. The evolutionists propounded a number of theories regarding the origin of religion. The common assumption among nineteenth century evolutionists such as Tylor, Morgan, Spencer and others was that primitive religion grew out of ignorance and intellectual inadequacy. They emphasised the social usefulness of various religions, but looked at them as bodies of erroneous beliefs and illusory practices. The other approach was functionalist and was advocated by Durkheim, Radcliffe-Brown, Malinowski and Evans-Pritchard. They wanted to show that religion is essential to social cohesion and community feeling in society. According to Radcliffe-Brown, the existence and continuance of an orderly social life depended on the presence of collective sentiments in the minds of the individual members. Evans-Pritchard criticised the theories put forward to explain religion as fantasy or illusion. He criticised sociologists and anthropologists who imposed their own cultural criteria on a quite incompatible subject matter. He advocated the importance of analysing religious facts in relation to the entire institutional system of society.

The religious aspect of Adivasi societies has been studied by many, especially European travellers, missionaries, historians, etc. Broadly, these studies can be classified into four groups. The first group (Dehon, 1906; Ferreira, 1965; Roy, 1925 and others) gives ethnographic details about the religion of different Adivasi groups. The second group (Bose, 1941; Sachchidananda, 1964, 1970; Sahay, 1962 and others) of studies tries to depict the different cultural processes among Adivasis such as assimilation, Sanskritisation, the Adivasi-caste continuum, Christianisation, cultural changes, etc. Various movements such as revitalisation, Bhagats, messianic movements, etc., form a third group (Das, 1968–69; Paul, 1919; Sen, 1968; Swain, 1969 and others) of studies. While a fourth group (Banerjee, 1968; Hajra, 1970; Radcliffe-Brown, 1964 and others) describes relations between different Adivasi religions and their social structure. All these groups focus on the process of cultural transactions, contacts of 'little traditions' with 'great traditions'.[2]

These approaches have dominated the scene for years, but now efforts have been made to apply a different approach to the phenomenon of Hinduisation of the Adivasis. This new approach has seen the light of day during the 1990s and particularly after the demolition of the Babri Musjid at Ram Janma Bhumi at Ayodhya. The antagonism between Hindus and Muslims has come to a head in recent years. In this context, researches on Hindu nationalism have become an important area of study today (Bajaj, 1993; Graham, 1990; Iyer, 1991; Jayaprasad, 1991; Nandy et al., 1995; Panikkar, 1991; Rajkishore, 1995; Shourie, 1987). The rise of Hindutva and the BJP as a political party has opened new areas of research for scholars. They have now begun to look into this matter and how it effects the Dalits and other marginalised groups in India. Politics and society have once again become a major focus of inquiry. Recently, Yogendra K. Malik and V.B. Singh (1995) have made a praiseworthy study of this subject. In their book *Hindu Nationalists in India: The Rise of the Bharatiya Janata Party*, they have analysed the circumstances leading to the emergence of the BJP as a major political force in the 1980s and 1990s. The study has been a valuable contribution to the subject, but there are shortcomings in it. For instance, it covers the subject in broad outline but does not deal with local groups and events or regional tendencies. But, of course, efforts have been made in the right direction.

Achyut Yagnic (1995) has contributed an article titled 'Hindutva as a Savrana Purana', in which he has made an attempt to describe the rise of communal feelings among the Hindus in Gujarat. Recently, a political scientist, Ghanshyam Shah (1991, 1992, 1993, 1994, 1995) has written a couple of articles on the rise of the BJP in Gujarat. In one of these articles (1994) he tries to analyse the rise of the BJP among Backward Classes. Gopal Guru (1991), another political scientist, has pointed out in an article why certain sections of the Dalit community are getting attracted to the rightist movements; why and how these reactionary movements are coaxing Dalits into Hinduism and spiritualising Ambedkar (ibid.: 339).

Thus, we have two confronting views on the Hinduisation of certain social groups. According to the first view, the process of integrating Adivasis into Hinduism is a natural process. According to the other view, it is not natural but something imposed on them from the outside by the Hindus. I find both viewpoints extreme and according to my view, reality lies somewhere in between these two.

The present chapter will follow this line of approach. It describes how the Adivasis, particularly of south Gujarat, are Hinduised by Hindutva organisations which have successfully exploited religious beliefs and emotions for political purposes in order to increase the Hindu vote. The term 'Hinduisation' in this chapter is given not only a religious but also a political meaning. Hinduisation means that one group consciously manipulates others for its own material and political benefit. The manipulation is done in such a systematic way that the exploited group/section does not realise the intention and intricacies behind it. This chapter also briefly highlights the possible consequences of Hinduisation for the Adivasis. It is based on my long association with the Adivasis of Gujarat. I have referred to secondary sources for necessary supplementary information.

THE ADIVASIS OF SOUTH GUJARAT

As the name itself indicates, the Adivasis are considered the original inhabitants of Gujarat. They constitute about 14 per cent of the total population and are divided into 17 groups and each of them is further subdivided into five or six subgroups. The main subgroups among the Adivasis of south Gujarat are Gamit, Chodhari, Dungari Bhil, Rathava, Tadvi, Vasava, Dhodiya, Halpati (for details of such groups, see: Joshi, 1996; Lobo, 1996; Patel, 1996a, 1996b, 1996c; Pinto, 1996; D.S. Punalekar 1996; S.P. Punalekar, 1996; Shah, 1994).

There are also differences of status among them. Except for the Dublas, they are concentrated in certain areas on the eastern frontiers of the hilly tract of the Sahyadris and Satpuda ranges and hence have become a politically very significant group. The Adivasis of south Gujarat are concentrated in the eastern belt,[3] which covers eight districts, namely, Dang, Valsad, Surat, Bharuch, Vadodara, Panchmahal, Banaskantha and Sabarkantha. Some Adivasi regions (Desai, n.d.) are rather poor in infrastructure facilities and are also agriculturally backwards. The living conditions in Gujarat were so poor that the Adivasis were not able to earn enough to survive throughout the year in their native place, hence they migrated to other areas (Patel and Desai, 1992). About a quarter million Adivasis migrated as seasonal workers. Poverty, illiteracy, bad health, unemployment, lack of drinking water, etc., are urgent problems. Of course, a few Adivasis have been fortunate enough to take advantage of government aid schemes since 1960 and find a place in the mainstream culture of Indian society. Adivasis were considered to be outside the Hindu social system and they were not included in the governmental SC aid programmes because they did not have the stigma of untouchability. Ghurye (1963), considered Adivasis as backward Hindus.

INFLUENCE OF HINDUISATION ON ADIVASIS

The influence of Hindu religion on the Adivasi community has early beginnings. Old Adivasis in the interior villages of the Bharuch and Vadodara districts revealed in talks that their forefathers were often helpful in guiding pilgrims, who came for *parikrama* on the banks of the Narmada. The Narmada parikrama covers the area from Bharuch of Gujarat to Amarkantak in Madhya Pradesh. While visiting one shrine after another in the hills, the Adivasis used to beat drums to scare away animals. The annual fairs and *hat*s (weekly markets), considered as an integral part of Adivasi culture, were also important meeting places for Adivasis and Hindus. There are several studies available that have brought to light how the Adivasis have absorbed certain elements from the Hindu religion. These studies deal with the religious beliefs and rituals of the Adivasis. There appears to be much similarity between the various beliefs and practices of the Adivasis and the Hindus. Singh (1993a), Sahay (1967, 1980), Srivastava (1958) and others have shown how some of the Adivasi groups have been integrated into the Hindu social order.

Although the impact of Hindu religion on the Adivasi community has been great in the last decade or so, it did in fact begin a long time ago. Evidence is found in some of the temples, for instance in Surpaneswer in Rajpipla taluka and Hanfeswer in Chhotaudepur taluka in south Gujarat, which point to the fact that the spread of Hindu gods and goddesses in the Adivasi region has early beginnings. There are a few old Hindu shrines and temples from ancient times on the bank of the river Narmada. All these temples have been centres from which Vedic culture has spread in the Adivasi region. The temples in the Adivasi belt are living examples of the cultural synthesis between Hindu and Adivasi traditions (Gazetteer of India, 1979).

The Brahmin priest served as a model for the Adivasis and through him they learnt to imitate the beliefs and lifestyle of the Hindus. Priests, generally, do not take meat or alcoholic drinks, which is common among Adivasis. The Brahmin bathes regularly and wears a sacred thread. We noticed that temples on the banks of the Narmada provide shelter to the *yatris* (pilgrims) and utensils for cooking. In Hanfeswer, we heard that the priest did not encounter any difficulty in doing his duties as the upper-caste people stayed in Naswadi, Chhotaudepur, Vadodara, etc., offering grains and other necessities to the temple as *dan* (gift).

The princes also encouraged Hindu religious activities. I was told that the prince of Rajpipla attended the *mela* (fair) of Surpaneswer regularly around the beginning of the ninth century. Some of the temples in the Adivasi belt are considered important *dhams* (sacred places). There are many instances in which the local raja has contributed to the renovation of a temple from time to time before Independence. In some places, the rajas employed Brahmins to perform regular worship in the temple and manage its affairs. In Hanfeswer I was told that land was given to the priest for the maintenance of the temple. In Hanf village, thousands of rupees had been invested for water supply in the village. Government officials, politicians and social workers sometimes pay visits to the temple and they always show a readiness to help in all possible ways.[4]

The process of Hinduisation was speeded up after the middle of the nineteenth century in the region. This rule introduced certain procedures and regulations that increased the interaction of the Adivasis with others. The influx of moneylenders, traders, contractors and non-Adivasi peasants further accelerated the process. Hinduisation was given a fresh impetus in the nineteenth century with the new Bhakti movements (Singh, 1993a: 11). The great influence of these movements on the Adivasi people has been one of the important instances of the interaction of the Adivasi people with Hinduism.

The Hindu revival movement or neo-Hinduism,[5] which emerged in the first decade of the present century, is also part of the campaign to bring the so-called lower social groups under the spiritual and social umbrella of Hinduism. It makes it possible for such lower groups to rise in the social scale. This possibility fulfils the aspirations of many Adivasis, particularly the ambitious ones and it also gives them a new sense of identity. One of the aims of the new Hindu revival movement has been to prevent Christian influence on the Adivasis and to purify them so that they become acceptable to upper-caste Hindus.[6]

The influence of Hindu movements in the Adivasi area is quite old. Lal (1977, 1982) has described such movements in the southern Gujarat Adivasi belt in the period 1920–50. Recently, Lobo has studied the phenomenon and he found such Hindu sectarian movements in various talukas of Surat and the Bharuch districts. Some of the most prominent Hindu sects are Sanathan, Mokshmarg, Satkeval, Nairant, Ramand (belonging or relating to the Ramanuja sect), Kabir, Swadhyay and Jaygurudev (for details about each sectarian movement and its spread see Lancy Lobo [1992, 1995]). The Adivasis, particularly the educated ones, have joined different Hindu movements and are now emulating the Hindus in order to win acceptability and esteem among caste-Hindus (Lobo, 1992: 54). It is to be noted here that the Gandhians have implemented some welfare measures for the uplift of the Adivasis and are trying to civilise them (Desai, 1982; Joshi, 1992, 1996; Punalekar, 1993; Shah, 1995). Affiliation to such movements means cultural change, a new lifestyle (dress, decorum, rituals, customs and practices) and a new sense of identity.

The interaction between Adivasis and Hindus has augmented in scope due to better communication and to the fact that Adivasis have been constantly on the move as seasonal migrant workers. The district gazetteer on Vadodara (Gazetteer of India, 1979: Vadodara) noted that as a result of the intensive interactions of the Adivasi people with the Hindus, they no longer remained isolated. Their religion, language, habits and social customs, are being greatly influenced by the Hindu community to which they bear close linguistic and racial affinities (ibid.: 190–91).

CHANGING ADIVASI CULTURE

The Adivasis, though rich in local culture, began to feel inferior to people of non-Adivasi culture since the introduction of the market economy by the caste-Hindus in this region from the middle of the nineteenth century. Since then, Adivasi culture has greatly changed and a mixture of Hindu and Adivasi elements are found in their socio-cultural life. We observed during our stay in Adivasi areas that the *bedevo*, that is, the Adivasi priest, was increasingly losing his importance in the cultural and ritual life in the community. He is gradually being replaced by the Brahmin priest. Many Adivasis have begun to believe that calling a Brahmin priest for sacred rites is a sign of progress. This is true for most Adivasis such as the Dungari Bhils in the interior. Now Brahmins are officiating at rituals and ceremonies, at birth, marriage, death, etc., among Adivasis. We observed that our neighbour, a Brahmin priest, at Vaghrali village in Rajpipla taluka, where my institute, the Centre for Social Studies, has opened a field office for monitoring and evaluation work of the Narmada Dam project, had no spare time as he was continuously busy in performing one or the other religious activities among the Adivasis.

Today Adivasis are gradually adopting the Brahmanical value system. They have also started performing the *shraddha* (last rites) and the *chhathi puja* (religious worship for strength) ceremony. Their food habits are also changing in imitation of upper-caste Hindus. In this regard, the impact of Guru Vishvanath Maharaj among the Dhanka Tadvis, who are found in 72 villages of Rajpipla taluka is quite visible. Many Dhanka Tadvis have become vegetarians and teetotallers. Adivasi folk culture and traditional habits are changing under the cultural impact of upper-caste Hindus. The leaders among the Adivasis are influenced by Brahmanical ideas. Many Adivasi groups today have crystallised into two socially different groups. These groups are identified as the Bhagats and non-Bhagats in Dhanka Tadvi; and Variela and Sariela among the Chaudharas. The former group, which has adopted many Brahmanical customs, believes itself to be more advanced in its sociocultural life than the latter group (Joshi, 1995; Patel, 1996c; Punalekar, 1996; Shah, 1994). They also observe certain specific rules and procedures. For instance, the Bhagat Tadvi generally eat first when attending weddings among the non-Bhagat Tadvi people. Their utensils and drinking pots are of brass.

Traditional Adivasi culture is different from that of the Hindus. For example, the Adivasis have no concept of temples such as the Hindus have. They generally have their own *devasthan*, in which they keep small clay horses and cows and stones painted red.[7] The Adivasis offer goats, fowls and liquor to their *devasthan*s on social and cultural occasions. Liquor forms an integral part of Adivasi life. This is altogether different from the customs of upper-caste Hindus. But now they have begun to worship gods and goddesses from the Hindu pantheon. In many Adivasi houses, one will find photographs of Hindu gods and goddesses.

Stephen Fuchs (1973: 73) has pointed out that various Hindu deities like Vishnu and Shiva play an important part in the religious life of the primitive Adivasis. The panth (a Hindu sectarian movement) has also played a major role in changing the lifestyle of especially upper-class Adivasis. It is well-known that Adivasis, who are members of the Hindu panth, have stopped worshipping their traditional Adivasi gods. Instead they now worship Hindu gods (Shah and Shah, 1993: 335). Something similar has taken place in the case of festivals. Ind, Kunvari, etc., are the original festivals of the Adivasis in Gujarat, but now they have started celebrating Hindu festivals such as Diwali, Holi, Navratri, Ganesh Chaturthi, Ram Navami, etc. I was told that there is a big celebration of the Ganapati festival in Vansada taluka of Dharampur district. The Bania shop-keepers provide the necessary financial means for these activities. During my stay in different Adivasi villages, I noticed that the Adivasis are fully committed to Hindu beliefs and customs. Like

Hindus, they believe in the existence of a divine spirit, theories of birth and rebirth, *paap* (sin) and *punya* (merit), etc.

The influence of the Hindu caste has been very strong on the Adivasi social structure. Like Hindus, the Adivasis also have caste characteristics such as social divisions, hierarchies, endogamy, restrictions on food and drink, etc. The notion of purity and pollution has become firmly entrenched, particularly among educated and middle-class Adivasis. Many social anthropologists and sociologists such as Bose (1941) and Kalia (1961) have called attention to the fact that the Adivasis have borrowed ideas and institutions heavily from the Hindus.

Although the effect of Hinduisation on Adivasis can be easily seen, it is difficult to assess accurately the extent of its influence. Consulting the census report is one way of doing it. Within the period 1921–81, only 6 per cent of the Adivasi population identified themselves as Adivasis, whereas 87 per cent claimed that they were Hindus[8] by religion and 7 per cent claimed to be Christians. Scholars like K.S. Singh (1993a) and J. Troisi (1979), however, believe that in spite of the fact that Adivasis claim to be overwhelmingly Hindu or Christians, the Adivasi religion has not disappeared as many feared. According to K.S. Singh, a great many non-Brahmanic rituals and ideas still survive.

RELIGIOUS PRACTICES IN ADIVASI REGIONS

Numerous religious activists and leaders of various movements have been campaigning among Adivasis in order to propagate their ideas. The Nath Panthi Bhakta Parivar has been active in Adivasi areas in expounding its philosophy of religion. Its aim is to convince the Adivasis that the ultimate goal of religion is to realise God. *Bhagvat kathas* have been held by them at various places in the Adivasi-dominated regions. The Nath Panthi Bhakta Parivar's message is that through the medium of katha (story telling), man can attain the highest level of spiritual life. Saint Shri Laxmi Chand Bapu is propagating Hindu religion in Mahuva taluka through the Ramdev Bapu Parivar Nainas Nath. He is achieving his ends through *satsang* (spiritual gathering), *gaa-shala* (devotional gatherings), education, etc. Yog Vedant Samiti is active in one of the most backward taluka areas,

Dharampur, in south Gujarat. Shri Sureshanandji, a follower of Shri Ashramam Bapu, teaches a philosophy of life and advises people not to be too materialistic but to set apart some time for spiritual matters also. Gayatri Shaktipith is campaigning in Adivasi areas in order to make people aware of the modern nature of *Bhartiya* Vedic Shastras. I came across a few Adivasis who had learnt the Gayatri Mantra by heart and who repeated them at social gatherings and ceremonies.

The efforts to spread Vedic *sanskriti* culture in Adivasi areas has been made for many years. For instance, Pandit Satvalekar, who received the honour of Padma Bhushan, came to Killa Pardi near Vapi in 1948 and began his work through the Swadhyay Mandal. He has also translated the Vedic texts and rituals for the use of the tribals of this area. His activities have been concentrated in the southern part of Gujarat. The Ram Sevak samitis are working for *Hindujagran* in these areas.

Ram katha, Bhagvat katha and lecture series by various saints such as Morari Bapu,[9] Praful Shukla, Chhote Morari Bapu, Swami Shri Viditatmanand Saraswatiji, Nilesh Bapu, have been organised at various places in the Adivasi area of south Gujarat. The Adivasis, who reside in the adjoining areas, took part in these activities and received them very well.[10] These religious leaders emphasise the importance of Bhartiya sanskriti. They also advise people to liberate themselves from the bad habits of drinking and smoking, etc. They speak in favour of *lok seva, satnaj seva, arogya seva, vidya dan, sarva dharm sambhav* (these are some of the servise oriented organisations), etc. Several saints have settled permanently in towns in the Adivasi area and founded religious trusts such as the Sitaram Seva Trust, Sanskriti Parivar, etc. They often attend religious programmes and teach their philosophy.

The masterminds behind the Hindutva campaigns have realised that the mere existence of temples in the Adivasi localities will not drastically change the situation in the long run. They constantly feel threatened by Christian missionaries.[11] The role of Arya Samajists in Gujarat is quite important in the Hinduisation of the lower social groups, including Adivasis. The Arya Samajists realised the mistakes of orthodox Hindu leaders long ago. They have come to see the seriousness of the situation and are aware of the possible threat to the Brahmanical social order, which, it is feared, probably cannot survive if the age-old oppressive and inhuman practices towards Dalits are not changed into something more constructive. Swami Sachchidanand, an Arya Samajist, has, through his books and speeches, called for a change in the policy towards Dalits in Gujarat.[12]

To oppose the work of the missionaries and to propagate Hindu ideology among the Adivasis, some of the campaigning Hindu movements such as the Swaminarayan Movement have institutionalised their activities. They have started schools and recreation centres in the Adivasi region. They have purchased hundreds of acres of land in the Adivasi areas in Chhotaudepur and Dediyapada talukas. They have started schools, dispensaries, hospitals, welfare centres, etc. The Adivasis were easily won over because the state had failed to help them. The Hindu sampradayas have started introducing Hindu ideas into the community beginning with Adivasi boys at an early age.

The saints have not only confined their activities to religion but have also engaged in welfare work. For instance, Prafulbhai Shukla, a well-known saint in Gujarat, organised a katha in an Adivasi-dominated village for the renovation of a school building and for opening a science line in the village high-school.

Temple-building activities are quite visible in Adivasi villages[13] and remote villages are not neglected. Pinto (1996) observed that over the past 10 years there has been a steady increase in Hindu shrines and temples. He cited a follower and propagator of the Bhatiji Movement on the fact that 350 shrines have been built by this movement alone in the past five years in three Adivasi talukas. Nowadays almost every village has its own temple. Adivasi gods and goddesses are sometimes systematically replaced by Hindu idols. Pinto (1995) has recorded one such instance in which an Adivasi god was replaced by a Hindu deity. This is rather common and has happened in other places in India also.[14]

The Swadhyay Parivar[15] is also an organisation working in the Adivasi area. It was founded by Shri Pandurang Shastri Athavale. He concentrates on community building that cuts across caste and class. He has initiated various programmes among which Gharmandir[16] is one. As pointed out earlier, in traditional Adivasi culture there is no concept of temple. Athavale has found a remedy for that by consecrating Gharmandir and Amrutlaya[17] even in remote villages. His seventy-second birthday was celebrated at the village of Umergao in an Adivasi area. I was also present at this celebration together with more than a million other participants, who came mostly from lower and middle castes, including Adivasis and Harijans. His seventy-fifth birth anniversary was celebrated in several places. Between 17 and 18 February 1995, a big celebration was organised at Vadodara and hundreds of Adivasis participated in it. Athavale took advantage of these opportunities and spoke in favour of Hinduism and the importance of the Gita.

Nowadays one will find that different kinds of Hindu religious activities have been developed in Adivasi Gujarat. There seems to be a keen competition in the celebration of kathas, festivals and *yagna*s (fire sacrifices). Various Hindu movements and sampradayas (schools of thought or traditions) have also intensified their activities. The founding of religious trusts, the renovation of temples and construction of Hindu temples are common events in the Adivasi region.

Athavale has not confined himself to the devotional field, but has also implemented programmes that are economically helpful to the Adivasis. He has opened technical training centres, locally known as 'manav pratishtha kendras'. Adivasi children are given the benefits of practical training such as sewing, carpentry, electric motor rewinding, repairing vehicles, etc. The Parivar also gives interest-free loans to the trainees. The ideas of Athavale have also fascinated some of the intellectuals of Gujarat. The Adivasi families who have benefited from these programmes have started performing trikal sandhiya (prayer performed three times a day—morning, mid-day and evening) and they also regularly listen to discourses on the Bhagavat Gita (Dilip Shah, n.d.).

Religious institutions have launched other activities. The Vanvasi Kalyan Parishad Sidumbar in Dharampur taluka in Gujarat runs several schools and Prafulbhai Shukla has been made trustee in some of the educational foundations. The president of the Gayatri Parivar arranges multiple weddings free of cost at the temple at Bandar Road. The Gayatri Shaktipath runs a low-cost ayurvedic dispensary and bal mandir, it provides library services and performs Gayatri yagnas. Tailoring classes free of cost are also provided. The Gayatri Parivar has for the current year planned 1,001 yagnas in the villages of Navsari taluka.

THE RISE OF THE BJP

The rise of the BJP has been phenomenal in the past decade. The election results show that the BJP has made rapid progress in winning seats at all levels, that is, from the village to the centre. The BJP, which won two seats in the 1984 elections, emerged as the single largest party in the Eleventh Lok Sabha. The number of Adivasi Members of Parliament (MP) was also higher in the BJP than in other political party including the Congress. In this Parliament, the total number of Adivasi MPs was 41. Out of that, the BJP had 11 (the figure is based on Vajpayee's lecture in Parliament). The BJP, in fact, broadened its base in all pockets of Gujarat and became the ruling party in the state. In the Gujarat state assembly, 26 seats were reserved for Adivasis, out of which 14 belonged to the BJP. The election result of the panchayats in 1995 showed that the BJP won 82 per cent of the seats and came to power in 18 out of the 19 districts in Gujarat with a two-thirds majority in the Adivasi-dominated districts such as Valsad, Bharuch, Surat and Panchmahal. The trend was also visible in the election of the taluka panchayats, where the BJP won 44 out of the 54 taluka panchayats in six Adivasi districts of Gujarat (Joshi, 1996).

Ghanshyam Shah (1994) observes that the BJP is also gaining ground among the Dalits and Adivasis in urban areas, which is something new. This is amazing because up to now the Adivasis used to back the Congress party. The Adivasis remained with the Congress even during non-Congress rule in the state. Till 1995, the Congress had a monopoly in the districts and taluka panchayats in the Adivasi areas. The question that arises is how has the BJP managed to gain such an influence among the Adivasis? According to former prime minister, Atal Bihari Vajpayee, the rise of the BJP did not come about all of a sudden but was the result of systematic efforts over the past 30 years. The BJP has succeeded in undermining the growing solidarity among the SCs, STs, OBCs and other minorities and instead replaced it with a loyalty to the upper castes. Many will see the sudden rise to power of the BJP in the failure of the Congress party. According to the followers of the Phule–Ambedkar ideology, the Mandal Commission imposed a unity among the SCs, STs and the OBCs, which in turn constituted a major threat to the Brahmanical

social order. The Congress failed to maintain its upper-caste hegemony in Indian politics. The BJP made an ideological unity out of
caste divisions and the Hinduisation of Adivasis is one step in the
policy of maintaining status quo in the Brahmanical social order.

THE BJP: WOOING THE ADIVASIS

Besides stirring up Hindutva feelings, the BJP has tried to win the
people's confidence through unique programmes such as the 'Sarkar
Prajana Dware' (government on the doorstep), Gokul Gram Yojana,
Rojgar Mela and Kuvar Bainu Mameru. In the Sarkar Prajana Dware
programme, BJP ministers along with government officials visit
villages and try to solve their problems on the spot. The BJP has very
cleverly used such tactics in order to improve the image of the party.
The Adivasi people liked this style as they have had only bad
experiences with government bureaucracy. The BJP successfully
carried out such campaigns[18] in 10 places in Surat till September 1995
and found solutions to about 3,000 problems, which had remained
unsolved for years. Generally, the cases involved were related to
roads, health, dams, electricity, irrigation, transportation and drinking
water. With such campaigns, the BJP tried to win the people over
by sanctioning on-the-spot projects valued at several million rupees.
They responded to the demands of the people and programmes were
initiated or halted as per the people's wish. Another initiative was to
launch programmes for providing employment for unemployed
youth. One such programme was implemented in Gandevi taluka of
Valsad district, where 678 unemployed youth were given jobs. The
BJP deputy chief minister also distributed machines and tools for
tailoring, wiring, etc.

The BJP has also begun to arrange multiple weddings[19] for
Adivasis. At election time, the BJP also arranged several *sammelans*
(gatherings), group meetings, door-to-door campaigns and the like in
Adivasi areas. In one campaign, a BJP minister contacted around
400–500 Halpati families, assisted by local Adivasi leaders. Generally,
BJP leaders used to announce projects to be implemented in the near
future by the BJP government such as the installation of electricity
and handpumps, the building of schools and the like. Such occasions
used to attract great numbers. At one time so many Halpatis turned

up that one was led to believe that it was a lok darbar (people's court). The air rang with the slogans of *Bharat Mata ki Jai* (Hail Mother India) and *Vande Matram* (Bow to Mother India). The Halpatis promised the BJP overwhelming support in the next election. The strategy of the BJP has been to expose the neglect and want of concern of previous governments towards the Adivasis and then to present themselves as the only reliable alternative.

The Adivasis of Rajpipla taluka have been demanding the regularisation of forest land since 1956. The Congress promised to consider the question in 1974, the present BJP government, however, immediately passed a resolution to regularise 65,000 hectares of land as a concession to Adivasi demands. In election speeches they used to first tarnish the image of the Congress party and then present the BJP as the true friend and sympathiser of the Adivasi cause and the only party able to save Hindu dharma (that is, the Hindu *rashtra*) from outside attacks. During its 111 days in power, the BJP took numerous steps for providing welfare to the people. The Gokul Gram scheme was meant to benefit 6.2 million Adivasis. The poorest among the poor like the Kotvaliyas, who are one of the most backward Adivasi tribes in Gujarat, were to be helped under this scheme. Hopes were raised among the poor and the image of the BJP greatly improved as a result. The BJP used every platform, state or centre, to spread the message that their's was the only party that was fully committed to the Adivasi cause. The party also succeeded in convincing the masses that they were the real guardians of national interests.[20]

ADIVASI EMOTIONS EXPLOITED BY THE BJP

As discussed earlier, in Gujarat there are many saints such as Morari Bapu, Praful Chandra Shukla, Asharam Bapu, Pandurang Athavale and Swami Sachchidanand, who are trying to rejuvenate the Hindu religion in order to bring different social groups into the Hindu fold. Though they may apply different approaches, they have one thing in common: they work for Hindu unity by incorporating the tribals into the Hindu fold by equating Hinduism with Indian nationalism.

The role of *sadhu*s and saints has become crucial, particularly at the time of elections. Praful Shukla lives in an Adivasi area and he openly propagates BJP viewpoints, while others such as Morari Bapu,

Pandurang Athavale and Asharam Bapu advise people to vote for the party which works for the preservation of Hindu sanskriti.

According to the followers of Phule and Ambedkar, all these saints aim at one and the same thing, that is, unity based on Hindu religion, but their style of persuasion may differ. Various religious and political leaders have been constantly drumming up religious and political feelings of fear and insecurity by repeating the idea that the Hindu religion is endangered, that unless they are united, Hindus would soon belong nowhere, that their nation was in danger, its very existence threatened. Such propaganda created insecurity and also persuaded Adivasis to unite on the basis of Hindutva.

Hindutva activists in most taluka headquarters have founded *shakha*s, that is, branches of various Hindu organisations, such as Hindu Milan Mandir, Swaminarayana, Swadhyay, Ram Krishna, Radha Krishna, etc. There are also shakhas of the BJP, the RSS, the Akhil Bharatiya Vidyarthi Parishad (ABVP), the Shiv Sena, etc. They all aim at propagating Hinduism among the Adivasis. Helping them in many ways, they try to convince the Adivasis that they will benefit from Hinduism. They let them know that there is no harm in taking up arms in order to protect Hindus if the situation should demand such a course of action.

Adivasis have also been called upon to instigate communal riots against Muslims. Ghanshyam Shah (1994), Pinto (1995) and Lobo (1990) have described how Adivasis have been communalised very systematically by the the RSS, the VHP and the BJP and encouraged to turn against Muslims in the post-Babri mosque incidents. There are many initiatives taken for the Hinduisation of Adivasis, the most important being the 'the Ramshila Pujan', 'rathyatra' of Advani and 'Ramjyoti' and 'kar seva'. During the Ramshila Pujan in 1984, according to Pinto, a token collection of Rs 1.25 was taken from Adivasis with the question: 'Are you Hindus? If you are, then prove it by contributing Rs 1.25 for Ramshila Pujan. If not, then prove that you have come from a Muslim womb!' (Pinto, 1995).

There are also a number of other initiatives such as organising celebrations of Hindu festivals, road blocking, destructive activities, the celebration of Independence Day and Republic Day. The stickers of *Vande Mataram, Garv se Kaho Ham Hindu Hain* (Hail Mother India and Say with pride we are Hindus), etc., have become very popular

among Adivasis. Propaganda is spread to convey the message that
the Sangh Parivar, political parties such as the BJP, the Shiv Sena,
saints and sadhus are the real protectors of India, while others are
not. The Congress party especially portrayed as pro-Muslim and anti-
Hindu. The rathyatra campaign was successful in mobilising the
Adivasis for a Hindu celebration (S. Yagnic, 1995). Many mini-
rathyatras have been organised by Hindutva organisations in the
Adivasi regions of Gujarat.[21] Adivasis were encouraged to light the
fire from the Ramjyoti, which was carried by a mini-*rath*. Speeches
were also given to instigate Adivasis to drive out Muslims and
Christians (Pinto, 1995). The Adivasi youth have been especially
influenced by the Hindutva campaign. They openly attacked Muslims
and resorted to looting, arson and physical fights. Communal riots
have become a widespread phenomenon throughout the Adivasi belt
of Gujarat.[22] There have also been instances of attacks on Muslim
*dargah*s (sacred places of Muslim saints) and shrines.

POLITICAL STRATEGIES TO WIN OVER THE ADIVASIS

Religious leaders have also played a major role in polarising religious
life in India. Activists from Hindu organisations like the VHP and
the RSS have very systematically used Adivasi politicians, bhagats
(religious leaders), sarpanchs, police patels and some primary schoolteachers for spreading their radical Hindu views and for instigating
communal riots. Muslims are accused of destroying Hindu shrines,
for being exploiters of Adivasis and for causing them many ills and
much trouble. Expulsion and elimination of Muslims was proposed
as a solution (Pinto, 1995: 2418). In all these campaigns, the tactics
employed were to portray Adivasis as Hindus and Muslims as their
enemies. An Adivasi teacher told me that in those days feelings of
communalism were so widespread that real ills like poverty, illiteracy,
disease, exploitation, indebtedness, pauperism and land alienation
were non-existent to the Adivasis. For them the main problem was
the Hindu–Muslim controversy as it was for the majority of Hindus.
Growing expectations especially among the educated Adivasi youth
have accelerated Hinduisation and the BJP's influence among the
Adivasis.

Dipika Chikhaliya, a famous actress, who performed the role of Sita in the television serial *Ramayana*, made speeches at various places at the time of elections in Adivasi areas. In a meeting at Mandvi, she severely criticised the Congress party and emphasised that the misrule of Congress in Gujarat was the root cause of all evils. She spoke in favour of BJP rule in the state for the protection of Hindu sanskriti. Bharatiya Janata Party politicians at the state as well as national levels have made the Congress party responsible for poverty, unemployment, rising living costs and corruption. Lal Krishna Advani, the then national president of the BJP, at mass meetings in two Adivasi-dominated talukas, Vyara and Bardoli, pointed out that the nation had made no progress at all during the past four-and-a-half decades of Congress rule.

The BJP has also very skillfully made use of Adivasi leaders in its campaigns. For instance, at Dholikui village of Mahuva taluka, a big *sammelan* (gathering) was organised under the chairmanship of Chandubhai Deshmukh, a BJP Adivasi president in Gujarat. He did not mince words and criticised the Congress for having allowed corruption to grow like cancer, for having neglected local needs related to roads, drinking water, electricity and irrigation. He then highlighted the BJP's programmes, which were to be implemented out of concern for Adivasi needs, provided the party got sufficient support in the elections. He called attention to Congress corruption in shares, sugar, Bofors; he mentioned the corruption case during the rule of the ex-chief minister, Amarsingh Chaudhare and said that the Congress had made no inquiries into the theft of Rs 250 million in Bharuch district and of Rs 140 million in Surat district. He concluded his speech with the question: Are you going to vote for such a band? Are you going to support a party involved in so much racketeering?

Bharatiya Janata Party supporters visited most Adivasi areas during election campaigns. Now the prestige of the Congress party has diminished throughout the Adivasi belt.[23] In remote villages nobody knew about the BJP four or five years back, now numerous followers have been recruited from there. The BJP has succeeded in nurturing feelings of hatred towards the Congress party, especially among young people who have begun, rightly or wrongly, to accuse the Congress of having kept them backward with the ulterior motive of using them as a permanent vote bank. The question of identity has become important to many Adivasis and a recognition as Hindus is the fulfilment of an aspiration for a larger identity now much in demand among the Adivasis.

The issue of a common civil code has also been raised and the fact that Hindus have suffered differential treatment in their own country has been criticised. Anti-Muslim feelings have been so vigorously propagated by Hindutva supporters that the average educated person does not remain unaffected by its impact. Congress influence has been further weakened due to infighting among Adivasi leaders. A few Congress politicians have criticised the Congress policy towards the Adivasis. Pratap Gamit, the chairman of the Adivasi Corporation in Gujarat and a member of the Legislative Assembly (MLA) (independent), at a meeting in the village of Khutadia in Vyara taluka, criticised some well-known Congress Adivasi leaders for not having defended Adivasi interests. Because most Congress leaders have been found wanting in most respects, Hinduisation has progressed to such an extent that the Congress influence is rejected and only the BJP is tolerated. The result of this development is visible in the elections to the panchayats, corporations and Parliament.

ADIVASI CONSCIOUSNESS

Many Adivasis now feel that the Hindu religion is their own. 'We are Hindus' is a widespread feeling among them. They identify themselves with a larger religious *quam* (community). Their customs and codes of social behaviour are guided by the Hindu religion, which is altogether different from other quams such as those of the Muslims, Sikhs and Parsis. They want to be recognised as Hindus and, therefore, they enter Hindu names in the census paper as well as in school certificates and other documents. Today Adivasis are accepted, at least nominally, as part and parcel of the Hindu community. This phenomenon came to light at the time of communal riots. The Adivasis proved their solidarity with the Hindu community in turning against the Muslims. A small group of Adivasis, who have political aspirations, has been instrumental in securing votes of the Adivasi masses for the BJP upper-caste politicians. In return, these Adivasi politicians have been rewarded by the upper-caste BJP.

A special kind of Adivasi self-consciousness is now emerging. It is interesting to observe that on one hand, the religious leaning towards Hinduism has been increasing, especially over the past 10 years, while on the other hand, Adivasi self-consciousness and self-respect and insistence on rights have also shown a rising trend. A few Adivasi leaders are now becoming aware of their situation. They increasingly feel that the Aryans (Hindus) have made their lives intolerable. They have begun to realise that the present government will not solve their problems. A few Adivasi politicians have also realised how biased the state is, not only towards Adivasis but also towards other lower social groups. Their demand for autonomy should be seen in this context. This demand, however, is not new. It was made in the 1960s also (Desai, 1971), but now it has erupted so violently that it has embarrassed the government.[24]

Adivasi leaders claim that they are the original inhabitants of the land but were driven to the hills by the conquering Aryans. There is also a feeling of growing hatred towards the Hindus,[25] particularly towards the upper castes. They allege that the Hindus have imposed their beliefs, their faith and their culture on the Adivasis in the name of the so-called 'mainstream' tradition (see the handbill by Adijati Vikas Paksha, n.d.). Adivasi leaders are trying hard to unite the Adivasis against upper-caste exploitation. Of course, this new Adivasi self-consciousness has been frowned upon by BJP Adivasi leaders. It has been realised that Adivasi and other groups from the lower social orders have begun to think for themselves. On the basis of their own experience, the oppressed groups of Indian society includ-ing the Adivasis have begun to critically observe the day-to-day behaviour and attitudes of the upper castes. A new type of conscious-ness has emerged in the 1990s. Adivasis have become aware of their numerical strength and the fact that they have been politically manipulated by non-Adivasi Hindus. To remedy this situation they have begun to assert themselves. Upper-caste Hindus have begun to realise the long-term consequences of this development and are taking preventive measures (Adhvaryu, 1981; Augustine, 1984; Lobo, 1993; Parmar, 1993; Shah and Shah, 1993). Some Adivasi leaders demand autonomy and are suspicious of democracy. According to them, the democratic system made up of MPs, ministers and the bureaucracy is a Western invention and quite incompatible with their own sanskriti or tradition. A committee (including a Gujarat MP, Ramjibhai Damor) brought this up in Parliament on 17 January 1995.

CONCLUSION

Theoretically, Adivasis do not have a caste, but caste-like elements are found in Adivasi society. The influence of Hinduism on the social and religious life of the Adivasis has been considerable, particularly in the last 10–15 years. The slow process of Sanskritisation, which has been going on for a long time, has prepared the ground for the Hinduisation of the Adivasi people. This is reflected in their social consciousness, in the vision they have for themselves and their society, in their hopes and expectations. The Hinduisation of Adivasis has indirectly resulted in the consolidation of inequality. Ghanshyam Shah (1994) has rightly observed that the Sanskritisation of the Backward Classes has reinforced the caste system and the dominance of upper-caste Hindus. The communalism of the Adivasis and their participation in the riots against Muslims is the public expression of their Hindu identity. Although there has been a significant influence of Hindu society on the Adivasis, it is also a fact that they have not given up their traditional values and belief systems altogether. But, the BJP and other Hindu organisations such as the RSS, the ABVP, Bajarang Dal, Shiv Sena, the Hindu Milan Mandir, the Arya Samaj, saints and sadhus and some Adivasi politicians have succeeded in inculcating the Hindutva ideology in the minds of the Adivasi people. In fact, many have seized the opportunity to embrace Hinduism, which is the religion of the majority and considered to be one of the oldest religions in the world. The adoption of a wider identity is the crux of the matter for the Adivasis, but Hindutva supporters on the other hand are aware of the importance of keeping the Adivasis within the Hindu fold in order to secure Hindu hegemony. Thus, it may be said that both parties, that is, the Adivasis and the supporters of the Hindutva cause have had a common interest in promoting the process of Hinduisation. Having chosen Hinduism, Adivasis have accepted the social and theological implications of their new religion and indirectly recognised the supremacy of the upper castes. Whether this consolidation of the Hindu social order will last or not only time will tell.

NOTES

1. Adivasis are considered to be the original inhabitants of the country. They are known by various names, namely, Vanyajati, Vanvasi, Paharia, Adimjati, Janjati, etc. In the various census papers, the Adivasis are referred to under the following headings: Adivasi form of religion, animists, hill or forest Adivasis, primitive Adivasis, Adivasis, etc.

2. K.S. Singh (1993b) does not agree fully with such a typology. He argues that '... the great and little traditions are conceptual categories set up by scholars. They are based on the intellectual perception from above not peoples' perception from below. For an adivasi, worshipping in the sacred groves ... is neither great nor little. It is his own tradition which gives him his identity and a feeling of cultural continuity.'

3. In south Gujarat, the total Adivasi population is distributed as follows: Dang, 93 per cent, Valsad, 55 per cent, Bharuch, 45 per cent and Surat, 42 per cent. Within this district, Adivasis are found concentrated in a few talukas. For instance, in Bharuch they are more common in talukas such as Dediyapada, Sagbara, Valia, Rajpipla and Jhagadia. In Surat, they are concentrated in Uchchal, Vyara, Mahuva and Songdh talukas. In Valsad, they are found in talukas such as Vansada and Dharampur. Dang district is full of Adivasis.

4. The building of temples in the Adivasi belt and its impact on the Adivasi people needs an extensive and systematic study. It is also important to study the role of Hindu kings, mainly because they invited numerous Hindus from outside to settle in their kingdom. These settlers increased the Hindu pressure on local Adivasis.

5. Hindu movements are basically well structured. These Hindu revival movements have spawned numerous groups, which have concentrated in different pockets and also reached many Adivasi villages. It is widely believed that Hindus promoted this movement in order to prevent the conversion of Adivasis to Christianity. Christian missionaries have been working in the Adivasi region for the past hundred years. Some Adivasis have been converted to Christianity, mainly because they were exploited by Hindu landlords, rajas, traders and police officers. The missionaries gave the Adivasis material benefits and protection and helped them fight their exploiters.

6. They try to make the Adivasis abstain from meat, liquor, tobacco, etc. They try to make them 'human', teach them to respect others, to set apart time for devotion to the divine spirit, etc. They also teach them the importance of certain symbols, the wearing of the sacred thread, putting *tilak* on the forehead, making certain saints their gurus, etc. They give them a new identity, which is supposed to be socially and economically higher and more attractive than the one they at present have.

7. The Adivasis worship malevolent spirits mainly because they want to protect themselves from natural calamities such as droughts, earthquakes, epidemics, etc. They offer special sacrifices to these spirits at certain occasions to win their favour. Most of the names of Adivasi gods refer to forests, hills, rivers, etc. Now some Hindu gods and goddesses have crept in. They also worship their ancestors and invariably invoke the blessings of ancestors at every social occasion. Functionalists like Durkheim, Radcliffe-Brown and Malinowski have interpreted this phenomenon as a source of stability.

8. There are many reasons for Adivasis to join the Hindu fold. K.S. Singh (1993b), who has done admirable work in 'the People of India Project', considered three factors in the Hinduisation of Adivasis. First, Hindu Mahasabhahad identified as Hindus those persons whose religion has not originated outside India. Second, some Adivasi groups have demanded to be recognised as Hindus, and third, a majority of the census officials were Hindus, and they have registered Adivasis as Hindus.

9. For instance, Morari Bapu is working full time for the survival of Hindu sanskriti (culture). He has performed Ram katha at several places in Adivasi towns such as Shinor, Vyara, Mandvi, Santrampur and Sisodra. He has also been invited on several occasions to give speeches. The first Ram katha in an Adivasi area was organised at Vyara in October 1995. On this occasion, the Bajarang Dal organised a 4 km *pothi yatra*. Morari Bapu has tried to introduce Ram to the Adivasis and every day more than 50,000 Adivasis participated in the katha where meals were also served. Morari Bapu's birthday was celebrated with Ramotsav and distribution of Ganges water. The expenses were covered by a wealthy trader from Surat. On the last day Bapu performed *arti* (act of veneration) and representatives from each Adivasi group, Harijans and Muslims participated in the ceremony and Babu finally gave to his devotees the mantra of *Ram hi kevalprempyala* (only Ram is full of love, therefore he should be worshiped).

10. Morari Bapu is one of the well-known saints, who recites the *Ramayana* in most Adivasi areas of Gujarat. He has an influence not only on educated and urbanite Adivasis, but also on the illiterate Adivasi masses. Nandu Bhagat of Khroda village is one of his devotees. He gave up dacoity and drinking after listening to Morari Bapu 10 years ago. He began chanting *Ram jap* (invocation of Ram in prayer) and gradually learnt the whole *Ramayana* by heart. From evening to early morning, he performs the Ramayana katha with a small group of Adivasis as part of a campaign. He has also begun to expose tricks employed by Christian missionaries to convert Adivasis to Christianity. He advises the Adivasis to embrace the Hindu religion. He has probably organised more than 150 kathas with thousands of participants.

11. A drastic change has taken place in the Hindutva policy, especially after the mass conversion of Harijans to Islam in 1981 at Minakshipuram, Tamil Nadu. Dalit demands are no longer opposed directly. Instead, Hindus have begun to present themselves as the true well-wishers of the Adivasi cause.

12. He has written extensively in local newspapers and has published more than 20 books. The purpose of his writings is to expose the orthodox and inhuman practices of Hindu religion. Swami seems to be strongly opposed to the traditional Hindu varna system. He has devoted an entire book to it in which he highlights the inhuman and discriminatory attitude of the savarnas (upper-caste Hindus) to those at the bottom of society.

13. Temple-building activity is on in a big way in this region. Local people are mobilised for this purpose. Temples have been constructed in several Adivasi talukas. Twenty-five years ago, the first temple of Akshar Purushottam Swaminarayan was built at Mandvi. This was the first temple in the eastern belt in south Gujarat, but now there are many. Recently, the *mahila*s (women) of Vyara taluka arranged a Ram katha by Nilesh Bapu, which took place over nine days, in the interior village of Chodchit in order to collect money for the construction of a Jalaram Bapu temple at Songdh.

14. The Jagannath Temple in Orissa was probably an Adivasi temple origi-nally, but gradually it was changed into a Hindu temple. A study made by Annacharlotte Eschman (1986) shows how Hinduisation has been at work in many places. In Orissa, in Bastar, at Mysore, and in West Bengal we meet the same pattern: deities from the Hindu pantheon replace local folk deities.

15. The teachings of Shri Pandurang Shastri Athavale, a Brahmin from Maharashtra are focused on the study of self. He has been active as a teacher of spirituality for 50 years. Today he probably has a following of more than 3 million people, spread over 125,000 villages in India and abroad. Devotees are mainly recruited from the lower layers of society. They are invited to participate in activities such as (*i*) *swadhyaya*, (*ii*) *Bhakti-pheri* (devotion march), *trikal sandhya* (pray three times), (*iii*) *yogeshwar krishi* (community farming), (*iv*) *matsyagandha*, (*v*) *bal samskara kendra, Shri darshanam* (visit and homage to the Lord), etc. The upper and lower castes often work together. Athavale Shastri is trying to bring about a social, economic, emotional and political 'revolution' through spiritual revolution. Swadhyaya is a study of self through group encoun-ters. This self-understanding is holistic in nature and includes the social, economic, political, psychological and philosophical dimensions of hu-man personality. Bhakti-pheri is a devotional tour of the *swadhyayee*s for spiritual development. They do not seek any material things. With the Lord in their hearts they visit villages to spread the message of the Gita. Swadhyayees spend a minimum of 15 days in a year in villages. Yogeshwar

krishi is farming in the name of God. Swadhyayees cultivate plots of land in the name of the Almighty and use their farming skill in his service. Matsyagandha is the representation of floating temples. A crew of 6–10 swadhyayee fishermen working as devotees are carried on these floats. The sons of these devotees offer a part of their earnings from the sea to Lord Yogeshwar. When enough fund is accumulated, it is used to buy motorised fishing boats. These boats are called matsyagandhas. Bal samskara kendras are the centres for child development that the swadhyaya runs in the locality, neighbourhood or village, where it is at work. In such centres, women participants of the swadhyaya spend time with children. Usually this is done once a week.

16.   There is a belief that God comes weekly to each of the Adivasi families and that their house becomes a gharmandir. The swadhyay Adivasi families meet in such houses every evening to pray to God. The campaign has had some impact as far as cleanliness, rejection of liquor and meat are concerned.

17.   Amrutlaya is a simple structure for worship. By using locally available materials, the Adivasis build a hut for their *shram bhakti* (devotion). There is no idol in the temple except the pictures of Krishna, Shiva and Pandurang Shastri. It is also used as a community centre where they deliberate on their problems. Amrutlaya is open to all including Harijans. Even Muslims come to perform namaz (worship) there.

18.   At one such campaign, a BJP minister said that his party had found solutions to questions concerning housing, allotment of residential plots, distribution of 10 kg of grain free of cost, interest-free loans of Rs 2,000 for petty businesses, legalisation of forest land, clothes for school-going children, wheat at the rate of Rs 2 per kg, Rs 5,000 at the time of marriage, Rs 200 for widows, working women hostels in cities, debt relief of up to Rs 10,000, etc. The BJP minister along with social assistants contacted 200–300 Halpatis in the adjoining areas.

19.   A second multiple-wedding ceremony for Adivasis was held under the auspices of the Adivasi Vikas Mandal of Kamrej-Palsana Vibhag. This ceremony was held at the Swaminarayan Sanskriti Dham in Ladvi. Many Adivasi leaders and saints were present. The social welfare minister also honoured this function with his presence. Blessings were bestowed on the 45 couples who were married at this ceremony. The minister pointed out that the present government was much concerned about the welfare of people from the lower classes including the Adivasis. He announced some government schemes to be implemented soon, including Kurvarbai nu Mameru, Saraswati Sadhana Yojana and the 'Manav Garima Yojana'. etc. Premswaroop Shastriji, who is in charge of the Swaminarayan Sanskrit Dham in Ladvi, advised Adivasis to seek education and to assimilate with mainstream Hindu tradition. He was also in favour of helping people enslaved by addiction.

20. Some Adivasi leaders have become strong supporters of Hindutva organisations. At one Adivasi gathering at which I was invited as a guest speaker, I saw that a few Adivasi party leaders shared the dais with upper-caste leaders from the BJP. In their speeches, upper-caste leaders did not miss the opportunity to drum into the heads of their listeners that the BJP was a real friend working for the uplift of the Adivasi people. They also called attention to the fact that they had given positions of power to Adivasi leaders. Finally, they turned against the Congress party, whom they strongly criticised for the injustices committed against the Adivasi people.

21. In October 1995 (from 2 to 20 October) an Ekatma Yatrawas was organised by the Vishwa Hindu Parishad (VHP). This yatra covered the distance from Kanyakumari in the south to the Himalayas in the north. The purpose of the yatra was to promote awareness about Hindutva in the nation. It was felt that a national and religious awakening would take place simultaneously. The yatra was attended by 200 million people from 350,000 villages. It comprised about 45,000 public meetings. The yatra was attended by 5.4 million people in five zones of the Surat district. Around 2.2 million people participated in smaller yatras associated with the Ekatma Yatrawas. Twenty-two smaller yatras and an equal number of dharma sabhas were held. The yatra covered 790 km and in 976 villages, a pot of water from the holy river Ganges was set up. About 21,100 villages were included in the campaign. Kamedrasinh, the person in charge of the Gujarat Ekatma Yatra said in his address that such a yatra was necessary to save the country and its religion (Nandy et al., 1995).

22. Some of the faculty members of the Centre for Social Studies in Surat launched a study of their own in order to investigate communal riots among Adivasis in Gujarat in 1993. I was associated with this project and collected some information through personal interviews and observation of the communal situation in Sagbara and Dediyapada talukas of the Bharuch district. I also read reports from other parts of south Gujarat.

23. In the last week of February 1995, a public meeting of Adivasis was held at the Adivasi village of Uchchal. The state president, Kashiram Rana said that the Congress was losing its importance in the south Gujarat region. The taluka presidents invited were Adivasis from Uchchal, Nizar and Navapur talukas. They emphasised in their speeches that the Adivasis have now realised that the Congress has not been a spokesman for the poor or for the Adivasi people.

24. Recently, Chhotubhai Vasava, Ramanbhai Chaudhari and some others held a meeting in the Adivasi area, first in Nizer, later in Mandvi, on the eve of the last parliamentary elections. They succeeded in mobilising thousands of Adivasis from all over the Adivasi belt of Gujarat. For the first time, all the chairs on the dais were occupied by only Adivasi leaders.

25. Adivasi leaders appealed to Adivasi masses to free themselves from the clutches of the Hindus. In a handbill published by the Adivasi Vikas Parishad in Panchmahal district, an emphatic appeal was made for Adivasis to demand their own state—Bhilistan. Adivasis were encouraged to liberate themselves from Hindu slavery. The handbill described how in former times the invading Aryans developed the varnavyavastha (hierarchical division of social group based on race and colour) to keep the Adivasis down; and to make their ideology of suppression perfect they made it part of a religious cosmic order.

REFERENCES AND SELECT BIBLIOGRAPHY

Adhvaryu, Bhanu (1981) *Agnigarbh Valia*. Surat: Socialist Study Centre.

Adijati Vikas Paksha (n.d.) Handbill of the Adijati Vikas Paksha. Dahod: Adijati Vikas Paksha Trust.

Allen, Douglas (ed.) (1993) *Religion and Political Conflict in South Asia, India, Pakistan, and Sri Lanka*. New Delhi: Oxford University Press.

Augustine, P.A. (1984) *Suppression of Valia Tribals: A Case Study of Human Rights Violation*. New Delhi: Indian Social Institute.

Bajaj, Jitendra (ed.) (1993) *Ayodhya and the Future of India*. Madras: Centre for Policy Studies.

Banerjee, S. (1968) *Ethnographic Study of the Kuvi-Kandha*. Memoir No. 21, Calcutta: Anthropological Survey of India.

Bidwai, Praful, Harbans Mukhia and Achin Vanaik (eds) (1996) *Religion, Religiosity and Communalism*. New Delhi: Manohar.

Bose, N.K. (1941) 'The Hindu Method of Tribal Absorption', *Science and Culture*, 7(4), October: 188–94.

Campell, James M. (1988) *Hindu Castes and Tribes of Gujarat*. New Delhi: Vintage Books.

Das, A. (1968–69) 'Impact of Christianity on Tribals', *Adibasi,* 10(1), April: 87–96.

Dehon, P. (1906) 'Religion and Customs of the Uraons', *Memoirs of the Asiatic Society of Bengal*, pp. 121–81.

Desai, I.P. (1971) 'The Slogan of a Separate State by Tribals of South Gujarat', *ICSSR Research Abstract Quarterly*, 1(4), February: 118–27.

———. (1976) *Profile of Education among the Scheduled Tribes of Gujarat*. Surat: Centre for Social Studies.

———. (1982) *Vedchhi Andolan* (in Gujarati). Surat: Centre for Social Studies.

Desai, Kiran (n.d.) 'Adivasis of South Gujarat' (MS). Surat: Centre for Social Studies.

Eschman, A. (1986) *The Saorias of the Rajmahal Hills*. Berkeley: University of California Press.

Ferreira, John V. (1965) *Totemism in India*. Bombay: Oxford University Press.

Fuchs, Stephen (1973) *Aboriginal Tribes of India*. New Delhi: Macmillan India.

Gazetteer of India (1979) *Gujarat State. South Gujarat Districts*. Ahmedabad: Gujarat State Publications.

Ghurye, G.S. (1963) *The Scheduled Tribes*. Bombay: Popular Prakashan.

Graham, B.D. (1990) *Hindu Nationalism and Indian Politics: The Origins and Development of Bhartiya Jana Sangh*. Cambridge: Cambridge University Press.

Gujarat State Gazetteers (1979) *Vadodara District*. Ahmedabad: Government Printing Stationary and Publications, Gujarat State.

Guru, Gopal (1991) 'Hinduisation of Ambedkar in Maharashtra', *Economic and Political Weekly*, 26(7), 16 February: 2819–23.

Hajra, D. (1970) *The Dorlas of Bastar*. Memoir No. 16. Calcutta: Anthropological Survey of India.

Hardiman, David (1984) 'Adivasi Assertion in South Gujarat: The Devi Movement of 1922–23', in Ranajit Guha (ed.), *Subaltern Studies III: Writings on South Asian History and Society*, pp. 134–51. New Delhi: Oxford University Press.

Hasan, Mushirul (1991) 'Adjustment and Accommodation: Muslims after Partition', in K.K. Panikkar (ed.), *Communalism in India: History, Politics and Culture*, pp. 62–79. New Delhi: Manohar.

Herbert, Spencer (1876–96) *The Principles of Sociology*. 3 Vols. London: William and Norgate.

Iyer,V.K. Krishna (1991) *Politics and Religion*. New Delhi: Konark Publishers.

Jayaprasad, K. (1991) *RSS and Hindu Nationalism*. New Delhi: Deep and Deep Publications.

Joshi, Satyakam (1992) 'Forest Co-operatives of South Gujarat', Ph.D thesis. Surat: South Gujarat University.

———. (1995) 'Congress Debacle in Panchayat Poll', *Mainstream*, 33(44), 23 September: 11–14.

———. (1996) 'Gamits of South Gujarat', in N.N. Vyas (ed.), *Tribal Encyclopedia*. New Delhi: Discovery Publishing House.

Joshi, Vidyut (1980) *Ashramshalao Ek Adhyayan: Adivasi-Shikshano Ek Samajshastriya Abhyas*. Ahmedabad: Gujarat Samajik Seva Mandal.

Kalia, B. (1961) *Tribal Elements in Hinduism*. New Delhi: Munshiram.

Lal, R.B. (1977) 'Socio-Religious Movements among South Gujarat Tribes' (mimeograph). Ahmedabad: Gujarat Tribal Research and Training Centre.

———. (1982) 'Socio-Religious Movements among South Gujarat', in K.S. Singh (ed.), *Tribal Movements in India*, Vol. 2, pp. 285–308. New Delhi: Manohar Publication.

Lobo, Lancy (1990) 'Communal Riots in Tribal Dediyapada and Sagbara during October–November 1990, A Report' (MS). Surat: Centre for Social Studies.

———. (1992) 'Religious Sects among the Tribals of South Gujarat' (mimeograph). Surat: Centre for Social Studies.

———. (1993) 'Suppression of Valia Tribals and Their Assertion', Paper presented at a seminar on 'Bastar: Pro-Imperialist Development Strategy versus People Struggles', Nagpur. Surat: Centre for Social Studies.

———. (1994) 'Suppression of Valia Tribals', *Economic and Political Weekly*, 15 January: 1189–96.

———. (1995) 'Religious Movement among Tribals of Gujarat', Paper presented in the 'National Seminar on Social Identities: Religion, Region and Language in Contemporary India', 14–15 September, Surat.

232   ARJUN PATEL

Lobo, Lancy (1996) 'Choudhuries of South Gujarat', in N.N. Vyas (ed.), *Tribal Encyclopedia*. New Delhi: Discovery Publishing House.
Malik, K. Yogendra and V.B. Singh (1995) *Hindu Nationalists in India: The Rise of the Bharatiya Janata Party.* New Delhi: Vistaar.
Mohapatra, E.B. and J. Swain (1969) 'Conversion to Christianity', *Man in India*, 49(3), September: 253–58.
Nandy, Ashis, Shikha Trivedi, Shail Mayaram and Achyyut Yagnic (1995) *Creating a Nationality: The Ramajanmabumi Movement and Fear of the Self.* New Delhi: Manohar.
Panikkar, K.K. (ed.) (1991) *Communalism in India: History, Politics and Culture.* New Delhi: Manohar.
Parmar, Rameshchandra (1993) *Agnikund Valia, Bhartiya Dalit Panther.* Ahmedabad: Bharatiya Dalit Panther.
Patel, Arjun (1996a) 'The Dungari Bhils of Baroda District of Gujarat', in N.N. Vyas (ed), *Tribal Encyclopedia*. New Delhi: Discovery Publishing House.
———. (1996b) 'The Rathwas of Baroda District of Gujarat', in N.N. Vyas (ed.), *Tribal Encyclopedia*. New Delhi: Discovery Publishing House.
———. (1996c) 'The Tadavis of Bharuch District of Gujarat', in N.N. Vyas (ed.), *Tribal Encyclopedia*. New Delhi: Discovery Publishing House.
Patel, Arjun and Kiran Desai (1988) 'Review of Literature on Adivasis Studies', *Souvenir*, MRS. Dept. Surat: South Gujarat University.
———. (1992) *Migrant Labour in Rural Gujarat.* Surat: Centre for Social Studies.
Patel, Arjun and Ghanshyam Shah (1993) 'Tribal Movements in Western India: A Review of Literature'. Occasional Paper No. 15. Surat: Centre for Social Studies.
Patnaik, N. (1963) 'From Tribe to Caste: The Juangs of Orissa', *Economic and Political Weekly*, 15(18), 4 May: 741–42.
Paul, K.T. (1919) 'How Missionaries Denationalise Indians', *International Review of Missions*, 8(4), October: 92–105.
Pinto, Stany (1995) 'Communalisation of Tribals in South Gujarat', *Economic and Political Weekly*, 30(39), 30 September: 2873–77.
———. (1996) 'Vasavas of South Gujarat', in N.N. Vyas (ed.), *Tribal Encyclopedia*. New Delhi: Discovery Publishing House.
Punalekar, D.S. (1996) 'Choudhuries of South Gujarat', in N.N. Vyas (ed.), *Tribal Encyclopedia*, pp. 243–65. New Delhi: Discovery Publishing House.
Punalekar, S.P. (1990) 'Descriptive Study of Dhodias of Surat', Ph.D thesis. Surat: South Gujarat University.
———. (1993) 'Structural Constraint in Tribal Education: A Case Study of Tribal Community in South Gujarat', *The Indian Journal of Social Science*, 6(1): 32–47.
———. (1996) 'Dhodias of South Gujarat', in N.N. Vyas (ed.), *Tribal Encyclopedia*. New Delhi: Discovery Publishing House.
Radcliffe-Brown, A.R. (1964) *Andaman Islanders.* Cambridge: Cambridge University Press. (First published in 1922.)
Rajkishore, C. (ed.) (1995) *Ayodhya Aur Use Age* (in Hindi). New Delhi: Vani Prakashan.
Roy, Sarat Chandra (1925) *The Birhor: A Little Jungle Tribe of Chotanagpur.* Ranchi: Man in India Publications.
Sachchidananda, S. (1964) *Culture Change in Tribal Bihar.* Calcutta: Bookland.

Sachchidananda, S. (1970) 'Tribe-Caste Continuum: A Case Study of the Gond in Bihar', *Anthropos*, 65: 973–97.

Sahay, K.N. (1962) 'Trends of Sanskritization among the Orans', *Bulletin of the Bihar Tribal Research Institute*, 4(2), September: 89–102.

———. (1967) 'A Study in the Process of Transformation from Tribes to Caste: Parahiyas of Lolki: A Case Study', *Journal of Social Research*, 10(1), March: 64–89.

———. (1980) 'The Transformation Scene in Chotanagpur: Hindu Impact on the Tribals', in P. Dasha Sharma (ed.), *Sarat Chandra Roy Commemorative Volume: The Passing Scene in Chotanagpur.* Ranchi: Maitryee Publications.

Sen, Jyoti (1968) *Community Development in Chotanagpur.* Calcutta: Asiatic Society.

Shah, Dilip (n.d.) 'Rural Reforms through Swadhyay Bhakti' (MS). Surat: South Gujarat University.

Shah, Ghanshyam (n.d.) *Gujaratna Adivasio.* Surat: Centre for Social Studies.

———. (1991) *Adivasio: Gaikale one Aje.* Surat: Centre for Social Studies.

———. (1992) *Caste Association and Political Process in Gujarat.* Bombay: Popular Prakashan.

———. (1993) 'Tenth Lok Sabha Elections, BJP's Victory in Gujarat', in Asghar Ali Engineer and Pradeep Nayak (eds), *Communalisation of Politics and 10th Lok Sabha Elections,* pp. 142–65. Also in *Economic and Political Weekly*, 16(51), 21 December 1991: 2105–8.

———. (1994) 'The BJP and Backward Castes in Gujarat', *South Asian Bulletin*, 14(1): 5–12.

———. (1995) *Politics of Scheduled Castes and Tribes.* Bombay: Vora & Company Publications.

———. (1996) 'Gujarat: BJP's Rise to Power', *Economic and Political Weekly*, 13–20 January: 1023–28.

Shah, Ghanshyam and Arjun Patel (1984) *Economic Differentiations and Tribal Identity.* New Delhi: Ajanta Books International.

———. (1985) 'A Profile of Education among the Scheduled Tribes in Gujarat', in Ghanshyam Shah (ed.), *Tribal Education in Gujarat.* New Delhi: Ajanta Books International.

———. (1991) 'Tenth Lok Sabha Elections. BJP's Victory in Gujarat', *Economic and Polit al Weekly*, 26(52), 21 December: 1827–31.

———. (1993) 'Tribal Movements in Western India: Review of Literature'. Occasional paper No. 15. Surat: Centre for Social Studies.

Shah, Ghanshyam and H.R. Chaturvedi (1983) *Gandhian Approach to Rural Development.* New Delhi: Ajanta Books International.

Shah, Ghanshyam and Kalpana Shah (1993) 'Police Adivasio par Gujarelo Atanb: Maljipura Gamni Dastur', *Padkar*, 10(4): 62–75.

Sharkir, Moin (ed.) (1989) *Religion, State and Politics in India.* New Delhi: Ajanta Publications.

Shourie, Arun (1987) *Religion in Politics.* New Delhi: Roli Books International.

Singh, K.S. (1993a) 'Hinduism and Tribal Religion: An Anthropological Perspective', *Man in India*, 11(2), March: 74–87.

———. (1993b) *The Scheduled Castes*, People of India, National Series Vol. 2. New Delhi: Oxford Universit Press.

Sinha, Surajit (1965) 'Tribe-Caste and Tribe-Peasant Continuum in Central India', *Man in India*, 45(1), January–March: 57–83.

Skaria, Ajay (1992) *A Forest Policy in Western India. The Dangs: 1800s–1920s.* Cambridge: University of Cambridge.

Srivastava, S.K. (1958) *The Tharus: A Study in Culture Dynamics.* Agra: Agra University.

Swain, J. (1969) 'Conversion to Christianity', *Man in India*, 49(3), September: 128–35.

Troisi, J. (1979) *Tribal Religious Beliefs and Practices among the Santhals.* New Delhi: Manohar.

Tyler, E.B. (1920) *Primitive Culture*, Vol. 1 (sixth edition). New York: G.B. Putnam and Sons.

Vidyarthi, L.P. (ed.) (1967) *Applied Anthropology.* Allahabad: Kitab Mahal.

Yagnic, A. (1995) 'Hindutva as a Savrana Purana', *Communalism Combat*, 5(45): 31–35.

Yagnic, S. (1995) *Saffronite Swagger.* Madras: Earthworm Books.

10

Ambedkar's Daughters: A Study of Mahar Women in Ahmednagar District of Maharashtra

TRAUDE PILLAI-VETSCHERA

INTRODUCTION

Indian and international scholarship has for a long time shown special interest in the castes that are 'at the bottom of Indian society'. Accordingly, a large number of books and articles have been published on castes which were formerly called 'Untouchable', but later on 'Harijans' (children of God), somewhat patronisingly, and nowadays mostly 'Dalits' (that is, suppressed). The last name has a special appeal at least to the educated members of these communities, who prefer to call themselves 'Dalit' rather than 'Harijan', and are wary of the term 'Untouchable' or 'ex-Untouchable'.

A lot has been written also on Indian women. In recent years, women's studies have appeared in many languages, Indian and foreign, with the focal points ranging from 'abortions of female foetuses' to 'bride-burning' and the ideology of 'sati'. But, amazingly, there is little interest in Dalit women. Most of the women's studies concentrate on middle-class women, among whom very few are Dalits, because only an estimated 5–10 per cent of Harijan women are able to lead a middle-class life. On the other hand, in the general literature of Dalits, usually no special attention is paid to women and their specific problems.

In this chapter, I intend to deal with the Mahar women of Ahmednagar district in the Indian state of Maharashtra.[1] The Mahars are the predominant and most numerous Dalit community in this area. More than other castes of a similar ranking, they avoid their proper caste name when speaking about themselves, but refer to themselves as Harijans or Dalits.[2] Apart from the Mahars, the Mangs (rope-makers), the Chamars (shoemakers), the Mochis (leather-workers), the Dhavars (tanners), the Lohar Ghisadis (iron-workers), the Kaikadis and Buruds (manufactures of different types of baskets), the Telis (oil pressers), the Kumbhars (potters), the Tambolis (sellers of pan-leaves) and other minor low castes are found in the same area. Due to lack of time I could not talk with women of all these communities. The Mahars, even if they are poor, certainly belong to the better-placed groups within the category, and not everything which can be said about them will necessarily also hold true of the other ex-Untouchable castes of this area.

In this context, a few words have to be said about Ahmednagar district. The district of Ahmednagar is located partly in the Upper Godavari Basin and partly in the Bhima Basin, the interfluve in-between forming the extensive Ahmednagar Plateau. The district has a total area of 17,048 sq. km and a population of 2,708,309, according to the 1981 Census report. Out of the population of 2,708,309 in the district, 87.02 per cent live in rural areas and only 12.97 per cent in urban areas. The SCs form 10.62 per cent (in Shevgaon taluka 14.2 per cent) of the population of whom the Mahars are by far the most numerous. Besides them, the important SCs in the district are the Mangs, Chamars, Dhors, Bhangis, Holars and Tirgars. Actually, the Mahars alone number about 10 per cent (according to Swart [1947], in some districts even between 12 and 18 per cent) of the population, but in the census reports those who have been converted to Buddhism or Christianity are not enumerated as SCs anymore.

I was told repeatedly by different people and on different occasions that the Dalits in the Ahmednagar district are compara-tively better off than the Harijans in other areas of Maharashtra as, for example, in Marathwada. A few informants suggested that the reason might be a comparatively high number of Dalit Christians in the district (and, therefore, also quite a few Dalits with higher education). However, the suppression of low castes in Ahmednagar district is said to be 'not so bad'. Low castes could take water from village wells; temple entry was no problem and if somebody, because of his caste, was not permitted to enter a temple, the newspapers reported the case and there was a public discussion. Caste barriers are not as rigid anymore as they had been formerly: for a marriage, for example, friends belonging to different castes may be invited. At a banquet, guests belonging to higher orders may not accept the food that has been prepared by low castes; but the same people may accept food at the house of a low-caste friend when they visit and are invited to have a meal. Generally, men are said to have more problems in overcoming caste barriers, whereas 'women have learned to help each other'.

CLICHÉS AND REALITY: LAZINESS AND LOOSE MORALS

Many high-caste Hindus have certain ideas in mind about people belonging to the lower orders: ideas that they are dirty, lazy, quarrelsome, not reliable, that the women enjoy much more freedom than rural high-caste women and above all that 'they [the women] have no morals and therefore deserve to be raped' (see, for example, Pawade, 1995: 145). What Lannoy says about the relationship between high-caste and tribal societies, the latter of whom he considers the 'antipodes' of the former, to a large extent holds true also of the relationship between dominant high and suppressed low castes:'Dominant people like those they hold in subjection to remain as they imagine them—lazy, feckless, libidinous—because it confirms their self-image as industrious, orderly, adult, and socially organized ... the subject-people represent *a negative identity* in the unconscious of the dominant—what it has been warned not become...' (Lannoy, 1974: 169).

I feel that the two main points are the alleged laziness of the Dalit castes and the alleged low moral standards of their women. Taking into consideration the situation of Mahar women in the Ahmednagar district, it can be shown that these clichés do not hold true in daily life. Usually, Dalit women work hard and very often work much more than their menfolk. Very few Mahar women have a regular job with a fixed salary. And the few who do work in factories usually get no contract and are often cheated. As a rule, men get better payment than women for the same type and amount of work. But, as it is, most Dalit women in the area can find work as daily field labourers only, usually for four to five days per week. Apart from working in other people's fields, the women have to do all the household chores.

Their husbands do not help them, as they consider household work degrading. For many women that means that they go to bed at 11 o'clock at night and they have to get up again at four or five in the morning, light the fire, cook the morning meal and send the children off to school. Then they go to work for eight or nine hours in the fields. And if they do not find work as field labourers, they walk long distances to collect wood or grass. They sell one bundle for the price of Rs 20–25 in the bazaar.

As far as the idea of 'loose morals' is concerned it can be shown as false. It is the upper-caste people who portray the Dalit women as having loose morals because they do not conform to the upper-caste Hindu ideals.

Mahar women in general have more freedom than women of tradition-bound higher Hindu castes or of the Muslim community. Like other low-caste women, they can move about rather freely, once they are married. Without much difficulty, a woman can leave her husband if she is treated badly in his house and live with another man of the same community.

Today, through the Sanskritisation process, the Dalits are losing their cultural world view. They are being influenced more and more by the upper-caste Hindu world view. The practices and values of the high castes have been accepted to a large extent at least by those Dalits who consider themselves 'educated'. The high-caste norm that a woman should not live alone, but stay at first with her father, then with her husband, brother, son or, at least, with a 'male friend' is influencing the lives of the Dalit women in this area. Traditionally, Dalit women were freer in their social, economic and religious sphere. Unlike the upper-caste women who used to remain at home, the Dalit women had to work for their bread mostly outside their home. Hence, they were more economically independent than upper-caste women.

But, today, the Sanskritic values of the upper-caste have influenced the lives of Dalit women. For example, the traditional freedom enjoyed by Dalit women is under constrain. As soon as a man is in the house, the woman is always under his control and has a subordinate position. She cannot invite her relatives when she so feels, but has to welcome her husband's relatives, cook for them and serve them whenever they come on a visit. She cannot keep her earnings for herself. Often the man takes the money that she earns to buy country liquor and gets drunk. On the other hand, if a woman wants to buy a sari, she cannot do so independently, even if she has earned the money. She has to tell her husband and he will buy her clothes. Professor Chavan, a social activist who is involved in the Dalit movement in Nagar district, narrates the impact of Sanskritic values on Dalit women in these words: 'Dalits have taken over the idea that the husband is like a god. In society a Dalit has a low position and he is treated badly by the high castes. Then he comes home, and at least here he wants to be treated with respect.'

For the women, that means that the men take absolute precedence over their wives. They take the decisions, they take the money and they eat first: if something remains, the women may eat it. The men eat as long as they are hungry, sometimes nothing is left and the women go to bed hungry. This 'respect' for men finds expression also in religious practices. Many married Mahar women fast twice a year for the sake of their husbands and they celebrate *vata savitri* in May/ June, walking seven times round a banyan tree, worshipping the tree and praying for the 'grace to be married seven times to the same husband'.

At any rate, the fact of a stricter control of women has also a positive aspect, for even Dalits agree that in this area, sexual molestation of Dalit women by high castes has somewhat decreased during the last 20 years. Even now, Dalit women working for 'rich men' become victims of rape and do not dare to speak up, or they are given money and everything is hushed up (see also Pillai-Vetschera, 1994: 43). But such cases have decreased and the situation has improved, even if it has not changed completely.

HIGH-CASTE WOMEN AND DALIT WOMEN

Repeatedly I would hear statements to the effect that 'tensions in the villages did not exist so much between the castes, but more between men and women, and that in the villages nowadays there was little difference between women of higher castes and of Harijan communities. Both groups had to work in the fields, high castes in their own, low castes in other peoples' fields'. One would also hear that 'women had fewer children now, not more than two or three'. These opinions were not held by the general public but by social workers, who go regularly to the villages and also have contact with Dalit women.

Talking about caste tensions and the present situation of the Harijans in the villages, the Mahar women felt that there was some improvement compared to earlier times. Formerly, they were not permitted to touch anything in the village and old women even today do not dare to take water from the village tank and ask women of higher castes to fill up their pots. While this discussion was going on, the young women spoke in loud voices, whereas the old ones just smiled and nodded. The new generation has no inhibitions any more about using the wells of the high castes. They take the water themselves and feel that life has become slightly better. But they object to still being called Harijans or Backward Classes. These remarks were sufficient to show that caste tensions do exist, even if they are not always evident. During the whole discussion, a woman of the Maratha caste had been standing with a group of Dalits, with shabby clothes and dishevelled hair, her outward appearance did not immediately betray her higher caste. She had been listening quietly, but when the Mahar women complained about being called Harijan, she suddenly spoke up: 'No, that can never stop; God will not permit that all should be regarded as equals.' The amicable atmosphere was spoilt; the women started arguing in high-pitched voices and the Maratha woman left soon thereafter. Similar incidents may be observed quite frequently. Although they are neither dangerous nor serious, they show that tensions between women of different castes do exist and that the traditional behaviour patterns have not been given up completely.

As for the tension between the sexes, there also seems to be a difference between higher and lower castes. According to the statements of hospital doctors, cases of physical violence against women (above all, wife-beating) are less frequent among the higher castes but are more frequent among the lower castes. Very often money is the cause and usually women are reluctant to disclose what has happened in their homes. When they come to the hospital they complain at first about 'pains'. When they are asked how they had hurt themselves, they say that they had had an accident, for example, with a bullock. It is only after prolonged discussions that they admit that they have been beaten up by their husbands.

As far as working in the fields is concerned, low-caste, and sometimes also high-caste women, work. Even in a rich house, the daughter-in-law will usually be ordered to work in the fields at least until her first child is born. The difference between high and low castes has already been mentioned. Dalit women mostly work for an official wage of Rs 20–25 (and very often the actual wage they receive is Rs 15 only) for eight hours in other people's fields.[3] Women of the higher castes work in their family's fields or they supervise the female field hands. Even if the amount of work is the same, the differences are there. High-caste women have the disadvantage that they cannot move about freely and are restricted to the family fields. Besides, they do not receive cash for their work. On the other hand, working for money outside one's own house or field is considered a loss of prestige and, therefore, not an option available for women of high castes.

One more point has to be taken into consideration. Joint families are more frequent among higher castes; Mahars and other Harijan communities, who possess little or no land, often live in nuclear rather than in extended families (with an aged father or mother to be looked after). In joint families, work in the house and fields are divided between the women of the family. Sometimes there may even be servants to help out with the work and there is always someone to look after small children. Dalit women, on the other hand, often have to manage all the work alone or with the help of their daughters.

Nowadays, educated couples have two or three children. But, generally, family planning is more common among the higher castes. During the Emergency, the government tried to enforce population control using force and villagers in the district would often hide in the sugarcane fields for fear of forceful sterilisation. Today the situation is different. 'Even if someone wants to apply for a government house, he does not have to produce a certificate to show that "the operation" had been performed', I was told. There are still large families with many daughters among the Dalits, whereas the number of children in higher-caste families is generally small. The reason is evident. During pregnancy, higher-caste women undergo medical tests (for example, ultra sonography) to determine the sex of the foetus. This costs about Rs 250. If the foetus is found to be female and there is already a daughter in the family, the woman often goes in for an abortion, which is performed in most of the local hospitals.[4] Scheduled Castes women cannot generally afford such medical tests. Sometimes they have a number of daughters until finally the eagerly expected son is born. The consequences are disastrous for Dalit women.

The value of girls has decreased among Harijan castes, whereas among higher castes the situation is slowly changing in favour of girls. There, girls are getting rarer, they are appreciated and pampered and sometimes people, who have had two or three sons look forward to having a daughter. Some of these 'precious daughters' are already married, and expecting mothers in Maharashtra usually go to their parent's house for their first delivery and are taken to the hospital by their parents. Their fathers, who never bothered what happened to their own wives when their children were born, jump up and down whenever their daughters scream during delivery and the mothers get angry. I overheard a women saying: 'It is painful to give birth to a child, but the girl will survive. I have borne five or six children and this man never bothered what happened to me. Now, with his darling daughter, he completely loses his head ....'

CHANGES IN MARRIAGE PATTERNS AND MARRIED LIFE

The Indian caste system is regarded as the oldest hierarchical system in the world. Caste ranking within the system depended to a large extent on the sexual purity of the women. Each community tried to control female sexuality through rules and regulations, very strict ones among the high castes, less severe ones—permitting more freedom to women—among the lower orders. Thus, every caste has established marriage patterns, which are allegedly kept up, above all, by the tradition-bound women. However, nowadays changes can be observed in the Ahmednagar district

Cross-Cousin Marriage

Formerly, among the Mahars, cross-cousin marriages used to be common, that means, a boy was married to his *mama's* (mother's brother's) daughter. In this type of marriage, the girl already knew the family members of the boy and the adjustment of the girl in the boy's house was easy. Nowadays, marriages are often arranged with families from distant villages and no longer between cross-cousins. Monetary considerations play an important role in selecting a bride or a bridegroom for one's own son or daughter. Newly married girls of 13 or 14 years of age are sent to their husbands' villages to live among complete strangers. They do not know anyone and have nobody to talk to. They are uneducated and when they are maltreated in their in-laws' house, they are as a rule at a complete loss about what to do and naturally have no courage to approach the gram panchayat or ask other people for help.

Dowry Instead of Bride Price

Until a few decades ago, bride price was paid among the Mahars. W.Q. Swart made a study of the Mahars of the Ahmednagar district in 1947 and spoke of a 'substantial gift of money and clothes' that had to be given to the girl's father to secure a bride. The money that the girl's father received was called *dejabhoja*. But, about 25–30 years ago, it became more common for the girl's side to pay dowry, which is called *hunda* in Marathi. Many Dalits of this region are of the opinion that this change is due to 'education'. The higher Hindu castes usually pay dowry, whereas among many tribes and nomadic castes of Maharashtra, bride price is more common. 'Education' thus means nothing but to imitate the higher castes.

Nowadays, both among the educated and uneducated Dalits, dowry is paid. Compared to higher castes there is at least one advantage. After marriage, there is usually no harassment of the young wife for more money. Besides, tensions may be slightly less than among the high castes, since young Dalit couples normally do not live with the boy's parents. Instead, they construct their own hut as soon as they can afford it, thus living at some distance from the mother-in-law who is said to always play an important role in the harassment of young wives.

The reasons given for the shift from bride price to dowry are manifold. Many people seem to consider it prestigious to behave like the high castes. ('Dowry is only there for the educated, uneducated people do not give it.') However, bride price has disappeared among the 'uneducated' Dalits also. The changes are ascribed to overpopulation, especially to the surplus of girls in the caste. The fathers and sons say: 'We can see many girls, the people have to get rid of their daughters, so let them pay dowry.' The main reason seems to be the idea that the girls should be settled well by getting them married into a somewhat wealthy family. This is expensive. A common belief among the villagers is: 'If we give more money, the girl will be happy.' The women repeated it all over again, 'We are prepared to give money, my own daughter should be better off than I am.' Under such circumstances not only does the amount of dowry go up, but also the age of girls at marriage goes down. For if there is a marriageable boy in a slightly wealthy family, especially if they own some land, the parents of a girl get scared that somebody 'might snatch him away' and they try to arrange the match as soon as possible. Thus, in Dalit families with little or no formal education most girls are married off when they are between 12 and 15 years old. An uneducated girl of 17 is already considered 'old' and has little chance for a good match. The legal age for marriage (18 for girls, 21 for boys) is hardly ever observed.

However, the amount of dowry also depends on the girl's education and to a smaller extent on her 'beauty', above all, on the colour of her skin. For a dark girl with two or three years of schooling, the dowry is higher than for a girl with a job and maybe fair skin. Boys with some regular income said they could get about Rs 10,000 and one or two *tola*s of gold as dowry. Besides, they expected their future wife to work and contribute to the family income.

If a father is too poor or has too many daughters, he tries to marry them off without paying a dowry. This usually happens when girls are married off to much older men, to widowers with children, to men who are permanently without work or who have physical defects or to men who are known to be notorious drunkards. A girl may also be given in marriage as a second wife to somebody who is already married. Polygamy is illegal, but exists nevertheless. In the rare case of a police inquiry, the husband's statement that 'he is too poor to afford to maintain two wives' is said to be sufficient to keep the police from interfering anymore. And even if it is known that the second wife is treated badly and has to work like a slave, usually nobody bothers to help her. Such 'second-rate weddings' are performed without a big feast, the girl is taken to the man's house and married off with the simplest ceremony possible. All the women said that they knew of many such cases. 'Once the girl is gone, she is gone forever, and nobody bothers, not even her family.'

Whereas the higher castes are said to try to keep good relations with the in-laws, Dalit parents often seem to feel that their obligations are over once their daughter is married. Sometimes desperate young wives are taken back by their parents, but frequently they are told, 'You have another name now, and we have done everything.' Neighbours normally do not interfere, even if they know that a young woman is being maltreated. Usually her native village is far away and in the new village she is only a daughter-in-law.

While bride burning for the sake of dowry seems more frequent among higher castes, cases of suicide or attempted suicide are becoming common among Dalits today. This was confirmed by a woman doctor in a private hospital of this region (Ahmednagar district), who said sadly, 'Women of all castes kill themselves'. Mostly the girls burn themselves—that is easier than jumping into a well. All of them have kerosene, which they pour over themselves, and matches to light themselves up. The people who bring the young women to the hospital try to pretend at first that a cooking accident had taken place. In all such cases, the police has to be called, the government hospital has to be informed and only then can the girl be accepted as a patient even in a private hospital. When the girls die (in most cases they do), the government hospital has to be informed again for the post mortem.

Divorce

Perhaps the number of suicides of young Mahar women began to go up because a new attitude towards marriage has been forced on them.

Formerly it was relatively easy for a Dalit woman to obtain a divorce. When a wife felt she was being treated badly by her husband, she could leave him without major problems, returning to her parents' house or she started to live with another man (*ghara ghusane*, see Pillai-Vetschera, 1994: 50). Nowadays, divorce seems much more difficult, at least for women. A man, who wants to get rid of his wife, sends her home for a festival or for the delivery of her first child and does not bring her back. A Dalit woman, on the other hand, is nowadays not supposed to leave her husband but to stay with him, even if she suffers. When there are quarrels, she may only hope that everything will return to normal. She cannot leave his house and her children. For the sake of 'society' she is expected to put up with everything. ('What will people say if I leave the house or if I talk back.') Many wives are scared of being beaten by drunken husbands ('with any object that might be at hand.') And they still find no way to leave the man. I doubt whether 20 or 25 years ago women would have made statements like the ones I heard during my study. For example, they say, 'Our men don't treat us as badly as animals, this means that the men are good.' Somehow, I got the sad impression that these women felt that suffering was an essential part of a woman's life and nothing could be done about it.

Widow Remarriage

Remarriage of a widow was regarded as inauspicious by the Mahars even earlier. The bride and the groom had to cover their faces with cow-dung in order to avert evil from themselves and from the people who took part in the ceremony, and the groom had to spend the night after the wedding in the jungle. It was considered inauspicious for other people to see his face early next morning. These customs have disappeared, but the attitude towards widow remarriage has not changed. On the contrary, formerly only an older woman with children 'who were big enough to look after their mother' and who wanted to remarry was regarded with disapproval. For a young woman with one or two children there were no problems, and her parents arranged for her remarriage soon after she became a widow. Today the general opinion among the Dalits is that 'low-caste women cannot marry once their husbands die'. They also believe that 'if a widow is young and her parents permit it, she can marry again, but if she has children, she must not remarry'.

High-Caste Brides

The control of female sexuality is considered one of the keys to understanding caste and the ranking of castes properly. Caste members have to ensure that 'low quality blood does not enter the caste through men of lower caste' (Das, 1992: 74). If low-caste men have access to high-caste women, not only is the women's purity in danger, but also the social rank and status of the whole jati. Female sexuality, therefore, was always strictly controlled among the higher castes and sexual relations outside marriage strictly forbidden. Marriage was between equals and, if not, hypergamous: women moved up in hierarchy with the help of money. To give a daughter to someone down the hierarchy was strictly forbidden from the early times onwards and, especially in north India, the bride-giving family is considered of lower status vis-à-vis the family that accepts the bride.

The situation has changed in Maharashtra. A number of educated Mahar boys are married to high-caste girls. Dalit girls, on the other hand, practically cannot marry Brahmins, even if according to the ancient law and tradition this type of hypergamous *anuloma* marriage would be more acceptable than hypogamous *pratiloma* marriage. One of the Dalit leaders told me.

> In college, Marwadi or Brahmin girls fall in love with Mahar boys, who are sometimes rather handsome. On the other hand, a Brahmin will not accept a Mahar girl. Only a girl from his caste will be accepted by his family and she has to pay a dowry. A Mahar father does not protest if his son wants to marry a Brahmin girl. But he will not permit him to marry a Chamar or a Mang girl. Many RPI leaders in Maharashtra are married to Brahmin women. Likewise, Ambedkar's son and grandson married high-caste women.

In an article published in *Dalit Voice*, Kumar warned Dalits in 1990 of the 'fair-skinned Aryan sex bombs' and the danger of one-sided inter-caste marriages, propagated by 'socialist Brahmins' in order to avoid dowry and to get their daughter's future children entitled to the 'much-hated reservation benefits'. Dalit girls, who were not accepted as brides by the high castes and rejected by the men of their own caste, had no other possibility but to become prostitutes (Kumar, 1990: 14).

Certainly cases of Mahar–Brahmin marriages are not so many that one has to worry seriously about the Dalit girl's future. But the fact remains that Dalit girls are hardly accepted as brides by high castes. On the other hand, Mahars, who consider themselves superior to other Harijan communities of the area, will not at all tolerate mixed marriages with castes whom they consider lower in ranking, namely, the Mangs, Dhors and others. 'You see, all people are not equal', I was told. 'The castes have different cultures, languages and behaviour. The Mahar are higher, the Mang or Dhor are lower, and we cannot give our daughters to them or accept their girls. If such a marriage took place, the couple could not live here; they would have to go away.' Even conversion to another faith does not change this attitude. Caste is much more important than religious denomination. A Mang Christian will not marry a Mahar Christian, but within the Mahar community Hindus, Buddhists and Christians may marry freely. Especially in the case of the Mangs, the traditional antagonism between the Mahars and the Mangs makes a marriage between individuals belonging to these two communities even more impossible. In most places, the two castes even today avoid taking water from each other's wells.

EVERYDAY LIFE

Economic Conditions

Compared to 10 or 20 years ago, today there are more families in the community who seem economically well-off. There are a few families who 'became richer than they themselves had expected', but the majority of the Dalits still live in poor conditions and it seems that the gap between the rich and the poor has become wider. The main complaints of the poorer women were that they did not have good houses, had few work opportunities and that they earned only Rs 15 per day. Old women do not find work and depend on their daughters-in-law. Men spend a lot of money on alcohol. Often there is no money to buy vegetables and oil.

One of the main problems, in this draught-stricken area of Maharashtra has always been the lack of water. The soil is good and everything grows well, provided there is enough rain. In the last three or four years, with the monsoons failing to a large extent, the wells have had to be dug deeper and deeper, an undertaking which only the rich can afford. The water that can be pumped up goes to the fields of the rich farmers, whereas the poor remain without it and their fields dry up completely. In February and March 1996, the river beds were dry, the water pumps in the living quarters of the Dalits sometimes did not give water for two or three days. The rich have bigger vessels, servants to fetch water and the possibility to store more water. The women of poor families have to queue up for water and they cannot store much in their houses.

However, the water problem may sometimes also help to over-come caste barriers. In one village, recently, women of all the castes took out a *morcha* and went with empty water pots to the panchayat office and sat down there to demonstrate that they had no water. In another village without water, the villagers decided to dig a ditch to get access to a pipeline, which was only one mile away. Besides the low castes, a few Marwadis and one Brahmin family also live in that village. The Brahmin woman was teased by the others because nobody believed that she would participate in the work. But she told them, 'Do you think that I cannot dig, or do you think that I do not need water?'

Apart from water, another big problem for Dalit women, who cannot afford to buy kerosene, is the problem of procuring fuel for cooking. Men think that it is easy for the women to use dry *babul* twigs, which the trees shed and which can be collected. The women know that there are not enough twigs. When possible, they make cow-dung cakes or they walk far to collect wood.

Earlier, Mahar men often went to big cities like Mumbai or Pune to earn money for their families, when there was no chance for work in the villages. Nowadays, husbands and wives often work for sugarcane factories, which have mushroomed in the area, and undertake sugarcane cutting. Sugarcane is cut thrice, after which the soil gets exhausted and the plants are removed. Sugarcane factories have contracts with farmers who had been given loans to plant sugarcane. When the cane has to be cut, the factories employ labourers who are transferred from one place to another until all the sugarcane fields, whose owners have a contract with the factory, have been harvested. This results in work for six to eight months, during which period the labourers are always on the move. Many villages seem half-deserted when the Mahars go away to cut sugarcane. Children remain with their grandparents or neighbours: the older ones sometimes have to leave school and are taken along by their parents. While the labourers are employed, they can hardly be traced, as they are made to shift from one village to another. If somebody at home falls sick during their absence, nobody can inform the labourers; the neighbours usually do not want to spend money to take the infirm to hospital. When the sugarcane workers return home, they may sometimes find that a family member has died during their absence.

Working in the sugarcane fields, the Dalit labourers are also prone to be bitten by snakes. When it starts raining, the number of snake bites increases considerably and six to eight patients may be rushed to the hospital in one day. Even during the night, the snakes may easily enter the huts, which the workers put up for the duration of their stay. The snakes seek shelter from the cold and rain and often they sting the inhabitants of the huts. The treatment for a snakebite costs between Rs 3,000 and 4,000. Even if only a part of the cost is to be paid, a substantial part of one's earnings has to be spent to save one's life.

Bonded labour in this area is rare, although there are a few cases of people who have been trying for the last 40 years to get rid of their debts. It is quite common that somebody 'sells' himself for one year and works like a slave for another person, but 'usually only men do such things'.

Tensions

According to K. Pawade, Dalit women live in permanent tension:

> ...they have to take water from upper-caste wells, go to the nearby fields of the upper castes for defecation, and are beaten up by high-caste women when they do not want to work for them like slaves. They live in permanent fear that they might get beaten up or burnt or that something might happen to their husbands and children. (1995: 145)

The situation does not seem to be so bad in the Ahmednagar district. Dalit women emphasised that they had no major problems with the higher castes. But within their Dalit community, compared to men, it is the women who have more worries and tensions. During my fieldwork I came across some Dalit women who said, 'Dalit women have no *chappals* (slippers) and their clothes are often worn out. Often they cannot sleep for they think, "What shall we eat tomorrow, what will happen tomorrow." For women this is a bigger problem, because they are worried about the children. Men don't worry so much. But women do not know how to get money for education.'

The women also pointed out the differences between the higher and lower castes:

> In the higher castes, the men bring home the money and not the women; women look after the household, but not outside affairs. We, Harijan women, are 'allowed' to earn money and our men have less tension, because they can count on us. Somehow, we always manage to find some money and prepare something to eat. And if a woman works well, her husband relies on her more and more, and she has to work more and more.
>
> Often our men sleep quietly, and we cannot sleep, because we think of our work and money. The men go to the bazaar, roam around and enjoy themselves. We always stay behind and work. We have no time like that.

Political Awareness

Where elections are concerned, most women do not decide for themselves for which party they will vote. In the villages, the men often discuss these matters and decide, together with their sarpanch, in favour of a political party. Once the decision has been made, the elections become a 'family business'; the men announce their decision and the women vote for the party their husband has 'chosen'. When Indira Gandhi was head of the Congress, some women were impressed by her and voted for her 'because she was a woman'. Usually women do not take part in rallies, etc. The general opinion is that 'There is no use for elections, because for us nothing ever changes. Nobody does anything for us, neither the RPI nor the Congress.'

In the panchayat samitis, nowadays, two seats are reserved for women, one from the high castes and one from the low castes. That sounds impressive, but usually women who do not have the courage to speak out are chosen for the posts. Often the meetings take place after nine o'clock in the night and while the men are well prepared and know what will be discussed at the meeting, the women, who have been working the whole day, are not informed about the issues under discussion and hence cannot participate in the proceedings. Often they do not have an opinion of their own. The decisions are taken by their husbands, who instruct the women what to say. A special name is in use for such husbands: sarpanch *pati*, 'the sarpanch's husband' which implies that the husband is for all practical purposes the sarpanch.

Self-Esteem

Talking to young Mahar women, I got the impression that compared to many women of their generation, they were outspoken and self-conscious. But what is the actual situation? How do the women see their position in the family and society, what about their self-respect? To give a general answer is difficult. Naturally much depends on the women's age and whether she is a newly-wed wife, a mother of sons, a middle-aged mother-in-law, or an old and weak woman, who cannot earn her living anymore and has to be cared for. Women belonging to this last group especially have little self-esteem. They nod apologetically when the daughters-in-law repeatedly mention the fact that nobody wants to employ old women anymore and they seem to consider themselves a burden to their families. They are also the ones who cling to traditions, which younger women may reject as unjust. And even though they themselves are badly suppressed by the caste system, they endeavour to keep up the rules and laws of their own sub-caste (for example, that low-caste people should not take water from the village well, that the husband has a right to beat his wife, and so on).

Education is as important as the age factor. Uneducated girls think and behave differently from those who have received a better formal education. The latter will not keep quiet so easily when they have something to say, whereas the former think twice before talking back because they are scared. 'If I say something wrong, or if I do something wrong, my husband might leave me. I am not educated. When a woman is young and has a long life in front of her, she has to adjust and keep quiet' was more or less the answer that I frequently got. An 'uneducated' woman often feels at a loss outside her own village and cannot do anything independently. When she falls sick she does not even know which bus to take to reach the hospital and she is scared of arranging anything by herself.

Uneducated young women will not open their mouths when their mother-in-law is present, whereas others may even contradict the mother-in-law, who usually is less educated. When, for example, a sick child is taken to hospital, the mother-in-law will often take all the decisions and the child's mother is brought along only as a 'milk-cow'. But, if the young woman is educated she will want to talk with the doctors and take the necessary decisions herself. Similarly, educated young women make up their minds—sometimes even against their mother-in-law's will—to participate in the vaccination programmes for their children; or they take them to mother-and-child care programmes—without asking permission or seeking help from the husbands or mothers-in-law. Often these independent women manage to influence the uneducated girls of the village towards self-reliance also.

Welfare organisations, which began programmes for women in the villages, had their pertinent experiences. In the beginning, women often refused to speak in public about their needs and problems. ('In our village it has not happened that women stand in front of men and talk.') Many men are convinced that women themselves are not able to decide whether they want to participate in such programmes or not. I had the opportunity to be present at a mahila mandal meeting. The high-caste schoolteacher, who was asked to give a talk on the occasion, said that 'women alone cannot do anything at all; the men should tell their wives, sisters, and daughters-in-law to participate in all the mahila programmes'.

To take decisions without feeling convinced that they have the support of their men is probably the main difficulty for many Dalit women in the villages. They have been conditioned to have no faith in their own decisions. Usually when a project for women is to be started in a village, the men have to be approached first. When the men have approved it, the women are eager to participate, but then they expect that the social workers will organise everything and just tell them what they are supposed to do. Most women lack self-confidence and faith in their own abilities. When they are put to work, they usually do well, but it generally takes time to convince them that they can carry on a project alone, without further help from social workers and without the men telling them what to do next. However, once they have realised that they can manage alone, this helps to build up their self-esteem and may gradually lead to the desire to change things in the village.

Sister Franziska, a social worker who has dedicated many years of her life to the uplift of Dalit women through mahila mandal programmes in the villages, told me: 'The women are able to learn, and sometimes they even learn faster than the men would want.' In villages, where the projects have gone on for some time, the attitude of the women towards men seems to change a bit. When major decisions have to be taken and the men come for the meeting, it may happen that a low-caste woman, who is in charge, asks the sarpanch, the village teacher and other important persons, one after another, to give their opinion.

In the area under survey, two organisations run mahila mandals: the one discussed earlier is based in a local hospital, the other is run by a congregation of Catholic nuns nearby. In the mahila groups, the women learn to save small amounts of money every month. Also, projects like producing calcium powder to make *rangoli*, making *papad* and *agarbatti*, grinding *dal*, etc., are carried out. Some women, who work as daily labourers, can be employed at a fixed salary in these programmes. It has been noticed that the women get their ration cards (which they also need to take part in elections or to apply for a government house). In one village a watershed project has been started, in another a poultry farm will be opened. All these activities have brought changes in the attitudes of the Dalit women.

The activities of the mahila mandals help to overcome caste barriers. Often it can be observed that in the beginning, low-caste women will not sit next to high-caste women, or they get up when high-caste women arrive. Slowly the situation changes: after the programmes have been going on for some time, all women sit together and work together on their projects. When lists of participants in an event have to be compiled, it is only a person's first name that is written down nowadays whereas formerly the caste name was also listed.

Mothers and Daughters

As discussed earlier, it is clear that education can make a difference in the behaviour and self-esteem of Dalit women. We would expect that mothers of young daughters would have understood the situation and would have tried to give the girls a better education. Unfortunately, the circumstances are often adverse. First, of all, the relevant infrastructure in small villages does not exist. There may be only a primary school in the village, high schools are often miles away. When there is no bus, the problems become almost insurmountable. Boys are allowed to walk to school and come back in the evening, but young girls are not permitted to go anywhere alone, especially if it gets dark, as this would mar their reputation. Normally, people do not bother much about married women, who move about alone in the fields, but they are concerned about unmarried girls.

Of course boarding schools are a good solution for village girls and nowadays parents are eager to get their daughters accepted in hostels, even if some years ago many were reluctant to send the girls away from home. If one belongs to a Dalit community, there is also a monthly grant of Rs 30 per child towards hostel expenses. Nowadays, sometimes problems arise when some of the girls in the hostels get used to an easier way of life and do not want to go back to their villages. They get used to luxuries like bathrooms, electricity, a fan and water inside the house. In the villages all these amenities are missing.

However, many girls are not permitted to stay for long even in the boarding school. When there are more children in a family and both parents work, an older girl usually has to stay at home and look after her younger brothers and sisters, whereas the boys are permitted to continue going to school. Even if the mother does not leave the village in order to do sugarcane harvesting, she has often to rely on the help of her daughters to keep the family going. As mentioned earlier, the Mahars usually do not live in joint families and a woman with small children cannot run the household satisfactorily, fetch water and earn money if she has no one to help her. Often tensions arise in families when daughters are asked to stay at home, while their brothers, who may not be as good students as the girls, are permitted to go to school. Many women feel that they deprive their children of their childhood due to economic constraints.

Higher education for most girls, therefore, seems beyond their reach, even if Christian and Buddhist Mahars especially are very keen on getting their children educated. Nevertheless, in most villages only one or two Dalit girls manage to pass their senior secondary certificate (SSC) examination in a couple of years. Girls, who reach the tenth standard and fail are usually not permitted to repeat the class and are married off at the age of sixteen or seventeen. Very few Mahar girls in the area of Shevgaon village in the so-called famine belt of Ahmednagar district finish college and get a graduate degree. They can find work as schoolteachers, in post offices, and so on. If they graduate college and marry, their husbands decide whether they may work or not. In most cases, a family is glad if their daughter-in-law has a well-paid job.

DALIT MOVEMENT AND WOMEN

All over India, Dalit organisations are active and are forcefully demanding human rights of which they have been deprived for centuries. Unfortunately, this Dalit movement has to struggle with a number of external and internal problems, above all the problems of unity. Not only are the Dalits split up into many castes and sub-castes, but there are also divisions within sub-castes in the villages. Everyone wants to demonstrate that he is better than his neighbour and is not really keen on helping his caste members to rise up in society. So far as the Mahars are concerned, it can be observed that those who have come up in life, try to move as far as possible from the *maharvada* and do not bother anymore about their caste fellows. So, on the one hand, we get the feeling that even in a small Dalit community, there is little willingness for earnest cooperation. On the other, there are people who want to extend the Dalit movement to large sections of the Indian population and include not only the Harijans in it, but also the BCs, OBCs, Adivasis, landless labourers and the like, extending the term to such an extent that 70 per cent of India's population would be included under the label.

In our context the question to be asked is: What does 'Dalitness' mean for women and what does the Dalit movement do for them? It has become fashionable among many Dalits to refer to themselves as Adi-Dravidas, implying that their castes belong to the autochthonous groups who had inhabited the country before the invasions of the Aryans. Women in Dravidian society had a good position. The love poems of the ancient Tamil Sangam literature show that women were comparatively free, could choose their husbands, work together with their menfolk and move freely (Subrahmanian, 1966). Later on, the women of the 'Untouchable' castes enjoyed much more freedom than the women of the high Hindu castes; divorce was possible, widow marriage practised, the virginity of the bride was not as important as among the high castes and girls were appreciated at least as valuable working members of the family, for whom the bridegroom's family had to pay a substantial amount of money (see Deliege, 1997).

Today the position of Dalit women in their society seem to have changed drastically. How did these changes come about? Women, and especially Dalit women, are often blamed for being 'traditionalists'. 'They trudge along as they have always done and they have no interest in improving their situation, so what can we do?' a Mahar told me. If the women sustain traditions, how were all these changes possible? Old women still remember that when they were young, bride price had to be paid, but they cannot explain how and why dowry has taken its place and why they were not able to prevent the changes. It seems that the explanation is a simple one: Even if many Dalits nowadays say that they do not believe in 'Sanskritisation', they, nevertheless, have adopted from the high castes those behavioural patterns, which appeal to them, such as depriving the women of their freedom; but at the same time they have retained some of their traditional practices such as sending their women outside their home for manual labour. A Dalit patriarchy has developed in which Dalit men use the same mechanisms to subjugate their women as high-caste men had done for ages against their own women and also against the Dalits.

As far as I can see, the Dalit movement as it exists today, has done much for a handful of male Dalit intellectuals, less for the great majority of Dalit men such as improving their position within the family, and nothing for Dalit women. The only way out of the dilemma confronting the women would be to initiate their own Dalit movement, because given the Dalit men's attitude towards their women, no major changes may be expected from that side in the near future. Dalit women have also arrived at the same conclusion. On 11 August 1995, the National Federation of Dalit Women (NFDW) was formed in Delhi, to liberate Dalit women from all oppression (Guru, 1995: 2548–50). Two main issues stand out as important factors in Dalit women's liberation: The first is male dominance and patriarchy within the Dalit community and the other is the role of caste in determining Dalit identity. It is felt by the members of NFDW that the caste factor does not get adequate recognition in the analysis of women's problems by non-Dalit, middle-class, urbanised women activists. In fact, caste is very important because it gives definitions to the term Dalit. The influence of the NFDW is still not widespread. Whether these Dalit women will be able to create a strong and effective movement remains to be seen. The problems that have to be tackled are many and till now the number of Dalit women with higher education is small. In my opinion, better education for the girls belonging to the low castes is a precondition for any further improvement.

NOTES

1. The material presented in this chapter was collected during a stay in Ahmednagar district, to be exact, in and around Shevgaon, a small town in this district, in February/March 1996. I wish to express my gratitude to Kondiram Raju Ingle, Amita Patil, Professor Chavan and the Mary Sisters, who helped me in different ways to collect the material. The sisters and doctors of Nityaseva Hospital, Shevgaon, not only provided valuable information but also provided accommodation during that period.
2. This coincides with observations made by Moffatt (1979: 119) and Charsley (1996: 17) in south India, namely, that 'Harijan' became 'the preferred name of particular castes, usually one only in any particular area'.
3. For the same amount of work, men receive Rs 25–30 per day.
4. The estimated number of such abortions is about 200,000 per year (Arora, 1996: 420).

REFERENCES AND SELECT BIBLIOGRAPHY

Arora, D. (1996) 'The Victimising Discourse—Sex-Determination Technologies and Policy', *Economic and Political Weekly*, 31(7), February: 420–24.
Charsley, S. (1996) '"Untouchable": What is in a Name?', *The Journal of the Royal Anthropological Institute*, 2(1): 1–23.

Das, V. (1992). *Structure and Cognition* (second edition). New Delhi: Oxford University Press.

Deliege, Robert (1997) *The World of the 'Untouchables': Paraiyars of Tamil Nadu.* New Delhi: Oxford University Press.

Guru, G. (1995) 'Dalit Women Talk Differently', *Economic and Political Weekly*, 30(41/42), October: 2548–50.

Kumar, S. (1990) 'Dangers of Dalit Boys Marrying Brahmin Girls', *Dalit Voice*, 9(6): 8–9.

Lannoy, R. (1974) *The Speaking Tree.* New Delhi: Oxford University Press.

Moffatt, M. (1979) *An Untouchable Community in South India.* Princeton: Princeton University Press.

Pawade, K. (1995) 'The Position of Dalit Women in Indian Society', in B. Das and J. Massey (eds), *Dalit Solidarity*, pp. 145–64. Delhi: ISPCK.

Pillai-Vetschera, T. (1994) *The Mahars.* New Delhi: Intercultural Publications.

Subrahmanian, N. (1966) *Sangam Polity.* Bombay: Asia Publishing House.

Swart, W.Q. (1947) 'The Mahar Folk' (MS). Ahmednagar: Ahmednagar College.

11

The BSP in Uttar Pradesh: Whose Party is It?

CHRISTOPHE JAFFRELOT

D r Ambedkar, the architect of Dalit politics in India, oscillated between two different strategies so far as party-building was concerned.[1] To begin with, he founded a party aiming at the rural and urban workers, the Independent Labour Party (1935). Then he focused not on a socio-economic class any more, but on a status group, the Dalits, by launching the Scheduled Castes Federation (1942). And finally he reverted to a mixed approach that was intended to woo all the depressed categories of the lower castes by initiating the Republican Party of India (1956), which came into existence after Ambedkar's death in 1957.

Kanshi Ram, who inherited some of the legacy of Dr Ambedkar, followed a similar political trajectory. He first established, in 1981, the Dalit Shoshit Samaj Sangharsh Samiti (DSSSS, committee for the struggle of the community of the oppressed and the exploited), a party in whose name the word 'Dalit' had the strongest connotations. The DSSSS was immediately associated with the Untouchable castes. But three years later, he built the Bahujan Samaj Party which aspired to represent the 'Bahujans', that is, all those who were both socio-economically backward and from a low status group.

In practice, Ambedkar could never attract support from large groups, except from his own caste, the Mahars of Maharashtra. But the BSP, while it has largely remained confined to one state only, Uttar Pradesh, seems to have become more than the party of one jati and even more than a Dalit only party.[2]

PARTY OF THE DALITS, OR PARTY OF THE CHAMARS?

While Ambedkar's party remained identified with the Mahars, the BSP's core group may not even be the Dalits, but the Chamars, the largest Untouchable caste of north India. Kanshi Ram himself was born in 1932 in rural Punjab—his native village Khwaspur is situated in the district of Ropar (Parliament of India, 1992: 326)[3]—in a family of Ramdasias, Chamars converted to Sikhism, though he made a point to keep his caste a secret. In an interview he gave me 10 years ago, without disclosing his caste, he underlined that his first environment was not as oppressive as the one Untouchables suffered elsewhere 'because of the Sikh religion, and more especially because most of the Chamars have adopted the Sikh religion;[4] there was somewhat upward mobility'.[5]

An Attempt at Constructing a Dalit Vote Bank in UP

The other major figure of the BSP, Mayawati, is also a Chamar. She is from Uttar Pradesh (her native village, Badalpur, is located in the district of Ghaziabad). Though she was brought up in Delhi, Mayawati was successful in her studies in another UP town, Meerut (where she did her BA and BEd.) before returning to Delhi for her LLB. She became a schoolteacher in 1977 and her first political experience took place during the same year within the Janata Party. Three years later, she was preparing for the Indian Administrative Service examination when she met Kanshi Ram[6] who persuaded her to enter politics. In 1984, she left her job to devote herself to the BSP. She became chief minister of UP for the first time in 1995— she was to occupy this post two more times.

The BSP projected Mayawati as a source of pride after she became chief minister of UP. Her accession to the topmost position in UP was part of a deliberate strategy: considering this first short-term as CM, she declared in an interview: 'my biggest achievement has been consolidation of the dalit vote bank' (*The Pioneer*, 23 October 1995, p. 9). She became an icon and also became adept at manipulating symbols especially the pan-Dalit symbol that Ambedkar is today all over India. Agra University was re-named Dr Bhimrao Ambedkar University. New districts were carved out and renamed after Dr Bhimrao Ambedkar and Mahamayana, the mother of Buddha. The

Agra stadium was named Eklavya, etc. More importantly, dozens of statues of Ambedkar were put up across the state to impose Dalit presence all over the public space.

But the consolidation of the BSP's Dalit vote bank also resulted from the special treatment Mayawati granted to the Dalits. They benefited from some concrete measures during the four-and-a-half-months of Mayawati's first government. Originally, the Ambedkar Village Scheme allotted special funds for socio-economic development for one year to villages which had a 50 per cent SC population. Then Mayawati extended this programme in June 1995 to those villages which had a 22–30 per cent SC population and on top of it, in 1997–98, 10 villages with a cent SC population of 30 per cent or more were selected in each assembly constituency. All in all, 25,434 villages were included in the Ambedkar Village Scheme. The Dalits of these villages received special treatment since roads, hand-pumps, houses, etc., were built in their neighbourhoods.[7] Sudha Pai underlines the fact that 'The Jatavs in our sample villages, described the 1995 Mayawati government as "our government" and were quick to point out the benefits they had received' (2002: 129–30). When Mayawati came back to power in 1997, the Ambedkar Villages Programme (AVP) was revived in a big way under the direct supervision of the chief minister, who admitted that she was focusing her attention 'on one section of society', that is, the Dalits.[8] The Rs 3,500 million scheme covered 11,000 villages. In addition, 15,000 Ambedkar statues were installed throughout UP, one of them, in Lucknow at an estimated cost of Rs 250,000. Also, in Lucknow, the Rs 1,200 million Ambedkar Udhyan (park) assumed colossal dimensions with five 12 feet tall bronze Ambedkar statues. But has the BSP reached out to all sorts of Dalit groups, or has it remained confined to the Chamars—also known as the Jatavs in UP—as suggested by Pai?

Capitalising on the Jatav Movement

The BSP borrowed a large part of its political culture from the Chamars, not only because its leaders came from this caste, but also because the Chamars have been the largest caste group in UP (12.5 per cent of the population according to the 1931 Census, as against the Brahmins who form 9.2 per cent of the population) and the most

politicised caste of Dalits in northern India since the 1920s (see
Briggs [1920] and Kshirsagar [1994]). To begin with, they remained
imbued with the ethos of Sanskritisation, as evident from the
religious style of Swami Achhutanand, the first Dalit leader of north
India and the founder of the Adi-Hindu movement (see Jigyansu
[1960] and Gooptu [1993]. Their craze for Sanskritisation found its
clearest expression in the name Chamar activists gave to their caste
at the turn of the twentieth century: 'Jatavs', from Yadu, the founding
father of a dynasty of Kshatriyas.[9] Owen Lynch points out that, at
that time, 'The Jatavs were not attempting to destroy the caste system;
rather they were attempting to rise within it in a valid, though not
licit, way' (1969: 75). But the influence of Ambedkar made a strong
impact on the Jatav movement in the 1940s, including in terms of
conversions from Hinduism to Buddhism—so much so that the
'Buddhist identity has replaced Sanskritic Kshatriya identity' (ibid.:
206, see also p. 93). This process was especially strong in west UP
where, unsurprisingly, the RPI made electoral inroads in the 1960s.
As a result, the RPI won eight MLA seats in 1962 and 10 in 1967,
as against respectively three and five in Maharashtra, the party's
original stronghold. The RPI performed so well thanks to the grass-
root work of dedicated activists such as B.P. Maurya, who, however,
defected to the Congress in the early 1970s.[10]

Thirty years later, the BSP recaptured the same segments of the
Dalit population. For instance, it carved a niche for itself in Agra.
During the 1995 municipal elections, the BSP won 32 seats out of 80.

The BSP absorbed parts of the Jatav culture to such an extend
that one of the mottos in which its ideology got encapsulated, was:
Tilak, tarâjû aur talvâr isko mâro joote char, which means, 'The tilak
[emblem of the sectarian affiliation of the Hindus which is applied
on the forehead and symbolises the Brahman], the balance [symbol
of merchants castes] and the sword [symbol of warriors castes], hit
them with their shoes [that is, with the symbol of the Chamars who
work the leather]' (Kanshi Ram, 1992a: 67).

The Chamar Core Group of a Dalit Nebulae

The BSP has attracted the UP Chamars in large numbers because
this caste owned a small elite which could not find a niche for itself

in any other party. The Census of India shows that in UP the literacy rate among the SCs rose from 7.14 per cent in 1961 to 10.2 per cent in 1971, 15 per cent in 1981 and 27 per cent in 1991. The Chamars benefited more than any other caste from the progress made by the SCs in terms of education, not only because they were the largest Dalit caste (they constituted 56.6 per cent of the SC population of UP in 1991, as against the Pasis, who formed 14.6 per cent of the SC population), but also because they modernised more quickly.

This modernisation process was partly due to the relative affluence resulting from their activity as shoemakers. Some of the leather workers became artisans or even traders. But this upward social mobility was boosted after Independence by the reservation system which enabled thousands of Dalits to join university and the public services in even larger numbers. In Uttar Pradesh, among the cadres from the IAS, the SC officers 'form the largest number next to the Brahmins and Kayasths' (Ramaseshan, 1995: 73). Yet, these officers felt frustrated because they were denied 'important posts in the districts as well as the state capital' (ibid.). The BSP cadres came first from this new, frustrated Dalit elite which had already been the main supporters of the BAMCEF. Pai has shown that the BSP activists belonged to a new generation of young, educated Dalits. Out of 66 BSP MLAs in 1993, 16 had a BA, seven had an MA, 15 had an LLB and one a Ph.D; three years later, out of 67 MLAs, 24 had a BA, two had an MA, 19 had an LLB and one had a Ph.D (Pai, 2002: 96).

But why did these young Dalit activists opt for the BSP? Kanchan Chandra argues convincingly that they did so because 'each of these men was seeking better economic opportunities and higher status recognition than his parents, and each found these in politics' (Chandra, 2004: 185ff). But why not in other, more established parties? The Congress, the first choice of the Dalits after Independence, should have been a more natural avenue for upward socio-political upward mobility. But the party has remained upper-caste dominated till today, as evident from the social composition of the party apparatus as well as the status of its elections candidates (see Jaffrelot [2003]).[11]

In contrast, the new Dalit leaders who captured the most important posts within the BSP were Chamars. According to K. Chandra, 85 per cent of the state-level posts of the BSP in UP were cornered

by Chamars in 1995–96. None of them went to the Pasis or leaders
from any other Dalit caste (Chandra, 2004: 189). In fact, Pasis (pig
herders), Balmikis (sweepers), Khatiks (meat-cutters) and others
dislike the Chamars because of their socio-economic and poitical
ascent. They also resent the way they cornered the reservation quotas.
Such an alienation of minor Dalit jatis recalls the reaction of non-
Mahar Dalit groups vis-à-vis Ambedkar's parties in Maharashtra: the
Mangs and Chambhars preferred to vote for the Congress or other
parties (including the Shiv Sena) instead of joining hands with the
Mahars, a group whose domination they resented a lot. Similarly, in
UP, the Balmikis support the Congress or the BJP, partly because of
their leaning towards Sanskritisation and partly because they offer
an alternative to the BSP (see Jaffrelot et al. [2002]). K. Chandra
insists that the BSP 'does not do well among Chamars because
Chamars are naturally attracted to it. Rather, it obtains the support
of Chamar voters only when it supersedes the competition as channel
to office for Chamar elites from across subdivisions among Chamars,
and not otherwise' (Chandra, 2004: 170). I would propose a different
view. Certainly, the key element in the attractiveness of the BSP for
the educated Chamar leaders was the opportunities it offered them;
but so far as the voting pattern of the Dalits of UP is concerned,
the identification of the BSP as a Chamar or a Jatav party played
a role in attracting more Chamar/Jatav voters and for repulsing
Dalits from other jatis. Identity politics and political cultures keep
some explanatory potential in this context and a rational choice-
oriented interpretation is bound to underestimate this potential. In
fact, a purely rational choice-oriented kind of interpretation, which
would ignore the impact of sentiments of belongingness, could not
explain the scope of the pro-BSP Chamar vote.[12]

Indeed, surveys indicate that most of the voters of the BSP come
from the Chamars who were already the mainstay of the RPI when
the party made some incursion in UP in the 1960s. (In 1962, the
electoral slogan of the RPI was '*Jatav Muslim bhai bhai, Hindu kaum
kahan se aye?*'—'Jatavs and Muslims are brothers, where do the
Hindus [community, nation] come from?' [cited in Duncan, 1979:
286]). Table 11.1 shows that in the second half of the 1990s, when
the BSP really took off electorally, about three-fourths of the
Chamars voted for it.

TABLE 11.1

Caste and Community of the BSP Voters (in percentage)

CASTES AND COMMUNITIES	1996 VIDHAN SABHA ELECTIONS	LOK SABHA ELECTIONS		
		1996	1999	2004
Upper castes				
Brahman	–	–	2	5
Rajput	–	–	1	4
Banya	–	2.9		
Others	–	2.9	5	10
Intermediate castes	–	1.9		11
OBC				
Yadav	4	4.3	4	9
Kurmi	27	–		
Koeri	–	24.7		
Pal/Gadaria		11.8	13	
Others	Lower OBCs: 19	Peasant: 16.7; Artisan: 14.9; Others: 20.6		Other OBC: 16; MBC: 17
SCs	65			71
Chamar		73.8	74	
Pasi		45.7		
Others		60.6	39	
Muslims	5		5	10
Muslim (low)		6.5		
Muslim (high)		3.1		
Others		23.1		

SOURCES:　CSDS data unit, *India Today*, 31 August 1996, p. 53; Kumar (1999: 822) and *Frontline*, 19 November 1999, p. 41 and *The Hindu*, 20 May 2004.

In 1996 and 1999, to get three-fourths of the Chamar votes was a major achievement in a state where this group represented the largest caste. But confining itself to the Chamars was also a dangerous limitation. The BSP seemed to be facing the same difficulty as Ambedkar's political parties since the Independent Labour Party (ILP), the Scheduled Caste Federation (SCF) and the RPI had not been able to significantly attract voters beyond the Mahars in Maharashtra and the Chamars in Uttar Pradesh.

However, the BSP is not a Chamar party only, as evident from the fact that more than 45 per cent of the Pasis voted for its candidates in the 1996 Lok Sabha elections. It is not even a Dalit only party: in the same election 24.7 per cent of the Koeris voted for it and in the assembly elections, 27 per cent of the Kurmis did the same. Interestingly, in 2004, 9 per cent of the Yadavs—the vote bank par excellence of the Samajwadi Party (SP)—supported the BSP and 16 per cent of non-Yadav OBCs as well as 17 per cent of the MBCs (Most Backward Castes) did the same.

In 1999, however, the BSP received only 13 per cent of the non-Yadav OBC votes. At that time, the Kurmis had deserted the party[13] largely because of the splits orchestrated by Kurmi leaders such as Raj Bahadur and Jung Bahadur who formed respectively the BSP (R) and the Bahujan Samaj Dal, while another Kurmi leader from the BSP, Sone Lal Patel created the Aapna Dal. But a significant section of the Koeris supported it.

Sudha Pai argues that these splits resulted from inner tensions between Kanshi Ram and the OBC leaders of the BSP. According to Pai, in the mid-1990s, 'Kanshi Ram holds that lower backwards are not as politicised as the dalits and lack both a strong leadership and an understanding of the need to unite and fight the savarnas' (Pai, 2000: 40). As a result, the BSP allegedly developed a Dalit-oriented policy: 'In its post-bahujan phase, social justice has been defined not only as retributive but also *exclusive*, i.e., meant only for the dalits and not the entire bahujan community' (ibid.: 42). According to Sudha Pai, the BSP changed its strategy once again in 1999 when 'the leadership decided to broaden the base of the party by giving tickets to carefully selected candidates belonging to the Muslim community, upper and backward castes, in the 1999 Lok Sabha elections thereby increasing its share of seats' (Pai, 1999: 3100). This reading of the BSP's electoral strategy is not entirely convincing. In fact, the BSP had always tried to attract OBCs by giving them tickets at the time of elections, including in what Sudha Pai calls the party's 'post bahujan' phase.

THE BSP, ALSO A PARTY OF THE OBCs AND THE MUSLIMS

When he lived in Maharashtra, Kanshi Ram was very critical of the RPI's tendency to work only among the Dalits and even more especially among the Buddhist Mahars: 'Nothing can be achieved in a democracy by working with a particular community.'[14] For him, the RPI by focusing so much of its attention on the Dalits was betraying Ambedkar. His reading of *Annihilation of Caste* had convinced him that any organisation based on one particular community would fail.[15] As Gail Omvedt emphasises, Ambedkar considered that Dalits, tribals and Backward Castes were 'natural allies' against the *savarnas* (upper castes) and that the Dalits needed to make alliances with these other subalterns (Omvedt, 1998: 224).

However, for suggesting an alternative strategy he drew his inspiration not so much from Ambedkar as from Phule who used the Aryan theory to his own advantage: the fact that the origins of the upper castes could be traced from Aryan conquerors enabled him to argue that they descended from foreigners and that their culture, including the caste system, was alien to India's original people who, for him, were the ancestors of the low castes, those who he called the 'bahujan samaj' (the majority community) (Phule, 1991).

Kanshi Ram drew his inspiration from this theory for endowing the lower castes with an ethnic identity. He transposed the motif of the Aryan invader versus the oppressed 'bahujan samaj' in the democratic context of India:

In a democracy, the one with the larger number of votes forms the government. The *bahujan samaj* accounts for 85% of the votes. It is a shame that the foreign Aryans constituting 15% are ruling over the 85% .... The Aryans have exploited us. An Aryan ruler can never work for our betterment .... When our ancestors from the *bahujan samaj* were ruling over his country, India was known world wide for its prosperity. The *bahujan samaj* can rule this country even today.... (Kanshi Ram, 1997)

Right from the beginning, Kanshi Ram included the religious minorities in his definition of the Bahujan samaj since, even though those who did not descend from low caste converts did not belong to the pre-Aryan society, they suffered from the same oppression of the upper-caste Hindus. On 14 October 1971, Kanshi Ram created 'The Scheduled Castes and Scheduled Tribes, Other Backward Classes and Minority Communities Employees Association'. Kanshi

Ram, considered, at that time, that the most urgent need of the Bahujan samaj was to organise its elite, which was, like him, a product of reservation in the education system and largely employed in administration. He then defined the Bahujan samaj in opposition to the twice-born upper castes, the savarna, whom he also called the 'Manuwadi', those who follow the varna system as codified by Manu's *Dharmashastra*.[16]

Capitalising on this organisation he had set up in Maharashtra, Kanshi Ram created in 1978 an all-India association called the All-India Backward (SC, ST, OBC) and Minority Communities Employees Federation (BAMCEF) whose aim was still to organise the elite of the Bahujan samaj, wage earners having intellectual qualifications and benefiting from quotas. BAMCEF made rapid headway and reached a degree of critical mass because of the growing number of educated SC civil servants. But it was not intended to organise the Dalits only. Kanshi Ram did not content himself with a unionist kind of stategy either: he wanted to play a political role too. In 1996 he told me: 'I still want my people to advance socially and economically. But I have realised that unless we are having political clout, we cannot advance much on those sides.'[17] Kanshi Ram was walking in the footsteps of Ambedkar, who also considered that capturing power had to be a priority.

Kanshi Ram launched the DSSSS in this perspective. In spite of its name, the party was not supposed to target the Dalits specifically. In fact, in addition to Shudras and tribals, the DSSSS also tried to attract Muslims, especially in UP. Dr Mahsood Ahmed, a temporary lecturer at Aligarh Muslim University became one of the full-time organisers of the DSSSS in 1983 (Mendelsohn and Vicziany, 1998: 224–25) in order to serve this expansion scheme. In 1987, the launch of the BSP amounted to a change of name more than a change of strategy. Kanshi Ram continued, indeed, to defend the interests of the OBCs as much as those of the Dalits.

Kanshi Ram and the OBCs

Even before the Mandal affair exploded in 1990, when the debate (in the Lok Sabha and outside) on the Mandal Commission Report was gaining momentum, Kanshi Ram emphasised the claims of the

OBCs. This is evident from one of his speeches during the election campaign for the Vidhan Sabha of Haryana in 1987:

> The other limb of the Bahujan Samaj [in addition to the Scheduled Castes] which we call as OBC or Other Backward Classes, needs badly this party [the BSP]. Thirty-nine years after independence, these people have neither been recognised nor have they obtained any rights. Improvements have been introduced in the legislation for the Scheduled Castes and the Scheduled Tribes, but nothing similar has happened for these people. The truth is that the government of this country is not ready to recognise them. In accordance with section 340 of the Constitution, which was drafted by Dr. Ambedkar for the welfare of these people, the Kaka Kalelkar and Mandal Commissions were constituted, but the reports of both the commissions were thrown in the waste paper basket on the pretext that they had identified 3,743 castes which could not be called Other Backward Classes. Our central government is not ready to recognise any of these castes. When these castes are not even recognised, where is the question of obtaining their rights? (Kanshi Ram, 1992b: 23)

Kanshi Ram thus admitted that in some respects the condition of the SCs was better than those of the OBCs. He thus recognised that the SCs and the STs had a larger presence in the bureaucracy than the OBCs because of reservations:

> In this country, out of the 450 District Magistrates more than 125 are from SC/STs but those from the OBCs are very few.... The number of OBC is 50 to 52% but we don't see any of them as District Magistrate. The issue, which is special for us, is that reservation is not a question of our daily bread, reservation is not a question of our jobs, reservation is a matter of participation in the government and administration. We want participation in the government and administration of this country. There is democracy in this country. If in the republic 52% of the people cannot participate, then which is the system in which they can participate? (Kanshi Ram, 1992c: 58)

Similarly, he noted in 1994, that of some 500 IAS officers in UP, 137 were SCs whereas there were only seven OBCs (six of them were Yadavs) (Mendelsohn and Vicziany, 1998: 224). One of the BSP's slogans has been '*Mandal ayog lâgû karo, kursî khâli karo*' (Implement Mandal Commission [Report] or vacate the seat [of power]). This was part of Kanshi Ram's strategy of constituting the Bahujan samaj into a political force and therefore the BSP undoubtedly benefited from the atmosphere created by the 'Mandal affair' and tried to tap the OBC vote at the time of elections.

After gaining power in 1995, Mayawati announced that the OBCs would benefit from 27 per cent of the state budget. Some castes that had been neglected by the administration and which belonged to the lower stratum of the OBCs—popularly known as Most Backard Classes—were included in the OBCs' list and the Nishads (boat-people also called Mallahs or Kewats) got the privilege of hiring plots of sandy land running alongside the rivers.

Similarly, the Muslims were designated for receiving the same grants as SC children and Mayawati implemented the recommendations of the UP Backward Classes Commission which insisted, in a report of 11 July 1994, that the low caste Muslims should benefit from reservations in the state administration. Mulayam Singh Yadav had not been in favour of such a measure because it was bound to reduce the quotas which the Hindu OBCs tended to monopolise. Mayawati granted the Muslims 8.44 per cent of the 27 per cent due to the OBCs. A comparable proportion—8 per cent—of posts of police officers were also allegedly reserved for Muslims.[18]

Electoral and Party Politics: Beyond the Dalit Threshold

The BSP's ambition to become more than a Dalit party became clear in the 1980s when it nominated non-SC candidates at the time of elections in UP. In 1989, when BSP MLAs were elected for the first time, a majority of its successful candidates were not Dalits (four Muslims, three OBCs and five SCs). In 1991, the results were even more striking since none of the BSP Dalit candidates were returned to the assembly whereas 11 OBCs and one Muslim joined the Vidhan Sabha on a BSP ticket. Since then, the electoral outcomes have been more balanced. But in 1993 and in 1996, the OBC MLAs were still 10 percentage points ahead of the SC MLAs (44.7 per cent as against 34.3 per cent and 38.6 per cent as against 29.5 per cent in 1993 and

TABLE 11.2
Caste and Community of the BSP MLAs (1989–2002)

CASTE AND COMMUNITY	1989	1991	1993	1996	2002
Upper castes			1.5	13.5	16.2
Brahman			1.5	4.5	6.8
Rajput				6	6.8
Banya					1.3
Bhumihar				1.5	1.3
Kayasth				1.5	
Intermediate castes	22.8	91.4		1.5	1.3
Jat				1.5	1.3
OBC			44.7	42	39.7
Yadav	7.6	16.6	14.9	1.5	2.7
Kurmi	7.6	16.6	7.5	12	10.9
Lodhi			1.5	1.5	4.1
Koeri					1.3
Shakya				1.5	1.3
Rajbhar		8.3	2.9	3	1.3
Saini					2.7
Pal/Gadaria				6	2.7
Kashyap					1.3
Kushwaha			1.5	6	2.7
Muraon/Maurya				3	2.7
Nishad		8.3	1.5	4.5	1.3
Bhagel				1.5	1.3
Gujar					1.3
Other	7.6	41.6	14.9	1.5	2.7
SCs	38.4		34.3	27.2	25.9
Jatav				16.6	20.5
Passi				7.6	4.1
Khatik				1.5	
Other				1.5	1.3
Muslim	30.7	8.3	16.4	16.6	10.9
Non-identified			2.9		
Total	100	100	100	100	100
	N = 13	N = 12	N = 67	N = 64	N = 73

1996 respectively). Though the percentage of the Muslim BSP MLAs is declining, from 16.4 in 1993 to 10.9 in 2002, their share remains high (see Table 11.2).

However, one should not look only at the caste break-up of its MLAs, but also at the social profile of the candidates to analyse the strategy of the BSP. I did this research for the 1996 assembly elections (see Table 11.3). Then the SC candidates were only 29 per cent of the total number, whereas the OBCs were 34 per cent and the Muslims 18 per cent. Interestingly, the OBC candidates of the BSP were relatively more successful since there were almost 40 per cent OBCs among the party MLAs and only 28 per cent among the SCs. This gap suggests that the BSP owns a fully transferable Dalit vote bank and get an additional support from the OBC voters when the party candidate belongs to the OBC category. Interestingly, this interpretation does not apply to the Muslims who may adopt more systematically a strategic vote in order to beat the BJP candidate.

TABLE 11.3

Caste and Community of the BSP Candidates in the 1996 Assembly Elections in Uttar Pradesh

CASTE AND COMMUNITY	%
Upper castes	17.5
Brahman	4
Rajput	8.2
Banya	1.3
Khattri	1.6
Bhumhiar	0.6
Kayasth	0.9
Others	0.9
Intermediate castes	1.6
Jat	1.6
Other backward classes	34.4
Backward castes	11.8
Kurmi	6.3
Yadav	1.9
Lodhi	1.9
Most backward castes	22.6
Pal/Gadariya	1.9
Teli	0.3
Kachhi/Kushwaha	2.3

(Table 11.3 Contd.)

(Table 11.3 Contd.)

CASTE AND COMMUNITY	%
Gujjar	0.9
Nai	
Nishad	1.9
Baghela	0.6
Kumhar	0.3
Sunar	0.3
Chaurasia	0.3
Rajbhar	2.3
Shakya	1.6
Kashyap	0.6
Prajapati	1.3
Chaukan	0.9
Vora	0.3
Saithwar	0.9
Bair	0.3
Saini	1.6
Maurya	2.3
Others	1.3
SCs	28.3
Chamar/Jatav/Dhore	19.1
Kori	0.9
Pipil	0.3
Dhobi	0.6
Khatik	0.3
Dusadh/Pasi	4.2
Katheriya	0.3
Kuril	0.6
Chilpkar	0.3
Balmiki	0.9
Others	0.3
Muslim	17.5
Christian	0.3
Non-identified	0
Total	100
	N = 303

SOURCES: Interviews in the BSP office of Agra, *Bahujan Sangathak*, 11 Novembre 1996; *National Mail*, 20 September 1996.

The share of the OBCs is even more important among the state party office-bearers than among the BSP candidates to the assembly elections (see Table 11.4). By contrast, the Dalit office-bearers are almost as few as the upper castes! Interestingly, the president of the Uttar Pradesh BSP has been an OBC for years, ever since Sone Lal Patel (a Kurmi) was replaced by Bhagwat Pal (a Gadariya), who was himself replaced by Dayaram Pal, another Gadariya.

A majority of the lower caste leaders of the BSP come from the MBC and not from larger, dominant BC such as the Yadavs. In fact, Yadavs were important till the mid-1990s but their role diminished

TABLE 11.4

Caste and Community of the BSP Office-bearers in UP (1996–2000)

CASTES AND COMMUNITY	OFFICE-BEARERS OF THE EXECUTIVE COMMITTEE OF THE BSP IN UP	
	1996	2000
Upper castes	13.7	14.3
Brahman	10.3	10.7
Banya	3.4	3.6
Other backward classes	44.2	46.5
Backward castes	6.8	7.2
Kurmi	3.4	3.6
Lodhi	3.4	3.6
Most backward castes	37.4	39.3
Pal/Gadariya	3.4	3.6
Kachhi/Kushwaha	3.4	3.6
Gujjar	3.4	3.6
Nai	3.4	3.6
Nishad	3.4	7.1
Kumhar	3.4	3.6
Rajbhar	6.8	
Saini	3.4	7.1
Others	6.8	7.1
SCs	17.2	21.4
Chamar/Jatav/Dhore	10.5	3.6
Khatik	3.4	3.6
Dusadh/Pasi	3.4	3.6
Others		10.7
Muslim	10.5	7.1
Non-identified	13.7	10.7
Total	100	100
	N = 29	N = 28

SOURCE: Interviews in the BSP office in Agra.

after the SP—a Yadav-dominated party—and the BSP developed hostile relations. The relations between the BSP and the SP deteriorated soon after their electoral success in 1993. First, the BSP was worried about the 'Yadavisation' of the state initiated by Mulayam Singh Yadav. Second, the Yadavs, who were anxious to improve their social status and to keep the Untouchables in their place, reacted violently to the Dalits' efforts to achieve social mobility. The OBCs and the Dalits' class interests are clearly contradictory in some regions of UP. While in east UP 'the OBCs and the Scheduled Castes labourers have a common enemy: the old élite' (Lerche, 1998: A-33). made up of the upper-caste ex-landlords, elsewhere the Untouchables are often landless labourers or cultivators with a very small plot who work for OBC farmers: their class interests then are virtually antagonistic. Conflicts about the wages of agricultural labourers and disputes regarding land ownership have always been acute, but became more frequent since both groups—the Dalit and the OBCs—had become more assertive after the 1993 elections.

The situation was almost the same with the Kurmis. Their position has remained influential within the party, but their presence has also decreased after the splits mentioned earlier. Obviously, these OBCs do not belong to the same world as the Dalits. They often employ—and exploit—the Dalits as labourers whereas the MBCs and Muslims have a similar class status.

To cope with the rise of the OBCs and more especially with the party of the Yadavs, that is, the SP, the BSP developed two strategies. First, it joined hands with the BJP, an upper-caste dominated party which was equally anxious to sandwich Mulayam Singh Yadav. When the BSP put an end to the coalition with the SP, it became actively involved in another alliance with the BJP, in an even more favourable position since on 3 June 1995 Mayawati became chief minister of the UP government with the BJP's support. The alliance of the BSP with the BJP epitomised the convergence between Dalit and upper-castes leaders against the OBCs and above all against the Yadavs, who were now posing a threat as much to the SCs as to the élite landowners and civil servants because of Mulayam Singh Yadav's reservation policy.[19]

Second, the BSP decided to focus on the MBCs. As a result, the list of the BSP candidates started to include people from many small, dominated castes such as the Nishads, Sainis, Shakyas, Baghels, Kashyaps, Rajbhars, etc. The MBC MLAs and office-bearers of the BSP of UP come today from a dozen different jatis, whereas its SC MLAs are almost all Jatavs. But the former are in larger numbers anyway.

To sum up: even though within the UP branch of the BSP, power always laid in the hands of a Chamar, Mayawati, the BSP's image as a 'Dalit party' needs to be amended since the SCs do not represent the largest number of office-bearers and party candidates (or MLAs) in UP. This picture, however, is more in tune with the social profile of its electoral basis which suggest that the BSP may be less a Dalit party than a Chamar party.

CONCLUSION: THE BSP, NEW CATCH-ALL PARTY?

Kanshi Ram, like Ambedkar, promoted the formation of a socio-political coalition gathering together ascriptive groups with similar social and economic status. Ambedkar had oscillated between this position and the defence of the Dalits alone, but had opted for a larger front in the end. Kanshi Ram did the same on behalf of the Bahujan samaj and, in contrast to Ambedkar, succeeded in partially uniting the SCs—mostly Chamars—and in rallying around this core group some OBC castes—mostly MBCs—and some Muslims whose socio-economic condition has declined, especially among the *ashlaf* (lower castes). The party's social basis remains relatively narrow anyway. It is not exclusively a Dalit party any longer, but it is not a party of the low caste either since a mere fraction of the OBCs vote for its candidates. In addition, the BSP is not even the party of the SCs. It is still identified with the Chamars, just as the RPI tended to be 'a Mahar party' in Maharashtra.[20] Balmikis and Pasis vote for other parties, partly to distinguish themselves from the Chamars whose hegemony they fear—the former for the BSP, the latter for the Janata Dal because of Ram Vilas Paswan.[21]

In order to further broaden the social basis of the party, the BSP leaders have decided to approach the upper castes too. Since the mid-1990s, the party has made it a point to give tickets to a significant number of upper-castes candidates and to appoint a similar number of office-bearers from the upper castes too. In both cases, the percentage of the upper castes in question approximates their share in the total population, that is, 15–20 per cent. This is in tune with Kanshi Ram's assumption that assemblies should reflect the composition of society, a principle which echoes the theory of mirror representation.[22] In the 1999 Lok Sabha elections, the BSP continued with this policy. Kanshi Ram decided explicitly to nominate candidates in proportion to the caste and community break-up of society. Out of 85 candidates, he fielded 17 Muslims (20 per cent), 20 SCs (23.5 per cent), 38 OBCs (45 per cent) and 10 upper castes (12 per cent)— five Brahmins and five Rajputs (*The Hindu*, 11 August 1999, p. 9). In 2002, the BSP did the same during the UP assembly elections: it gave tickets to 37 Brahman, 36 Rajputs and 86 Muslims. In 2004, this strategy started to bring some dividends since 5 per cent of the Brahmin voters, 4 per cent of the Rajputs and 10 per cent of the Muslims cast their votes in favour of the BSP according to a CSDS survey.

Among the upper castes, the Brahmins seem to be the favourite target of the BSP. In May 2005, the party coined a new slogan '*Brahman–Dalit bhai-bhai*' and Mayawati decided to set up 'Bhai-chara samiti' (brotherhood committee) in all the assembly constituencies with Brahmins as presidents and Dalit as secretaries! (*Central Chronicle*, 16 May 2005).

Sudhir Chandra Mishra, the new general secretary of the BSP, is the main architect of this policy. But Mayawati has invested a lot of time and energy into it, as evident from the series of 'Brahmin sammelans' she has organised across UP, including in Lucknow where the 'Brahmin maha rally' marked the culmination of 50 'Brahmin jodo sammelans' (Brahmin enrolling conferences). Interestingly, in Lucknow, Mayawati was greeted with Brahmanical rituals, a group of priests chanting Vedic hymns while she was presented with a silver axe, the mythical weapon of Lord Parashuram—a Brahmanical icon (*The Hindu*, 10 June 2005).

At the same time, the BSP targeted Mulayam Singh Yadav's social stronghold, the Yadavs, by organising 'Yadav sammelans' at all major places in UP. The party even set up a Yadav Vikas Manch (*The Hindu*, 22 January 2005).

Generally speaking, the OBCs were bracketed together with the Dalits during the new campaign Mayawati launched in the fall of 2005 for the fulfilment of quotas and the introduction of reservations in the private sector, not only for Dalits and OBCs, but also for the tribals (*The Hindu*, 20 September and 6 October 2005).

The BSP is trying its best to broaden its social basis beyond its traditional Dalit support by reaching out to new groups. For Mayawati, this needs to be done for presenting the party as a credible alternative to the other party in the fray in UP. In a way, she is oscillating the same way as Ambedkar did more than half a century ago. The fate of Dalit politicians remains the same, but the BSP may have accumulated enough strength for achieving more than its predecessors. On top of it, the party seems to be in a position to overcome the transition to a new leader, Mayawati, who became party president in 2003, after Kanshi Ram—who died recently—suffered a terrible stroke. The political resilience of Mayawati is remarkable so far, but the judiciary may hinder her career anyway.

Appendix: The Electoral Performance of the BSP

TABLE A.1

Percentage of Votes Polled by the BSP during the Last Six General Elections

YEAR	CANDIDATES	WINNING CANDIDATES	% OF VALID VOTES
1989	246	3	2.07
1991	231	2	1.61
1996	117	11	3.64
1998	251	5	4.7
1999	N.A.	14	4.2
2004	435	19	5.3

SOURCES: Election Commission of India (1990: 7, n.d.: 9, 1996), Rao and Balakrishnan (1999) and Yadav and Kumar (1999: 120–26).

NOTE: The growth of the BSP enabled the party to obtain from the Election Commission the status of national party after the 1996 elections.

TABLE A.2

Electoral Performance of the BSP in Five States of North India during the General Elections of 1989–99 (in Percentage of Valid Votes)

STATES	HARYANA	PUNJAB	UTTAR PRADESH	MADHYA PRADESH	JAMMU AND KASHMIR
% of SCs in					
1991	19.75	28.31	21.05	14.5	N.A.
1989	1.62 (0)	8.62 (1)	9.93 (2)	4.28 (0)	4.06 (0)
1991	1.79 (0)	No election	8.70 (1)	3.54 (1)	No election
1996	6.6 (0)	9.35 (3)	20.61 (6)	8.18 (2)	6 (0)
1998	7.7 (1)	12.7 (0)	20.9 (4)	8.7 (0)	5 (0)
1999	1.7 (0)	3.8 (0)	22.1 (14)	5.2 (0)	4.8 (0)
2004	4.9 (0)	7.7 (0)	24.7 (19)	4.7 (0)	2.2 (0)

NOTE: Numbers in parenthesis indicate seats.

TABLE A.3

Performance of the BSP in the Assembly Elections of UP

YEAR OF ELECTION	1989	1991	1993	1996	2002
Seats	13	12	66	67	98
Percentage of votes	9.4	9.3	11.1	22.6	23.1

TABLE A.4

Region-wise Vote Share of the BSP in the Elections of the 1990s (in percentage)

(REGIONS)	ASSEMBLY ELECTIONS		LOK SABHA ELECTIONS	
	1991	1993	1996	1999
Uttarakhand	3.5	4.2	10.1	6.7
Rohilkhand	5.9	2.7	20.5	22.6
Upper Doab/West UP	3.5	5.7	18.5	23.8
Awadh/Central UP	8.8	5.6	18.8	22.8
Lower Doab/Central East UP	10.2	9.9	22.8	22.8
Bundelkhand	20.3	26.1	25.8	28.9
Poorvanchal/East UP	13.5	21.9	20.2	23.6

SOURCES: *Frontline*, 3 December 1993, p. 24; 15 November 1996, p. 22 and 19 November 1999, p. 41.

NOTES

1. I have made this argument in my book, Jaffrelot (2005).
2. In 1998, I argued that the BSP was more than a Dalit party, but this interpretation needs to be revisited because the statistical basis for such an interpretation was then based on a couple of elections only. See Jaffrelot (1998).
3. Mendelsohn and Vicziany give another date for Kanshi Ram's birth—1934 (Mendelsohn and Vicziany, 1998: 219).
4. In fact, the proportion of the Hindu Chamars is still very high in Punjab. In the 1931 Census, they were 62.1 per cent, as against 14.4 per cent of Sikh Chamars.
5. Interview with Kanshi Ram, New Delhi, 12 November 1996.
6. The same year her family converted to Buddhism.
7. The best account of the AVP, with special references to Meerut district, is Pai (2002: 126–49).
8. Interview in *India Today*, 11 August 1997, p. 33.
9. After the publication of the white paper which was to be the basis of the 1935 Government of India Act, the Agra-based Jatav Conference sent a memorandum to the deputy secretary to the Government of India where it was said:

> The Jatavs are the descendants of Yadu, the founder of Jadav [*sic*] tribe, from which the great Hero of Maha Bharat, Lord Krishna, came. But this position of superiority could not remain intact. Our community fell down from that great height to this degraded status in the Hindu fold ... our present position is the outcome of the age-long inhumane oppressions of Brahminism on the Kshatriyas. We, Kshatriyas of the past, are labouring under various sorts of disabilities, restrictions and religious injunctions imposed on us by the Orthodox Hindus .... But we are at loss to understand the exclusion of our (Yadav) Jatav community from the list of the Scheduled Castes given in the White Paper. The result of this horrible negligence would, no doubt, be the sacrifice of the interests of our community. (Memorandum of Jatav Conference of Agra, in IORL/P&J/9/108)

Such a discourse suggests that, while the Jatavs were eager to benefit from reservations for the SCs, their movement was still operating in the framework of Sanskritisation.

10. Interview with B.P. Maurya in Delhi, 7 November 1997.
11. K. Chandra underlines that 'Congress leaders themselves readily acknowledge that the representational blockage for Scheduled Castes elites in their own party pushed them towards he BSP' (Chandra, 2004: 187).
12. K. Chandra argues that the 'Chamars' do not really exist and cannot, therefore be motivated by such an identity: 'The category "Chamar" is an aggregate rather than an individual category, no different from the

category "Scheduled Caste" [sic]' (Chandra, 2004: 168). It is now common knowledge that all identities are constructed not only with some cultural symbols, but also with some material interests in mind. But once the identity-building process has reached a certain stage, people believe in this construction. Chamars or Jatavs consider they form a group in today's UP, like Muslims in spite of even more dramatic status-based divisions.

13. Till the mid-1990s, the BSP succeeded in attracting Kurmis of the region between Faizabad and Banda.

14. Cited in Kanshi Ram (1997). Kanshi Ram had appreciated Maurya's attempts at federating the SCs and the Muslims under the banner of the RPI in UP.

15. One of the BSP slogans is: 'Bâba terâ mission adhûrâ Kanshi Ram karenge pûrâ' (Baba [Saheb Ambedkar] your unfinished work will be fulfilled by Kanshi Ram).

16. Kanshi Ram talks of 'Manuwadi' versus 'Manavwadi', those who believe in men as human beings. His hostility to Manu led him to ask for the removal of the statue of Manu from the premises of the Jaipur High Court (The Hindu, 5 September 1998, p. 4).

17. Interview with Kanshi Ram

18. BSP (1996). The Muslims also appreciated the way the Mayawati government resisted the Vishva Hindu Parishad's attempt at organising an important event at Mathura for Krishna's birthday in September 1995. On this site, that the VHP claimed to be Krishna's birthplace, stands a mosque and the VHP's intention was, like in Ayodhya, to mobilise the Hindus in order to 'reconquer' a Muslim space. Mayawati allowed the VHP's function to take place provided that it was held more than 3 km away from the mosque.

19. This rapprochement of groups which were poles apart in the social structure was justified in those terms by Kanshi Ram: '... we can take the help of the BJP to advance our national agenda. We feel that the upper castes will be more amenable to social transformation than the intermediate castes' (Interview of Kanshi Ram in Frontline, 28 June 1996, p. 35).

20. Mayawati, while confessing that she feared for her life, declared in late 1998: 'If I am killed, members of the Chamar community would create a havoc' (The Hindu, 12 December 1998).

21. Besides, the BSP recruits most of its supporters from the younger generations while their parents still vote for the Congress. But the party may therefore grow incrementally in the long run and, in the meantime, use its young partisans to convince their parents.

22. Political theories tell us that there are two kinds of representation, one which is based on the returning of individual deputies by abstract citizens to houses of representatives and the other which emphasises the

social identities of the represented and the representatives—mirror-representation (see Pitkin [1967]).

REFERENCES AND SELECT BIBLIOGRAPHY

Ambedkar, B.R. (1936) *Annihilation of Caste*. Jallandhar: Beema Patrika Publications.

Briggs, G.W. (1920) *The Chamars*. Calcutta: Association Press.

BSP (1996) *Mukhya lakshay evan apil* (in Hindi). New Delhi: BSP.

Chandra, K. (2004) *Why Ethnic Parties Succeed: Patronage and Ethnic Head Counts in India.* Cambridge: Cambridge University Press.

Duncan, R.I. (1979) 'Levels, the Communication of Programmes, and Sectional Strategies in Indian Politics, With Reference to the Bharatiya Kranti Dal and the Republican Party of India in Uttar Pradesh State and Aligarh District (UP)', Ph.D. thesis, University of Sussex.

Election Commission of India (1990) *Report on the Ninth General Elections to the House of the People in India, 1989.* New Delhi: Government of India Press.

———. (n.d.) *Report on the Tenth General Elections to the House of the People in India, 1989.* New Delhi: Government of India Press.

———. (1996) *Statistical Report on General Elections, 1996 to the Eleventh Lok Sabha*, Vol. 1. New Delhi: Government of India Press.

Gooptu, N. (1993) 'Caste and Labour: Untouchable Social Movements in Urban Uttar Pradesh in the Early Twentieth Century', in P. Robb (ed.), *Dalit Movements and the Meaning of Labour in India*. New Delhi: Oxford University Press.

Jaffrelot, Christophe (1998) 'The BSP in North India. No Longer Just a Dalit Party', *Comparative Studies of South Asia, Africa and the Middle East*, 18(1): 35–51.

———. (2003) *Indian Silent Revolution: The Rise of Lower Castes in North Indian Politics.* New York: Columbia University Press.

———. (2005) *Dr Ambedkar and Untouchability: Analysing and Fighting Caste.* New York: Columbia University Press.

Jaffrelot, Christophe, J. Zérinini and J. Chaturvedi (2002) 'The BJP and the Rise of Dalits in Uttar Pradesh', in R. Jeffrey and J. Lerche (eds), *UP 2000*, pp. 128–46. New Delhi: Manohar.

Jigyansu, C.P. (1960) *Swami Achhutanand*. Lucknow: Bahujan Kalyan Prakashak.

Kshirsagar, R.K. (1994) *Dalit Movement in India and its Leaders*. New Delhi: MD Publications.

Kumar, P. (1999) 'Dalit and the BSP in Uttar Pradesh', *Economic and Political Weekly*, VIII(2), 3 April: 822.

Lerche, J. (1998) 'Agricultural Labourers, the State and Agrarian Transition in Uttar Pradesh', *Economic and Political Weekly*, XIV(3), 28 March: A-33.

Lynch, O. (1969) *The Politics of Untouchability: Social Mobility and Social Change in a City of India.* New York: Columbia University Press.

Mendelsohn, O. and M. Vicziany (1998) *The Untouchables. Subordination, Poverty and the State in Modern India.* Cambridge: Cambridge University Press.

Omvedt, G. (1998) 'Peasants Dalits and Women: Democracy and India's New Social Movements', in M. Mohanty, P.N. Mukherji and O. Tornquist (eds), *People's Rights: Social Movements and the State in the Third World*, pp. 86–102. New Delhi: Sage Publications.

Pai, S. (1999) 'BSP's New Electoral Strategy Pays Off', *Economic and Political Weekly*, 30 October: 3100.

———. (2002) *Dalit Assertion and the Unfinished Democratic Revolution: The Bahujan Samaj Party in Uttar Pradesh*. New Delhi: Sage Publications.

———. (2004) 'The BSP in Uttar Pradesh', *Seminar*, 471: 40.

Parliament of India (1992) *Tenth Lok Sabha Who's Who*. New Delhi: Lok Sabha Secretariat.

Phule, J. (1991) *Slavery—Collected Works of Mahatma Jotirao Phule, Vol. 1*. Bombay: Government of Maharashtra.

Pitkin, H.F. (1967) *The Concept of Representation*. Berkeley: University of California Press.

Ram, Kanshi (1992a) *Bahujan Samâj ke lye âshâ kî kiran*. New Delhi: Bahujan Publications.

——— . (1992b) 'Bahujan Samaj Party aur Haryana Pradesh ke chunav', in Kanshi Ram, *Bahujan Samaj ke lye âshâ kî kîran*. New Delhi: Bahujan Publications.

———. (1992c) 'Azadi ke 44 sal bad bhi bahujan samaj (anusuchit jati, janjati, pichre varg va dharmic alpasankhyak) anyaya tyachar ka shikar', Kanshi Ram, *Bahujan Samaj ke lye âshâ kî kîran*. New Delhi: Bahujan Publications.

——— . (1997) *Aaj ke neta/Alochnatmak adhyayanmala*. New Delhi: Rajkamal Prakashan.

Ramaseshan,R. (1995) 'Dalit Politics in U.P.', *Seminar*, January: 73.

Rao, G.V.L. Narasimha and K. Balakrishnan (1999) *Indian Elections: The Nineties*. New Delhi: Har-Anand.

Yadav, Y. and S. Kumar (1999) 'Interpreting the Mandate', *Frontline*, 5 November: 120–26.

PART

IV

VI

12

Ambedkar's Interpretation of the Caste System, its Economic Consequences and Suggested Remedies[1]

SUKHADEO THORAT

CASTE SYSTEM VERSUS INEQUALITIES

Historically, the caste system has formed the regulatory base for the social, cultural and economic life of the people in India. Ambedkar devoted considerable intellectual efforts to understand the nature of the caste system, its consequences on the status of groups, particularly those located at the bottom of the caste hierarchy, and also suggested the possible remedies for the discrimination-induced deprivation in Indian society. This chapter discusses Ambedkar's interpretation of the caste system, its economic consequences and suggested remedies for the discrimination and deprivation face by the low caste Untouchables in particular.

Ambedkar recognised that caste as a system of social and economic governance or organisation (of production and distribution) is essentially based on certain customary rules and norms, which are unique and distinct. In general, a caste-based society and economy is one in which property rights, as also occupations are hereditary, compulsory and endogamous. The organisational scheme of the caste system is based on the division of people into social groups (or castes) in which the civil, cultural, religious and economic rights of each individual caste are pre-determined or ascribed by birth and made hereditary. Moreover, endogamy remains the central feature of the caste system. The assignment of civil, cultural and economic rights, however, is unequal and hierarchal. The system also provides for a regulatory mechanism to enforce the social and economic organisation through the instruments of social ostracism (or a system of social and economic penalties) and reinforces it further with justifications from the philosophical elements in the Hindu religion (Ambedkar 1916 and 1987). It is these features, which make the institution of caste rigid, stubborn and change-resistant.

These features imply that the Hindu social order is based on three interrelated principles, namely, (*i*) predetermination of social, religious and economic rights of each caste based on birth, (*ii*) the unequal and hierarchical (graded) divisions of these rights among the castes and (*iii*) provision of strong social, religious and economic ostracism supported by social and religious ideology to maintain the Hindu social order. In Ambedkar's view, the doctrine of inequality is the core, the heart, of the Hindu social order. What is important is that the philosophical elements of Hinduism also directly or indirectly support this system. This leaves no difference between legal philosophy (the laws) and moral philosophy (morality) in Hinduism. What is legal also becomes moral. There being no distinction between the legal and the moral, morality becomes a social and binding force on all (Ambedkar, 1987).

The notion of 'human rights' under the Hindu social system takes a specific meaning. It becomes clear that unlike other human societies, the Hindu social order in its classical form does not recognise the individual and his distinctiveness as the centre of the social purpose. The unit of the Hindu society is not the individual. Even the family is not regarded as a unit of society except for the purposes of marriages and inheritance (ibid.). The caste system is also governed by the principle of rank and gradation, insofar as the rights increase in ascending order from the Untouchable to the Brahmin. It is a hierarchically interlined system. Within this framework, castes are artfully interlined with each other in a manner such that the right and privileges of the higher castes become the disabilities of the lower castes, particularly the Untouchables. In this sense, in Ambedkar's view, caste cannot exist in a single number. Caste can exist only in plural numbers. There cannot be such a thing as caste as a singular phenomenon. Any single caste cannot be viewed in isolation and can only be understood as a pyramidal structure or maze. So castes need to be conceived as a 'system' of societal governance, which are interlinked in unequal measures of social, cultural, religious, economic relations with each other.

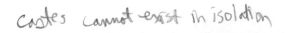

Isolation and exclusion (social and physical) of the Untouchables is also a unique feature of the Hindu social order. Ambedker observed,

> Classes or social groups are common to all societies, but as long as the classes or social groups do not practice isolation and exclusiveness they are only non-social in their relations towards one another. Isolation and exclusiveness makes them anti-social and inimical to one another. (Ambedkar, 1987)

REMEDIES FOR DISCRIMINATION AND INEQUALITIES

The caste system's fundamental characteristic of fixed civil, cultural and economic rights for each caste, with restriction for change implies 'forced exclusion' of one caste from the rights of the other castes. Exclusion and discrimination in civil, cultural and, particularly, in economic spheres such as occupation and labour employment is, therefore, internal to the system and a necessary outcome of its basic features. Since the rights of each caste are fixed and compulsory, the institution of caste necessarily involves forced exclusion of rights of one caste from the rights of another. It is necessary to recognise that though an unequal and hierarchal assignment of economic rights restricts, obviously, the freedom of occupation and development, leading to inter-caste inequalities, it may not necessarily lead to deprivation and poverty among them. That is, deprivation is avoidable if every caste person has access to reasonable sources/resources of livelihood in his assigned occupation. However, in the case of the lower castes, particularly the Untouchables, exclusion leads to deprivation and poverty insofar as they are denied of all sources of livelihood, except manual labour which consists of assigned occupations considered to be polluting and inferior and service to the castes above them. Therefore, their exclusion has multiple dimensions and is simultaneously comprehensive and results in their severe deprivation as a social group. Besides, the Untouchables also suffer from social and residential separation, isolation due to the practice of untouchability. The concept of purity/pollution brings in an additional dimension to their discrimination and exclusion and, in more respects than one, further segregates them from the human capability and capacity building processes.

The practice of caste-based exclusion and discrimination thus, necessarily involves a failure of entitlement, not only to economic rights, but also to civil, cultural and political rights. It involves what has been described as living-mode exclusion, exclusion from political participation and exclusion and disadvantage in social and economic opportunities (United Nations, 2004). This form of exclusion could take the following forms:

(a) The exclusion and denial of equal opportunities in the economic sphere would necessarily operate through market and non-market transactions and exchange. First, such exclusion may be practiced in labour markets through the denial in hiring for jobs, in the capital markets through the denial of access to capital, in agriculture (land) markets through the denial of the right to sell/purchase/lease land, in the input markets through the denial in sale and purchase of factor inputs and in the consumer markets through the denial in sale and purchase of commodities and consumer goods.

(b) In the civic and cultural spheres, the Untouchables may face discrimination and exclusion in the use of public services like public roads, temples, water bodies, land for grazing and common use; access to institutions, either public/government or private delivering services like education, health, housing and other public services.

(c) In the political sphere, the Untouchables may face discrimination in the exercise of political rights and in participation in the decision-making process.

(d) Due to physical segregation and social exclusion on account of the notion of untouchability, they may suffer from general societal exclusion.

Ambedkar also devoted considerable intellectual efforts to suggest remedies for the exclusion and discrimination-induced deprivation, particularly of Untouchables and the structural inequalities in Indian society. In order to get insights into the evolution of Ambedkar's approach, it is necessary to go back to the formative stage of the present policies for which systematic intellectual efforts were made by Ambedkar since the early 1920s.

Beginning his articulation in 1919, he deepened and enriched his set of remedies with systematic efforts throughout the 1930s, 1940s and the 1950s.

A systematic articulation of his arguments were made by Ambedkar in his first statement submitted in January 1919 to the Southborough Committee at the time of the reform of the Government of India Act, 1919. About a decade later, Ambedkar submitted two statements—one to the Simon Commission in May 1928 and another at the First Round Table Conference, 1930. The final statement—'State and Minorities—What are Their Rights and How to Secure Them in the Constitution of Free India'—was made at the time of the framing of India's Constitution in 1947. These statements indeed provide insights into the evolution of Ambedkar's thinking on the problems of Indian society and his remedies to solve the problems of the Untouchables, in particular, and of the deprived sections of Indian society, in general. In their intellectual exercise, these documents are basic to the understanding of the malady of Hindu society and the remedies proposed by Ambedkar against the denial of equal opportunities to the Untouchables (Ambedkar, 1919, 1928, 1930, 1946).

From his writings of the 1920s through the 1940s, it becomes clear that Ambedkar grounded the case of remedies for the discrimination of Untouchables on the historical and prevalent denial of basic human rights and rights to development to them. In 1919, in his first systematic written statement, Ambedkar argued,

Not only the untouchability arrested the growth of personality of untouchables but also comes in the way of their 'material well being'. It deprived them of certain civil rights…. The untouchable is not even a citizen. Citizenship is bundle of rights such as personal liberty, personal security, right to hold private property, equality before law, liberty of conscience, freedom of opinion, and speech, right of assembly, right of representation in country's Government, and right to hold office under the state. The untouchability of untouchables puts these rights far beyond their reach.[2]

Substantiating the claim before the Simon Commission, Ambedkar argued, about ten years later in 1928, at the time of reform of the Government of India Act, that:

Depressed classes cannot be employed in the army, navy, and
police because such employment is opposed to the religious notion
of majority. They cannot be admitted in schools, because their
entry is opposed to the religious notion of majority. They cannot
avail themselves of Government dispensaries, because doctors
will not let them cause pollution to their persons or to their
dispensaries. They can not live cleaner and higher life, because to
live above their prescribed position is opposed to the religious
notion of majority. (Ambedkar, 1928)

Ambedkar adds,

So rigorous is the enforcement of the social code against the
Depressed classes that any attempt on the part of Depressed
classes to exercise their elementary rights of citizenship only ends
in provoking the majority to practice the worst forms of social
tyranny known to history. (ibid.: 445)

Repeating the same argument in the plenary session of the First
Round Table Conference in November 1930, Ambedkar said,

What is worse is that these servility and bar to human intercourse,
due to their untouchability, involve not merely the possibility of
discrimination in public life, but actually work out as a positive
denial of all equality of opportunity and the denial of those most
elementary of civic rights on which all human existent depend.
(Ambedkar, 1930: 504)

And finally, 17 years later, in 1947, while justifying the need for
safeguards against discrimination for the Scheduled Castes in the
constitution of independent India, Ambedkar argued, 'Unequal
treatment has been the inescapable fate of the untouchables in India'
(Ambedkar, 1946: 406–7) and added that 'in country like India where
it is possible for discrimination to be practiced on a vast scale and
in a relentless manner, fundamental rights have no real meaning for
untouchables' (ibid.).

A close look at the four memorandums prepared and presented
by Ambedkar, in fact, capture his interpretation of the problems of

the Untouchables. In his view, the problems of the Untouchables are rooted in the denial of basic human rights to them, which are essential for the growth of human beings. Therefore, Ambedkar grounded the justifications for remedies fundamentally on the denial of human rights, citizenship rights and other rights.

We also see the broadening of the solutions ever since Ambedkar first articulated his formal position in 1919, which took a definite shape in 1946. Ambedkar suggested the use of multiple remedies in combination to ensure equal opportunity and fair access, participation and representation to the Untouchables in the social, political and economic processes in society.

Some of the measures suggested were—the provision of equal rights to all; legal safeguards against violation of rights in terms of punitive measures; measures to ensure equal access and participation (through a reservation policy) in civil, political and economic spheres; and in addition, a definite strategy of the state aimed at the development and empowerment of Untouchables to compensate for denial of equal opportunities in the past.

Let us discuss the logic and reasons behind each of these measures:

EQUAL RIGHTS

The guarantee of equality before law and possession of equal rights common with other citizens of India in all public spheres was suggested as an initial pre-condition. This required the abolition of the customary laws governing the institution of untouchability and the caste system.

LEGAL SAFEGUARDS AGAINST VIOLATION OF RIGHTS

Guaranteeing equal rights, however, is not enough unless adequate legal safeguards and protection accompany them when the rights are violated. Ambedkar emphasised that equality of opportunities is impossible under the Indian societal situations, which do not recognise equality and where attempts by Untouchables to secure equal rights are opposed by the high castes. Those in the government, particularly the executive and civil service, Ambedkar felt, also opposed the equality of opportunity. Therefore, the larger remedy, according to Ambedkar, should not only imply that the Untouchables have the same rights that every other community has, but that there is a mechanism that provides legal ways and means by which the

Untouchables are protected in the exercise of these rights. That is, legal penalties exist against the infringement of their rights.

Ambedkar suggested legal safeguards against the practice of caste discrimination both for the private and the public sectors. He wrote 'Discrimination against citizens by government officers in public administration or by private employers in factories and commercial concerns on the grounds of race or creed or social status should be treated as offences' (Ambedkar, 1946: 396).

The private sector is defined in a manner so as to include not only employment but also commercial concerns, involving transactions in various markets. In the context of punitive measures associated with social boycott, Ambedkar clarified that spheres under the private sectors be included under 'commercial concerns'. Private spheres included renting and use of houses (housing market) and land (agricultural land market and lease market), hiring of workers (employment market), undertaking business with another person (capital, products and consumer markets), rendering and receiving any service (transactions and services carried through market and non-market channels) and things which are commonly done in the ordinary course of business (ibid.: 399).

Looking at it from the perspective of the market economy, the spheres that are included in the definition of private sectors for legal safeguards include transactions in various markets and non-market channels, such as all factors market (that is agricultural land market, labour market, capital market), product and consumer market, private housing market, educational institutions and exchange undertaken in other services necessary for any business activity and other provisions related with social needs.

STRATEGIES FOR EQUAL ACCESS (FAIR SHARE), PARTICIPATION AND REPRESENTATION

The anti-discrimination measures in the form of 'equality before law' and 'legal safe guards against violation' have their limitations. The laws only prevent members of society from taking steps that puts minorities in disadvantageous situations in the market and other spheres. Despite laws, the Untouchables may, however, not enjoy fair access and participation in economic, social and political processes due to the practice of discrimination and opposition by the high caste.

In this context, Ambedkar observed, 'In a country like India where it is possible for discrimination to be practiced on a vast scale and in relentless manner fundamental rights can have no meaning' (Ambedkar, 1946: 408).

Therefore, in addition to legal safeguards against discrimination there is a need to have strategies that provide fair and adequate access and participation in the legislature, executive, government services, educational institutions and other processes (spheres).

The legal measures have their limitations in ensuring fair participation of discriminated groups, therefore, the legal safeguards need to be supplemented by methods like 'reservations' that facilitate equal share, representation and participation to the discriminated groups in various spheres. Therefore, Ambedkar suggested measures to ensure fair access and participation in various spheres, which include legislative bodies, the executive, public services, educational institutions and all public spheres by representation in proportion to the population. These are, in fact, proactive measures on the part of the government to provide equal access and participation in various public spheres.

REMEDIES VIS-À-VIS THE STRUCTURAL INEQUALITIES ASSOCIATED WITH THE HISTORICAL PRACTICE OF EXCLUSION

Ambedkar also recognised that the present-day poverty, deprivation and marginalisation of the Untouchables were deep-rooted and hence a solution of present deprivation cannot be effective if one does not take into account the effects of historical denials. These denials do bear upon their present capabilities to gainfully engage in available opportunities. The measures in terms of equal laws with legal safeguards and measures for fair representation and participation in public spheres (in the form of a reservation policy) have their limitations to overcome the poverty and deprivation. The historical exclusion and isolation in the past is reflected in the abject lack of resources (agricultural land and non-land assets), education, employment and lack of basic civil, cultural rights for development. Hence, while anti-discriminatory measures are necessary, they are ineffective when it comes to overcoming the cumulative deprivation caused by historical exclusion and isolation in the past. Therefore, certain policies are required to compensate the discriminated group of Untouchables for the historical denial of ownership of resources, denial of access to education, employment and social needs. Ambedkar recognised this historically-rooted limitation of anti-discrimination policies of legal and fair participation.

In his view, the real solution lay in removing the structural inequalities caused by past exclusion and isolation in more fundamental ways and he thus suggested the policy of 'structural equalisation'. In his systematic and comprehensive elaboration on this issue, he suggested dual remedies: first, a set of policies/remedies relating to the safeguards against discrimination in the present or current discrimination, as discussed earlier, and second, strategies to over-come deep-rooted deprivation caused by the historical exclusion and isolation of the Untouchables. Emphasising the solution against structural inequalities, Ambedkar observed,

> There can be no doubt that in view of the circumstances, the uplift of the Depressed Classes will remain a pious hope unless the task is placed in the forefront of all governmental activities and unless equalisation of opportunities is realised in practice by a definite policy and determined efforts on the part of government. (1930: 553–54)

For this purpose, Ambedkar suggested a couple of main/important measures: The first fixed a clear responsibility on the state to develop policies and programmes for the educational and economic devel-opment of the SCs. Such policy are suggested specifically with respect to education and economic development. The denial of the right to education, property rights and business has led to high illiteracy, landlessness and lack of ownership of capital assets or business. Therefore, Ambedkar put singular responsibility on the state for the development of education and for the enhancement of the owner-ship of capital assets in terms of agricultural land and other capital assets. Ambedkar suggested few remedies to achieve this goal.

In the economic sphere, Ambedkar put responsibility on the state for providing access to agricultural land and capital to the SCs and others. He suggested a more radical remedy in the form of 'state socialism' for protection against economic exploitation.

His observation was,

> The main purpose behind the clause is to put an obligation on the
> state to plan the economic life of the people on the lines which
> would lead to highest point of productivity without closing every
> avenue to the private sector and provide for the equitable
> distribution of wealth. The plan set out in the clause proposes state
> ownership in agriculture with collectivised method of cultivation
> and a modified form of State Socialism in the field of industry.
> It places squarely on the shoulders of the state the obligation to
> supply capital necessary for agriculture as well as for industry. It
> also proposes state owned insurance system. (Ambedkar, 1946:
> 408)

Ambedkar also suggested a statutory obligation to maintain a
separate administrative division to deal with their problems, that is
'to watch the interests of the Depressed classes and promoting their
welfare' and argued for representation of the Untouchables in the
process of preparation and formulation of the general policy of the
government so that they could influence the decision-making process
with their presence at all levels. In this respect, Ambedkar observed:

> Just as it is necessary that the Depressed Classes should have the
> power to influence governmental action by seats in the Legislature
> so also it is desirable that the Depressed classes should have the
> opportunity to frame the general policy of the government. This
> they can do only if they can find a seat in the Cabinet. (1930: 554)

Thus, the participation of the Depressed Castes in the policy-
making process in the various arms of the government through
representation in the legislature, the executive and the public services
was considered essential and necessary by Ambedkar. For him, merely
representing the 'interests' of the Dalits was not enough. Ambedkar
believed that the interests of the discriminated groups could be
meaningfully ensured by their participation in the decision-making
process at all levels. He recommended participation of the Dalits in
the democratic polity at all levels from legislation to execution of

policies and measures, which would regulate the working of modern Indian society and its institutions. In this manner, in the conceptual scheme and vision of Ambedkar, representation and participation were fused together. His arguments for reservations in the Indian conditions were an innovative and original formulation that sought to bring together the requirement of representation and participation of marginalised groups through an elaborate system of rights. For ensuring participatory democracy and equal opportunity, rights embodied in the constitution were emphasised by Ambedkar. He was aware that if a society practices discrimination, then the impetus for change could only be located in the state, outside and autonomous of society and its practices. Since historically, society has practiced discrimination and isolation of a certain group of individuals through a hierarchical arrangement, Ambedkar recommended fair terms for their inclusion in the democratic polity, economic and social and cultural life. Bearing in mind the discriminatory attitude of society, he advocated an elaborate system of safeguards to ensure an inclusive, equal and participatory polity through rights, embodied in the constitution. The fact that historical discrimination was still pervasive and prevalent in Indian society, Ambedkar argued for intervention in ways that society reproduces itself, so as to arrest the retrogressive practices and ideas on which much of the social order was based, presenting itself as 'natural'.

It is also necessary to emphasise that Ambedkar suggested con-stitutional obligations on the state to undertake developmental measures—not just leaving the state's efforts to the voluntary initiative of the legislature and the government. In a statement/ scheme submitted to the Round Table Conference in 1930, Ambedkar (1930) observed,

In and for each Province in India, it shall be the duty and obligation of the Legislative and the Executive or any other Authority established by law to make adequate provision for the education, sanitation, recruitment in public services and other matters of social and political advancement of Depressed Classes.

In a similar manner, he also suggested safeguards against the failure of administrative authority to implement the statuary and other provisions of advancement for the Depressed Castes.

CONCLUDING OBSERVATIONS

This journey through the formative stage of the evolution of a policy on the remedies for structural inequalities associated with the institution of the caste system and untouchability, in general, and discrimination and deprivation of the Untouchables, in particular, from 1919 to 1946 provides insights into Ambedkar's interpretation of the caste system and its consequences. Ambedkar articulated the remedies in successive stages from 1919 till 1947, which ultimately culminated in the present policy at the time of the framing of the Indian Constitution in 1950.

Ambedkar suggested two sets of remedies. A set of remedies against continuing (present) discrimination and another set of remedies against the historical deprivation of the Untouchables due to the denial of economic, civil and cultural rights to them and the past structural inequalities of the Indian society.

Three safeguards were suggested to ensure that the practice of untouchability and caste discrimination did not carry on. These were (i) the safeguards against present discrimination were to include provisions of equal rights, (ii) legal safeguards in the form of preventive laws against the violation of the legal rights, and (iii) proactive measures to ensure that the discriminated groups had a fair share in and participated in the legislature, executive, public services, education and other public spheres (in the form of a reservation policy).

Given the limitation of these measures (which are used as safeguards against discrimination in the present) as solutions to the problems of deprivation due to historical exclusion, Ambedkar also suggested more fundamental measures for addressing the issue of 'structural inequalities' and suggested developmental measures for equalisation through 'state socialism', specifically in the economic spheres.

In Ambedkar's view, equal rights would provide the legal framework, overturning the unequal customary legal framework of the institution of the caste system and untouchability. Legal safeguards in the form of punitive laws would provide protection against violation of laws against discrimination in public and private spheres and the proactive measures would provide for fair share, participation and representation through reservation in public spheres as a safe-guard against present discrimination. The strategy against structural inequalities as compensatory measures for past denial of economic and education rights would help to empower the discrim-inated groups and reduce inequalities between them and other sections of Indian society.

NOTES

1. The original manuscript of this paper has been edited by Miss Dilshad Godrej Kapadia.
2. In this respect Ambedkar suggests: 'Discrimination against citizen by government officers in Public administration or by private employers in factories and commercial concerns on the grounds of race or creed, or social status shall be treated as an offence. The jurisdiction to try such cases shall be vested in a tribunal to be created for the purpose' (Moon, 1979: 256, 261).

REFERENCES

Ambedkar, B.R. (1916) (1936) 'Caste in India: Their Mechanism, Genesis and Development', in B.R. Ambedkar, *Annihilation of Caste*. Jullandher: Bheema Patrika Publications.
———. (1919) 'Evidence before the Southborough's Committee on Franchise', in Vasant Moon (ed.) (1979), *Dr. Babasaheb Ambedkar—Writings and Speeches*, Vol. 1. Bombay: Education Department, Government of Maharashtra.
———. (1928) 'Statement Concerning the Safeguards of the Depressed Classes as a Minority in the Bombay Presidency and the Changes in the Composition of and the Guarantees from the Bombay Legislative Council Necessary to Ensure the Same under Provincial Autonomy Submitted by Depressed Class Institute of Bombay', in Vasant Moon (ed.) (1982), *Dr. Babasaheb Ambedkar—Writings and Speeches*, Vol. 2. Bombay: Education Department, Government of Maharashtra.
———. (1930) 'Proceeding of Round Table Conference, (1) Plenary Session, Fifth Sitting, 20th November 1930, Need for Political Power for Depressed Classes, (2) In Sub-Committee No. III (Minorities) Second Sitting, 31st December 1930, Government of India', in Vasant Moon (ed.) (1982), *Dr. Babasaheb Ambedkar—Writings and Speeches*, Vol. 2. Bombay: Education Department, Government of Maharashtra.
———. (1946) 'States and Minorities—What are Their Rights and How to Secure Them in the Constitution of Free India'. Memorandum submitted on behalf of the All India Scheduled Caste Federation.

Ambedkar, B.R. (1987) 'The Hindu Social Order—Its Essential Features', in Vasant Moon (ed.), '*Dr. Babasaheb Ambedkar—Writing and Speeches*, Vol. 3, pp. 95–115. Bombay: Education Department, Government of Maharashtra.

Ambedkar, B.R. and Rao Bahadur R. Srinivasan(1930) 'A Scheme of Political Safe-guards for the Protection of the Depressed Classes in the Future Constitution of Self-Governing India', Appendix to the Report of Sub Committee No. III (Minorities), in Vasant Moon (ed.) (1982), *Dr. Babasaheb Ambedkar—Writings and Speeches*, Vol. 2. Bombay: Education Department, Government of Maharashtra.

Banerjee, Biswjit (1991) 'Job Discrimination and Untouchability', in Nancy Birdsall and Richard Sabot (eds), *Unfair Advantage—Labour Market Discrimination in Developing Countries*, pp. 183–205, World Bank Studies. New York: World Bank.

Birdsall, Nancy and Richard Sabot (eds) (1991) *Unfair Advantage—Labour Market Discrimination in Developing Countries*, World Bank Studies. New York: World Bank.

Darity, Jr. William (ed.) (1996) *Economics and Discrimination*, Vol. 1, An Elgar Reference Collection. New York: Edward Elger Publishing Ltd.

———. (2000) 'Tracing the Divide: Inter-group Disparity Across Countries', *Eastern Economic Journal*, 26(1): 78–97.

———. (1997) 'Reparations', in Samuel L. Myers, Jr. (ed.), *Civil Rights and Race Relations in the Post Reagan-Bush Era*, pp. 113–47. London: Praeger.

Darity, Jr. William and Steven Shulman (1989) *Question of Discrimination—Racial Inequality in the U.S. Labour Market*. Middletown, Connecticut: Wesleyan University Press.

Haan, Arjan De (1997) 'Poverty and Social Exclusion: A Comparison of Debates on Deprivation'. Working Paper No. 2, Poverty Research Unit at Susex. Brighton: University of Sussex.

———. (2003) 'Extreme Deprivation in Remote Areas in India: Social Exclusion as the Explanatory Concept', Conference on Chronic Poverty, April, session 'Social Exclusion, Rights and Chronic Poverty', Manchester.

Lal, Deepak (1988) 'Hindu Equilibrium', *Cultural Stability and Economic Stagnation*, Vol. 1. Carendor: Oxford.

Moon, Vasant (ed.) (1979) *Dr. Babasaheb Ambedkar—Writings and Speeches*, Vols. 1 & 3. Bombay: Department of Education, Government of Maharashtra.

Nescah, D. (1997) *Discrimination with Reason? The Policy of Reservation in USA, India and Malaysia*. New Delhi: Oxford University Press.

Thorat, S.K. (1996) 'Ambedkar on Economics of Hindu Social Order: Understanding Its Orthodoxy and Legacy', in Walter Fernandes (ed.), *The Emerging Dalit Identity*, pp. 201–28. New Delhi: Indian Social Institute.

———. (2002) 'Oppression and Denial: Dalit Discrimination in the 1990s', *Economic and Political Weekly*, 9 February.

Thorat, S.K. (with R.S. Deshpande) (1999) 'Caste and Labour Market Discrimination', *Indian Journal of Labour Economic*, Conference Issue, November.

Thurow, Lester C. (1969), *Poverty and Discrimination*. Washington, DC: The Brookings Institution.

United Nations (2004) *United Nation Human Development Report–Culture and Liberty*. Geneva: United Nations.

13

Dalits and Economic Policy: Contributions of Dr B.R. Ambedkar[1]

GAIL OMVEDT

INTRODUCTION: DALITS AND THE ECONOMIC DEBATE

'Ambedkar would have supported devaluation!' This claim by Dr Narendra Jadhav of the Reserve Bank of India shocked me at a time when all progressives seemed to be automatically opposing devaluation as a part of liberalisation.[2] But, while this most highly placed economist of Dalit background was a supporter of liberalisation, others have been equally vociferous in arguing that the 'new economic policy' will effect Dalits most harshly, with much-needed reservations lost to privatisation and cutbacks in social spending hitting the rural poor the hardest (see Teltumbde, 1997; Thorat, 1997).[3] Still others have argued that participation in a world economy has been part of the Dalit heritage since Mohenjodaro while the Aryan Brahmins and their heirs prefer a closed economy.[4]

There was a time, before the collapse of communism in the Soviet Union, that debates on economic policy had a clear 'left–right', progressive–conservative line-up. Socialists and progressives pushed for a greater role for the state, if not in building socialism then at least in assuring welfare where markets failed, while rightists hailed the market. Those days are gone. Today the most notorious reactionaries on social issues, from Pat Buchanan to Zhirinovsky, join with old leftists and trade unionists in calling for protectionism. The former socialist countries are forging a path towards capitalism, the Asian ones are under the leadership of communist parties. On the other hand, fervent free-marketers such as the 'Freshmen Republicans' of Newt Gingrich in the USA have discovered the virtues of at least some subsidies. In India, the BJP and CPI(M) alike have opposed 'Dunkel' tooth and nail while in opposition, but have promised that 'reforms will not stop' while in power: the effective debate now is only over the speed and type of reforms. Socialism is seemingly dead, but the market has hardly triumphed, welfare survives and people everywhere behold the doings of their political classes and intellectual leaders with scorn and puzzlement. Rethinking is clearly necessary.

Bhimrao Ramji Ambedkar, 'Babasaheb' to his Dalit followers, received his degree in economics from Columbia University. In spite of an event-filled political life, he found time to write numerous books, many dealing directly or indirectly with economic theory. In these days of intellectual confusion, can we find any guidance in the Dalit tradition, as compared to the Marxist one? This chapter takes a brief look at Ambedkar's theorising.

AMBEDKAR'S ECONOMIC THEORY: THE STAGE OF ECONOMIC TRADITIONALISM

Ambedkar—even more than Marx—was primarily a political activist, though with a Ph.D in economics. He had little time for deep academic research, but was immersed in the turmoil of his times. This is reflected in his economic thinking, which broadly went through three stages. The first was in his early, more academic economic writings of the 1920s (especially *The Problem of the Rupee and the Evolution of Provincial Finance in British India* [Moon, 1990c]) which gave strong anti-imperialist but fairly orthodox liberal economic assessments of British rule.[5] The second was in the 1930s and 1940s when as a central figure in the social and national movements of the period he was heavily influenced by traditional Marxism in the field of economics, a period that climaxed with the slogans of 'state socialism'. During this period, Ambedkar used a kind of 'dual systems' approach in which Brahminism and capitalism were seen as parallel systems of exploitation. The third period was towards the end of his life, marked by his historical researches on caste, Hinduism and Buddhism, when he sought a total alternative in Buddhist philosophy.

In the 1920s, employed as a professor at Sydenham College, Ambedkar spent his time reading and working and preparing the base for a surging Dalit movement. This included the organisation of the

Bahishkrut Hitakarni Sabha and the first great campaign (later to be memorialised as the 'Untouchable Liberation Day') for water in the Mahad Tank Satyagraha. It might be noted that the Mahad Tank Satyagraha was organised in the Konkan region, an area that was later to become the centre for a united Mahar-Kunbi movement against the Khoti landlord system. But, with a pace somewhat slower than that of later years, Ambedkar found time for two major economic treatises. Both followed fairly conventional economic thinking and both also had important similarities with the Indian economic nationalists—with the *Evolution of Provisional Finance* (Moon, 1990c) taking a harsh stand against much of British policy.

The *Problem of the Rupee* (ibid.) was the book that justified Narendra Jadhav's contention that Ambedkar would have supported devaluation. In the final sections of the book, Ambedkar dealt with the devaluation controversy of his day. Strikingly, at that time it was the Indian bourgeoisie who wanted a low rupee against the pound, while the British bureaucracy wanted a high rupee—the first, undoubtedly because they were primarily in an industry which had been a world leader from the very beginning (the textile industry), the second at least partly because of personal interests which would have preferred to be able to buy more pounds from their rupee salaries when they retired.

Ambedkar's own position was to argue for a moderately low rupee. In the course of his discussion, however, he did something which few in the devaluation debate of the 1990s had done: he gave a class analysis of the (at least temporary) effects of devaluation—arguing that entrepreneurs and the self-employed (from businessmen to farmers) would benefit from a low rupee, while wage and salary owners (from bureaucrats to daily labourers) would benefit from a high one which would keep consumer goods cheaper.[6] Ambedkar's recommendation was, therefore, one which he consciously saw as a compromise between workers and capitalists—a devalued rupee but not quite as much as the Indian bourgeoisie would have liked.

AGAINST BRAHMINISM AND CAPITALISM

Ambedkar did not remain a 'conventional economist' for long. In the 1930s and 1940s, under the impact of a mass upsurge, the pressures of the Great Depression and the evidently successful economic progress of the USSR and the working-class radicalism this gave birth to, he turned to the left. This was the period when his Dalit-based Independent Labour Party joined with communists to organise peasants and workers and he formulated the struggle as being against both 'capitalism' and 'Brahmanism'. In the largest peasant march of the 1930s, organised to demand the abolition of the Khoti landlord system in the Konkan, he told the rally that 'in regard to the toiler's class struggle, I feel the Communist philosophy to be closer to us' (*Janata*, 15 January 1938). Later that year, at a conference of Dalit railroad workers, he said:

> There are in my view two enemies which the workers of this country have to deal with. The two enemies are Brahminism and Capitalism.... By Brahminism I do not mean the power, privileges and interests of the Brahmins as a community. By Brahminism I mean the negation of the spirit of Liberty, Equality and Fraternity. In that sense it is rampant in all classes and is not confined to the Brahmins alone though they have been the originators of it. (reported in *The Times of India*, 14 February 1938)

These were years in which the pages of the *Janata*, Ambedkar's weekly, were filled with reports of the struggles of workers and peasants against 'capitalists and landlords' as well as the fight of the Dalits against atrocities. Ambedkar did not have much time for theoretical writing in this period of tumultuous organising, but his programmes and speeches indicate that he accepted broadly the Marxist analysis of class struggle so far as economic issues were concerned. What this led to, though, was a kind of a *dual systems theory*, which saw capitalism and Brahminism (casteism) as separate systems of exploitation, one to be fought by class struggle, the other by caste struggle.

The climax of this approach in many ways came with the writing of *States and Minorities* (Moon, 1990a), proposed to be a draft of sections of the Constitution. Here Ambedkar gave a severe critique of capitalism and called for the nationalisation of land and basic industries, explicitly calling this 'state socialism'. In a sense, the term 'state socialism' indicated his difference with the communists, in that in contrast to a revolution under 'working class leadership', state ownership was to be written into a democratic constitution. At another level, the phrase simply made the assumption of a mechanical Marxism that 'socialism' or collective ownership of the means of production was equivalent to *state* ownership.

There were, however, many problems with the 'dual systems' of Brahminism and capitalism. These became clear in *State and Minorities* itself, which seemed to contain two rather disparate sections, one advocating land nationalisation and state socialism, the other calling for separate village settlements of Dalits. The connection between the two was not clear. The problems of any 'dual systems theory' remained: seeing separate systems of class and caste exploitation left unchallenged by the Marxist assumptions of a class analysis accepted the idea that 'class' dealt with the economic issues while the 'caste' system of exploitation was at a cultural and ideological (superstructural) level. The dual systems of 'capitalism' and 'Brahmanism' provided useful rhetoric and a rule of thumb for analysis, but this left the question of the connection between the two systems completely unresolved. And if other systems of oppression (for instance 'patriarchy' and 'national oppression') were also included, then such an approach would simply yield to an unwieldy amalgam of many disparate 'systems' of exploitation. In other words, the dual systems theory could not give an integrated, holistic explanation. It reflected Ambedkar's initial grappling with Marxism, when he insisted that 'caste' be added to a class approach (and even that it should have priority) but did not develop an overall alternative theory.

BUDDHISM VERSUS MARXISM

If 'capitalism and Brahminism' were the themes of the 1930s and 1940s, the last years of Ambedkar's life were preoccupied with Buddhism and from time to time with the question of Buddhism and Marxism. But, the framework of thinking was different. Whereas in the 1930s and 1940s, Ambedkar had tended to see dual systems of exploitation, increasingly he came to give weight to caste and Brahminism and to try to theorise these in a way that would provide a unifying theme for the entire society. In the process, he also came to question his earlier acceptance of a mechanical class approach and of 'state socialism' as the solution to economic exploitation. In his search for a 'single system' theory, Ambedkar began to look towards Buddhism as the solution not only to problems of caste but also to economic exploitation.

We do not have to seek far for the reasons for this change. One was 'internal': that is, the logic of a dual systems theory was inadequate in the sense that it gave no idea of the connection between Brahminism and capitalism. Making 'class' the economic base and 'caste' a political-ideological superstructure tended to give legitimacy to the mechanical Marxist position that the base was primary and that caste was a secondary issue. This was unacceptable to Ambedkar and other Dalit-Bahujan activists.

But, the other reason for disillusionment with the existing theory of Marxism was *external*, the result of historical experience. On the one hand, Ambedkar had an on-going struggle with the Indian communists, who saw him only as a party bourgeois misleader. On the other hand, the world context was changing. In the 1930s and 1940s, the revolutionary claims of mechanical Marxism appeared justified by world events; depression, war and revolution abounded and the Soviet Union seemed to be able to achieve both equality and impressive economic growth. By the 1950s, these conditions had reversed themselves. Capitalist growth in the West was showing a new dynamism and its proletariat was becoming integrated into the system. And, the Soviet 'model' was beginning to tarnish; the state was not withering away, it was showing its dictatorial face in a way clear to all. In this context, Ambedkar began to define himself not so much as a socialist but as an equalitarian who was equally devoted to freedom and a moral community life. His earlier definition of 'Brahmanism' had seen it as the negation of the ideals of liberty, equality and fraternity; now he returned to this theme. As his conclusion to a draft essay on Buddha and Marx says:

> Society has been aiming to lay a new foundation as was summarised by the French revolution in three words, fraternity, liberty and equality. The French revolution was welcomed because of this slogan. It failed to produce equality. We welcome the Russian revolution because it aims to produce equality. But it cannot be too much emphasized that in producing equality society cannot

afford to sacrifice fraternity or liberty. Equality will be of no value without fraternity or liberty. It seems that the three can coexist only if one follows the way of the Buddha. Communism can give one but not all. (Moon, 1990b: 462)

What did Ambedkar mean by 'the way of Buddha'? He could not finish the book he proposed on this, but the essay on 'Buddha or Karl Marx' gives some indications of his thinking. The essay begins with an outline of Marxist propositions and states that most of these have been historically invalidated: the proletariat has not become increasingly immiserated and revolutionary; the state has not withered away after revolutions. Marx's assertions of private property as the origin of exploitation and of class conflict remain, in Ambedkar's words, 'a residue of fire, small but still very important' (ibid.: 444), but now he sees the way to overcome the exploitation of private property in a radically different way. In other words, with this Ambedkar rejects state socialism, nationalisation and the dictatorship of the proletariat as solutions to the problem of exploitation and turns to Buddhism for an alternative. And here he comes up with what may be called a 'moral economy' solution to the problems of exploitation. This was not simply a matter of a stress on non-violence as opposed to violence.

Ambedkar had never rejected Marxism simply because of the role of force in its philosophy; unlike Gandhi he did not see non-violence as an absolute or religiously based principle. In this essay he expands on what he feels is a more practical Buddhist attitude towards violence. His argument is that we cannot (and Buddha did not) renounce force when it is necessary to obtain justice. '[Buddha] certainly would not have exempted property owners from force if force was the only means for that end', Ambedkar writes (ibid.: 451). But this kind of force was not necessary, he argues, first because equality and the abolition of private property was achieved in the Bhikku Sangha through voluntary means and, second, because morality and a welfare state could ensure that private accumulation of wealth did not lead to impoverishment.

Thus, a long Buddhist parable in the essay describes how the rule of 'righteousness' rather than the 'rule of law (force)' is necessary to maintain the prosperity of the kingdom. The role of the state (as symbolised by the righteous king) seems to be twofold: one is *the guarantee of property and protection to all in the kingdom* and the second is *direct action to remove property by 'providing wealth to the destitute'*. The second is crucial; in fact, it is the failure to remove poverty which leads (in the parable) to the downfall of society.

But Ambedkar assumes here that property and wealth accumulation will continue, though under state regulation. In regard to this, Ambedkar makes an important contrast between Buddhism and Christianity. Christianity gives a high value to poverty and other-worldliness, Buddhism does not—and Ambedkar believes it was superior precisely for this reason: 'There is no Sermon on the Mount to be found in the Buddha's teachings. His teaching is to acquire wealth' (Moon, 1990b: 460). For householders, lawful and moral accumulation of wealth is praised:

> Thus to acquire wealth legitimately and justly, earned by great industry, amassed by strength of the arm and gained by the sweat of the brow is a great blessing. The householder makes himself happy and cheerful and preserves himself full of happiness; also makes his parents, wife and children, servants and labourers, friends and companions happy and cheerful, and preserves them full of happiness. (ibid.: 461)

Ambedkar in this essay thus talks of equality but not of 'socialism'. Similarly, in his speech introducing the Indian Constitution, he refers to 'social democracy' rather than socialism (Moon, 1993: 1216). Was he having doubts about the value of socialism as defined in terms of collective ownership of the means of production? Or were these responses only due to the situation: after all, a summing up of the debate on the constitution was not a place to talk of socialist ideals since no one had, at that time, seriously proposed that independent India define itself as socialist state.

But, if Ambedkar maintained a socialist ideal, it must have been in a very different form than the traditional understanding of socialism at the time. Socialism was defined in terms of 'collective ownership' and Ambedkar's identification of this as 'state ownership' was similar to the confusion shown by all the Marxists of his day. Soviet developments (and the continual communist defence of the 'dictatorship of the proletariat') identified this, in turn, with dicta-torship or the use of force. This is perhaps why in this essay, Ambedkar continues to emphasise equality but does not use the word socialism and explicitly rejects the abolition of property by force. 'Equality' is to be maintained by voluntary communism in the Bhikku Sangha and poverty is to be remedied by the redistributive activities of the state. Thus, by the end of his life Ambedkar can be called a 'socialist' only if socialism is defined in terms of the value of equality and not as equivalent to the collective ownership of the means of production.

AMBEDKAR AND THE MORAL ECONOMY

Today, provoked by the failures of 'state socialism' and by the resurgence of issues of identity, culture and spirituality, many socialist activists and theorists are centring their attack on the immorality of commercial capitalism and writing about the need for a 'moral economy'. Ambedkar would have agreed, and the need for 'morality' in the economic and political ordering of society was one of the crucial points of his criticism of the Marxism of his day.

At the same time, Ambedkar's 'moral economy' differed crucially from the version being put forward by many in India (and other countries) today. Today, most of the progressives arguing for a 'moral economy' in the abstract, do so basing themselves on a criticism of the 'immorality' of the 'market economy' and the meaninglessness and destructiveness of 'economic growth for its own sake' also avoid this issue. But, the guiding theme for their 'moral economy' is a neo-Gandhian Hinduism, in which 'Indian (Hindu) spirituality' and the 'limitation of needs' are praised. On these points, Ambedkar would have thoroughly disagreed. Morality in economic life required, according to him, a firm rejection of the pseudo-morality of traditional 'Hinduism', it had to be grounded in the three revolution-ary values of 'liberty, equality and fraternity' and it presumed the overcoming of poverty through the development of human produc-tive forces. Ambedkar sees these as (not Western but) universal ideals and as necessary for the welfare of the Bahujan samaj.

This is clear in an early essay of Ambedkar, a review of a book by Bertrand Russell. In contrast to the Gandhian notion of 'limitation of needs', Ambedkar never accepted the equation of morality with suffering, poverty, asceticism or renunciation of money and consumption. As he wrote:

> This time-honoured complaint of the moralists against 'love of money' is only a part of their general complaint against the goods of the world and finds its justification in the economic circumstances which gave rise to this particular belief.... At a time when the whole world was living in 'pain economy' as did the ancient world and when the productivity of human labour was extremely low and when no efforts could augment its return, in short when the whole world was living in poverty, it is but natural that moralists should have preached the gospel of poverty and renunciation of worldly pleasures only because they were not to be had. (Moon, 1990a: 489)

Ambedkar's moral economy, then, was to be one of abundance and wealth accumulation. His rejection, in *Buddha or Karl Marx*, of the Christian glorification of poverty is consistent with this. It seems at the end of his life he returned to his first insight, 'the trouble... is not with property but with the unequal distribution of it' (ibid.: 491).

At a time when many environmentalists, once again, are preaching an anti-developmentalist ethic and urging a return to traditionalist practices, this basic philosophical outlook is important. Ambedkar would certainly have been aware of the problems of ecological destruction caused by unregulated overproduction, but he would even more certainly have seen the solution to this in a form of *sustainable development*, not a rejection of development as such. Ambedkar here shares with Marx a positive appraisal of economic development—the development of the 'forces of production' and the potentials of wealth, choice and freedom made possible by this. He has no inclination towards the ascetic 'limitation of needs' and rejects what he calls a 'pain economy'. Thus Ambedkar's 'moral economy' which is outlined in a very sketchy way in *Buddha or Karl Marx* is not contrasted either to a market economy or a planned economy as such but rather presents some alternatives that will make both market and state work for the good of the people.

It has three basic elements: (*i*) the role of the state was seen to be in providing 'protection' and the removal of poverty; (*ii*) the role of the market was to be in the production and accumulation of wealth by individual householders (modified by moral concerns); and (*iii*) the role of community, which would give equality, was seen in the development of a voluntaristic equalitarian communism in the Bhikku Sangha.

AMBEDKAR'S ECONOMIC THEORY AND ECONOMIC REFORMS

One should not make too much of *Buddha or Karl Marx*; it provides at most a direction of economic thinking but by no means does it provide a fully developed economic theory. Would Ambedkar have opposed privatisation or supported liberalisation? Statements at this level remain to a large degree speculation. But, it seems clear that a large part of his approach, finally, would have been pragmatic, looking for the most effective combination of state, market and community roles; that he would have been clearly for the kind of globalisation that would aid the Dalits and other sections of the poor to establish their full place in a world heritage; that he would have been concerned both with all-round economic growth and its impact on the poorest and most deprived sections of the community. He would clearly have given overriding power to the state unlike many of those who speak in his name and refer only to his period of advocacy of 'state socialism'. He would not deny the occasional need to use state power to override property rights, he would see acquisition not as an evil but as part of a process of wealth creation. And, he would look to voluntary sharing in a community of concern as the primary means of achieving equality.

NOTES

1. An earlier version of this chapter was published in the Omvedt (1997).
2. This statement was made by Dr Narendra Jadhav at a seminar on 'Dalit Middle Class', Pune University, Department of Politics, 1994. See also his speech at the Vichar Vedh Sammelan in Nasik, December 1996, where he elaborated on the distinction between 'open economy' or *khule*

arthavyavastha, and 'free economy' or *mukt arthavyavastha*: the latter is the pure 'free market' of ideologues, the former emphasises a crucial role for the state especially in regulation, social services and infrastructure.

3. See Anand Teltumbde (1997) and Sukhadeo Thorat (1997). These were papers for a seminar on the 'Impact of New Economic Policy on Dalits' organised by the Department of Sociology, University of Pune, on 9–11 December 1996; the collection is to be published in a book edited by P. Jogdand.

4. See the articles in *Bahujan Sangharsh*, by Nagesh Chaudhuri (1994), Divakar Bhoyar (1994) and Siddharth Kamble (1994).

5. Where not otherwise cited, references to Ambedkar's writings are to the volumes edited by Vasant Moon and published as *Dr B.R. Ambedkar: Writings and Speeches*.

6. In evaluating this issue today, it might be noted that the salaries of workers in the organised sector (both public and private) are three to five times higher compared to those who are 'self-employed' in the unorganised sector. It might also be asked why the Indian policy-makers (the nationalists of the 1920s) changed their position after Independence to maintain a currency kept artificially high by world market standards: here the interests of the bureaucracy plus a new push for 'import-substitution industrialisation' built a group of industrialists who benefited from a high rupee and hence cheaper imports (reported in *The Times of India*, 14 February 1938).

REFERENCES AND SELECT BIBLIOGRAPHY

Bhoyar, Divakar (1994) 'Dunkel, GATT and Bahujans', *Bahujan Sangharsh*, 30 April.

Chaudhuri, Nagesh (1994) 'What Policy Should We Take Towards Dunkel?', *Bahujan Sangharsh*, 30 April, Editorial, pp. 1–2.

Jogdand, P.G. (ed) (2000) *The Impact of New Economic Policy on Dalits*. Pune: University of Pune.

Kamble, Siddharth (1994) 'What is the Dunkel Draft?', *Bahujan Sangharsh*, 30 April, pp. 32–39.

Moon, Vasant (compiler) (1990a) *Dr. B.R. Ambedkar: Writings and Speeches, Vol. 1, Mr. Russel and the Reconstruction of Society*. Bombay: Education Department, Government of Maharashtra.

———. (1990b) *Dr. B.R. Ambedkar: Writings and Speeches, Vol. 3, Buddha or Karl Marx*. Bombay: Education Department, Government of Maharashtra.

———. (1990c) *Dr. B.R. Ambedkar: Writings and Speeches, Vol. 6, The Problem of the Rupee and the Evolution of Provincial Finance in British India*. Bombay: Education Department, Government of Maharashtra.

———. (1993) *Dr. B.R. Ambedkar: Writings and Speeches, Vol. 13, Dr. Ambedkar as the Architect of the Indian Constitution and His Speeches in Parliament—1946 to 1956*. Bombay: Education Department, Government of Maharashtra.

Omvedt, Gail (1997) 'Dalits and Economic Policy: Contributions of Dr B.R. Ambedkar', *Fourth World*, 4(1): 22–26.

Teltumbde, Anand (1997) 'Impact of New Economic Policy on Dalits in India', Occasional Paper Series 1. Pune: Department of Sociology, University of Pune.

Thorat, Sukhadeo (1997) 'New Economic Policy and Its Impact on Employment and Poverty of the Scheduled Castes', Occasional Paper Series 2. Pune: Department of Sociology, University of Pune.

14

Reservation Policy and the Empowerment of Dalits

P.G. JOGDAND

INTRODUCTION

Compensatory discrimination sometimes called 'protective discrimination', is a government policy and programme of 'preferential treatment of historically disadvantaged sections (Scheduled Castes and Scheduled Tribes) of the population' built into the constitution and then implemented through subsequent legislation and judicial decisions. It was one of the means chosen to achieve the ends of liberty, equality, justice and fraternity enshrined in the constitution. In pursuance of the constitutional provisions for the historically disadvantaged, the central and state governments have adopted a number of measures for the economic, educational and social uplift of these disadvantaged groups. These measures may be classified as the protective, developmental and welfare schemes to empower the Dalits of India.

Within this broader compensatory discrimination policy, the aim of establishing job reservations or quotas in government service and public sector undertakings has been to create a just society by providing a helping hand to the disadvantaged sections of Indian society. Specifically, job reservations are intended not just to provide a few jobs to some individuals, but to uplift and empower as well as provide them with opportunities for both social and economic mobility. Indeed, job reservations have served as one of the means by which members of historically disadvantaged groups, Dalits and tribals in particular, have gained some sort of social mobility through individual mobility.

CONSTITUTIONAL SAFEGUARDS

Article 14, which enjoins upon the state not to deny to any person 'equality before law or equal protection of the laws', carries special significance in the context of Indian society which hitherto was socially graded facilitating elevation of some and degradation of others. Article 15 prohibits the state from making discrimination on grounds of religion, race, caste, sex, or place of birth. The constitution was amended in 1995 (Seventy-seventh Amendment Act, 1995). This amendment restored reservation for the promotion of the SCs and STs by inserting Clause 4(a) in Article 16. Article 16(4)(a) mentions that 'nothing in this article shall prevent the State from making any provision for reservations in matters of promotion to any class or classes of posts in the services under the states in favour of the SCs and STs which in the opinion of the state, are not adequately represented in the services under the State'.

The Indian Constitution has fully recognised the need for the development of the weaker sections both socially and educationally. It has also abolished the practice of 'untouchability' and declared it as an offence punishable in accordance with the law (Article 17). As per this article, we have legally abolished untouchability and hence there is no room for it. The constitution has not only granted to every citizen of India the right to profess any religion (Article 25), but it also has included in the fundamental rights that no citizen will be discriminated on the basis of religion, race, caste or sex (Article 15).

The constitution also provides reservation of seats for the backward sections in the Lok Sabha (Article 330) and in the Vidhan Sabhas (Article 334). Out of the 545 seats in the Lok Sabha, 106 seats are reserved for the weaker sections. In pursuance of Article 332, reservation of seats for SCs and STs in the state Vidhan Sabhas (legislative assemblies) is provided.

In accordance with the constitution (Seventy-third Amendment) Act, 1992, seats in panchayats (from the village to the zila parishad level) are reserved for weaker sections in proportion to their population at the respective level in direct election.

On the economic front, the constitution not only prohibits any form of forced labour (Article 23), but also makes special provision for people of the backward sections of society to be provided reserved posts in various government departments both at the central as well as state level (Articles 16, 320, 335). These reservations have been offered according to their percentage of the total population of the country. Article 46 of the constitution offers a special provision to promote with special care the education and economic interests of the weaker sections and it offers them protection from social injustice and all forms of exploitation.

In addition to these safeguards in favour of the weaker sections, some protective and anti-exploitative measures have been provided. These measures include the Untouchability Offences Act, 1955 (UOA), Protection of Civil Rights, 1976 (PCR). Actually, the UOA of 1955 was amended and renamed PCR in 1976 with more severe punishments included for the violation of civil rights. Since PCR did not cover all cases of atrocities on the weaker sections, vital steps to prevent atrocities on these sections was taken by Parliament in 1989 by enacting the Scheduled Castes and Scheduled Tribes (Prevention of Atrocities) Act, 1989.

So the Constitution of India has provided all the possible basic and human rights to the weaker sections and even has empowered the president of India to appoint a special officer or a commissioner in order to see to the working of these constitutional safeguards and report the same to the president.

Besides all these provisions in favour of the weaker sections, the government of India has been implementing several other plans for the last 50 years within the provisions of the constitution. In the First Five-Year Plan, the policy measures were largely confined to educational facilities, allotment of wastelands and reservation in government services. The same approach continued in the Second Five-Year Plan as well. In the Third Plan, the assistance in educational development received high priority with additional emphasis on technical and vocational training. In the Fourth Five-Year Plan, the emphasis on education continued. In the Sixth Plan, significant modification was made in the strategy towards the economic development of these sections. In this plan, the Special Component Plan was adopted in order to quantify the flow of funds and benefits from various sectors to the weaker sections. In the Seventh Plan, emphasis on beneficiary-oriented programmes of socio-economic uplift of weaker sections continued. In the Eighth Five-Year Plan, education and the programmes of economic development received high priority. The programmes during the Eighth Plan were to be tuned to meet the specific needs of these communities.

The approach paper to the Ninth Five-Year Plan observed that all programmes meant for the weaker sections would be so designed as to empower them and provide both social and economic mobility.

In addition to the funds allocated for the benefit of SCs and STs, a number of other schemes have been launched by the government from time to time. For example, Intergrated Rural Development Programme (IRDP), National Rural Employment Programme (NREP), (Training of Rural Youth for Self-Employment (TRYSEM), Jawahar Rojgar Yojna, Tribal Development Programmes, Special Component Plan and the Scheduled Castes Development Corporation.

There are several other temporary schemes like the National Safai Karmacharis Development Corporation, post-metric scholarships to upgrade the merit of SC and ST students, book banks, centrally-sponsored schemes for boys and girls hostels, aid to voluntary organisations and the Dr Ambedkar Foundation, which were initiated to enhance the development of the weaker sections in non-traditional occupations.

THE POSITIVE EFFECTS OF COMPENSATORY DISCRIMINATION

The spread of education among the SCs and STs has been a major part of the government programmes since the early 1950s. It mainly includes financial support in the forms of scholarship stipends at the school and college levels, construction of hostels for students of this community, reservation in engineering and medical colleges and other facilities. As stated earlier, Article 46 of the Constitution of India refers to the special care to be taken by the state for the promotion of education among the SCs and STs. The policies of the government have led to improvements in the access of the Dalits to educational services. Literacy rates of these sections, as shown in the report of the ministry of human resource development, *Education for All—The Indian Scene*, 1993, indicates an increase in the literacy rate among SCs from 21.4 per cent in 1981 to 37.4 per cent in 1991 and among STs from 16.4 per cent in 1981 to 29 per cent in 1991. The literacy rate among SC males increased from 31.1 per cent in 1981 to 49.9 per cent in 1991 and among ST males from 21.5 per cent in 1981 to 40.6 per cent in 1991. The literacy rate among SC females increased from 10.9 per cent in 1981 to 23.8 per cent in 1991 and among ST females from 8 per cent in 1981 to 18.2 per cent in 1991. As is evident from this report, the main problems of these communities on the educational front is the high level of illiteracy, massive drop-out at middle and high school levels and limited access to higher education (see Table 14.9) This has happened despite progressive educational programmes for these sections in our country.

Thus, undeniably, the protective discrimination policy and other policies and programmes initiated by the Indian state have helped, to a large extent, the weaker sections in getting access to different jobs in government departments, public sector undertakings, political arena and educational institutions. At least at the aggregate level, their recruitment has been in proportion to their population. Overall, these state policies have produced substantial redistributive effects. Reserved seats provide a substantial legislative presence. The reservation of jobs has led to a substantial increase in their earnings and has provided them security, information, patronage and prestige.

However, after 1991, with the introduction of the new economic reforms, which were aimed at privatisation and reduction in the role of the government, the employment of SCs and STs has declined both in absolute numbers and in proportion. The new economic measures have reversed the positive trends set in since 1956 (see Table 14.8). Moreover, evidence suggests that such redistribution is not spread evenly throughout the beneficiary groups. Further, it indicates that the weaker sections are not a homogeneous group in terms of their socio-economic problems. However, they are homogeneous as far as their social and cultural identities are concerned. Hence, there is a demand that the plan and policies of the government must concentrate on the unique problems of each section and caste in a region and that there must be rigorous implementation of specific and target-oriented schemes.

Admittedly, the SCs and STs have certainly benefited from the safeguards offered by the government as stated earlier since they have realised the benefits of education. They are engaged in educating their children and improving the socio-economic status of their families. Evidence suggests that they have achieved some measures of success in the present social system. The overall impact of all these policies is, though limited, certainly positive in the sense that at least a small section of SCs and STs have got access to government jobs and the legislatures. However, the poor and needy, who constitute a majority, are outside the vortex of these developments. This can be seen in the latest report of the commissioner for SCs and STs (Government of India, 2001). In this report, a stock taking has been done with a view to measuring the trends of progress of these sections. The Commission has provided some meaningful data and indicators regarding population, literacy, occupational profile and representation in services to get an overview of the development that has taken place with regard to SCs and STs in the last 50 years. According to this report, the share of SCs and STs in these indicators of visible progress of India is dismal. All efforts are concentrated only in providing reservation in services, which also has not reached the prescribed limit. The Commission observed that representation should be ensured in respect of population, literacy, occupational profile and representation in services for visible progress of these groups. Emphasis should be given to the promotion of entrepreneurship and upward mobility among SCs and STs.

They should be encouraged to take up self employment in all sectors of economic development through training, education and provision of financial and other facilities. Many activities are considered necessary for the development of SCs and STs and there should be policy to contain built in safeguards to ensure a fair share of the benefit to these groups. This should be built in mechanism to provide substantial share and role to such representations from the SC/ST for ensuring the effective working of all these safeguards. (Government of India, 1998: 20) (see Tables 14.1–14.9)

THE NEED FOR CLARITY ABOUT JOB RESERVATIONS

When weighing the recent decisions, as well as the earlier judgements on this issue and the misunderstandings created by the opponents of the reservation policy, it is necessary to review the entire job reservation policy so as to avoid further distortions and misconceptions.

Although this policy has been in place for the past half century, neither its beneficiaries nor the general category people have been happy with its consequences. The anti-reservationists believe that their merit is being ignored while its beneficiaries think that this package is not being implemented properly and consequently their social status has not been enhanced to the degree expected. As a result, job reservations have become a sensitive and controversial issue. The SCs and STs were demoralised by the Supreme Court arguments that where there is reservation there is no merit and that reservation is 'contrary to the national interests'. Not only were these arguments insulting, but they also ignored the harsh reality of caste prejudice in the selection and promotion process. Two decisions of the Supreme Court on the reservation issue have created a lot of hue and cry. The first, delivered on 10 August 1999, ruled that in the competitive examinations for government or public sector jobs there can not be a wide disparity between minimum qualifying marks for candidates in the reserved category (that is, SCs, STs and OBCs) and candidates in the general category (that is, everyone else). Moreover, no special provisions for candidates in the reserved category are permitted for admission (as students) into super-speciality courses as that would be contrary to national interests. The next blow came barely a month later when the same court ruled that reservations should not be applicable in cases of job promotions. A five-judge constitution bench headed by the chief justice of the Supreme Court held that Articles 16(4) and 16(4)(a) of the Constitution 'do not confer any fundamental rights nor do they impose any constitutional duties of enabling provisions vesting a discretion in the state to consider providing reservations if the circumstances so warranted'.

These two articles of the constitution are concerned with equality of opportunity in matters of public employment for SCs, STs and OBCs. The court also overruled an earlier judgement which had held that a government rule could be issued either to provide for reservations or to relax the rules for reserved category candidates. The court also held that the 'roster point' promotees (reserved category) could not count their seniority in the promoted category from 'the date of their continuous officiation' in the promoted posts vis-à-vis the general category candidates who were senior to them in the lower category and who were later promoted.

The evidence shows that a lot of misconceptions about job reservations have been generated in the minds of the people. For example, the general category people feel that they do not get jobs because of this policy which is therefore responsible for their unemployment; caste is strengthened by it; merit and efficiency in educational institutions and administration have vanished as a result of it. As a matter of fact, new jobs are not being created in the market and so there is a lot of resentment in the minds of the people at large. Even among the Dalits, the unemployment rate is quite high. At the beginning of the twenty-first century, it is imperative that we see these distortions for what they are and portray the real picture.

We categorically state that the charges of the anti-reservationists and the successive verdicts issued by the Supreme Court go against the very spirit of the Constitution of India. Reservations were challenged through courts immediately after the adopation of the constitution. The entire history of reservations in independent India has several stages where crucial decisions have moulded its implementation. In several cases, the constitution was amended so as to sustain this policy. The main intention behind the reservation policy was to give social justice and thereby empower the Dalits and the tribals. This policy of job reservations intends to bring about proportional equality, as it is a mode of distributing benefits based on the proportion of the population, that is, 15 per cent for the Dalits and 7.5 per cent for the STs. It is based on the principles of distributive justice and of compensation for past disadvantages. All in all, it has been a project of 'capacity building' among the weaker sections of Indian society. Although theoretically sound in conception,

TABLE 14.1

Representation of SCs and STs among Employees in Public Sector Banks, 1986–96 (14 Nationalised Banks, State Bank of India and its Associate Banks)

YEAR	1986		1996	
	SCs	STs	SCs	STs
Officers	7.30	1.84	11.11	3.65
Clerks	13.63	3.70	14.69	4.71
Sub-staff (including sweepers)	24.94	4.39	30.00	5.54

SOURCE: Government of India, 1998.

TABLE 14.2

Representation of SCs, STs, OBCs and Others in Different Categories of Posts in the Indian Embassies (in percentage)

CATEGORY	SC	ST	OBC	UPPER CASTE
Group A	8.0	1.00	0.00	91.00
Group B	4.20	0.60	5.00	94.00
Group C	4.30	1.20	1.50	93.00
Group D	7.0	1.00	0.20	91.83

SOURCE: Government of India, 1998.

TABLE 14.3

Representation of Different Social Groups as Judges and Additional Judges in the High Courts

YEAR	TOTAL	SC	ST	OTHERS
March 1982	325	4 (1.23%)	–	321 (98.77%)
March 1993	547	13 (2.38%)	4 (0.73%)	530 (96.89%)

SOURCE: Government of India, 1998.

TABLE 14.4

Representation of SCs and STs in the Services of the Central Public Sector Enterprises as on 1 January 2000

GROUP	TOTAL NUMBER OF EMPLOYEES	SCs	PERCENTAGE	STs	PERCEN-TAGE
A	204,127	21,125	10.35	6,057	2.97
B	175,159	19,355	11.05	7,317	4.28
C	1,013,917	191,931	18.93	85,744	8.46
D (excluding safai karamcharis)	407,425	91,729	22.51	46,463	11.40
Total	1,800,628	324,140	18.00	145,581	8.09
Safai karamcharis	27,903	20,412	73.15	878	3.15
Grand total	1,828,531	344,552	18.84	146,459	8.01

SOURCE: Government of India, 2001.

TABLE 14.5

Representation of SCs and STs in the Services of the Central Ministries, Departments and their Subordinate Offices

GROUP	TOTAL NUMBER OF EMPLOYEES	SCs	PERCENTAGE	STs	PERCEN- TAGE
A	93,520	10,558	11.29	3,172	3.39
B	104,963	13,306	12.68	3,512	3.25
C	2,396,426	378,115	15.78	145,482	6.07
D (excluding sweepers)	949,353	189,761	19.99	66,487	7.00
Sweepers	96,435	63,233	65.57	5,314	5.51
Total (excluding sweepers)	3,544,262	591,740	16.7	218,653	6.17
Total (excluding sweepers)	3,640,697	654,973	17.99	223,967	6.15

SOURCE: Government of India, 2001.

it has shown some unanticipated results over the last fifty years. Tables 14.1–14.9 provide data both about the results of the reservation policy and about trends in its implementation.

One can see in these tables the job categories for which the SC and ST quotas have been filled. They are heavily concentrated in the lower level, Class III and Class IV jobs, whereas there is a heavy backlog in the higher-level Class II and Class I services. There is also a heavy backlog in almost all institutions. There are 239 universities (including 12 central universities) in the country in which 23 per cent of the jobs are reserved for Dalits and STs. Accordingly, almost 69,000 individuals should have been employed through the reserved quotas in these universities. However, only 2 per cent of the 23 per cent posts have been filled. In its report, the National Commission has expressed its dismay over this sorry state of affairs. There is no quota in the judiciary. In March 1993, only 13 of the 547 judges and additional judges in the high courts throughout the country were Dalits and only four were STs. Although their share has increased

TABLE 14.6

Employment Profile of SCs and STs in the Central Government

GROUP	TOTAL		SC		PERCENTAGE OF TOTAL		ST		PERCENTAGE OF TOTAL	
	1965	1995	1965	1995	1965	1995	1965	1995	1965	1995
Class I	19,379	65,408	318	6,637	1.64	10.12	52	1,891	0.27	2.89
Class II	30,621	108,857	864	13,797	2.82	12.67	103	2,913	0.34	2.68
Class III	1,082,278	2,341,863	96,114	378,172	8.88	16.15	12,390	133,179	1.14	5.69
Class IV (excluding sweepers)	1,132,517	1,041,082	101,073	221,380	17.75	21.26	38,444	67,453	3.39	6.48
Total (excluding sweepers)	2,264,795	3,557,210	198,369	619,986	13.17	17.43	50,989	205,436	2.25	5.78
Sweepers	–	177,527	–	78,719	–	44.34	–	12,269	–	6.91
Grand total	2,264,795	3,734,737	198,369	698,705	13.17	18.71	50,989	217,705	2.25	5.83

SOURCE: Government of India, 1998.

NOTE: Figures relating to sweepers in 1965 are included in the figures for the Class IV Group.

TABLE 14.7
Occupational Distribution at the All-India Level

CATEGORY OF WORKERS	GENERAL				SCs				STs			
	1961	1971	1981	1991	1961	1971	1981	1991	1961	1971	1981	1991
Cultivators	52.78	43.38	41.53	39.74	37.76	27.87	28.17	25.44	68.18	57.56	54.43	54.50
Agri-labour	16.71	26.32	25.16	19.66	34.48	51.74	48.22	49.06	19.71	33.04	32.67	32.69
Household Industry	06.38	3.55	3.99	02.56	06.56	03.33	03.31	02.41	02.47	01.03	01.42	01.04
Other workers	24.13	26.75	29.32	38.04	21.20	17.06	20.30	23.08	09.64	08.37	11.84	11.76

SOURCE: Government of India, 1991. See also Government of India, 1998.

over the years, even then it is almost nothing in proportion to their percentage of the population. It may be further observed from these figures that the number of cultivators decreased in all categories over a period of three decades from 1961 to 1991. But the decrease has been sharp among general and ST categories compared to the SCs. Although the number of agricultural labourers has increased in all categories, the increase has been more among the SCs. In household industries, the share of all the communities has decreased, but the decline is much more among SCs than amongst the general categories and STs. Other workers occupation includes industry and the service sectors. The number of other workers has witnessed an increase in all sections of the main workers though the increase in the general category has been much more than amongst SC and ST categories. Keeping in view the new economic policies and reforms, special care is required to be given for SCs and STs in providing employment in industrial and service sectors.

According to the National Sample Survey data, the employment generation rate among Dalits is negligible. With the introduction of the New Economic Policy (NEP) there has been 'jobless growth' in the country. Moreover, the government has recently privatised the insurance establishment and intends to transfer other public sector responsibilities such as transport and banking to the private sector. Given this scenario, it is unfair to hold the reservation policy responsible for the unemployment of general category people.

Table 14.8 shows the unemployment rate of the SCs vis-à-vis the others for 1977–78, 1983–84, 1993–94 and 1999–2000. The

TABLE 14.8
Unemployment Rate

YEARS	SCs				OTHERS			
	UPS	UPSS	CW	CD	UPS	UPSS	CW	CD
1977–78	1.23	N.A.	2.93	6.73	1.57	N.A.	2.15	3.90
1983–84	1.10	0.76	3.22	7.16	1.30	1.90	2.15	4.03
1993–94	0.90	0.60	1.97	4.30	1.20	0.90	1.60	2.70
1999–2000	1.20	1.00	2.50	5.00	1.60	1.20	2.50	3.50

SOURCE: National Sample Survey, 1977–78, 1983–84, 1993–94, 1999–2000.
NOTES: UPS–Usual Principal Status, UPSS–Usual Principal and Subsidiary Status, CW–Current Weekly Status and CD–Current Daily Status.

unemployment rate of the SCs are much higher than that of other workers based on current weekly and current daily status in 1977–78, 1983–84 and 1993–94. Higher unemployment rate of Dalits worker indicates a possible existence of caste-based discrimination against Dalits workers in hiring. Second, it is important to note that there has been a continuous decline in the unemployment rate under all status both for SCs and others between 1977–78 and 1993–94. After 1993–94, however, for the first time, there has been an increasing trend in the unemployment rate during the liberalisation period. Thus, it is quite clear that during the 1990s, the employment rate declined and there was a corresponding increase in the unemployment rate. This indeed reversed the favourable trend in employment experienced during the pre-liberalisation period as stated earlier. One estimate indicates that 'during the period 1992–99, the total employment opportunities in public sector undertakings (PSUs) under Group A, B, C and D (except sweepers) shrank from 2,152,650 to 1,800,628 registering a 16.35 per cent decline and the job opportunities for SCs also declined'.

EDUCATIONAL SCENARIO

The spread of education among the weaker section has been a major part of the government programmes since the early 1950s. It mainly includes financial support in the forms of scholarship (GoI) stipends at the school and college levels, construction of hostels, reservations for students of this community in engineering and medical colleges and other facilities. As stated earlier, Article 46 of the Constitution of India refers to the special care to be taken by the state for the promotion of education among the SCs and STs. The policies of the government have led to improvements in the access of these sections to educational services. Literacy rates of these sections, as shown in the report of the ministry of human resource development (*Education for all—The Indian Scene*, 1993), indicates an increase in the literacy rate among SCs from 21.4 per cent in 1981 to 37.4 per cent in 1991 and amongst STs from 16.4 per cent in 1981 to 29 per cent in 1991. The literacy rate among SC males increased from 31.1 per cent in 1981 to 40.6 per cent in 1991 and among ST males from 21.5 per cent in 1981 to 40.6 per cent 1991. The literacy rate among

SC females increased from 10.9 per cent to 23.8 per cent in 1991 and among ST females from 8 per cent in 1981 to 18.2 per cent in 1991. As evident from this report, the main problems of these communities on the educational front is the high level of illiteracy, a massive dropout rate at the middle and high school level and limited access to higher education. This has happened despite progressive educational programmes for these sections in our country.

The data shows that there has been a significant improvement in the gross enrolment ratio of the Dalits. However, the worrying feature is the high dropout rates in children from Dalit communities (see Table 14.9).

TABLE 14.9
Dropout Rate amongst SC and ST Children

LEVEL OF EDUCATION	DROPOUT RATE OF SC CHILDREN		DROPOUT RATE OF ST CHILDREN	
	1981–82	1990–91	1981–82	1990–91
Primary	59.21	49.35	74.00	62.52
Middle	74.76	67.77	84.99	78.57
Secondary	85.72	77.65	91.65	85.01

SOURCE: Report of the National Commission for Scheduled Castes and Scheduled Tribes, *Fourth Report, Vol. I*, 1996–97 and 1997–98, pp. 47, 50.

It is seen that during the period 1981–82 to 1990–91, the dropout rate of the SCs has come down by 10 per cent at the primary level, 7 per cent at the middle level and 8 per cent at the secondary level, thus showing a very slow pace of improvement.

As far as ST students are concerned, Table 14.9 shows that during 1981–82 to 1990–91, the dropout rate was to the tune of 11 per cent at the primary level, 6 per cent at the middle level and 7 per cent at the secondary level.

Some of the special programmes, which have had a significant impact on improving the educational status of the Dalits include elementary education, post-metric scholarships, book banks, hostel for boys and girls, ashram schools in tribal areas, national overseas scholarships, coaching classes and allied schemes. Admittedly, these schemes have contributed significantly in raising the educational status of the Dalit students. However, the desired results have not been achieved to the extent expected because of numerous factors. Globalisation has come to halt it. It has set a new paradigm that negates the premise of the welfare state, which had enabled the educational progress of the Dalits. It is the commercialisation of education, its elitist orientation and the all-pervasive ethos of the free market that are injurious to Dalit interests.

THE POLITICS OF RESERVATION

It seems that the government and its implementing agencies are playing politics over the job reservation issue. This is evident from the caste politics of Jats in Rajasthan. Political analysis indicates that the BJP did succeed in winning over a large section of the Jat community from their traditional allegiance to the Congress (I) Party by assuring them that their demand for Backward Class status would be granted. Similar demands are being made by Brahmins in Tamil Nadu, UP and other places.

The time limit for reserved seats in elected bodies, which was due to expire in 2001, has been extended by the government for another ten years. However, this time limit has nothing to do with reservations in educational institutions and jobs in the public sector. Extending political reservations without any forceful demand being made for it is useful to the political parties because representatives elected from reserved constituencies must serve the interests of their respective parties rather than of their own Dalit people. Hence, political reservations tend to produce accommodating rather than forceful, articulate and independent leaders among the Dalits. The politics of de-reservation, of interchangeability and not maintaining the 'roster' properly, of appointing general category people to reserved posts for years together, of keeping reservation at the 'entry point' only and filling vacancies with personnel on deputation are some of the tricks being employed to keep Dalits and tribals out of positions of significant power and responsibility.

All this shows how constitutional rights and directive principles are being sabotaged by using flimsy rules and regulations. In addition, there is no uniformity in allocating the benefits of reservations to the 'quota people' in the different states of the country. This has created considerable confusion in the minds of the people. No department has evolved a foolproof system for the proper implementation of job reservations. No study has been made so far on whether, in a multi-stage administrative system reservation at the entry point alone can ensure due representation for members of historically disadvantaged groups in subsequent stages as well. The anti-Mandal riots by the upper castes shows the extent of the politicisation of the reservation programme in India.

UNINTENDED CONSEQUENCES

As stated earlier, the reservation policy has produced some unintended consequences such as patron–client relationships between donors and recipients within the administrative system; reservations has become a controlling device to keep Dalit beneficiaries silent on key issues since government employees are supposed to be apolitical; it has led to the emergence of a Dalit middle class whose autonomy is curtailed; a welfare mentally which seems to have developed among the beneficiaries of reservations; the placing of these beneficiaries in a separate and stigmatised category; the legitimisation of caste labels. It seems that the Dalits have realised by now that the various provisions vis-à-vis the reservation policy is a piecemeal device. The Dalits believe that this policy has neutralised them politically. Further it is observed that their occupational dependence on the reservation policy discourages their political activism. Thus, this policy operates as a 'mechanism for social control' (Lelah Dushkin, 1972: 217). The correlation between the ritual status bestowed by caste and the social class of a person has not yet been broken down. One of the purposes of the job reservation policy had been to break this correlation by opening up middle class and professional jobs to people of low ritual status, but this purpose has not been fulfilled as yet. Admittedly, the patronage has created political consciousness among the beneficiaries. As a matter of fact, the reservation policy has not helped the larger Dalit masses to improve their lot, but, on the contrary, it has helped to create a microscopic class among the Dalits. While the system was originally designed to promote the 'uplift' of whole groups, it has at best proved to be of some help in individual social mobility at the expense of group stagnation (Glass, 1982: 118). Though some progress has been registered by these people, yet the path has been beset with many problems.

POSITIVE CONSEQUENCES

Yet, despite its limitations, this policy has brought a few positive changes among Dalits and tribals. Individual mobility is one of the positive changes. It has also provided social security or private security to the family members of the beneficiaries (one estimate states that six to seven persons are dependent on each beneficiary). Dalits and tribals have gained in status, although they have paid a heavy price for it.

Since the reservation policy has produced some positive social returns, it is necessary to invest in this policy and implement it as originally intended so that the goals enshrined in the constitution can be fulfilled in a better way in the days ahead. What the Dalits and tribals want is to be judged on the basis of their achieved status instead of their traditionally ascribed (caste) status. Further, they expect that the general category people should give up a 'labelling approach' towards the beneficiaries of job reservations. If the prescribed job quotas are properly filled with full commitment, this capacity-building project among the historically disadvantaged may not remain a distant dream, but will help to solve this historically inherited problem of caste discrimination in a more logical way in the future.

Discussions of the job reservation policy in the light of the recent Supreme Court decisions may enable us to understand the magnitude of the caste problem in India and will help us to distinguish realities from misconceptions in the minds of our people. It is not fair either to the beneficiaries of job reservations or to the opponents of this policy to play politics over this issue. If we continue on such a course, reservation will remain a perennial source of problems, perpetuating a host of vested interests, which will prove very expensive to Indian society.

THE PROCESS OF EMPOWERMENT

It is amply clear that in a changing situation the weaker sections would need more and not less support and protection from the state. They would need more stringent application of protective legislatures; more and more help and rigorous implementation of the provisions meant for them. Above all, there is need for more and better 'conscientisation, and 'politicisation' of this segment of the under-privileged to fight back the onslaught of globalisation and liberalisation which are likely to affect their need of survival and growth. However, issues of development and social justice are not merely matters of state-sponsored schemes or programmes, they essentially constitute a strength in getting access to and control over social resources. All these schemes will help them to improve their life condition and life chances. In fact, the process of growth with social justice should inspire the members of these sections to rely on self-help and utilise all available opportunities to reconstruct their life on a firm footing.

But ultimately, what does empowerment mean as far as the weaker sections in Indian society are concerned? Empowerment is not a thing or an object. It is self-help. This depends on self-effort and psychological mobilisation of people, deprived people in this case. It is necessary that individuals feel empowered to successfully undertake the task of re-fashioning the conditions of their living in a way that emancipates them from hopelessness, passivity and degraded life conditions. Empowerment in this connection incorporates attitudinal change and acquisition of material resources. In short, empowerment is nothing but a state of mind. It reflects self-confidence, self-reliance and the determination to fight for one's rights and interests. This can only be acquired through self-cultivation and sustained through action.

Empowerment in this context is seen as a way of addressing the problem of rights that are not enforced. It is further seen as a condition or an aspect of building economic and social capabilities among individuals, classes and communities. The idea behind empowerment is to bring about social change from a hierarchical to an egalitarian type of society.

It is against this background that the whole issue of empowerment and thereby social development of weaker sections in India needs to be looked into. It is evident from the growing consciousness among these sections that they have now started asserting themselves vehemently with a view to changing the hierarchical structure sustained by the dominant sections of society. Now they are initiators of social transformation and thereby the process of empowerment. The conscious castes and tribes have come forward and started waging protests against the oppression and multiple deprivations to which they were subjected for centuries. It is through their political outfits that they are trying to capture political power on the one hand and to change the notion that they are the 'vote banks' on the other. They are protesting for their 'human rights' and for their due share in the overall development process. This new awakening has not only provided them a basis for establishing their self-respect, self-determinism and honour, but has also led them to protest against the domination of upper castes and classes in Indian society. It is through their writings and sociocultural organisations that these segments of the society are mobilising people to fight for their democratic rights and interests and thereby develop their capabilities.

Hence, empowerment in this context is to be understood in terms of bringing them out of their degraded social status, acute poverty and deprivation. In other words, empowerment of weaker sections means progress in their overall socio-economic conditions and upward enhancement in their status. In short, to be empowered, the weaker sections will have to articulate and address their genuine issues in a more organised fashion and put pressure on the state for its effective intervention in the future. But the empowerment of these sections must be sought within the framework of democratic politics. Therefore, the state has a special responsibility to carefully tackle this agenda set by the weaker sections and ensure capacity building in them.

REFERENCES AND SELECT BIBLIOGRAPHY

Chalam, K.S. (1999) 'Economic Reforms and Welfare of Scheduled Castes', Paper presented at the national seminar on '50 Years of Independence: Economic Development of Dalits', organised by the Department of Economics, University of Hyderabad.

D'souza, Victor S. (1990) *Development Planning and Structural Inequalities—The Response of the Underpriviledged*. New Delhi: Sage Publications.

Dushkin, Lelah (1972) 'Scheduled Caste Politics', in J. Michael Mahar (ed.), *The Untouchables in Contemporary India*. Tucson, Arizona: Arizona University Press.

Gaikwad, S.L. (1999) *Protective Discrimination Policy and Social Change*. Jaipur and New Delhi: Rawat Publications.

Galanter, Marc (1997) 'Pursuing Equality: An Assessment of India's Policy of Compensatory Discrimination for Disadvantaged Groups', in S. Kaviraj (ed.), *Politics in India*, pp. 187–99. New Delhi: Oxford University Press.

Glass, R. (1982) 'Divided and Degraded: The Downtrodden Peoples of India', *Monthly Review*, 34, July–August: 118.

Government of India. (1991) *Census Report, 1991*, Series 1, Paper-I, Union Primary Census Abstract for Scheduled Castes/Scheduled Tribes. New Delhi: Government of India.

———. (1998) 'National Commission for Scheduled Castes and Scheduled Tribes', *Fourth Report*, Vol. I, *1996–97 and 1997–98*. New Delhi: Government of India.

———. (2001) 'National Commission for Scheduled Castes and Scheduled Tribes', *Sixth Report, 1999–2000 and 2000–2001*. New Delhi: Government of India.

Jogdand, P.G. (2000) 'Job Reservations: The Issues and The Facts', *Dalit International Newsletter*, Waterford CT, USA.

———. (2003) 'Empowerment of Weaker Sections', in Ramashray Roy (ed.), *The Federal Experience—India and Russia*, pp. 104–13. New Delhi: Shipra Publications.

Ministry of Human Resource Development, Government of India (1993) *Education for All—The Indian Scene*. New Delhi: Government of India Press.

Patil, Ravi (2000) 'Globalization and Dalit Labour Market: A Sociological Analysis', Paper presented at the national seminar on 'Contemporary Dalit Situation—Challenges and Vision', organised by Dr Babasaheb Ambedkar School of Thought, University of Mumbai, Mumbai, 9 April 2000.

Punalekar, S.P. (1999) 'Development against Empowerment of the Poor—A Case Study of Rural Dalit Masses', in S.M. Michael (ed.), *Dalits in Modern India*, pp. 303–20. New Delhi: Sage Publications.

Ram, Nandu (1988) *The Mobile Scheduled Castes: Rise of a New Middle Class*. New Delhi: Hindustan Publishing Corporation.

Roy, Ramashray (1999) *Dalits Development and Democracy*. New Delhi: Shipra Publications.

Thorat, S.K. (1999) 'Social Security in Unorganized Sector in India: How Secure are the Scheduled Castes', *The Indian Journal of Labour Economics*, 42(3): 451–70.

———. (2003) 'Ambedkar's Economic Ideas and Liberalization—Emerging Challenges Before Dalits', in Tharakam Bojja (ed.), *100 Years Of Reservations*, pp. 12–39. Hyderabad: RPI Publications.

15

Scheduled Castes, Employment and Social Mobility

RICHARD PAIS

When India became an independent nation, it confronted, among several other problems, social and economic backwardness of some sections of its people. The SCs were one of the groups that were most backward. The basic determinants of SC status were untouchability and impure occupation. Other determinants were their low economic, political and educational conditions. Though there have been many attempts towards Sanskritisation in modern times, they have not been able to achieve social mobility fully because of the ritual barrier. Given the structural limitation of the ritual barrier for social mobility, SCs have had to rely upon the principles of democracy and secularism in free India.

With the attainment of Independence, various government measures such as reservation, anti-untouchability and non-discrimination have widened the scope for social mobility in such areas as education, employment, industry, accumulation of wealth, acquisition of land, extent of political participation, etc. Employment is perhaps the most important among them. It is mainly through employment that there has been social mobility among SCs, which is manifested in changed family, marriage, religion and leadership structures as well as emancipation of members of these castes. Over the past 50 years, one thus expects a great deal of social, economic and cultural change to have taken place among SCs. However, sociologists and other social scientists need to examine from time to time the extent of change and obstacles to such desired changes. In this context, a question may be raised: Has occupational mobility significantly contributed to social mobility among the SCs? If so, what impact does social mobility have on the individual, group and caste? This chapter tries to examine these questions.

In the organised sector, SCs are employed in government and public sector undertakings. The government is regarded not just as one more employer but as the one that affords a degree of security, prestige and authority not obtainable elsewhere (Galanter, 1984: 84–85). For a broad sector of India's population, including both the established middle classes and many aspiring groups, government employment is the prime focus of ambition. In Galanter's view, because the government has been their benefactor and because their access to employment in the private sector has been severely limited, dependence upon the government for employment opportunities is especially pronounced among the SCs. Government employment is a matter not only of private ambition but of group advancement (ibid.: 85). Scheduled Caste leaders have seen in government employment not only career opportunities, but relief from unsympathetic and oppressive administration, facilitation of the utilisation of opportunities and readier access to benefits. Further government work is regarded as a source of prestige for both the individual and the group.

With the world population moving towards towns and cities, urban centres are increasingly becoming more and more important. In India, with urban population growth rising to 30 per cent (approximately), India can no longer be described as a land of villages. The volume of empirical research done on the Indian urban society is much less than that on rural society. Often the importance of urban centres is either minimised or altogether ignored on account of the small proportion of population living in them. Second, 'many have considered such basic institutions as caste and joint family as essentially rural in character, or as having their origin in rural society and therefore rural even if they occur in cities.... Fortunately there is now an increasing awareness among sociologists of the fact that India has had urban centres since the time of the Indus Valley Civilisation several centuries before Christ, and that towns and cities—small and large—existed in all parts of India throughout its recorded history' (Shah, 1988: 2).

The present chapter examines the extent of occupational mobility achieved by SC groups such as the Adi-Dravida, Mundala, Moger, Bakuda and others. It also examines the extent of social mobility as a result of employment analysed in terms of their social relations, changing attitudes and lifestyles. The research relating to this chapter was begun in the year 1990 as a study of SCs living and working in Mangalore urban agglomerations. Here SCs are housed in segregated colonies in different parts of the city. Until recently, they were engaged in menial jobs such as cleaning the streets, carrying night soil, cleaning latrines, transporting city waste, etc. Though some of them still continue in their traditional jobs in the city corporation, many have sought jobs in the state and central government departments, schools and colleges, hospitals and banks, etc., in Class I to Class IV positions (now Group A to D). The present chapter examines the question of social mobility of SCs as a result of employment in an urban setting, for urban society accepts changes and tolerates ambiguities more readily than rural society. Scheduled Castes living in urban areas also change more readily than their counterparts in rural areas.

Mangalore is the capital city of Dakshina Kannada district formerly known as South Kanara. It is one of the important cities on the west coast of India and its significance is derived from the seaport, which has been a trading centre for thousands of years. The present name of the city is derived from the tenth century temple of Mangala Devi, the presiding deity of Mangalore. From the beginning of the Christian era, Mangalore and the surrounding areas came under the domination of several Hindu dynasties such as the Chalukyas (AD 500–757), the Rastrakutas (AD 753–973), the Hoysalas (AD 1000–1346) and the Vijayanagara rulers (AD 1336–1646). From the sixteenth century onwards, it came under the influence of the Portuguese. In 1763, Nawab Hyder Ali took possession of the dominions of the Ikkeri rulers including that of Mangalore. With the death of Tipu Sultan in 1799, Mangalore and the Kanara region came into the hands of the British. With the arrival of the Basel Evangelical Mission in 1834, the city witnessed new economic activities such as printing, weaving and tile manufacturing. The missionaries introduced English education, started a printing press, a Kannada newspaper, handlooms and a tile factory. In 1866, Mangalore Municipality was established under the Madras Town Municipal Act, 1865. The year 1878 saw the arrival of Jesuits, who started a college, a hospital and a seminary. Mangalore was connected with the rest of the country by a railway line in 1909. With the inclusion of 14 village panchayats in 1980, the Mangalore City Corporation was formed.

Mangalore presents a mixture of communities, castes, religions, languages and cultures. Hindus, Muslims, Christians and Jains make up the major religious groups. Brahmins, Bunts and Billavas are the important Hindu caste groups. The other caste groups are the Gaudas, Vishwakarmas, Mogaveeras, Holeyas, Samagaras, Koragas, Kudubis and Male-kudias. The Adi-Dravidas, Bakudas, Mogers, Mundalas and Samagaras are the important SC groups found in Mangalore. A distinctive feature of these castes is *aliyasantana*, that is, inheritance through the female line. Roman Catholics and Protestants are the two important Christian groups. Kannada, Tulu and Konkani are the major languages spoken. Mangalore provides excellent facilities in education, health, trade and banking.

For this study, 220 SC persons constituting 10 per cent of the total SC employees working in government, public sector and semi-government undertakings were interviewed. A stratified random sample was found suitable for the selection of respondents. The primary classification of the employees was based on class of employment, that is, from Class I to Class IV. Women made up 22 per cent of the respondents. Adi-Dravida, Adi-Karaataka, Mundala, Mogera, Bakuda, Bhovi, Baira and Samagara were the important SC groups in this sample. All the respondents belonged to the Hindu religion and 160 (72.7 per cent) stated that their mother tongue was Tulu. Ninety-seven (44 per cent) were from Mangalore while the majority of others belonged to the Dakshina Kannada district and other districts of Karnataka. Six were illiterate, 61 were degree holders and others ranged in between with different educational achievements. Out of 220 respondents, only 16.4 per cent were not married.

The respondents differed according to age, income and type of family. The respondents may be described to be of a younger age group since a majority of them, that is, 46 per cent were in the age group of 31–40 years. There were 34 (15.5 per cent) persons in the age group of 18–30 years, 52 (23.6 per cent) persons in the age group of 41–50 years and the remaining 32 (14.5 per cent) persons in the age group of 51–60 years. In terms of income of the respondents, a majority were in the income group of Rs 1,000–2,000 per month

(45 per cent). About 28 per cent were in the income group of Rs 2,000–3,000 while about 25 per cent had a monthly income of more than Rs 3,000. Only two persons had an income of less than Rs 1,000 per month.

Studies have indicated several changes occurring in the urban family structure (Gore, 1970; Narayanan, 1989; Ramu, 1977). Urban families tend to be nuclear compared to rural families where joint families are common. In this study, three types of families were considered, that is, nuclear, extended and joint. A nuclear family consists of a married couple with or without unmarried children. An extended family consists of a nuclear family living with either parents or unmarried brothers and sisters or both. A joint family consists of two or more nuclear families. In this study, 15 (6.8 per cent) respondents were staying alone either in rented rooms or hostels. These persons were treated as members of a single-person house-hold. About half the respondents were the members of nuclear families; 66 (30 per cent) were from extended families and 26 (11.8 per cent) were members of joint families. Nuclear families were more among Class I and II employees.

INTERGENERATIONAL OCCUPATIONAL MOBILITY

Though it was difficult to compare the employment of the respondents with that of their fathers and grandfathers in order to evaluate intergenerational occupational mobility, an attempt was made to group the employment of fathers and grandfathers into Class I–IV as presented in Table 15.1.

From Table 15.1 we observe a remarkable intergenerational occupational mobility. The proportion of coolie workers has come down from 78 per cent in the grandfather's generation to 44 per cent in the father's generation. A significant factor is that fathers of 24 (10.9 per cent) respondents had taken up masonry or carpentry work, which was not found in the grandfather's generation. It is also a clear indication that even in rural areas SCs have changed their occupation.

TABLE 15.1
Intergenerational Occupational Mobility

CLASS OF EMPLOYMENT	OCCUPATION/EMPLOYMENT		
	GRANDFATHER	FATHER	RESPONDENT
Class I	–	–	7.28
Class II	–	2.73	10.45
Class III	5.00	22.73	56.82
Class IV	1.82	10.00	25.45
Coolie	78.64	44.09	–
Mason/Carpenter	–	10.90	–
Own agriculture	5.90	5.00	–
Crafts	1.82	0.91	–
Others	6.82	3.64	–
Total	100.00	100.00	100.00
Number	220	220	220

EMPLOYMENT AND MIGRATION

It is generally said that migrants are more enterprising than non-migrants. To ascertain such a relationship, the class of employment in this study was also compared with the rural–urban origin of the respondents and the same was compared with migrants from within the district of Mangalore, that is, Dakshina Kannada and migrants from outside the district of Mangalore, that is, non-Dakshina Kannada origin. The results are presented in Table 15.2.

TABLE 15.2
Employment and Migration

CLASS OF EMPLOYMENT	MIGRATION				TOTAL
	URBAN	RURAL	DAKSHINA KANADA ORIGIN	NON-DAKSHINA KANADA ORIGIN	
I	18.75	81.25	25.00	75.00	16
II	39.13	60.87	34.78	65.22	23
III	40.80	59.20	70.40	29.60	125
IV	48.21	51.79	80.36	19.64	56
Total	40.91	59.09	65.91	34.09	100
Number	90	130	145	75	220

The rural–urban background of the respondents in relation to the class of their employment as presented in Table 15.2 indicates that a majority of all the classes came from rural background. This is to be expected since employment, particularly in the organised public sectors, draws personnel from rural areas. Since these people are members of SCs and many of the SCs have been predominantly living in rural areas, only after employment do they migrate to the place of work in towns and cities. However, it is interesting to note that in the higher-class status of employment we find more people drawn from rural background than from urban. Thus, we find that 52 per cent of SCs in Class IV employment are from rural areas, while 81 per cent in Class I employment are from rural areas. In other words, it seems to suggest that members of the SCs from urban areas are given low status employment, while a greater number of rural SC members succeed in getting high-status employment.

This proves the fact 'that migrants are more enterprising than the locals. They are driven by the "achievement motivation"' (McCleland, 1961). Many a migrant is a first-generation learner who is drawn to the urban area for further study and employment. Once he is in employment, he tries to improve his employment opportunities. Further, he tries to satisfy his other needs of a house and marriage. But, his children lack his dynamism because the needs of the children are taken care of by the migrant father. This is the case with the Class IV employees, most of them are 'Paura karmikas' (scavengers) in the Mangalore City Corporation. As a result, mobility is not very high among them.

It appears likewise that the high-status employment in terms of Class I or Class II seems to be found to a greater extent among people from outside Dakshina Kannada. While 80 per cent of Class IV employees and 70 per cent of Class III employees are from the district, 75 per cent and 65 per cent of Class I and Class II, respectively, are from outside the district. This is also because of the achievement motivation mentioned earlier. People who are able to take greater risks are able to get a higher level of employment. Second, in Class I and II, employees are transferred from other districts and states.

RESERVATION AND EMPLOYMENT

The general attitude in any work organisation regarding the employment status of SCs is that they occupy their present positions because of their caste status and the policy of reservation. Most non-SCs, out of 40, with whom discussions were held, expressed this view. Whether such impressions are true or not, the majority (73 per cent) of the respondents attributed their present employment status to the fact that their caste was a SC and that they were eligible for reservation. They expressed the view that they would not have got the job under normal circumstances given that caste discrimination prevails in Hindu society. Merit as the reason for employment was given by only 12 per cent of the respondents. One respondent, who had risen through hard work and merit, lamented that his colleagues attributed all his achievements to his caste status.

Those who had responded that their employment was due to the policy of reservation were asked whether they thought that they would have got the job even without that policy? Only 32.7 per cent among them were confident that they might have got the job even without that policy. However, respondents in Class I positions had a relatively higher level of confidence, 60 per cent of whom felt that they would have obtained the employment on their own merit. Such a level of confidence decreases steadily as the grade of position declines. Several respondents remarked that 'merited' SC candidates should be recruited as 'general category' candidates thereby enabling many more SC candidates to get employment under the reservation quota. The remaining 67.3 per cent felt that due to their incompetence, prejudices of non-SCs and lack of opportunities, they might not have got the job without the reservation policy.

EMPLOYMENT OF FAMILY MEMBERS

One of the ways by which occupational mobility facilitates social mobility for the immediate members of the family is by helping them also to get better education and employment. It is now a well-established fact that a person already in employment acts not only as a chief source of information for others concerning employment opportunities in his workplace or elsewhere, but he also helps make the necessary contacts. Such networking has been a crucial link in the rural–urban relations in India. It is common among members of the upper castes, but it is also widely practised by members of the SCs. Indeed, SC employees in various organisations not only have their associations to promote employment opportunities for people from their own caste, but are also expected to be helpful in other respects. To throw light on this aspect, an attempt was made to find out to what extent the respondents had facilitated employment for their own family members.

About 54.1 per cent of the respondents reported having no unemployed members in their household. It seems that the proportion of the unemployed members in the household is in inverse proportion to the class of employment of the respondents. Thus, Class I and II officials have the least percentage of unemployed persons in their families whereas Class IV has the highest. Keeping in mind some of the assumptions that were made earlier, it seems that a class of high-status employment also facilitates employment for dependent family members. Either such dependent members perform well in their education and in entrance tests or interviews when seeking jobs, or the employment status of the respondents becomes instrumental in getting jobs for family members also. It is, however, not uncommon for respondents in Class III and IV to use their connections, based mainly on caste identities, with the officials in Class I and II to facilitate employment of their dependants in the family.

INTERPERSONAL RELATIONSHIPS AT THE PLACE OF WORK

Peer group acceptance is an important factor in one's occupation. Considering that caste identities of people play an important role even in formal organisations (Ramaswamy, 1982), SC employees are likely to face situations which are hostile. The hostility would come not merely because of their low-caste status, but also because of prejudices the upper castes may have towards their favoured status (such as reservation in education and employment). Indeed, due to this hostile atmosphere in the workplace, newly-employed SC persons tend to seek the support and cooperation of other SC employees. In order to assess the nature of work experience, the respondents were asked to describe the interpersonal relationships in the work-place and outside the workplace. The respondents were also asked to describe their relations with their colleagues as experienced in the beginning of their service and at present. Three categories were given: good, fair and caste-biased.

It may be seen from Table 15.3 that relationships seem to improve over a period of time. In the first place, nearly 161 (73 per cent) found the relationships to have been good at the beginning, which itself is quite a high proportion, and this has increased to 78 per cent at present. Those subjected to caste-biased relationships are few in proportion. Only 8 per cent experienced such a relationship at the beginning of their service. Here too, there was a marginal increase from the past to the present. Interestingly enough, it was observed that there was a uniform consistency in describing the kinds of relationships experienced at two different points of time. Thus, a person having had a good relationship at the beginning of his service tended to find it to be the same at present also. The fact that 78 per cent found interpersonal relationships at the workplace good and another 14 per cent fair, indicates upward social mobility. Those who viewed the relationships as caste-biased do not mean that they have not achieved any social mobility. Many of them have indeed a better economic status than their parents and others in their own caste. What they have not been able to achieve is acceptance by colleagues as fellow workers independent of their caste identity.

In contrast, there were also those who experienced peer discrim-ination right from the beginning. Their selection and employment seem to have been a bone of contention. The performance and the

TABLE 15.3
Relations with Colleagues in the Beginning and at Present

RELATIONS IN THE BEGINNING	RELATIONS NOW			
	GOOD	FAIR	CASTE-BIASED	TOTAL
Good	91.30	4.97	3.73	161
Fair	46.34	46.34	7.32	41
Caste-biased	27.78	16.66	55.56	18
Total	77.73	13.64	8.63	100
Number	171	30	19	220

impression left behind by the SCs earlier in the same workplace also tended to form the basis for judging a new entrant in the service. Thus, for instance, a new recruit may find the work atmosphere to be hostile if in the same office or in its branch several members of the SCs have been promoted from lower to higher cadres. Another feature of the nature of interpersonal relationships seems to be that it is determined by the cadre of employment. Persons belonging to Class I and II found the relationships to be good while it was the lower cadres that found them to be fair or caste-biased. It is necessary, however, to bear in mind that the very nature of bureaucratic organisation itself makes it possible for higher cadre officials to enjoy greater power and authority as well as relative isolation from fellow workers. Consequently, they may not encounter opposition as frequently as others.

SOCIAL RELATIONSHIPS OUTSIDE THE PLACE OF WORK

Social relationships at the workplace usually go beyond the formal place of work. Colleagues may frequently visit each other, families may meet and share common interests. Here, there may be a process of selection based on caste, region and language identities. To assess this, the respondents were asked whether other caste colleagues visited them in their homes and whether they accepted lunch, dinner or tea at their place. Only 22 per cent of the respondents reported that other caste colleagues did not visit them, whereas the rest confirmed that their colleagues visited their homes. Among those who received colleagues at home, it was found that most (45 per cent) visits were in response to special invitations. Twelve per cent reported that their colleagues paid visits only in work-related matters. In a way, these represent certain non-voluntary type of visits, as against casual visits, which were reported by 43 per cent of the respondents.

The reason why the colleagues of some SC employees do not visit their homes is that these SC employees do not invite nor show interest in extending the social relationship at the workplace to their colleagues and their families due to a sense of inferiority. Forty-one (18.6 per cent) of them have not invited colleagues even if there were special occasions; they felt that their invitations might not be accepted. The rest had either no opportunity to invite colleagues or their homes were far off. In this connection, the respondents were asked the hypothetical question whether other caste colleagues would have visited them more often if they had been caste-Hindus. A majority (60 per cent) of them felt positively. Some were of the opinion that if they had had low-caste status but had not been SCs, there would have been a better social relationship expressed in terms of visiting their colleagues in their homes and vice versa. Among those who did not agree, most pointed out that whether they had belonged to any other caste or community or not, there would have been no difference. Their colleagues would have visited them irrespective of the difference in caste. This really indicates a marked change in attitudes, which may result in better social relationships in future.

Given this situation, how often do SC employees visit colleagues from other castes in their homes? On what occasions do they pay visits? What is their experience? Nearly 80 per cent of the respondents said that they too visited the houses of their colleagues. The pattern of response indicates that most SC employees go to visit their friends only when invited (57 per cent) and only a very small proportion (10 per cent) visit others due to work-related matters. The number of casual visits, implying spontaneous calling on friends, are higher among people with high-class employment and lower among people with low-class employment. The implication of all this is that only a small proportion of employees have felt free to visit their friends casually, while the majority still feel constrained and wait for an invitation.

Many of those who do visit colleagues report that they had been subjected to discrimination. Discrimination is of various types such as being served food and beverages in different utensils, not being allowed to enter inner parts of the house, being served meals in a separate place, being served food either early or late and making sarcastic remarks about SCs and on the reservation policy, etc. As far as those who do not visit their caste colleagues are concerned (21.8 per cent), it was found that a majority did not pay visits because they were not invited. An equal number of respondents do not feel like visiting their colleagues either because they do not feel close to each other or because they wish to remain by themselves. The rest said that they do not like to mix with other caste colleagues. One respondent stated that he did not feel comfortable to go to other caste colleagues' houses because he did not know how they would treat him. Another respondent of Class IV said that she called on her caste colleagues only to do some menial work in their homes. She did this to earn some additional income. Another respondent was very cautious and went only to the homes of those colleagues who did not discriminate.

IMPACT OF EMPLOYMENT ON FAMILY AND CASTE COMMUNITY

This social mobility of a person has an important bearing on the family and the caste community. It is a common feature that migrants help their kith and kin. Since most of the respondents are first-generation government employees, their employment status is expected to have a socio-economic impact on their family and caste community. One of the most predominant ways of helping family and kin group members is by education. Nearly 80 per cent of the respondents reported that they had helped or were presently helping someone to be educated. It is found that high-ranking employees merely contribute financially, while only a small proportion of them contribute in kind. The reverse is the case as the rank of employees goes down. This is in keeping with the fact that people with low income can only afford the cost of books and clothes, which is usually given once a year. People with a higher income may be able to meet monetary needs which are perhaps more urgent than the need for books and clothes. Among the 46 respondents who did not help, 20 per cent of the respondents' relatives did not require any help. About 22 per cent of the respondents reported that their family members or relatives had not approached them for help. Further, because of their own poor economic conditions, about 43 per cent could not afford to help.

Considering the nature and extent of the problem of unemployment, it is quite natural to seek the help of a well-placed and well-employed person in the family to get a job. In this regard, about 48 per cent of the respondents reported that they had helped at least one family member or relative to get a job. A majority (64.76 per cent) of them could do so by using 'influence' among their urban contacts. Another significant proportion (36.19 per cent) guided others in getting a job. Some helped financially by contributing to a bribe and one official had helped by appointing a relative in a job since it was within his powers to do so. Those who reported not to have helped (52 per cent) pointed out that their relatives or family members did not require help; or that help was not asked for; or that they lived far away from relatives or family.

Apart from helping members of the family and kin group with education and employment, a considerable number of respondents had also helped SC persons, who were not necessarily related to them. Such beneficiaries were either from the native village or from the locality where they now lived. Here too, help was given as if it had been given to one's own relatives. This indicates a strong commitment to fellow caste members to improve their social and economic condition. In this regard, there is more or less uniformity among all the different groups of the SC employees. Such help indicates not only individual mobility but also group mobility. It is individual mobility because the social standing of such persons is held in high esteem by the community.

TYPES OF RESIDENTIAL LOCALITY

Studies in urban sociology have demonstrated that there exists a caste and class selectivity with respect to housing patterns (Rao, 1989). In keeping with the traditionally ascribed social status to members of the SCs it is possible even now to find in several cities and towns separate localities inhabited by them (D'Souza, 1978). The existence of distinct localities in the context of the present-day urban situation is also a result of the government's housing policy to benefit SCs. The result of such a policy is the formation of new localities. Shortage of housing in urban areas is common and traditional-minded house-owners are selective concerning caste and class of the prospective tenants. The concern for class is easily explained: ability to pay the rent. House-owners usually prefer their tenants to be of 'clean' castes. As a consequence, SC employees, who are not native nor property owners in the town or city where they work, are at a severe disadvantage. Notwithstanding their employment status, they may often be compelled to live in localities that are inhabited by people of lower economic and social status than themselves (Ram, 1988: 45).

In Mangalore too, like other towns and cities in India, SCs working in the corporation are housed in colonies. Some colonies are in the centre of the city and some on the periphery. About 41 per cent of the respondents live in such SC colonies and about 51 per cent live in localities where people of all castes and religions live, and the remaining 8 per cent live in predominantly Christian, Muslim or Hindu localities. It is to be noted that the residential pattern of SCs differ in terms of cadre of employment of the respondents, which is shown in Table 15.4.

TABLE 15.4
Class of Employment and Type of Residential Locality

CLASS OF EMPLOYMENT	TYPE OF LOCALITY			
	SCHEDULED CASTE LOCALITY	MIXED LOCALITY	OTHER CASTE/ RELIGIOUS LOCALITY	TOTAL
I	12.50	87.50	–	16
II	13.02	82.06	4.38	23
III	40.20	50.00	9.80	125
IV	66.07	26.79	741	56
Total	41.36	51.36	7.28	100
Number	91	113	16	220

Class I and II employees are found to be residing predominantly in 'mixed' residential localities where different castes are found. This suggests that they prefer to live and mix with members of other castes. Fifty per cent of Class III employees were residing in mixed localities whereas Class IV employees are found to be predominantly in SC colonies. In some instances, due to migration and urban growth, SC colonies around Mangalore have become residential areas for several caste communities including those of non-SCs. Recent SC migrants to the city with lower-class background prefer to stay in SC localities because land price and house rent is relatively cheaper there than in the other areas. Many respondents from these localities, who had built their own houses with modern amenities, had to content themselves with building their houses there rather than elsewhere because of the high cost of land in the other areas.

Neighbours of more than 90 per cent of the respondents knew their caste. Neighbours of 10 respondents did not know their caste background, while eight respondents were not aware whether or not the neighbours knew their caste background. The reasons for the lack of knowledge of caste background were in some cases that respondents had moved in recently; a few had deliberately not revealed their caste background to their neighbours. Some pointed out that nobody had asked about their caste background since they did not interact with their neighbours. The relationship with neighbours was reported to be good in 75 per cent of these cases, fair in 19 per cent and bad in 4 per cent of the cases. Five persons reported that they had no relationship of any kind with their neighbours. While good and fair relationships were reported among all the four classes, 'bad' relationships was found mainly among Class III and IV employees. The reasons for bad neighbourly relationships are caste-based discrimination, being avoided by upper-caste neighbours and drunkenness by fellow caste members followed by brawls, etc.

PERCEPTION OF SOCIAL STATUS

A multiplicity of criteria determines social stratification and status of people in a society. Some such criteria are landholding, education, income and influence; they determine the status of individuals and groups in society. Social status is ascribed by a group of people to an individual or to a group. In this sense, social status is something that a person or a group is given by other people in the community. In recent years, however, attempts have been made by sociologists and social anthropologists to assess social status as it is perceived by the people themselves, that is, subjective assessment of social status (Bailey, 1958; Ram, 1988). The respondents were asked to place themselves in one of four social status categories: lower, lower-middle, upper-middle and upper class. The results are shown in Table 15.5.

A majority of the respondents (62 per cent) claimed that their family enjoyed a status of lower-middle class. About 22 per cent of the respondents claimed to belong to the upper-middle class. Not surprisingly, it is a majority of high-ranking employees (Class I and II) who claimed to enjoy upper-middle and upper social status and it is Class III and IV employees who claimed lower and lower-middle

TABLE 15.5

Employment and Status of Family

CLASS OF EMPLOYMENT	STATUS OF FAMILY				
	LOWER	LOWER-MIDDLE	UPPER-MIDDLE	UPPER	TOTAL
I	–	18.75	68.75	12.50	16
II	–	56.52	39.13	4.35	23
III	4.80	76.00	19.20	–	125
IV	46.43	46.43	7.14	–	56
Total	14.54	62.27	21.83	1.36	100
Number	32	137	48	3	220

class social status. The reasons for respondents ascribing a particular social status to themselves were as follows: 214 educated respondents believed that it was education which gave them class status and social status. About 54 per cent of the educated respondents believed that their status was determined solely by their being employed in various government jobs, which in turn was a result of their educational attainment. Indeed, more than 92 per cent of respondents were of the opinion that there had been a significant change in their social status as a consequence of their employment. They claimed it was employment which had given them a better economic status and a markedly improved social respectability.

ATTAINMENT OF EQUALITY

The basic purpose of reservation in education and employment is to provide adequate opportunities for the socially and economically deprived sections of society. The intention was to raise the social status of SCs and OBCs whose social and economic status has been low. It was done through various protective measures and developmental programmes. How far has this concept of an egalitarian society been realised? The respondents were asked whether they considered themselves to be socially and economically equal to people from other castes. In respect of social equality, 64 per cent considered themselves to be equal to other castes. The reasons they gave for considering themselves equal to any other castes were: that they were as well or better educated than the others (27 per cent); that they did their work as well as the others (20 per cent); that they were not discriminated against by others (10 per cent); that they were human beings like others (40 per cent); that they had improved their own social status (10 per cent); that they conducted themselves as well as others (25 per cent). It may be pointed out that not only do employed SC members see themselves in social positions comparable with other castes, but such an attitude also reflects a high self-esteem. An explanation is needed as to why 36 per cent of the respondents considered themselves socially not equal to other castes. It is not enough that they themselves claimed equality, what is important, according to them, was that other castes should also consider them to be equal. Such an attitude was yet to be developed, it was felt. Many others (38 per cent) felt that they belonged to lower castes, while 33 per cent were of the opinion that untouchability still existed. Fourteen per cent felt that due to low income they could not be equated with people of other castes, who generally had a better income.

In terms of economic comparability with other castes, a good proportion of respondents (52 per cent) felt that they were equal to members of other castes. This was because they felt their income to be as good as that of others. In the case of 10 persons, their income was indeed high because their spouses were also well employed. About 48 per cent of the respondents who did not consider themselves equal to others felt that way because they either had a low salaried income or their income was through salary alone.

LIFE EXPERIENCE

The life of SCs has been full of deprivations, discrimination and low social status. This has been the experience until recently and continues to be so even now. Do the SCs who now have urban employment feel that their life is still filled with such hardship? To answer this question, the respondents were asked whether they regret having been born into a SC. A majority of the respondents expressed that they did not (64 per cent). This is a significant proportion considering that many of them had complained of social discrimination in their childhood and now in their work life. Yet, having no regrets for being born into a SC, they expressed not only pride but also the will to face the social situation. They also thought that their employment has given them a social and economic status that is much better than what their forefathers or counterparts in rural areas experienced. Among 141 who have no regrets, 55 like the caste into which they were born, 33 were able to rise in society (thanks to the facilities of the government) and 26 felt no discrimination. Only 36 per cent had regrets that they were born into SCs. This was due to the discrimination and low economic and social status that was accorded to them. One respondent remarked 'I do not know what bad things I have done in the past to be born into a Scheduled Caste. But I should live this life in a sincere way though it is difficult.' As may be anticipated, the pattern of response corresponds to the differences in the cadre of employment. The higher the employment status, the less the proportion of persons who regretted having been born into SCs.

CONCLUSION

An attempt as been made in this chapter to assess the opportunities for social mobility in SCs as a consequence of their employment. The differences in the cadre or class of employment were analysed specially to see whether such differences played a significant role in opportunities for mobility. In the first place, it was found that there had been a remarkable 'intergenerational mobility' in terms of the occupation of the respondents. For a majority of them, the respondents were the first in two or three generations to have held urban employment in the government or related departments. Thus, it ought to have meant a major change in the social and economic conditions of life for them. How was this change perceived by them and by others? What were the indicators of such a mobility? These were some of the questions that we attempted to answer in order to understand the process and nature of social mobility.

It may be noted that there seems to be a tendency for urban employed SCs to be confronted with a limit to social mobility. The evidence for this was borne out by the fact that a majority of those in high positions are from rural areas while a majority from urban areas are employed in lower positions. There is an indication of the reservation policy being more beneficial for higher positions than for lower ones. There seems to be a sense of self-confidence among some SC members who expressed the view that they would have got their jobs even without reservation.

There have been several indicators of changed social status and, therefore, of social mobility as the consequence of employment. This is evident, for instance, in the amicable social relationships they enjoyed with colleagues at the place of work and neighbours in the place of residence. There have also been instances of caste-biased relationships indicating social discrimination, but that has been the experience of a minority. Social mobility was also assessed by analysing the type of locality in which they lived. Those in higher positions of employment reside in 'mixed' caste localities, whereas those in lower positions are found to be living in areas known to be SC localities. Assuming that the changed social status of an individual would also reflect itself in the family, an analysis was made to bring this out. Many SCs have tried to help the members of their families in education and employment indicating that the process of mobility was not merely individual but tended to promote group mobility.

Although a positive picture emerges of the relation between employment and mobility, a few comments should also be made about the negative aspect of the picture. Although few in number, there were instances in which the respondents had clearly expressed caste-based discriminations and such experiences were associated with the employment cadre. Persons in lower positions found that their own colleagues and subordinates did not treat them as they treated members of other castes in the same positions. Most SCs are seen to exercise caution in their interaction with other caste colleagues. They do not, for instance, visit colleagues in their homes without a special invitation. They also avoid offering food and beverages to their upper-caste colleagues out of fear that the guests may be offended. A noticeable fact is that most of them ascribe an upper-middle or middle class status to themselves. They no longer meekly accept lower status based on their caste identity.

REFERENCES AND SELECT BIBLIOGRAPHY

Bailey, F.G. (1958) *Caste and Economic Frontier*. London: Routledge and Kegan Paul.
D'Souza, Victor S. (1978) 'Caste, Occupation and Social Class in Chandigarh', in

RICHARD PAIS

M.S.A. Rao (ed.), *Urban Sociology in India*, pp. 184–98. New Delhi: Orient Longman.

Galanter, Marc (1984) *Competing Equalities*. New Delhi: Oxford University Press.

Gore, M.S. (1970) *Immigrants and Neighbourhoods: Two Aspects of Life in a Metropolitan City*. Bombay: Tata Institute of Social Sciences.

McCleland, C. David (1961) *The Achieving Society*. New York: D. Van Nostrand Company.

Narayanan, Leile (1989) *Ethnicity in Urban Context*. Jaipur: Rawat Publications.

Ram, Nandu (1988) *The Mobile Scheduled Castes: Rise of a New Middle Class*. New Delhi: Hindustan Publishing Corporation.

Ramaswamy, S. (1982) *Caste Identities and Occupation in South India*. New Delhi: Inter-India Publications.

Ramu, G.N. (1977) *Family and Caste in Urban India*. New Delhi: Vikas Publications.

Rao, Ranga A.V.P. (1989) *Urbanization, Occupational Mobility and Social Integration*. New Delhi: Deep & Deep Publications.

Shah, A.M. (1988) *Division and Hierarchy*. New Delhi: Hindustan Publishing Company.

About the Editor and Contributors

THE EDITOR

S.M. Michael is Reader at the Department of Sociology, University of Mumbai, and Honorary Director, Institute of Indian Culture, Mumbai. He is a member of the visiting faculty at the Anthropos Institute, Bonn, and Magdeburg University, both in Germany. Dr Michael is a consultant to the Vatican's Pontifical Council for Inter-Religious Dialogue as well as Chairman of the Bombay Archdiocesan Commission for Inter-Religious Dialogue.

His published work includes *The Cultural Context of Evangelization in India* (1980), *Anthropology as a Historical Science: Essays in Honour of Stephen Fuchs* (co-edited, 1984), *Culture & Urbanization* (1989), *Anthropology of Conversion in India* (1998), *Culture and Nationalism: Clarifying the Cultural Reality of India* (co-edited with Leela D'Souza and Rowena Robinson, 2000), *Globalization and Social Movements: Struggle for a Humane Society* (co-edited, 2003), *Communal Harmony, Secularism and Nation Building* (2005), and about 60 articles in national and international journals.

THE CONTRIBUTORS

Timothy Fitzgerald is professor of social anthropology at the Department of International Culture, Aichi Gakuin University, Japan. He graduated from King's College, London (B.A. in religious studies, Ph.D in philosophy) and the London School of Economics (M.Sc in social anthropology). He has been to India several times to research Ambedkar Buddhism.

Mahesh Gavaskar is Assistant Editor, *Economic and Political Weekly*, Mumbai. He has done his research on the works of Jotiba Phule and Dr B.R. Ambedkar. He has published articles on culture and contemporary politics in various journals. He also writes for Marathi newspapers and magazines.

Gopal Guru is professor of politics and public administration at the University of Pune. He has been Honorary Professor at Delhi University. His area of specialisation is contemporary social movements in India with special reference to Dalits in Maharashtra.

Christophe Jaffrelot is the director of CERI (Centre d'Etudes et de Recherches Internationales) at Sciences Po (Paris), and research director at the CNRS (Centre National de la Recherche Scientifique). He teaches South Asian politics to doctoral students at Sciences Po. He is also the director of a French quarterly journal, *Critique Internationale*.

P.G. Jogdand is professor of Sociology at the University of Mumbai and Co-ordinator of the Special Assistant Programme of the University Grants Commission. He is also the Co-ordinator of Dr Babasaheb Ambedkar Centre for Social Justice at the University of Mumbai.

Gail Omvedt is professor of sociology at the University of Pune. She is a scholar-activist working with new social movements, especially women's groups and farmers' organisations. Her academic writings include several books and articles on class, caste and gender issues, most recently *Reinventing Revolution: New Social Movements in India* (1993) and *Dalits and the Democratic Revolution* (1994).

Richard Pais is Professor and Head, Department of Sociology, St. Aloysius College, Mangalore. He is the founder secretary of Mangalore Sociology Association and organising secretary of the Twentieth All India Sociological Conference held at Mangalore University.

Arjun Patel is professor of sociology, Centre for Social Studies, South Gujarath University, Surat. He is a scholar-activist working with exploited masses of Gujarat. His publications are in the field of social movements as also in the field of empowering tribals and Dalits.

Traude Pillai-Vetschera teaches anthropology at the University of Vienna, Austria. She has been doing field studies among the Adivasis of Rajasthan and among Mahars in Maharashtra. Her main publications include *The Mahars: A Study of their Culture, Religion and Socio-Economic Life* (1994) and *Der Prinz aus der Mangofrucht* (1989).

S. Selvam is Professor in Sociology. He has taught at the Department of Social Work, University of Delhi. His publications are in the areas of secularisation, community development and communication, specialising in the Social Organisation of the South Indian Temple.

Shrirama is University Professor and Dean of the Faculty of Social Sciences, Pt. Ravishankar Shukla University, Raipur. Over the last 30 years she has undertaken interdisciplinary research work on the dynamics of Indian society and culture based on the sociological analysis of Sanskrit texts right from the *Rigveda* to the *Smritis*. She has authored (with Indradeva) *Growth of Legal System in Indian Society* (1980), of which a Russian translation has also been brought out.

K.P. Singh is Dr Ambedkar Fellow at the University of Wisconsin-Madison, USA and has been conducting research on issues related to caste, race, ethnicity, social movements in India and the United States of America. He has produced a TV documentary on 'Dalit Vision for the 21st Century'.

Sukhadeo Thorat is Chairman, University Grants Commission (UGC). He is Professor of Economics at the Centre for the Study of Regional Development, Jawaharlal Nehru University, New Delhi. He served as the Director of Indian Institute of Dalit Studies, New Delhi.

John C.B. Webster taught history at Baring Union Christian College in Batala, Punjab (1963–76) and served as director of the Christian Institute of Sikh Studies from 1971 to 1976. He is the editor of the *Dalit International Newsletter*. Among his most recent publications are the *A History of the Dalit Christians in India* (1992) and *From Role to Identity: Dalit Christian Women in Transition* (1997). At present, he is engaged in several research projects in modern Indian history.

Index

Adi-Hindu movement, 263
Adivasi areas, spread of Vedic
  sanskriti culture in, 213
Adivasi belt, temples in, 208
Adivasi community, impact of
  Hindu religion on, 208
Adivasi consciousness, 222, 223
Adivasi culture, and Hindu
  culture, difference between, 211;
  changes in, 210; influence of
  Hindu caste on, 212
Adivasi religions, categories of
  study of, 205
Adivasis, and Muslims, tension
  between, 220; BJP's influence
  among, 220, 221; changing
  lifestyle of, 211;
  communalisation of, 219;
  economically beneficial
  programmes for, 215;
  Hinduisation of 205, 207, 212,
  219, 220; of Gujarat, 207;
  religious aspect of, 104;
  religious practices of, 212; social
  and cultural life of, 204;
  subgroups among, 206
affirmative action, policy of, 175
African heritage, ideology of, 171
agricultural land and capital, access
  of SCs to, 296
Ahmednagar district, 236; Dalits
  in, 236
Aitareya Brahmana, 59, 60

alienation and conflict, aspects of,
  188
all-India Hinduism, 185
Ambedkar, Bhimrao 34, 119–22,
  132, 260, 306; and devaluation
  controversy, 304; adoption of
  the ideology of civil rights,
  171; analysis of Hindu
  ideology, 139; analysis of
  Indian society by, 143; Buddhism of, 147; *Annihilation of
  Caste*, 134; arguments for
  reservations by, 295; call for
  conversion by, 122; concepts of
  religion of, 133, 134; contribution to Dalits economic policy
  of, 302–14; controversy centred
  around, 126; criticism of
  Gandhi by, 136; economic
  reforms of, 312; economic
  theory of, 303, 312; economic
  thinking of, 303; elements of
  moral economy of, 312;
  embracing of Buddhism, 170;
  enlightenment of, 143; fight
  against Brahmanical Hinduism,
  121; influence of, 263; interpretation of the caste system,
  287–301; Jat Pat Todak
  Mandal, 135; life mission of,
  120; moral economy of, 310–
  12; on Buddhism, 138–41, 308;
  on Marxism, 308; on problem